THE KINGDOM OF WAALO
SENEGAL BEFORE THE CONQUEST

THE KINGDOM OF WAALO
SENEGAL BEFORE THE CONQUEST

BOUBACAR BARRY

DIASPORIC AFRICA PRESS
NEW YORK

Boubacar Barry is Professor of History at the University of Cheikh Anta Diop in Dakar, Senegal. He is the author of *Le Royaume du Waalo* (1972, 1985), translated into Spanish as *El Reino de Waalo* (2008); *Bokar Biro, Le Dernier Grand Almami du Fuuta Djalon* (1976), translated into Fulani as *Bokar Biro, Almaami Mawdo Sakkitoro on Fuuta Jalon* (1990); *La Sénégambie du XV ème au XIX ème: Traite Négrière, Islam et Conquête colonial* (1988), translated into English as *Senegambia and the Atlantic Slave Trade* (1998); *Sénégambie: Plaidoyer pour une histoire régionale* (2001), which has been translated into Portuguese (2000) and English (2001). He has also edited (with Leonhard Harding), *Commerce et Commerçants en Afrique de l'Ouest* (1993), and (with Pierre Sané), *Les Etats Nations face à l'Intégration Régionale en Afrique de l'Ouest* (2006 – 2012), in fifteen volumes.

This book is a publication of

DIASPORIC AFRICA PRESS
NEW YORK | WWW.DAFRICAPRESS.COM

Originally published in French as *Le Royaume du Waalo: Le Sénégal avant la Conquête* by Karthala, 1985, and © Karthala, 1985

First published in English by Diasporic Africa Press 2012 as *The Kingdom of Waalo: Senegal before the Conquest*

English translation © Diasporic Africa Press 2012

All rights reserved. No part of this publication may be reproduced or distributed in any form or by any means, or stored in a database or retrieval system, without the prior written permission of the publisher.

Library of Congress Control Number: 2012938852

Barry, Boubacar, *The Kingdom of Waalo: Senegal before the Conquest*.
Includes index.

ISBN-13 978–0–966–02011-3 (pbk.: alk paper)

Interior Layout by Phillip Gessert

Diasporic Africa Press uses environmentally friendly book materials, including recycled text paper that is composed of at least 30 percent post-consumer waste, whenever possible.

Printed in the United States of America on acid-free paper.

To my parents

and

In memory of Mamadou Saliou Balde who died in 1979 in Paris on the banks of the Seine, in the misery of exile.

CONTENTS

PREFACE BY SAMIR AMIN — i

FOREWORD — 1

PART I   ECONOMIC, POLITICAL AND SOCIAL SCENE OF WAALO IN THE SEVENTEENTH CENTURY — 21

CHAPTER 1   TRADITIONAL ECONOMIC ACTIVITIES — 23

CHAPTER 2   THE POLITICAL AND SOCIAL INSTITUTIONS OF THE KINGDOM OF WAALO — 31

PART II   WAALO SINCE 1659 UNTIL THE END OF THE EIGHTEENTH CENTURY: THE ERA OF THE SLAVE TRADE AND THE FORTIFIED COMMERCIAL TRADING POSTS — 47

CHAPTER 3   ATLANTIC COMMERCE IN THE ERA OF THE FORTIFIED TRADING POSTS — 51

CHAPTER 4   THE EVOLUTION OF THE KINGDOM OF WAALO FROM THE MIDDLE TO THE END OF THE SEVENTEENTH CENTURY — 67

CHAPTER 5   WAALO DURING THE LAST QUARTER OF THE SEVENTEENTH CENTURY: THE STRUGGLE FOR POWER BETWEEN BËR CAAKA AND YEERIM MBAÑIK — 89

CHAPTER 6   THE REIGN OF BRAK NDIAK ARAM BAKAR, CA. 1733–57 — 113

CHAPTER 7   CIVIL WAR AND THE FINAL DECLINE OF WAALO DURING THE FIRST BRITISH OCCUPATION OF SAINT-LOUIS, CA. 1758-83 — 117

CHAPTER 8   THE FRENCH RE-OCCUPATION OF SAINT-LOUIS (1783-1809) AND THE TUKULOR THREAT IN WAALO — 131

PART III	THE AGRICULTURAL COLONIZATION AND THE CONQUEST OF WAALO, CA. 1819-59	143
CHAPTER 9	AGRICULTURAL COLONIZATION OF WAALO, CA. 1819-31	145
CHAPTER 10	AGRICULTURAL COLONIZATION AND THE ECONOMIC, POLITICAL AND SOCIAL CRISIS IN WAALO	163
CHAPTER 11	THE PERIOD OF CONFLICTS AFTER ABANDONING THE POLICY OF AGRICULTURAL COLONIZATION, CA. 1830-40	177
CHAPTER 12	THE END OF THE WAALO KINGDOM AND THE EVOLUTION OF FRANCE'S COLONIAL POLITICS INTO THE SENEGAL RIVER REGION, CA. 1840-55	187
CHAPTER 13	THE ESTABLISHMENT OF COLONIAL ADMINISTRATION	201
CONCLUSION		215
POSTSCRIPT 1985	THE AGRICULTURAL COLONIZATION OF WAALO AND THE POLITICS OF THE DAMS	221
POSTSCRIPT 2012	MY LAND, MY LIFE SAMA SAMA SUUF BAKKAN	257
NOTES		263
INDEX		287

PREFACE

UNDERDEVELOPMENT AND DEPENDENCY IN BLACK AFRICA:
HISTORICAL ORIGINS AND CONTEMPORARY FORMS

SAMIR AMIN

Unity and Diversity in Black Africa

Contemporary Black Africa can be divided into wide regions that are clearly different from one another. However, it is more difficult to analyze these differences—and to study their nature, origin, and effects—than to see them.

The unity of Black Africa is, nonetheless, not without foundations. On the contrary, leaving aside the question of "race"—in Africa, "races" are no more homogenous nor less mixed, since pre-historical times, than are the other "races" (whether white, yellow, or red)—the common or kindred cultural background, and the striking similarities of social organization, make a living unity of Black Africa. This physical reality, extensive and rich, did not wait for colonial conquest to borrow from or share itself with the other wide regions of the Old World—the Mediterranean in particular, but also Europe and Asia. The image of an ancient, isolated, and introverted Africa no longer belongs to this age: isolation, naturally associated with a so-called "primitive" character, only corresponded to an ideological necessity born out of colonial racism. However, these exchanges did not break the unity of Africa. On the contrary, they helped assert and enrich the African personality. The colonial conquest of almost the whole continent strengthened this feeling of unity in Black Africa. Seen from London, Paris, or Lisbon, Black Africa appeared to European observers as a homogenous entity, just as the North Americans regard Latin America as a continent that extends south of the Rio Grande.

Looked at from the opposite point of view, that is to say from the inside, Black Africa, like Latin America, is just as extremely diverse. It is true that the present states are the result of an artificial carve-up, but almost nowhere does this constitute the sole or even the essential basis of their diversity. We would be wrong again to think that this pattern, however recent, has not yet left its mark on Africa and is not likely—for better or for worse—to consolidate itself, at least as far as the foreseeable future is concerned. Of even more significance, perhaps, are some 100 or 200 micro-regions, varying in width, which readily cross the frontiers of the present states. They constitute yet another aspect of the reality; they do not derive their definition from their geographical position alone, but above all because of the homogenous nature of their social, cultural, economic, and even political conditions. Between these two extremes—African unity and micro-regional variety—the continent can be divided into a few wide macro-regions. I propose to identify three, and shall discuss the basis for such a distinction.

Traditional West Africa (French West Africa, Togo, Ghana, Nigeria, Sierra Leone, Gambia, Liberia, and Guinea-Bissau), Cameroun, Chad, and the Sudan together constitute a first macro-region, which I wish to describe as *Africa of the colonial trade economy*. I shall give a precise definition to this term, which, unfortunately, is too often treated lightly. This integrated whole is clearly divisible into three sub-regions: (1) the coastal zone, which is easily accessible from the outside world, and which constitutes the "rich" area; (2) the hinterland, which mostly serves as a pool of labor for the coast, and as a market for the industries which are being established there; and (3) the Sudan, whose particular characteristics will be examined later.

The traditional Congo River basin (Congo-Kinshasa, Congo-Brazzaville, Gabon, and the Central African Republic) form a second macro-region, which I wish to define as *Africa of the concession-owning companies*. Here also it is necessary to explain how, over and above the difference in the policies and practices of the French and Belgian Governments, genuine similarities in the mode of colonial exploitation characterize the whole of the region, and this justifies its demarcation. The eastern and southern parts of the continent (Kenya, Uganda, Tanzania, Rwanda, Burundi, Malawi, Angola, Mozambique, Zimbabwe, Botswana, Lesotho, Swaziland, and South Africa) constitute the third macro-region, which I wish to call *Africa of the labor reserves*. Here also, apart from the varied nature of each country, the region was developed on the basis of the policy of colonial imperialism, according to the principle of "enclosure acts" which were applied to entire peoples.

Ethiopia, Somalia, Madagascar, Reunion, and Mauritius, like the Cape Verde islands on the opposite side of the continent, do not form part of these three macro-regions, although here and there are to be found some aspects of each. However, they also display features of other systems that have played an important part in their actual development: the slavery-mercantilist system of the Cape Verde islands, Reunion, and Mauritius; and the "pseudo-feudal" system of Ethiopia and Madagascar. Obviously questions of frontiers between the regions remain. Katanga, for example, belonged to the area of the labor reserves, and Eritrea to that of the colonial trade.

Toward a Periodization of African History

My proposed distinction is deliberately based on the effects of the *last* period in the history of Africa: that of colonization. It will be necessary to study how the dialectic reveals itself between the major colonial policies and the structures inherited from the past. To do so, we have to go back in time, and to distinguish four separate periods.

The pre-mercantilist period stretches from the earliest days until the seventeenth century. In the course of this long history, relations were forged between Black Africa and the rest of the Old World, particularly from both ends of the Sahara, between the savannah countries (from Dakar to the Red Sea) and the Mediterranean. Social formations emerged which cannot be understood if they are not placed, here as elsewhere, within the context of all the multitude of other social systems and their relationships with one another. During that period, Africa, largely, does not appear inferior or weaker than the rest of the Old World. The unequal development within Africa was not any worse than that north of the Sahara, on both sides of the Mediterranean.

The mercantilist period stretches from the seventeenth century to 1800. It was characterized by the Atlantic slave trade, and the first retrograde steps date back to this time. It was not only the coastal zone that was affected by this trade: there was a decline in productive forces throughout the continent. There were two distinct slave-trading areas: the Atlantic trade (by far the most harmful, due to the great numbers involved), which spread from the coast to the whole of the continent, from Saint-Louis in Senegal to Quelimane in Mozambique; and the Oriental trade operating from Egypt, the Red Sea, and Zanzibar, towards the Sudan and East Africa. This second type of mercantilist activity was carried beyond 1800, because the industrial revolution, which shook the foundations of society in Europe and North America, did not reach the Turkish-Arab part of the world.

The next period lasted from 1800 to 1880-90, and was characterized by attempts—at least in certain regions within the influence of Atlantic mercantilism—to establish a new form of dependence with that part of the world where capitalism was firmly entrenched by industrialization. These attempts, however, had very limited backing, as we shall see why later. The area of influence of Oriental mercantilism was not affected.

The fourth period, that of colonization, completed the work of the previous period in Western Africa, took over from Oriental mercantilism in Eastern Africa, and developed with tenfold vigor the present forms of dependence of the continent according to the models of the three macro-regions mentioned above. The present throws light on the past. The completed forms of dependence—which only appeared when Africa was actually made the periphery of the world capitalist system in its imperialist stage, and was developed as such—enable us to understand, by comparison, the meaning of previous systems of social relations, and the way in which African social formations were linked with those of other regions of the Old World with which they had contact.

The Pre-Mercantilist Period: Up to the Seventeenth Century

During this time, Black Africa was not on the whole more backward than the rest of the world. The continent was characterized by complex social formations, sometimes accompanied by the development of the state, and almost invariably based on visible social differentiations that revealed the ancient nature of the process of disintegration of the village community. The great confusion which arises in any discussion of traditional African society is due to a number of reasons, especially: (1) the scarcity of documents and remains of the past, leaving only the accounts of Arab travelers; (2) the confusion between the concepts of " mode of production" and "social formation" which calls for clarification and a basic differentiation; (3) the confusion between different periods of African history, particularly between the pre- and actual mercantilist periods and the justifiable concern of scholars to relate history in all its continuous detail, enhances this confusion; and last but not least, (4) the ideological prejudices against Africa, clearly connected with colonial racism.

This is why I have formulated three sets of propositions, so that we can see our way clearly through this history, without claiming to recast its evolution. My intention is to emphasize the main differences between the Africa of this period—the only true "traditional" Africa, neither isolated nor primitive—and that which followed.[1] The first thing to make clear is that a society cannot be reduced to a mode of production. This is an abstract concept which does not involve the notion of a fixed historical sequence with regard to the progress of civilization, from the first differentiated communities up to the capitalist form of society. It is feasible to distinguish five types: (1) the primitive community mode of production, the only possible one to come first, for obvious reasons; (2) the "tributary" mode of production involved the persistent parallel existence of a village community and a sociopolitical structure which exploited the former by exacting a tribute; this, the most common pre-capitalist mode, developed sometimes from earlier into evolved forms, when the village family community lost the right of land ownership to feudal masters; (3) the slave-based mode of production, which was less common but scattered; (4) the small-scale trade mode of production, quite common but never likely to form the main structure of society; and lastly, (5) the capitalist mode of production.

It is necessary to emphasize that social formations are *concrete* structures, organized and characterized by a *dominant* mode of production which forms the apex of a complex set of subordinate modes. Thus it is possible to have a small-scale trading mode linked to a dominant tributary ("early" or "developed feudal"), and even based on a slave or a capitalist mode of production. Likewise, the mode based on slavery may not be of the dominant type, and this seems to be the rule when it is related to a dominant tributary mode of production (or even a capitalist mode, as in the United States until 1865); and only in exceptional cases does it become dominant itself, as in the classical societies of ancient times.

Modes of production, then, do not actually constitute historical categories, in the sense of occurring in a necessary sequence of time. On the other hand, social formations have a definite age, reckoned based on the level of development of the productive forces. This is why it is absurd to draw any analogy between the same mode of production belonging to societies of different ages—for example, between African or Roman slavery and that of the nineteenth-century United States.[2]

Secondly, social formations cannot be understood when taken out of their context. Sometimes the relations between different societies are marginal, but often they are decisive. The problems connected with long-distance trade are thus very important. This is obviously not a mode of production, but a method of articulation between autonomous societies. This is the essential difference from internal trade, which is made up of exchanges between dealers in a particular society. Such exchanges are characteristic of the simple trading mode of production or that based on slavery (in this case a combination of both), which are elements of the society in question. But internal trade may also be an extension of long-distance trade, if the goods involved penetrate deeply within that particular society.

Long-distance trade brings into contact societies unknown to one another—i.e., it involves the exchange of products for which each is unaware of the other's cost of production, "rare" goods for which there are no substitutes in the importing country. As a result, the social groups engaged in that activity enjoy a monopoly position from which they derive their profits. Such a monopoly frequently explains the "special" nature of these groups, often specialized foreign traders belonging to a particular caste or ethnic community, for example the Jews in Europe and the Juula in West Africa. In this kind of trade, the subjective theory of value still had some significance, but it is meaningless when the respective trade partners know the cost of production of the goods, as in the capitalist system of exchange.[3]

This long-distance trade could, in certain societies, become a decisive factor. This is the case when only a limited surplus can be extracted from the producers in a particular society by the dominant local classes. The reason for this may be the low development of the productive forces, and/or difficult ecological conditions, or the successful resistance by village communities to the extraction of this surplus. In such a case, long-distance trade makes possible, through its characteristic monopoly profit, the transfer (not, of course, the generation) of a fraction of the surplus of one society to another. For the receiving society, this transfer may be of vital importance, and may serve as the principal basis of the wealth and power of the ruling classes. Civilization may then wholly depend on this trade, and any shift of trading centers can cause one region to fall into decadence, or create conditions for it to prosper, without bringing about either any regression or any noticeable progress in the level of its productive forces. This, in my opinion, is the explanation for the vicissitudes in the history of the Old World and the Mediterranean, particularly with regard to the so-called Greek miracle, and the prosperity and decline of the Arab world.[4]

The third point is that the African societies of the pre-mercantile period developed autonomously, although they followed a parallel course to that of the Mediterranean world, both Eastern and European. The semi-arid zone that stretches diagonally across the Old World, from the Atlantic coast to Central Asia, has always separated the regions that were ecologically conducive to a high productivity in agriculture: monsoon Asia, tropical Africa, and temperate Europe.[5] This zone has seen the birth of some brilliant civilizations, almost all founded on long-distance trade, particularly Greece and the Arab Empire, whose vicissitudes followed the course of this trade.[6] On either side, autonomous societies—those of feudal Europe and, at least, some of those of tropical Africa, particularly in the Sudan-Sahel region immediately south of the Sahara—developed along parallel lines, precisely because of the long-distance trade that linked them all. Thus one can say that this part of Africa was already fully integrated, as much as Europe, into the history of the world.

This is why the trans-Sahara trade was so significant. It enabled the whole of the Old World—Mediterranean, Arab, and European—to be supplied with gold from the main source of production in Upper Senegal and Asante, until the "discovery" of America. The importance of this flow can hardly be adequately stressed. For the societies of tropical Africa, this trade became the basis of their organization. The mining of gold under the orders of the king provided the ruling classes of the countries concerned with the means to obtain across the Sahara, on the one hand, rare luxury goods (clothes, drugs, perfumes, dates, and salt), and on the other, and in particular, the opportunity to establish and strengthen their social and political power by the acquisition of horses, copper, iron bars, and weapons. This trade thus encouraged social differentiation, and the creation of states and empires, just as it promoted the improvement of instruments, and the adaptation of techniques and products to suit local climatic conditions. In return, Africa supplied mainly gold, a few other rare products, notably gum and ivory, and some enslaved individuals.[7]

Some European historians, for obvious political reasons, have tried to confuse this trade between equal autonomous partners with the later devastating slave trade of the mercantilist period. The small number of black people in the southern areas of the Maghreb—a few hundred thousand compared with about a hundred million in America—shows the futility of this confusion. On the other hand, the stock of gold built up in Europe and in the East throughout these centuries, originating from tropical Africa, reminds us of the principal nature of this trade. After all, this is why the ideas that accompanied the traders were easily accepted—for example, the early adoption of Islam in the Senegal River areas. The important volume of this trade, its egalitarian nature, and the autonomous character of the African societies, are unambiguously described in the Arab literature of the period. Furthermore, one can understand the admiration expressed in the accounts of the Arab travelers if it is remembered that the development and structure of the societies of North and West Africa belonged to the same technological age, just as the place they occupied in the world system of the time was similar.[8] The link between the royal monopoly of the mining of gold, and its marketing by Muslim traders, forms the basis of the structure of these societies. These traders were, as was very often the case, organized in a kind of caste system, and here belonged to a religious minority.

For centuries, a bond, for better or for worse, united the Mediterranean societies and those of tropical Africa. The vicissitudes of one area had quick repercussions on the other, just as wealth and glory reached them all simultaneously. Thus, the gradual shifting of routes from west to east found a parallel shift in the civilization and power of the nations both in North Africa and in the West African savannah lands—reflected, for example, in the successive might of the ancient Empires of Ghana and Mali, the Hausa cities, Bornu, Kanem, and Darfur. This also explains why there was a crisis in Africa when the center of the newly born European mercantile capitalism moved from the Mediterranean towards the Atlantic. This shift, studied by Fernand Braudel with his usual talent and care for detail, heralded the decline, in the sixteenth century, of the Italian towns which, since the thirteenth century, had opened the way for a decisive evolution in the future history of mankind.[9] Similarly, we can say that this change was to cause the downfall of both the Arab world and the Sudan-Sahel regions of Black Africa. Soon afterwards, the presence of Western Europe along the coasts of Africa was to become a reality. This shift of the center of gravity of trade in Africa, form the savannah hinterland to the coast, was a direct consequence of the change of commercial emphasis in Europe from the Mediterranean to the Atlantic. But the new trade between Europe and Africa was not to play the same role as that of the preceding period; henceforth it was to take place under mercantile capitalism.

The Mercantilist Period (1600-1800)

As I have pointed out elsewhere, the mercantilist period saw the emergence of two poles of the capitalist mode of production: the creation of a proletariat resulting from the decline of feudal relationships, and the accumulation of wealth in the form of money.[10] During the industrial revolution, the two became united; money wealth turned into capital, and the capitalist mode of production reached its completed stage. During this long period of incubation covering three centuries, the American periphery of the Western European mercantile center played a decisive role in the accumulation of money wealth by the Western European bourgeoisie. Black Africa played a no less important role as the *periphery of the periphery*. Reduced to the function of supplying slave labor for the plantations of America, Africa lost its autonomy. It began to be shaped according to foreign requirements, those of mercantilism.

Let us finally recall that the plantations of America did not constitute autonomous societies, in spite of their slave-based form of organization. As I have argued previously, this mode of production was an element of a non-slave-based society, i.e., it was not the dominant feature of that society. The latter was mercantilist, and the dominant characteristic of the plantation economy was the trade monopoly which, under its control and for its benefit, sold the products of these plantations on the European market, thus quickening the disintegration of feudal relations. The peripheral American society was thus an element in the world structure whose center of gravity was in Western Europe.

The devastating effects of the mercantilist slave trade for Africa are now better known, thanks to the works of several historians free from the racist colonial prejudice. I wish here to mention a recent and brilliant study on the Kingdom of Waalo by Boubacar Barry, from which two main points emerge.[11]

First, while the pre-mercantile trans-Sahara trade, in which Waalo participated, had strengthened state centralization and stimulated progress in that autonomous Senegalese kingdom, the Atlantic trade which replaced it (as soon as the French settled in 1659 in Saint-Louis), did not give rise to any productive forces; on the contrary, this caused a disintegration of the society and of the Waalo state. This explains why force had to be used by the French to cut off the trans-Sahara links, to subjugate that region of Africa, and to alter its external relations to suit the requirements of the French trading post of Saint-Louis. African societies obviously opposed this worsening of their situation, and Islam served as the basis for their resistance.

The traders of Saint-Louis paid with weapons for the enslaved individuals they bought from the king (*brak*). This ruptured the former balance of power between (1) the *brak* who maintained a permanent army of captives (*ceddo*) under crown control, (2) the council of elders *(seb ak bawor)* which nominated him, and had a system of prerogatives superimposed over the collective clan-ownership *(lamanat)* of lands in the village communities, and (3) the village communities themselves, based on the *lamanat*. The customary dues paid by the traders of Saint-Louis encouraged a civil war which involved the *brak,* the *ceddo,* and the *kangam* (leading notables), and a ransacking of communities to obtain enslaved individuals. The Muslim priests *(marabouts)* tried to organize a resistance movement: their aim was to stop the slave trade, i.e. the export of the labor force, but not to end internal slavery. Henceforth, Islam changed its character: from being a religion of a minority group of traders, it became a popular movement of resistance. The first war led by the *marabouts,* 1673-7, failed in its attempt to convert the people of the Fleuve region and to stop the slave trade. A century later, in 1776, the Toorodo revolution in Tukulor country overthrew the military aristocracy and ended the slave trade. But in the Waalo Kingdom, being too near to Saint-Louis, the attempt by Prophet Diile in 1830 failed in the face of French military intervention in support of the *brak.*

Secondly, a study of the Waalo case is of special interest because the slave trade took place parallel to the trade in gum. However, the latter did not have the same impact on African society. The export of goods (instead of labor) does not necessarily have a devastating effect and may, on the contrary, lead to progress. This type of export was not characteristic of the mercantilist period for Africa as a whole, which almost exclusively supplied enslaved individuals. However, here, rather exceptionally, it played an equally important role, because the enslaved individuals, like the Galam gold, mainly followed the road to Gambia. However, gum was supplied by the Waalo, and in particular by the Trarza Moors. Either they could export this via Saint-Louis to the French alone, or via Portendick which was open to competition between the English and the Dutch. To cut off the Portendick route, the French helped the Trarza to settle in the Fleuve region, and to cross it during the "Gum War," in the first quarter of the eighteenth century. Such circumstances thus introduced a contradiction of secondary importance between the Waalo and the Trarza. It was this which explains the failure of the "War of the Marabouts" in the seventeenth century, led simultaneously by those who were hostile to the slave trade, and by the Moors who put increasing pressure on the Waalo in order to monopolize the gum trade.[12]

The mercantilist slave trade had similar devastating effects on all the regions of Africa where it took place. Along the coast, from Saint-Louis to Quelimane, it affected almost the whole of the continent, except the north-eastern area of the Sudan, Ethiopia, Somalia, and East Africa. The similarity between the history of the Waalo and that of the Kongo Kingdom should be recalled.[13] The slave trade here also brought about the disintegration of central authority, and led to anarchy which opened the way for the Yaga raids. Such examples abound. There were wars and anarchy almost everywhere on the continent, and the flight of peoples towards regions of shelter which were difficult to reach and very often poor—such as those of the so-called "paleo-negritic" peoples in the over-populated mountains of West Africa. It all ended with an alarming decrease in the population. The processes of integration were stopped, as well as the construction of large communities, begun in the pre-mercantilist period. Instead there was an incredible fragmentation, isolation, and entanglement of peoples, and this, as we know, is the root cause of one of the most serious handicaps of contemporary Africa.

It is necessary to conclude this section with the question of the Oriental mercantilist period. I have certainly hesitated to define in this way the relations of the Near East (Egypt and southern Arabia) with Africa of the Nile and the eastern coast, from the Red Sea and the Indian Ocean as far as Mozambique. Neither the Ottoman Empire, nor Egypt under Mohammed Ali, and still less the southern Sultanates, were mercantilist societies similar to those of Europe from the renaissance to the industrial revolution. The disintegration of pre-capitalist relations—the necessary condition for the formation of a proletariat—was almost non-existent. This was the obstacle which Mohammed Ali attempted to overcome by setting up an entirely new state apparatus. I do not propose to study this here, except to bring out the main trends in the evolution of the Sudan, which Egypt was to conquer in the second half of the nineteenth century.[14] It was during the pre-mercantilist period that two Sultanates were established here, based on long-distance trade with Egypt and the East: the Sultanate of Darfur, still powerful at the time of the Egyptian conquest, and the Sultanante of Fung, between the two Niles, weakened through the wars waged by Ethiopia. Mohammed Ali's aim was very simple: to loot the Sudan of gold, enslaved individuals, and ivory, and to export them in order to intensify the industrialization of Egypt. This was a process of primitive accumulation similar to that of the European mercantilist period, and this is the reason for speaking of Oriental mercantilism. The industrial revolution had already occurred, and this was known to the Pasha; consequently the pre-mercantilist period and that of the capitalist system were mixed up in an attempt to industrialize Egypt by raising finance through state taxation of the peasants, the monopoly of foreign trade and, whenever possible, the looting of the colonies.

Up to 1850, it was the Egyptian army itself which hunted for enslaved individuals and robbed the Sudan of local products. After that date, the soldiers handed the job to Sudanese nomads, particularly the Baqqara, who sold the enslaved individuals they seized to Turkish, Copt, Syrian, and European merchants established under the aegis of the Khedive. These operations quickly entailed changes in the social system of the nomads concerned; their clan organization was succeeded by "nomad feudalism," founded on a territorial basis, and dominated by warrior nobles. In the zones of agriculture that had been thoroughly conquered, the Egyptian army destroyed the old chiefdoms and subjected the villagers to a tax in kind—livestock and grain—for the purpose of feeding the administration and the army of the conquerors. *Shaykhs* were created by the Egyptians and made responsible for the collection of taxes; they rapidly became rich by this means. Moreover, the best lands were taken from the communities and given to Egyptian *beys* and to some Sudanese *shaykhs*. Peasants were taken from their villages and attached to these lands as half-enslaved individuals and half-serfs; the proceeds of their commercial farming went to swell the Egyptian Treasury. Other peasants, hunted by the nomads and impoverished by the *shaykhs*, flocked into the market towns, established by the army at cross-roads, and on the borders of the slave-raiding areas. A craft industry grew up, distinct from agriculture, while on the land given to the *beys* and *shaykhs* Egyptian farming methods were introduced with higher productivity. By 1870, it was feasible to replace the tax in kind with a money tax, because of the increased marketed surplus. The Sudan was becoming unified, islamized, and Arabized.

The Mahdist revolt, 1881-98, was a rebellion of those oppressed by that system: the people of the village communities, the slave-peasants of the estates, and the craftsmen, enslaved individuals and beggars of the market towns. The successful revolt drove out the Egyptian army, the *beys* and the *shaykhs*. However, after the Prophet's death, Khalifa Abdullahi changed the power structure of the Sudan. The military leaders of the revolt, whose origins were in the people, and the Baqqara warrior chiefs who joined it, reorganized to their advantage a state similar to that of the Egyptians; they seized the estates and levied taxes on their own account. It is true that the export of enslaved individuals was prohibited, but this had largely lost its old importance at the beginning of the conquest, because that labor force was now used on the spot. But the new state intended to continue exploiting the masses to its advantage and, for that purpose, destroyed the popular elements surrounding the Prophet. His family was imprisoned and several of the people's military leaders were executed. Furthermore, the Mahdist state resumed the export of enslaved individuals, but this time for its own benefit: the Khalifa organized slave raiding among the neighboring peoples of the Upper Nile, Darfur, and Ethiopia; he kept a large number to strengthen his army and his economy, but authorized Sudanese merchants to export some of them. The Khalifa's army, which had lost the popularity which made up its strength at the time of the revolt, did not resist the British colonial expedition at the end of the century.

The slave trade organized from Zanzibar in the nineteenth century certainly falls within a mercantilist framework. For centuries, Arab trade on the coast was carried out in a pre-mercantilist context, which brought these regions of Black Africa into contact with India, the Indian archipelago, and even China. Here products were more important than enslaved individuals, as is shown by the very small black population of southern Arabia and the countries bordering the Indian Ocean. There would seem to be one exception, at the time when the Khalifa of Abbasside was organizing sugar-cane plantations in Lower Iraq for which he imported enslaved Africans. This short period ended with the Qarmat revolt.

From 1850 the slave trade suddenly became much more intense. There were in fact two new markets: the island of Reunion, which was supplied in this way—although the enslaved individuals were disguised as "contract labor" since the British had abolished the slave trade—and the island of Zanzibar itself. In 1840, the Sultan had transferred his capital from Oman, and gradually established a slave plantation economy producing the cloves for which European trade now offered a market. Zanzibar, hitherto a trading post, now became a plantation on a model very similar to that of the Caribbean, Reunion, or Mauritius—the Arab West Indies. Thus, we once again see that integration into the world capitalist system was responsible for a devastating slave trade which had no resemblance to the long-distance trade of the pre-capitalist period.

Integration into the Full Capitalist System: The Nineteenth Century

The slave trade disappeared with the end of mercantilism, that is to say essentially with the advent of the industrial revolution. Capitalism at the center then took on its complete form; the function of mercantilism—then primitive accumulation of wealth—lost its importance, and the center of gravity shifted from the merchant sector to the new industry. The old periphery of the plantation of America, and its African periphery of the slave trade, had now to give way to a new periphery whose function was to provide *products* which would tend to reduce the value of both constant and variable capital used at the center: raw materials and agricultural produce. The advantageous terms under which these products were supplied to the center are revealed by the theory of unequal exchange.[15]

However, central capital had only very limited means of achieving that goal, until the end of the nineteenth century. It was only when monopolies appeared at the center that large-scale exports of capital became possible, and when henceforth central capital had the means of organizing directly in the periphery, by modern methods, the production which suited it under appropriate conditions. Until then the center could only rely on the ability of local social systems to adjust spontaneously, by themselves, to any new requirements. The Americans could do this in their own country; the British imperialists could impose this in India, as could the Dutch in

Indonesia. In certain Eastern countries, notably the Ottoman Empire and Egypt, the joint efforts of "spontaneous internal adjustment" and external pressure produced some results. This is not the place to trace that history. Even in tropical Africa some new crops were produced, exclusively due to the internal adaptation of African societies. There are a number of studies which are highly informative on the mechanism of these adjustments.

I wish again to refer to the exciting research of Boubacar Barry. The British Governor of Saint-Louis first formulated the project of establishing a colonial agricultural settlement in Waalo, making plantations for cotton, sugar cane, and tobacco, at the end of the eighteenth century; but it was put on the agenda again after the French Revolution, because of the slave revolt of Santo Domingo.

When Waalo was "bought" in 1819 by Governor Schmaltz, the experiment began. Barry analyses the causes of failure: the resistance of the village communities to their dispossession in favor of European planters, which had been agreed to by the aristocracy in return for extra "customary" benefits; and the lack of manpower, since there was no reason why the peasants should leave their communities and become proletarians on the plantations. The *brak* provided some warriors who for all intents and purposes were enslaved individuals—long-term recruits, *engagés à temps*. But the French settlement could only use "tinkering" methods. It was not until the colonial conquest that ample resources enabled a proletariat to be created: by taxation, by pure and simple dispossession, and by forced labor—in short, by all the methods used in Africa after 1880, which were similar to those used earlier by the British in India, the Dutch in Indonesia, the French in Algeria, and the Egyptians in the Sudan.

The fact remains that the Waalo agricultural settlement ended in failure in 1831. But the attempt had accentuated the people's hatred of the aristocracy, and had prepared the way for their conversion to Islam: outside the official authority, Muslim communities organized themselves defensively around the *serigne* (or *sëriñ*) to whom they paid tithes. When Faidherbe conquered the Waalo between 1855-9, with the intention of restarting the agricultural settlement, and at last procuring for French industry the cotton it needed, the vanquished aristocracy embraced Islam.[16] A new chapter opened, and we shall see later how the new production came to be organized in accordance with the requirements of the center. Thus Islam changed its structure a second time since instead of being a resistance ideology, it was now to become a powerful means of integrating the new periphery and subordinating it to the design of the center.

Other African societies made an effort to adjust to this project, even before they were conquered. Walter Rodney points out that throughout the Benin coast the enslaved individuals who were still raided, but who could no longer be exploited, were put to work inside the society to produce, among other things, the exports which Europe demanded.[17] Catherine Coquery-Vidrovitch has analyzed in these terms the prodigious development of Dahomean oil-palm groves.[18] Onwuka Dike shows how another society, that of the Igbo, unable to have recourse to enslaved individuals, nevertheless adapted itself, again for the production of palm oil for export.[19] Here again many more examples could be cited.

The constitution and subsequent destruction of Samory's Empire reveals another aspect of the mechanism of integration. The collection of products for export, and the conveyance of imports received in exchange, strengthened the position of the Juula Muslims, a minority inherited from the remote days of pre-mercantilism. The "Juula revolution" enabled them to establish a state that they controlled.[20] But this late episode occurred just at the beginning of the colonial period. Samory had scarcely founded the Empire, when it had to face the conquerors that destroyed it; they reorganized the channels of trade in the direction that suited them, and reduced the Juula to the subordinate functions of colonial trade.

Integration into the Full Capitalist System: Colonization

The partitioning of the continent, which was completed by the end of the nineteenth century, multiplied the means available to the colonialists to attain capital at the center. We must remember that their target was the same everywhere: to obtain cheap exports. But to achieve this, capital at the center—which had now reached the monopoly stage—could organize production on the spot, and there exploit both the cheap labor and the natural resources, by wasting or stealing them, i.e., by paying a price which did not enable alternative activities to replace them when they were exhausted.[21] Moreover, through direct domination and brutal political coercion, incidental expenses could be limited by maintaining the local social classes as "conveyor belts." Hence, the late development of the peripheral model of industrialization in Africa by way of import substitution. It was not until independence that the local elites who took over from the colonial administration constituted the first element of a domestic market for "luxury goods," according to inter-linking relationships that I have discussed elsewhere.[22] Hence, the markedly bureaucratic nature of the "privileged classes."

However, although the target was the same everywhere, different variants of the system of colonial exploitation were developed. These did not depend, or only slightly, on the nationality of the colonizer. The contrast between French direct and British indirect rule, so frequent in the literature, is not very noticeable in Africa. It is true that a few differences are attributable to the nationality of the masters. British capital, being richer and more developed, and having additionally acquired the "best pieces" of land, carried out an earlier and more through development than French capital.[23] Belgium, which had been forced to come to terms with the Great Powers, and had to accept the competition of foreign goods in the Congo, did not have the direct colonial monopolies which France used and abused to her advantage. Portugal similarly agreed to share her colonies with major Anglo-American capital.

In the region which I have called "Africa of the labor reserves," capital at the center needed to have a large proletariat immediately available. This was because there was great mineral wealth to be exploited (gold and diamonds in South Africa, and copper in Northern Rhodesia), and an atypical settler agriculture in the tropical Africa of Southern Rhodesia, Kenya, and German Tanganyika. In order to obtain this proletariat quickly, the colonizers dispossessed the African rural communities—sometimes by violence—and drove them deliberately back into small, poor regions, with no means of modernizing and intensifying their farming. They forced the "traditional" societies to be the supplier of temporary or permanent migrants on a vast scale, thus providing a cheap proletariat for the European mines and farms, and later for the manufacturing industries of South Africa, Rhodesia, and Kenya.[24]

Henceforth we can no longer speak of a traditional society in this part of the continent, since the labor reserves had the function of supplying a migrant proletariat, a function which had nothing to do with "tradition." The African social systems of this region, distorted and impoverished, lost even the semblance of autonomy: the unhappy Africa of *apartheid* and the Bantustans was born, and was to supply the greatest return to central capital. The economists' ideological mythology of the "laws of the labor market" under these circumstances, formulated by Arthur Lewis,[25] has been subjected to merciless criticism, and Giovanni Arrighi has restored the role of political violence to its true place.[26]

Until recently there was no known large-scale mineral wealth in West Africa likely to attract foreign capital, nor was there any settler colonization. On the other hand, the slave trade was very active on this coast, and caused the development of complex social structures which I have analyzed above. The colonial powers were thus able to shape a system which made possible the large-scale production of tropical agricultural products for export under the terms necessary to interest central capital in them, i.e., provided that the returns to local labor were so small that these products cost less than any possible substitutes produced in the center itself.

The net result of these procedures, and the structures to which they gave rise, constituted what I have called "Africa of the colonial trade economy" or, *l'économie de traite*.[27] These processes were, as always, as much political as economic, and included the following: (1) the organization of a dominant trade monopoly, that of the colonial import-export houses, and the pyramidal shape of the trade network they dominated, in which the Lebanese occupied the intermediate zones while the former African traders were crushed and had to occupy subordinate positions; (2) the taxation of peasants in money which forced them to produce what the monopolists offered to buy; (3) political support to the social strata and classes which were allowed to appropriate *de facto* some of the indigenous lands, and to organize internal migrations from regions which were deliberately left in their poverty so as to be used as labor reserves in the plantation zones; (4) political alliance with social groups which, in the theocratic framework of the Muslim brotherhoods, were interested in commercializing the tribute they levied on the peasants; and last but not least, (5) when the foregoing procedures proved ineffective, recourse pure and simple to administrative coercion: forced labor.

Under these circumstances, the traditional society was distorted to the point of being unrecognizable; it lost its autonomy, and its main function was to produce for the world market under conditions which, because they impoverished it, deprived the members of any prospects of radical modernization. This "traditional" society was not, therefore, in transition to "modernity"; as a dependent society it was complete, peripheral, and hence at a dead end. It consequently retained certain "traditional" appearances which constituted its only means of survival. The Africa of the colonial trade economy included all the subordination/domination relationships between this pseudo-traditional society, integrated into the world system, and the central capitalist economy which shaped and dominated it. Unfortunately, the phrase "colonial-type trade" has been used so frequently that its meaning has been reduced to a mere description: the exchange of agricultural products against imported manufactured goods.[28] Yet the concept is much richer: it describes analytically the exchange of agricultural commodities provided by a peripheral society shaped in this way, against the products of a central capitalist industry, imported or produced on the spot by European enterprises.

The results of this colonial-type trade have varied according to different regions of this part of Africa. To give honor where honor is due, it was British capital which initiated a perfectly consistent formulation of aims and procedures. At the beginning of colonization, when Lever Brothers asked the Governor of the Gold Coast to grant concessions which would enable them to develop modern plantations, he refused because "it was unnecessary." It would be enough, the Governor explained, to help the traditional chiefs to appropriate the best lands so that these export products could be obtained without extra investment costs. Lever then approached the Belgians and obtained concessions in the Congo, as we shall see why later.

I have analyzed elsewhere the conditions for the success of this colonial-type trade,[29] but these may be summarized as follows: (1) an "optimum" degree of hierarchy in a "traditional" society, which is exactly the case in those zones formed by the slave trade; (2) an "optimum" population density in the rural areas of 10-30 inhabitants per square kilometer; (3) the possibility of starting the process of proletarianization by calling upon immigrants foreign to the ethnic communities of the plantation zone; (4) the choice of "rich" crops, providing a sufficient surplus per hectare and per worker, at the very first stage of their development; and (5) the support of the political authority, making available to the privileged minority such resources—political and economic, especially agricultural credit—as would make possible the appropriation and development of the plantations.

The complete model of this colonial-type trade was achieved in the Gold Coast and German Togoland by the end of the nineteenth century, and was reproduced much later in French West and Equatorial Africa. This lateness reflected that of French capitalism, and was attributable to the attempts at quasi-settler colonization even under unfavorable conditions—for example, French planters in the Ivory Coast and in Equatorial Africa—and the corresponding maintenance of forced labor until the modern period, after World War II.[30]

This colonial economy took two main forms. Dominant in the Gulf of Guinea, where conditions enabled this kind of trade to develop, was the *kulak* class of indigenous planters of rural origin, who employed paid labor, and secured virtually exclusive appropriation of the land. On the other hand, in the savannah zone from Senegal through Northern Nigeria to the Sudan, the Muslim brotherhoods permitted another type of colonial trade: the production and export of groundnuts and cotton in vast areas subject to a theocratic power—that of the Mourid brotherhoods of Senegal, the Emirates of Nigeria, and the Ansar and Ashiqqa in the Sudan. They kept the form of a tribute-paying social system, but this was integrated into the international system, because the surplus appropriated in the form of tribute levied on the village communities was itself marketed. It was the Egyptian colonization in the Sudan which created the most advanced conditions for the development of this type of organization, which in that country tended towards a pure and simple latifundia system of large estates. The British merely gathered the fruits of this evolution. The new latifundia owners accepted the colonial administration after 1898, and grew cotton for the benefit of British industry. Powerful modern techniques were made available to them, notably large-scale irrigation in the Gezira.

There was a "second transformation of Islam" in West Africa, after the colonial conquest opened the way to the same kind of evolution, although less definite and slower. We have already seen that Islam in this region underwent a first transformation: from being the religion of a minority caste of merchants in the pre-mercantilist period, integrated into an animist society (hence similar to Judaism in Europe), it became the ideology of popular resistance to the slave trade in the mercantilist period. This second transformation made Islam—"restored" by the aristocracy and the colonial authorities—the guiding ideology of peasant leaders for the organization of the export production which the colonizers desired. The Mourid phenomenon of Senegal is probably the most striking example of this second transformation. The fact that the founders of the brotherhood, and some short-sighted colonial administrators, felt hostile to each other for some time, does not matter. Ultimately, the brotherhood proved to be the most important vector for the expansion of the groundnut economy, and for the submission of the peasants to the goal of this economy: to produce a large amount, and to accept very low and stagnating wages despite progress in productivity.

To organize this colonial-type trade it was necessary to destroy the pre-colonial pattern, and to reorganize the flows in the direction required by the externally orientated nature of the economy. For there had been, before, regional complementarities with a broad, natural forest-savannah base, strengthened by the history of the relations between the West African societies. The domestic trade between herdsmen and crop farmers, and in kola and salt, as well as the outflow of exports and the dissemination of imports, constituted a dense and integrated network, dominated by African traders. The colonial trading houses had to gain control of these flows and to direct them all towards the coast; that was why the colonial system destroyed African domestic trade and then reduced African traders—when they were not eliminated—to the role of subordinate primary collectors. The destruction of the trade of Samory, like that of the people of mixed blood in Saint-Louis, Goree, and Freetown, like that of the Hausa and Asante of Salaga, and of the Igbo of the Niger delta, bear witness to this other crippling socio-economic effect of *l'économie de traite*.[31]

Thus, the colonial trade necessarily gave rise to a polarization of dependent peripheral development at the regional level. The necessary corollary of the "wealth" of the coast was the impoverishment of the hinterland. Predisposed by geography and history to a continental development, organized around the major inland river arteries (thus providing for transport, irrigation, electric power, and so on), Africa was condemned to be only "developed" narrowly along the coast. The exclusive allocation of resources to the latter zone, a planned policy of colonial trade, accentuated this regional imbalance. The mass emigration from the hinterland to the coast forms part of the logic of the system: it made cheap labor available to capital where capital required this, and only "the ideology of universal harmony" can see in these migrations anything other than their impoverishment of the departure zones.[32] The culmination of the colonial trade system was a balkanization, in which the "recipient" micro-regions had no "interest" in "sharing" the crumbs of the colonial cake with their labor reserves.

Thus the bounties of the colonial trade were highly relative. However, it was impossible to implement this system in Central Africa, the third micro-region of the continent. To some extent, ecological conditions had protected the peoples who took refuge from the ravages of the slave trade in zones unlikely to be penetrated from the coast. The low population density and the lack of sufficient African hierarchies, made the colonial-trade model non-viable. Discouraged, the colonial authorities gave the country to any adventurers who would agree to try "to get something out of it" without resources—since adventure does not attract capital. The misdeeds of the concessionary companies have been duly denounced: between 1890 and 1930 they ravaged French Equatorial Africa with no result except a trivial profit. As for the Congo, it will be remembered that the Belgians welcomed Levers Brothers, after the firm's unsuccessful attempt to establish itself in the Gold Coast. Nevertheless, it was only after World War I, when the solution was adopted of having industrial plantations established directly by the major capitalists that a small-scale colonial-type trade infiltrated as an extension of the plantation zones belonging to foreign capital. As for French Equatorial Africa, this area had to wait until the 1950s before seeing the first symptoms. Thus the negative impact of this period, still omnipresent, justifies the name which I have given to the region—"Africa of the concessionary companies."

In all three cases, then, the colonial system organized the African societies so that they produced exports—on the best possible terms, from the point of view of the mother country—which only provided a very low and stagnating return to local labor. This goal having been achieved, we must conclude that there are no traditional societies in modern Africa, only dependent peripheral societies.

FOREWORD

Our previous study was about the kingdom of Waalo from the treaty of N'Gio in 1819 to the conquest in 1855, revealing to us the existence of a profound political, economic, and social crisis.[1] We observed that this crisis, which undermined this kingdom in the first half of the nineteenth century, had distant causes. Those causes essentially gave rise to upheavals, due to the misappropriations of the traditional trade routes of Africa towards the Maghreb, profiting the Atlantic commerce after the Portuguese discoveries of the fifteenth century. As Godinho said, this "victory of the caravel over the camel caravans" became one of the invaluable consequences in Africa, primarily on the Atlantic coast where the Europeans bought at the best price and in greatest quantity the merchandise traditionally imported from the Maghreb. Waalo, due to its geographical position on the mouth of the Senegal River—a natural route of penetration into the interior of Africa—and primarily because of its gate to the Atlantic, was very soon to experience contact with a Europe in search of new markets. Indeed, one can study for nearly four centuries the different forms of relations which existed between a kingdom of the coast and the different European powers. The relationships determined by the development of economic concerns did consecutively experience the phases of barter economy without territorial occupation, of fortified trading posts, of agricultural commerce, and finally that of territorial conquest, which ended in direct colonization in the second half of the nineteenth century.

Thus, in a study of the history of Waalo starting in the seventeenth century, the effect of that external factor—the arrival of the Europeans and their commercial needs—is a determinant. It determines the internal history of the land to a great extent. This is why we begin our study at the founding of the trading post of Saint-Louis in about 1659, which marks an important phase in the establishment of Europeans in Africa with its corollary, the slave trade, which constituted, with the gum trade, the economic foundation of their connections with Waalo and the neighboring kingdoms.

Nevertheless, the importance of the external phenomena that constituted major events for Africa has to be explained by a simpler theory capable of clarifying the internal history of Waalo. Because "our history needs to be written as history of our society...it must be treated as enjoying its own integrity, its history must be a mirror of that society, and the European contact must find its place only as an African experience."[2] The Waalo-Waalo (inhabitants of Waalo) in the framework of economic, political, and social institutions of their land, continually searched to resolve the problems which the evolution their society posed. This evolution is dominated by the will of the *brak* to inaugurate a central monarchy with the support of the permanent army of the *ceddo*, captives of the crown, which was constantly counterbalanced by that of members of *seb ak bawor* charged with his election and particularly that of the great chiefs of the provinces, or the *kangam*, jealous of their independence. Faced with the traditional political power continually more dominated by the Atlantic trade, and particularly as a consequence of the slave trade and the agricultural colonization, a new force linked to Islam, this time of the people, tried to resolve the general crisis of this quintessentially inegalitarian society and very often opposed the foreign presence in all its forms. Indeed Africa did not submit to its destiny with its arms crossed; it is thus that the history of Waalo from 1659 to 1859 is above all that of the response of an African coastal kingdom in defiance of the European conquest. It was the effect of that response, which continued throughout the colonial conquest, only a total and internal history of our societies can permit us to reach with more objectivity the study of our past which is required to guide and inspire our future. Also, the African historian, when he does not cease to write his past with reference to another history, this history which should generate a brilliant civilization, to avoid at last that stumbling block which has consisted of making nothing but an apology for our traditional societies or simply to deny them all historic interest. We do not need to define ourselves by relations to others, but rather in searching our own history and placing the domains of its internal dynamics correctly into the general evolution of humanity.

This objective quest for our past permits us thus to better grasp the economic and political reasons for the lagging behind of our societies, which more than the differences of civilization and culture are the source of all the prejudices to which African people are subjected. We hope when this internal study of a coastal kingdom will answer in part the fundamental question posed by the economic, political and social stagnation of Africa during the past four centuries, which preceded the colonial conquest. Unfortunately, that objective is largely limited because of the rarity of written documents, which prevents us from grasping in its entire dimension, the internal dynamics of the kingdom of Waalo.

We take advantage of this occasion to give credit to Vincent Monteil, the former director of Institut Fondamental d'Afrique Noire (I.F.A.N.), who, by facilitating our entry into this institute, gave us permission to start rather soon our studies of Africa in concert with researchers of all views and to materially accomplish this task. We equally thank his successor Pierre Fougeyrollas for the constant support that he gave us, as well as all of the research and administrative personnel of this institute, who each in his area, contributed to the accomplishment of this task. This work is the fruit of long archival research in the course of which we benefitted by the collaboration of Jean-Francois Maurel, conservator at the National Archives of Senegal, who, together with his personnel, is given here our recognition. The same recognition goes also to Mr. Timings of the Public Record Office, to Mr. Bridgewater at the British Museum in London, and also to Mr. Laroche of the National Archives of France, d'Outre-Mer (Overseas) section in Paris.

Waalo's history cannot be understood without the elucidation of that of the neighboring kingdoms. In this context, we are indebted to Oumzar Kane, Jean Boulegue, Guy Thilmans, Abdoulaye Diop, Pathé Diagne, Muhamed el Chenaffi and Moctar Ould Hamidoun. We equally thank the administrative authorities in the region of the Senegal River and of Mauritania for support which we received during our travels and we do not forget our *waalo-waalo* informants, too numerous to be cited here, but who by their attachment to their history helped us to understand their society.

On another level we also want to express our great gratitude to our compatriots Thierno Diallo, Ousmane Diallo and Saliou Balde, who during the last years spent together outside of the homeland, gave us at all times their moral and material support. Finally, we will not close without giving special thanks to our teachers: Professors Hubert Deschamps and Yves Person. The former accepted this work as a thesis and has followed it with interest, despite the distance, the development and the work. The latter, living in Dakar, has contributed to expand our view of African history and constantly encouraged us through his advice to write this history of Waalo.

The Problem of Sources

When one addresses African history, the rarity of written sources constitutes nearly always the first obstacle with which the historian collides. Nevertheless, Waalo, like most of the coastal kingdoms, benefits from documentation, written abundantly for the period after the Portuguese discoveries. It is thus that this period, which extends from the founding of the trading post of Saint-Louis in about 1659 to the annexation in 1859, is given priority in the history of Waalo, in light of the uncertainties of its beginning, which are hardly made clear in the oral tradition. The constant contact of Waalo with the principal European powers by way of the Atlantic commerce has permitted the publication of numerous accounts of voyages. Compiled works or direct testimonies constitute now the most important sources of the history of Waalo. These are, most rich in details, the reports of Claude Jannequin, Sieur de Rochefort in 1638, Dapper in 1668, Chambonneau in 1675, Barbot in 1681, La Courbe in 1685, Le Maire in 1688, F. Y. B. Gaby in 1689, Pierre Labarthe in 1784, Lamiral in 1780, Xavier Golbery 1785, Jean-Baptiste-Léonard Durand in 1785, Geoffrey de Villeneuve in 1785, etc.

The first category of the sources, which is by far the most important for the bygone periods, presents nevertheless the particularity to treat Waalo only through its trade relations. Testimonials of political and social institutions, speaking of the internal history of the land are poor and often treat the entire region of Senegambia, not taking into consideration the numerous confusions which they are hiding. Baron Roger has very well emphasized the misconception of the local realities concerning the opinion established by an inborn pride of the indigenes by saying: "Very few people have previously seen them. The Europeans have judged these people and things only from the decks of their ships. This is why this land is so little known."[3] However, the account by Chambonneau, between 1673 and 1677, constitutes an exception through the richness of its documentation of the history of the people of the Senegal riverbanks, which fills in the gap in the archives for the periods which were plunged into the darkness of time, several years after the founding of the trading post of Saint-Louis.

However, the archival documents constitute by far the second most important source for the history of Waalo, despite their discontinuity and their unequal richness concerning the time periods. We have at our disposal for the seventeenth and a large portion of the eighteenth century thirty files of the Fonds Colonies C6 in the national archives at Paris, which cover more of the history of commerce of Saint-Louis than the internal history of the adjacent lands. The unpublished account of Brasseur in 1776 is one of the rare documents that address the history of the populations of Senegambia. For the first period of the English occupation of Saint-Louis from 1758 to 1783, the files C.O. 267 of the Public Record Office in London include useful information, but a relatively poor one, because of not knowing the country, which the English occupied for a very short time. Thus, one can deplore the absence of details concerning the Toorodo revolution of 1776, which upset the political, social and religious conditions of that part of the Senegal River. Nevertheless, these documents permit us to date the definite decline of Waalo, due to the occupation by the Moors and the excessive demand for enslaved individuals for the Atlantic slave trade.

In contrast, the first half of the nineteenth century is extremely rich in archival documents, because of the sudden interest put on Waalo with the agricultural colonization of the land. Henceforth, the affairs of Waalo found continually a more important place in the correspondence of the Minister with the Governor, in the minutes of the Government Council, in the correspondence of the Governor with the leaders of French posts and local leaders. However, still at that stage the economic and commercial concerns constituted the backdrop of that enormous correspondence stored at the National Archives of Senegal and at the National Archives of France, d'Outre-Mer section, in Paris. The allusions to the internal history of Waalo are always linked to the hazards of the commerce of Saint-Louis. Any hindrance to the agricultural colonization or to free navigation on the river was enough to cause the governor to make a report of hostilities, always without discerning the local and profound reasons for the incident. Living on the edge of Waalo, despite constant contacts, the French did not see the consequences of the political events in a land they did not know very well. There again the wealth of documentation is more presumptive than real, when one wants to write an internal history of Waalo. The numerous missions sent during that period to Waalo had almost always economic (studies of agricultural possibilities or of the extension of commerce), or military goals (construction of the forts).

We have numerous, for the most part unpublished, accounts concerning Waalo, which deserve to be published. Among the most important, one should cite the chronicle of Pichon in 1823: *Apercus statistiques sur le Sénégal, colonie française sur la côte occidentale de l'Afrique.* This important account of 87 pages deals primarily with Waalo, and constitutes an inexhaustible source of information about the economic and physical geography of the land with several interesting details concerning local history. *L'Exploration au Sénégal, au lac Paniefoul et au Jolof* by Caille Huart and Pottin Paterson in 1839 gives us a description of the landscape, of the water management, of the production of the land and also of the habitat around Lake Guier. Finally, the richest is that by Monserat: *Précis des événements les plus intéressants qui sont arrivés dans le Sénégal chez les Maures et dans le Foula-Toro de 1839 à 1839.* For that period, dominated by agricultural colonization, we have here the first critical study by a contemporary warning about the major events that happened in Waalo. Monserat points out the errors and the motivations of the politics of Saint-Louis when confronting Waalo, better than the official correspondences. Thus, because of the abundance of details, this document is irreplaceable for understanding the internal evolution of the land.

For this first part of the nineteenth century we also have interesting publications; this is the case of the short report by Baron Roger entitled *Le Gouvernement, les mœurs et les superstitions des nègres du pays de Waalo en 1827.* This craftsman of the agricultural colonization takes first place in understanding Waalo, through his knowledge of the language and of the land where he stayed for a long time as well as inspector of the cultivations and then as governor. Despite his somewhat idealistic views of traditional society, one can only regret that his work *Mémoirs philosophiques et politiques sur la Sénégambia*, which was prepared during several years and from which this report is extracted, was never published. One cannot find a trace of Baron Roger's work where he announces the publication in his articles and works. The study by Father Boilat in his *Esquisses sénégalaises* includes good descriptions of the underprivileged social class of Senegal and the different economic activities with a very beautiful picture of the *linger* Ndaté Yalla and of *maaroso*. Unfortunately, one has to state that the interest given to political and social institutions and local history is strongly limited; we have nothing comparable to the wealth of observations made in the same period by a certain Thomas Bowdich concerning the Asante. It may very well be that the proximity of Waalo, its continuous relations with Saint-Louis, has made it a familiar subject in relationship to the rest of the continent, whereas the relative poverty of the land hardly prompted the enthusiasm of the explorers. This is why the majority of the great observers such as Mollien or René Caillé did not begin their reports until the borders of Waalo, fascinated as they were by the mysteries of the interior, the riches of Bambuk, striving to discover the route to Timbuktu, the sources of the Niger and the Senegal River or the high plateau of Fuuta Jaloo (Futa Jallon).

After the conquest of the land in 1855, the necessities of direct administration prompted Faidherbe to inaugurate indigenous politics based primarily on the knowledge of customs and lifestyles of the subjugated populations. We have since then numerous studies by Faidherbe and Paul Holle concerning Senegambia. For the most part, those works based on observation offer descriptions of the population often underpinned by the need to justify the colonial conquest. They are however very useful to measure the degree of resistance of the African societies at the moment of the colonial conquest. In addition, there have been brief studies about Waalo, which were made to facilitate the knowledge of the land to the newly arrived administrators. It is within that framework that one places the report by Flize about Waalo, and the important study in 1863 by Azan, who we are indebted for extensively utilizing oral tradition. Much later in 1946 Robin published, in the same framework, his *Essai sur l'ancien royaume du Walo*.

Finally, since the colonization, we have had numerous works concerning the history of Senegal in which that of Waalo is overwhelming. This is the case with those by Sabatier, Cultru and Villard who are dealing primarily with the work of France in this land. Fortunately, we have, for several years, serious studies that give us further insight into certain aspects of the internal history of Waalo. They include *La Sénégambia du XVe au XVI siècle* by Jean Boulègue, *La Compagnie du Sénégal de 1673 à 1696* by Abdoulaye Ly, *La Côte ouest atlantique de 1600 à 1800* by Jean Suret-Canale, *La France et les établissements français au Sénégal de 1713 à 1763* by André Delcourt, *L'Escla-*

vage au Sénégal de XVII au XIX siècle by Mbaye Gueye. Finally, addressing biases of the internal history of Waalo, the study of the development of Senegal from 1817 to 1855 by Georges Hardy sheds light on this first experiment in agricultural colonization, in which Waalo was the center. All these works allow us to see the evolution of the economic and commercial needs of France and the various forms of occupation in Senegambia.

Concerning the level of an internal study of the Wolof society, we have only the thesis of Boubacar Ly entitled *L'Honneur dans la société wolof et toucouleur* and the work of Pathé Diagne entitled *Pouvoir politique traditional en Afrique noire*. They are indispensible for grasping in depth the internal dynamics of the pre-colonial Wolof society.

However, faced with an abundance of relatively poorly written documentation, we have to relay on oral traditions, rich enough to fill in the gaps, in order to penetrate into the history of interior Waalo. Indeed, for the history of Waalo one has the advantage to have an oral tradition already elaborated and collected in the texts from various epochs. Le Brasseur in 1776 and Geoffrey de Villeneuve in 1784 talk extensively about the origin of the empire of Jolof and its break-up. Azan, in 1863, in collecting from the mouth of Fara Penda, the old chief of the royal family of *Loggar* and the Demba N'Diaye-An, a very intelligent old man renowned in the country for his prodigious memory, precious information concerning the history of Waalo. We have had, thereafter, irreplaceable works by the two authentic Waalo-Waalo (inhabitants of Waalo) Yoro Diaw and Amadou Wade. The first, Yoro Boli Diaw, is the principal source for the historic tradition of the Wolofs. Former chief of the county, this student of the École des otages (school of the hostages) from 1855 to 1860, has written a certain number of notebooks recounting the history, the lifestyles and the customs of the Jolof, the Waalo and the Kajoor. We can only regret the loss of these notebooks of which we have nothing but the commentaries made in 1912 by Gaden and in 1922 and in 1933 by Rousseau. Today it is of urgent importance to search for these notebooks, which constitute an important part of the cultural heritage of the Wolof societies.

The second, Amadou Wade, highly educated, retraced the history of the *brak* since Njaajaan Njay until the last *brak* Mó Mboj Maalik in his chronicle. Published in part in 1941 by Bassirou Cissé, this chronicle has been reprinted in its entity by Vincent Monteil in 1966. Reporting more details concerning the reigns of the *brak*s, than Yoro Diaw, this chronicle is indispensible for breaking the silence of the archives, while one knows that the authorities of Saint-Louis did not even make the effort to indicate the *brak*s by their names, when they happened to have to talk about this in their correspondence. This chronicle, despite its richness, poses nevertheless the problem of chronology, because everything is based faithfully on the historical framework, as proposed by Vincent Monteil from the deduction of the reigns, is not sufficiently critical. It is at that level, moreover, that the confrontation of the oral tradition with the rare written documents takes on its entire importance, since in a general way the oral tradition ignores unintentionally the external factor which is the European presence at Saint-Louis.

However, despite the existence of that important oral tradition recorded in writing, we have undertaken three study-excursions to Waalo in 1968, 1969, and 1970 to complete our documentation. We have visited the majority of the historic villages, such as Roos Beeco, Ndiange, Richard Toll, Khuma, Dagana, Tungene, Garak, Ndeer, Rooso and the land Trarza. One is first struck and above all disappointed by the absence of the new elements in comparison to the accounts of Azan, Yoro Diaw and Amadou Wade, which are based on principal sources among the last dispensers of the oral traditions. However, the contact with the Waalo has permitted us to observe in the behavior and the declarations of our numerous informants an unconscious historical attitude, in as much as the traditional Waalo continues to live in the heart of the people with their internal conflicts and their hereditary sensitivity of the past. Thus, one can perfectly understand the spirit of independence, which the *beetgo*, the powerful chief of the province adjacent to Saint-Louis, could have had, for his heirs talked of his relationship of suzerainty with the *brak*. Even more so, the ardor with which the actual descendents of the traditional aristocracy did vilify the "false Prophet" Diile (Diló), jeweler by origin, barely disguising their resentment to this man of a caste, who at the time of a power struggle had put into question the traditional social order. Finally, still today the opposition by a similar political party at Roos Beeco, of a descendant of the traditional chiefs and that of a captive of the crown: is it not the persistence of that fight for legitimacy, for the birthright against the power of the *ceddo* acquired thanks to the political crisis? This intensity of a mentality still faithful to traditional Waalo thus presents a problem of a certain form of permanence concerning political, social and economic structures for which the historian must provide an explanation. This is what we are going to attempt to do in this modest study and we apologize in advance about our insufficiencies in achieving such an objective, because of the particular character of the African history in gestation, and most of all because of the absence of any sources—written or oral—for certain periods.

GEOGRAPHIC FRAMEWORK OF THE KINGDOM OF WAALO

Traditional Limits

Waalo, at the time of its greatest extension, occupied a very large territory, mounted between the two banks of the Senegal River. The displacement of its borders is intimately tied to its history, dominated by the constant pressure of neighboring kingdoms. Thus, according to Yoro Diaw, "The border between Waalo and Fuuta goes from Be N'Denddi, a frequent pasture of the shepherds of the Fula, very close to Fanaye, which is the most important village since 1793." In that epoch the *almamy* Muslim Abdel Kader undertook in the name of the Prophet a holy war to uproot the villages N'Dierba, Bokhal, Gaya, and Réfo. His conquests moved this border to Fakanda, close to Dagana.

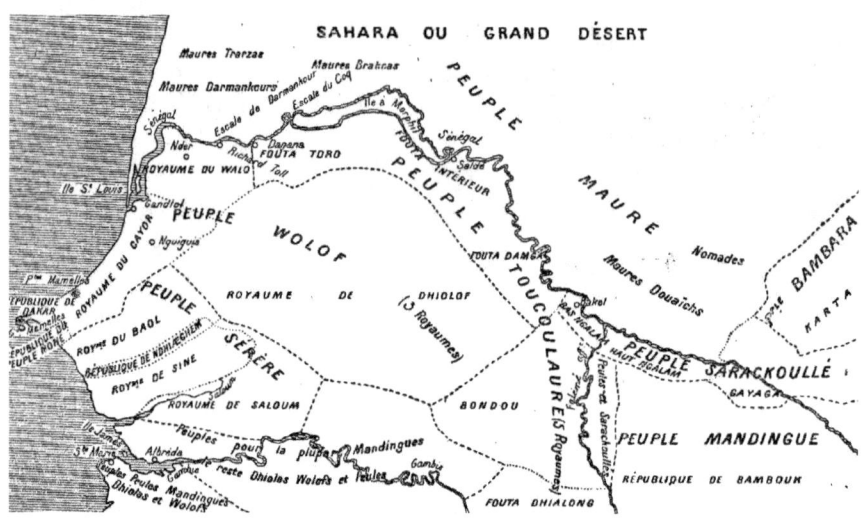

1853 Map of the peoples of Senegal, with the Kingdom of Waalo ("Royaume du Walo") and the island of Saint-Louis ("Ile S. Louis") in the west.

The Wolof Kingdoms in 1850.

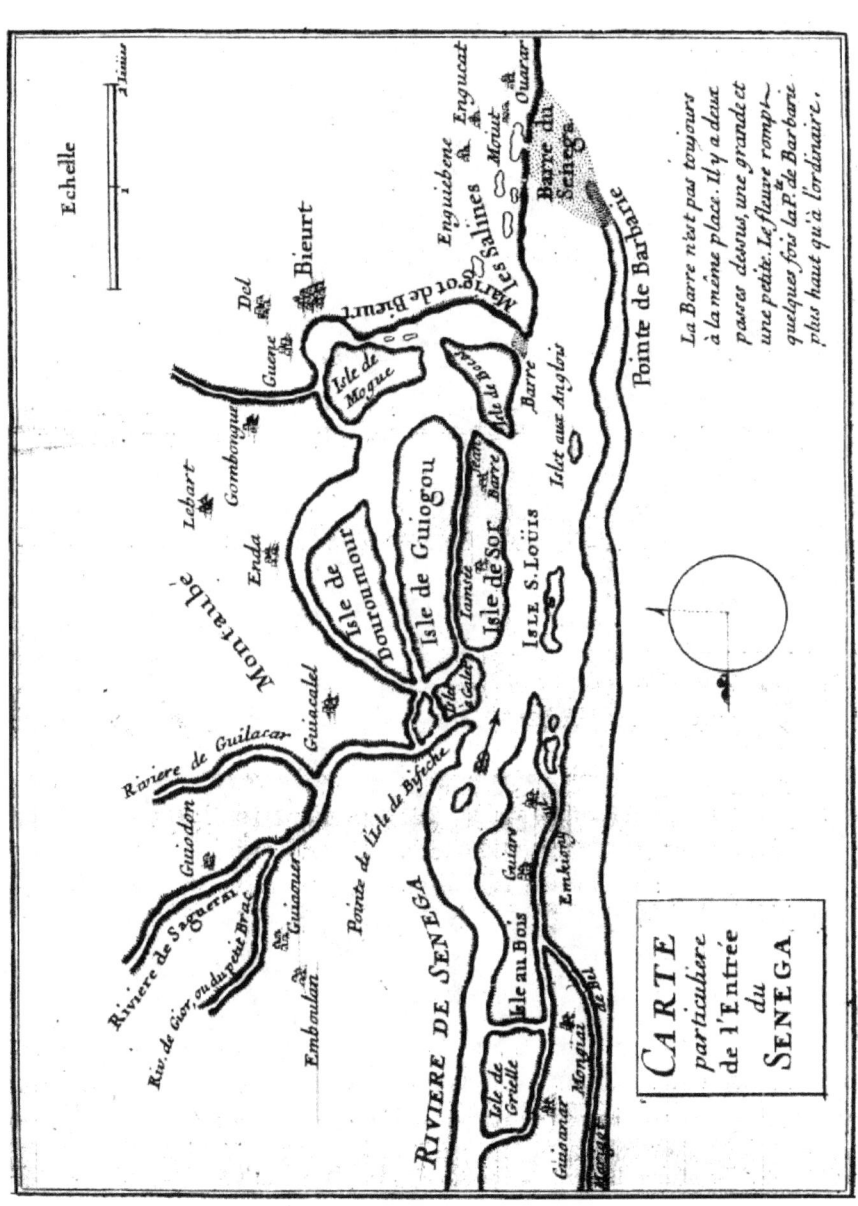

Early Eighteenth Century Map of Senegal.

Contemporary map of Senegal.

Bé N'Denddi was located in Senegal, east of the Kohrine forest and which leads to a long and large valley separating Waalo from Jolof when going south, then merges with that of M'Bunuune, serving as border between the two countries in the southwest. One of the numerous baobab trees of the desert in M'Bunuune, remarkable for its size and called Guy Juula, served in the past to mark this border. Three kilometers south at Siringe, an ancient village of Waalo, on the right bank of the marshland of Guiers, a tamarind-tree constituted another demarcation. There begins a territory 45 to 50 kilometers long and about thirty in width, where there was only one village in former times, called Budi, abandoned since a long time ago. This territory stops at about twelve kilometers from Gandiole, serving primarily in the east as a border between Waalo and Jolof and leaving to Waalo the village of Budi and the current province of the Kër Basin, while the ravine of Gallayele and its pits belong to Jolof. It serves subsequently as border between Waalo and Kajoor, leaving Waalo the now deserted village Mopp, those of N'gaye and M'Pall, the provinces Tuube and N'Gangunaye, the district Gandiole and Gelakle (salt lands) and in Kajoor the district Thiole, where Barale is the center.

On the right bank of the Senegal River, that is to say north, the border of Waalo and the lands of Trarzas extend sixty-five kilometers in the vicinity of the Senegal River. It rejoins the ocean following a straight line, punctuated by numerous wells and camp grounds that include: Tissilingue, wells at five kilometers from N'Gormadd, or the source of Lake Khomak (Cayar); Tandalha, wells and very popular camps; M'Balaytine, Gagarite, Tomogatine (Togomonte of the Wolof), village populated by the Wolof and wells; N'Dëngara, camp ground; Baridiane, village depopulated and destroyed a long time ago by the Moors, the wells of which are still maintained in good condition; Touaidirmi and M'Bëngarënde (or M'Nëgorëm), camp ground; and the ocean.[4] To sum it up, Waalo has borders to the north, the land of Trarza; to the east, the Fuuta Toroo; to the south, Jolof; to the Southwest, Kajoor; and finally to the west, the Atlantic Ocean. It is this location that explains to a large degree the turbulent history of the kingdom of Waalo, which was subjected constantly to the pressure of her neighbors.

The Physical Framework

Waalo is a vast sandy country, where the subsoil is clay or limestone and where there are almost no deviations in the terrain. The country is divided in two well distinct regions: The flat, limestone riverside of the Senegal River of an average length of 250 km and a width of 300 to 400 meters. This is the part, designated with the geographic term *waalo* and which corresponds to the terrains flooded by the flood-waters of the Senegal River. The rest of the land is essentially formed of sands and extends in the interior as far as Jolof; it is the *jeeri* sprayed exclusively by the often infrequent annual rains.

As can be seen, Waalo is dominated by the existence of the Senegal River, the valley of which constitutes the essential part of the land. As matter of fact, it is watered in all parts by the Senegal River, which divides itself there into several branches. It is the presence of the various marshlands of Gorom, Djën, Khassak and Mengueye of the Tawe, regularly conserving water during the entire year, without counting the huge Lake Guiers, which caused Robin to say, "Waalo is an amphibious kingdom." It is exactly at the bank of this lake and the long valley of the Senegal River where all the active life of the land is concentrated. All the villages of great importance are on the banks of the water and the name Waalo-Waalo, which the inhabitants are called, makes very clear their position on both sides of the Senegal River or Lake Guiers, in the flood-plane, the source of all agricultural life.[5] Chambonneau tells us in 1675 that "The villages are really close together, particularly near the rivers. Each is made up of about one hundred shelters and the biggest villages, which are very uncommon, do not exceed four hundred."[6] Consequently, one understands the importance of the river in that land, on the edge of the tropical world, dominated by two quite distinct seasons: one dry season, occupying half of the year, from November to June, during which everything becomes scorched under the effect of the east and northeast winds, and a rainy season in the course of which the irregular wetness regenerates all vegetation and allows cultivation on the *jeeri* from June to November.

Thus, the Senegal River and Lake Guiers constitute, through their fertile valleys, the nerve center of the economic life of Waalo, remaining of major importance throughout its history, because the devastation of their surrounding areas was sufficient to prevent all cultivation and reduce the land to famine. This is why the presence of the French on the Senegal River, and that of the Moors on the right bank and finally the thrust of the Fuuta on the east bank of Lake Guiers were crucial factors. Indeed, the rest of the land is composed of sands where some shepherd people wander, who moreover could neither cross there (the green surroundings of the river) during certain times of the year, nor graze their flocks. One can almost say without exaggeration that Waalo is a gift of the Senegal River, because of its importance to the history of the land.

Population

The population of Waalo is essentially composed of Wolofs, whose date of origin in the region has not been determined. It constitutes nevertheless the most ancient core and presents the same physical traits as the population of Kajoor, of Jolof and Bawol with who it shares the same language.

During the seventeenth century, we have nothing to assess the numerical importance of the Waalo-Waalo (inhabitants of Waalo) before the demographic drainage generated by the Atlantic slave trade. One can observe in Waalo the existence of minority populations: Moors, Fula and Sereers. But the fundamental fact is the linguistic, ethnic and cultural unity with the neighboring kingdoms, which it made for itself within the Empire of Jolof. The history of Waalo cannot be understood outside of that of the Wolof nationality. It is thus necessary to consider Waalo as an integral part of Jolof, before addressing the independent kingdom, the rise of which coincided with the definitive installation of the Europeans at the coast.

HISTORIC RECALL: WAALO AT THE BEGINNING OF THE FOUNDING OF THE FRENCH TRADING POST OF SAINT-LOUIS TO THE MID-SEVENTEENTH CENTURY

The valley of the Senegal River, at the same time a granary of millet and an excellent zone to raise livestock, is situated at the edge of the tropical world, which is regenerated by a yearly flooding and constitutes throughout the ages a privileged place of the convergence of different nomadic and sedentary people. Like the Nile, it gave birth very soon to political units, at best to organized states. It is there, in the part of the river basin in proximity with the mouth of the river, where without a doubt before the twelfth century the kingdom of Waalo was born, though its origins and developmental conditions remain obscure to the historian. The only elements which we possess rely on diverse versions through the oral tradition of the legend of Njaajaan Njaay, founder of the Empire of Jolof.[7] This tradition which places the reign to the end of the thirteenth century or the beginning of the fourteenth century allows us glimpses at the existence of political entities such as Waalo before the formation of Jolof. According to Rawane Boy, the Tuube were already populated by migrants who had come from Wuli, so to speak from the southeast of Senegal in about 1200.[8] In the history of Senegal, this date marks a phase of great population movements, the causes of which remain unknown to us. One can suggest with Rousseau, interpreting Yoro Diaw, the hypothesis according to which "The population of the six nations which for the ancient empire of Jolof was the consequence of the movements of the people of Sahel, or even of the Sahara, and their current population is at least as far as the nobles are concerned, due to the miscegenation of fractions of those white populations with the blacks of the South of Sahel, sufficiently advanced, so that these populations seem purely black today"?[9] This hypothesis raises more of a Muslim snobbery than an authentic reality and is nothing but a vague memory of the Almoravid movement. Indeed all the traditions agree in giving us an Arab or Berber origin of the founder of Jolof. Amadou Wade makes this founder the descendent of a certain Abu Bakr Ben Omar, an Almoravid warrior, who is no other than a descendant of Lamtuni,[10] which Geoffrey de Villeneuve calls Baisamsam.[11] Le Brasseur in 1778 designates him with the name Yaguiane and makes him the descendant of a certain Abouderdail, who came from the Orient "as envoy of Mohammed to make them know the dogmas and the sublimities of the Koran."[12] Beyond the legend, which has Njaajaan Njaay emerging from the waters of the Senegal River to assure the distribution of fishes among children, who were fighting with each other, we witness the formation of a huge political empire, resembling ancient Ghana (Wagadu), linked at that time to the expansion of Islam, and more precisely to the Almoravid movement. Thus, Waalo integrated itself into the vast empire of Jolof, grouping together Kajoor, Bawol, Sin Salum, and a part of Dimar. It seems that the Wolof language as well as the basics of the political and social institutions had Waalo, which is considered the cradle of Wolof civilization, as their seat of origin.

Waalo, although the vassal land of *buur-ba Jolof*, nevertheless conserved its individuality and Yoro Diaw shows us quite well how the *lamane* Diaw, who ruled Waalo before Njaajaan Njaay, conserved the important prerogatives in the political life of the country.[13] These prerogatives are particularly visible among the *seb akar bawor* or the assembly charged with electing the *brak* in which the descendants of *lamane* Diaw had a prominent place. Moreover, the Portuguese authors did not hestitate to draw attention to the fragility of the central power of *buur-ba Jolof* concerning the vassal nations. Thus, towards the middle of the fifteenth century "the authority of the king of Jolof over the vassal nations seemed to be most precarious. He received plenty of taxes and some horses per year, but they were located and relocated according to the will and preference of the lords."[14] This independence of the vassal kingdoms only accentuates itself in conjunction with the Atlantic commerce until the complete rupture towards the middle of the sixteenth century.

Indeed, in 1446 and 1448, Waalo and Kajoor were already open to Portuguese commerce. The upheaval of the traditional trading routes from the Maghreb to Africa for the benefit of the Atlantic route, constitutes the most important phase in the history of Senegambia through its political, economic and social consequences. During the centuries, the Trans-Saharan commerce constituted the only way of trading between this river basin and the exterior, mainly with Morocco. The formation of the Almoravid Empire established new ties between Senegal and western Maghreb, with Mauritanian Adrar, as relay stations on the route to Atlantic Sahara. Thus "from Aghmat, from the towns of Sous, from Noul, from the towns of the Anti-Atlas and from the land of indigo dye (Dara and Sidjilmessa) the convoys of camels carried away copper and fabrics, glass jewelry and other jewelry made of shells or stone, cowry shells and perfumes, medicines and dates. With these products the merchants of the North purchased in Ghana, in Aoudaghost and in Tacrour, gold, enslaved individuals, gum and grey amber."[15] The Trans-Saharan commerce was nevertheless limited, because of the long and difficult traversing of the desert, and its influence hardly touched the Atlantic coastline. But all the merchandises were carried from there and in great quantities by intermediaries of the Portuguese commerce. Indeed, the installation of the Portuguese at Arguin since 1445 stopped to a great extent the functioning of the nomadic camel drivers as intermediaries. This was the first victory of "the caravel over the caravan." Moreover, the commerce took place from then on at the mouth of the Senegal River, which since that epoch played the role of the major route of commerce and of penetration into the interior of Africa. Thus, Duarte Pacheco Pereira, who wrote in about 1506-1508, said that "Every year one could obtain from that river about 400 slaves and at other times less than half in exchange of horses and other merchandise."[16]

According to Fernandez, at the beginning of the sixteenth century there was also a little trade in gold, but lots in enslaved Africans. Indeed, as Godinho remarks on this fact concerning Senegal: "The *resgate* (ransom) of gold had never been important, contrary to the trade. At fault were the conditions for navigating the river. The falls of Felou (gigantic kettles) prevented [us from] reaching the great gold markets...Political reasons may have played an equal role, the Mandigues controlled the route through Gambia, whereas that of Senegal was under the control of the Tukulors and the Ouolofs. The Ouolof markets, endlessly supplying slaves, were badly supplied with the yellow metal and the Portuguese were only able to procure small quantities for themselves."[17] This explains why the Portuguese preferred to settle more solidly in the Gambia. However, we think that this is also due to the failure of constructing a fort at Waalo on the banks of the Senegal River, by Captain Pera Vaz, after Prince Bemoi's voyage to Portugal in October 1488, who had been unseated from power in Jolof. The objective of this fort was to open to Portuguese commerce the route from the fabled city of Timbuktu, considered as one of the "richest markets of gold in the world, where all of Barbary, from East to West until Jerusalem, supplies itself and stocks up."[18] Nevertheless, the Portuguese commerce, despite its importance relating to the Senegal River, became very soon the origin of the dislocation of the Jolof Empire. Indeed, "After having been forcefully disturbed by the Fula invasion of Koli, the empire of Jolof was definitely broken up, this time under internal pressure, at the time of the vassal kingdom of Kayor."[19] Kajoor, which benefited most readily from the advantages of the Atlantic commerce by its geographic position on the coast, made itself independent after the battle of Danki, during which the *buur-ba Jolof*, Lelefuuli Fakk, was killed. Dethie Fundiogu proclaimed independence and his son Amari Ngone, who had given his largest expansion to Kajoor, became the first *damel*. Yoro Diaw places this independence to 1549 and the oldest reference is that of Chambonneau, who travelled to Saint-Louis in 1675. In particular, Chambonneau said, "I have heard the negroes say that not a hundred and twenty years ago all these kingdoms were but one, which was called 'Guilolof,' that is to say 'Jalofes,' and the king was called Bourguiolof. Nothing is left of this kingdom but a small district, of which he who bears its name is the king."[20] This comes close to the date given by Yoro Diaw. For Jean Boulègue, "The secession of Kajoor may have taken place in 1530 and 1550 (and may not have been accomplished in only one battle, as tradition is stating)."[21] It is always that "Kajoor affirms itself from then on as the most powerful of the Wolof nations and as one of the most powerful ones of Senegambia."[22]

The independence of Kajoor inaugurated thus the process of the demise of Jolof, because as Chambonneau tells us, "This bold stroke caused others to do the same, and from one kingdom were created these four—Guiolof, Dhamel, Foules and Brak."[23] According to Yoro Diaw, *brak* Fara Penda Dieng is a contemporary of Amair N'Gone Sobel, who was the first independent *damel* of Kayor.[24] However, he does not seem to be the first independent *brak* of Waalo, because Gaden tells us that this was Kode Ndiureane, who liberated himself from the suzerainty of Jolof.[25] This says that Waalo, several years after its independence, which one cannot assign a precise date in so far as it became immediately the object of the covetousness of Kajoor and most of all that of the Deñanke empire in full expansion. Lavanha and Alvares d'Almeida demonstrate the possession of certain territories, facing the island of Saint-Louis, by the Kajoor, who even if they did not occupy all of Waalo "had at least one party, who represented the interest to give it the control of the mouth of the [Senegal] River."[26] Thus, the dividing of Tuube is significant, reflecting the pressure of Kajoor. After the breakdown of Jolof, the *brak* and the *damel* became each day more powerful and Tuube, an independent province, was divided in two: One part became the territory of the *brak* (the islands of Tuube), the other more important one, the territory of the *damel* (Tuube of the firm land).[27]

However, very soon the crisis of Kajoor-Bawol at the end of the sixteenth to the beginning of the seventeenth century aided the rise and power of the Fula Kingdom in Senegambia. It was at that period that the largest part of Waalo came under the suzerainty of Fuuta, because of the economic importance the coast had gained. The anonymous Spanish manuscript, brought to light by Jean Boulgue, gives considerable attention to the "Kingdom of Great Fulo" in about 1600, at the height of its prosperity, during which all the kingdoms of Senegambia paid it tribute.[28] Jannequin de Rochefort, in 1638, confirms the dominance of the Fuuta over Waalo, but already the ties are weaker, because of the inauguration of Samba Lame; at that time the accession to power of the vassal kings was pure formality.[29] The voyage of

Jannequin did indeed coincide with a new era of Atlantic commerce; to be sure, the Portuguese monopoly did disintegrate, opening the route to other European powers and especially to new forms of occupancy. The competition since thirty years of the French commerce at Dieppe and Havre was already mentioned by Richard Rainolds in 1591. In about 1600 Lavanha adds that "On that river it has been very many years that the French, the British and the Dutch traded a great quantity of hides, ivory and wax and their ships stayed there in great security, they had very friendly relations with the Blacks, who because of the continuous trades went to France and spoke French and there were some who intermarried with the French."[30] This foreign competition is such that Lavanha resumes the old project of constructing a fort at the mouth of the Senegal River in order to reserve exclusive commerce for that route and above all to be able to "clean the coast of corsairs as far as Sierra Leone" from this base.[31]

The importance of the Senegal River and its economic dimension appeared in the eyes of European powers as a natural route of penetration into the interior for the expansion of commerce. Indeed, as João Barbosa says, "the profit which one will draw from that fortress will be so great, only because of banning it to enemies, respectively the French, English and Dutch. Our people have benefited and there are hides in great quantity, ivory, gum, wax, amber which can be traded and they retain also a lot of slaves which the enemies do not retain because they do not use them."[32] However, the decline of the Portuguese commerce was irreparable, because at the start of the second quarter of the eighteenth century "Sugar replaced pepper, the route to Brazil cast a shadow over the route of the Cap."[33] This new source of wealth was thus very early the monopoly of the Dutch, the English and the French. The cultivation of sugarcane had, however, a basic requirement: the employment of a huge workforce at a cheap price which resulted in the complex phenomenon called the Atlantic slave trade. This new need would in several years precipitate the division of the coast into zones of influence, thus initiating the era of fortified trading posts engaged in commerce. Before recounting the formative history of the trading post of Saint-Louis, which played the leading role as provider of enslaved individuals for the Americas, inaugurating thus new connections between Africa and Europe, let us present a picture of the economy and the society of the kingdom of Waalo, which at that date consisted already of a state more or less independent of the Deñanke Empire.

PART I
ECONOMIC, POLITICAL AND SOCIAL SCENE OF WAALO IN THE SEVENTEENTH CENTURY

CHAPTER 1

TRADITIONAL ECONOMIC ACTIVITIES

Waalo is essentially an agricultural land. During that entire period, it retained the traits of a subsistence economy, based primarily on the products of the soil.

Agriculture

In this country, despite an environment of desolate regions, agriculture is the principal economy thanks to the river system that supports life and determines the cycles of activity in the Senegal River valley. November to June is the time of low waters and bustling agricultural work. On the previously flooded lowlands, called *waalo,* the peasants cultivate large crops of millet while the Fula and the nomads come to satisfy their thirst with the waters of the Senegal River. From June to November, the floods inundate almost the entire valley. During this time, the cultivation of land is practiced in the emerging zones or *jeeri,* while the flocks of nomads move away to pastures near or far.

The entire population depends on this cultivation of crops. As Dapper as said in the first half of the seventeenth century, "The Wolof people have exceptionally taken agriculture into their hearts...[Someone who shows himself to be negligent invites thus great disgrace and dishonor] because the highest nobles of the land join the workers in the fields, in such a way that the most elevated (in rank) and the least small and great, allow themselves to be employed for that purpose."[1] Chambonneau in 1674 precisely described for us this agrarian activity and listed the productions that essentially have remained permanent: "They have sort of a pick with which they scratch the earth a little. They sow millet twice a year that is to say small millet at the end of June, in order to harvest it in October and large millet after the water of the rainy season have quite dried away, this is at the end of February, so as harvest it in the month of June. They also sow little beans, rice, gourds and tobacco and plant cotton."[2]

The fundamental feature of this agrarian economy is the simplicity of the means of production. It sits on a framework of collectivist production based on lineage—or its substitute, the extended family. Indeed, the collective ownership of the earth was generally the rule in that region; different historical accounts from different periods recognize this unanimously. It is again Chambonneau who makes it clear: "They do not thirst after riches, everything is common amongst them, as regards real estate, for the land which they cultivate is not sold to them nor do they sell it. They take part of it where they like. If they do not find it good in one place, the following year they take another section of the land. Therefore, there are still two-thirds of it uncultivated and the same thing is true as regards forests and pastures."[3]

However, this description does not entirely account for the phenomenon of *property-rights* of that epoch. It shows in many ways the abundance of uncultivated land, the collective enjoyment of which did not pose problems at a time when population density was weak. But it ignores, likely through ignorance, the affiliations that existed already in that epoch: the *lamane* (the former land owner) and the village-collectives on one side and the king on the other. The *lamanat*, the oldest form of land ownership, was supplanted by the system of privileges as the monarchy ascended. With the monarchy came required payments of increasingly elevated rental fees.

Nevertheless, because of the autarkic (self-sustaining) character of the economy, the inalienable common right to the land was respected until French colonization. Thus pre-colonial Waalo did not yet experience a territorial crisis.[4] Agricultural activity was practiced primarily within the framework of a subsistence economy: "Each household only works at its *Tol* which are they arable lands, as much as the household needs for its own subsistence."[5] Production was geared toward need. As such, the women, for instance, wove "baskets of straw about three measures diameter and of a height of about seven or eight up right measures according to the size of their family and strive to gather into it enough grain which would according to their calculation provide subsistence for one year. The baskets containing the millet are covered with green herbs without there being dishonesty between one and the other or someone taking something from the other's baskets."[6] Thus, we observe here the presence of a rural economy of auto-consumption. It is one subjected to the frequent caprices of the river, the weather and most of all, the invasions of locusts during that period.[7]

Livestock Farming and Fishing

In this essentially rural economy, livestock farming and fishing complemented agriculture. In the expanse of the valley, there were granaries of millet and green pastures all year long. But to the north in Mauritania and to the south in Ferlo, an implacable sun scorched everything. Nomadic people constantly traversed the entire land. In March 1686, La Courbe, speaking of Boussart, described this zone of seasonal migration: "These are five or six villages on the shores of the water. All the surrounding land is flat and filled with pastures. The Moors, called Sargantes, who feed many of the camels and much livestocks come as far as this and pay some taxes to the lords of the land for letting them graze their livestock."[8] In the interior of the territories, as Perrotet says, "[A]fter Ntiago, the vegetation of trees makes room for vast natural praries which are annually submerged by the overflowing of the lake. The plains of grass, often perennial, and natural rice paddies are covered throughout the year with many herds of cattle and goats, belonging to different nomadic people, who are passing constantly through those areas."[9] This bucolic vocation of Waalo was the beginning of the continuous contact of the Waalo-Waalo with the Moorish nomads, providing a place for commercial exchanges as well as for numerous conflicts that punctuated their history.

Nomadic people held a monopoly on livestock farming, while the Waalo-Waalo dominated fishing—all the more so due to their proximity to the river with its numerous branches and the ocean. Dapper noted, "[T]he water of the rivers is also rich in fish, primarily in carps, crayfish and other fishes, particularly at certain times of the year. The seacoast also provides for people, which are located at the sea, quantities of various fishes, such as among others local bream and another type of fish called herkehan by them, the form of which resembles a salmon…When the people, who live at the seacoast, have not enough to eat in the fields, because of the scarcity of their crop, they then solve their problem by fishing and voyage with their little canoes, which seat three people, for a long distance on the sea without considering the weather or the wind. The fishing is done with a certain type of thrown net, with pulling nets and hooks."[10] Occupying a place in the framework of a subsistence economy long before the seventeenth century, fishing constituted a specialized activity, reserved for a caste, which Chambonneau called in 1675 "cubalots" (*cubbalo*).[11]

Hunting and Gathering

Hunting and gathering offered the richest possibilities in Waalo, thanks to the abundance of the flora and fauna during that period. Chambonneau described land animals in that the "quantity is so large that it is not possible to count them." He mentions the elephant, which provided ivory for commerce, as well as "the lions, leopards, bears and wolves and other ferocious beasts [that] are in great numbers in this land, this is why a black person never goes alone to a place from his hut unless he is equipped to defend himself with all the pieces of his armor as in war…" He further added, "France is not as populated by dogs, stags, roebucks, foxes, wild boars and rabbits as this land."[12]

Handicrafts

As with agriculture, handicrafts correspond primarily to exigencies of an economy of auto-consumption. It also highlights the different specialized activities performed by a well-defined social group—a caste. For as Dapper notes, "At the riverbanks of Zenega one hardly finds more than two professions, namely weavers and blacksmiths, which are both rudimentary craftsmen and have mediocre instruments, but carry out nevertheless their work reasonably well with them. Cowhides, from which they make shields, wrappings for weapons, shoes in the style of capuchin monks...They make suitable saddles, also in good style of this country and iron stir-ups and spurs with a pick, without having a wheel, that rotates, as in our country."[13] Chambonneau adds, "They know nothing of the many thousands of occupations there are in Europe. They have only four kinds of workmen, whom they call Rabeseyr, Tegue, Lobez and Cubalots. The Rabeseyr [*rabbser*] are those who work at making pieces of cotton clothes, Tegue [*tegg*] are those who work in gold, silver or iron, but they work so unhandily that, when they make a knife which cuts with two edges, they do not even have enough wit to fasten the blade properly. In addition, Tegue are all those who work at all objects made of leather, like horses' saddles, bridles, sandals, horns, amulet boxes and other artifacts, in which they enshrine their amulets, which they do very neatly. Lobez [*lawbe*] are those who work in wood, such as making canoes, bowls, mortars to grind millet, and pestles. Cubalots [*cubbalo*] are fishermen with the harpoon, the line and the nets."[14]

Local Commerce

This economy of subsistence inherently limits trading to a few rare products. Commercial activities were primarily conducted in small local markets through traditional trading between two complementary economies—in this case, the products of livestock farming against those of agriculture. Salt constituted the principal object of commerce. Thus Chambonneau reminds us that "(In the country of Brak) or to call it by a different name Hoüale they hardly take the trouble to sow their land at all, as much because the land is worth so little, as because of the water and salt marshes that cover the whole of this country for the greatest part of the year, as also for the handiness of the Niger and other little rivers which are there. They trade millet for salt and rolls of cotton in canoes."[15] According to La Courbe, "in Bouscart one makes the largest canoes that are on the riverside which they use to go and fetch salt from Biërt or from Maca and they later exchange it for millet in the country of Foules."[16]

Salt maintained its commercial importance during that entire period. The Kajoor and the Waalo became rivals for the possession of the rich salt deposits of Gandiole. According to Dapper, these yielded "beautiful white salt, transported through the entire land by camels and which has been also at other times carried across the sea to the Netherlands."[17]

After salt came fish as a commodity. Chambonneau details for us again that the "Blacks who inhabit the shores are all fishermen where they are making a great profit by drying the fish in the sun instead of salting it like we do, then they go sell it to those in lands which are remote from the riverbanks and to us."[18] Ultimately, the commerce in grain lay at the center of a local economy that did not use currency. Indeed, Chambonneau tells us, "All their trade is in barter, they do not make use of money."[19] Eventually, all these exchanges underwent a very large expansion after the founding of the French trading post of St. Louis. But here we are looking primarily at the nature of traditional Trans-Saharan commerce, which retained its importance despite the competition of Atlantic commerce.

Trans-Saharan Commerce

Until the Portuguese discoveries, the age-old path of the Atlantic Sahara constituted the only trade link between the river basin and the exterior. It was primarily at the riverbank, where the trade in salt, grains, and livestock dominated the traditional exchanges between the products of the Moorish nomads and those of the Waalo-Waalo farmers. However, the trade in horses and enslaved individuals constituted the major portion of the commerce early on. Chambonneau notes in 1674: "The horses are rare and more expensive than the captives, they are valued at ten or fifteen times more than a captive, they are not as big, not as large as in France and for the most part horses from Barbary which the Moors sold to them."[20] Barbot, who sailed to Goree in 1681, also remarked on the importance of the cavalry of the *brak*, which "has more horse (sic) in his army, than any of the other black kings of this country, because he can have as many horses as he pleases from the Azuaghe Moors his neighbours, (sic) of the country of Geehoa, in exchange for slaves…I have been told, that this king maintains five or six thousand horse (sic) after this manner which enables him to make frequent excursions into the dominions of his neighbours (sic) to get cattle, slaves or provisions."[21]

The constant demand of the King of Morocco for enslaved Africans to join his royal guard fueled such trafficking. Concerning this topic, Barbot tells us that under the Sultan of Morocco, Muley Ismaël, "the Moors of Morocco, Fez and Tarudant driving a considerable trade in Guinea, that is Genehoa, which is very advantageous on both sides. The Moors for some salt, little looking-glasses, and toys, carry home a considerable quantity of gold-dust, elephants-teeth, and numbers of Blacks."[22] In that line of commerce, the role of intermediary merchants was monopolized by the Berber (Amazigh) people of the Western Sahara—the Sanhadja most of all. The enforced shift of the Trans-Saharan commerce toward Arguin after 1455, and the importance that transatlantic commerce took on in the second part of the seventeenth century, did not fundamentally disturb the commercial role of the Moors. Moreover, they were able to integrate themselves very easily into the slave trade and maintained for a long time the monopoly of connections with the interior. In 1787, Lamiral comments on their predominant role:

> They are extremely active in the commerce, their commerce extends itself over all the productions of the land, gum, slaves, gold, ivory, horses and millet. They go to search for slaves and gold in the most distant areas, in five- to six-hundred locations with some beasts of burden, which are donkeys and camels, which carry salt, gun powder, scarlet, cloves etc. products of their trade with Senegal as far as the kingdom of Tombut and still farther to sell there the articles with great advantage with 300 percent profits.[23]

Thus, the battle "between the caravan and the caravel" continued to the riverbanks of Senegal. That competition between transatlantic commerce dominated by European powers and the Berber-dominated commerce of the caravan-leaders formed the backdrop of the economic history of the Senegal River until colonial conquest. It is at the center of the history of Waalo.

Habitat and Lifestyle

The technical level of this economy of subsistence sustained only a very simple lifestyle. One notices most of all the absence of urban centers, the great market towns. Thus, in 1675, according to Chambonneau, "the biggest villages which are very uncommon do not exceed four hundred huts."[24] These villages had no fortifications beyond picket fences. La Courbe describes for us the habitat in 1685:

> Some time after I retired to the hut, which one had assigned to me, it was like all of those of the Blacks of this land made of reeds, round, and covered with straw and resembled a small turret, the door, made like a shutter, served them also as a window. I found in this place a great illuminating fire, which served as a torch; deep inside it had a small plot made of clay, elevated a foot from the ground on fork-like supports, with two or three bulrush mats, one above the other and two large loincloths, one serving as sheet, the other as cover; there was no other furniture in this hut, except a chest, some pots filled with cotton and tobacco made of strong thick leather and a kind of little basket, which hung from the height of the hut with a lucky charm in it for its conservation.[25]

We observe here the presence of an essentially rural civilization characterized by simplicity of material needs. Their clothes were made from a cotton fabric, dyed "blue or black in marbled blue or in little chequers; that is as far as there art of dyeing extends."[26] Millet was the basic food; the Waalo-Waalo "live almost entirely on fish and milk products but because of the 'couscous'and 'sanglet,' which is their bread."[27] Life among the Waalo-Waalo was thus regulated by work in the fields, with occasional feasts to celebrate family events (marriage, circumcision, baptism, funeral) or religious ones (Gamu, Tabski, etc.). In the final analysis, it is this simplicity of lifestyle and of methods of production that explain to a large degree the economic stagnation that became a permanent trend in Waalo. Such stagnation reduced the tensions between the different societal classes.

CHAPTER 2
THE POLITICAL AND SOCIAL INSTITUTIONS OF THE KINGDOM OF WAALO

The political and social systems were closely intertwined in the kingdom of Waalo. The political system emerged out of the social, reflecting the different hierarchies of rank and of caste. The Wolof society was a non-egalitarian society *par excellence*; an individual's overall social standing arose directly from the status of his or her family. As Pathé Diagne remarked: "It is not the individuals but the families or lineages, which established relationships between each other of an order pertaining to the degree of freedom, the relationships of segregation concerning their activities, orders of distinction differently justified, relationships of simple contract of the *lamanal* type, relationships of sovereignty, of dominance or subordination, with economic consequences of greater or lesser range."[1]

The Social Structures

In Waalo society, lineage along with its substitute, the extended family, constituted the primary economic and fundamental social unit within the division of society into matrilineal and patrilineal clans. Matrilineal in origin, the family *meen* conceded its place in society to the patriarchal organization or *geño*. The process was especially perceptible among the peasants and the *ñeeño* (people of castes) whom, through the influence of Islam, inherited insignificant goods. However, the family *meen* did preserve all its prerogatives among the nobility, where it presided over the succession of political rights and goods.[2] Le Maire, in 1682, tells us: "The government there is monarchical and hereditary, but it is not the children of the king, who succeed him, it is his nephews, the children of his sister."[3] This society, divided into lineages, is strongly hierarchical, legitimizing subordinate relations among a free and a non-free class. Thus, one distinguishes three principal social groups: the *géér*, the *ñeeño* and the *jaam*.

The Géér or Free Persons

Géér form the superior class. The term *géér* defines, according to Yoro Diaw, "all persons of both sexes, immaculate of the blood of captives or that of the *ñeeño* from the royal princes until the last of the *baadolo*."⁴ Within this group, there were several hierarchies according to rank in society. The *garmi* (high nobility) had the right to the crown since the reign of Barka Bo M'Bodje, the first *brak* of Waalo, whereas the *tañ* were *garmi* through their mothers and could therefore not claim the throne.⁵ The *kangam*, below the royal family, provided the chiefs for the great territorial units, the districts or the villages. The *doomi-buur* were the third-ranking nobility, with the right to certain commanding positions of certain districts or villages. They were generally the *tara* children, the offspring of the marriage of a prince and a captive.

The *baadolo* constituted the bottom of the social scale of the free persons— the great multitude of peasants. The meaning of the term *baadolo* in Fulfulde, *wasde doole* ("having no power"), brings to mind the subordinate character of this class, helpless in the face of the nobility's power. However, neither Yoro Diaw nor the narratives of the European voyagers describe in detail this quintessential peasant class, which depended on the land. Their only guaranty of accomplishment lay in the work in the fields, which yielded the principal wealth of Waalo.

The Ñeeño

The *ñeeño*, also free, form the castes of artisans. This class is subdivided into as many castes as there are crafts; they are more or less ranked according to endogamy or level of regard (or contempt) by the *géér* class. Yoro Diaw, who calls them "the impure ones," distinguishes between three main categories of castes: the *Jëf-lekk*, the *Sab-lekk* and the *Bawlekk*.

1. The *Jëf-lekk* were those who made their living through a profession. One distinguishes among them the *tëgg* (blacksmiths and jewelers), the *wuude* (cobblers), the *rabb* (weavers), and the *lawbe* (woodworkers).⁶
2. The *Sab-lekk* were primarily musicians. There was the *tamakat* (the beater of the *tam-tam*) and the *xalambaan* (player of a kind of violin).⁷
3. The *Baw-lekk* or "griots" devoted themselves primarily to theatrical farces. They are the *gawlo* and the *géwël*.⁸

The Jaam

The *jaam*, or slaves, constituted the last social category. Among them, one distinguishes clearly between the *jaam sayor*— newly purchased enslaved individuals—and the *jaam juddu*, enslaved individuals born in the house (manor) of the master. Although as a whole at the bottom of the social scale, the enslaved individuals even within their social class had a certain hierarchy. The enslaved individuals of the king were above those of the manor. The slave adopted the status of his master in relationship to the individuals of his class. Thus, the royal captives were at the top of the slave hierarchy. According to Yoro Diaw:

> The captives of high families were constantly placed under the [domination] of the kings and of some commanding lords, under whom they had, during a long interval of time, produced generations, has given birth to classes superior to the other kinds of captives; which are arranged, as are their masters, in ranked sections according to their degree of superiority, forming the assemblages known by the French under the name of crown captives and in Ouoloff called *Feck-Bathétile* (from *feck* – troop; *ba* – to leave; *hetile* – still, encore). This word-for-word translation alone cannot bring out the correct and complete meaning of the composite for those who do not know Ouoloff. The word Feck Bathétile indicates that the crown captives, placed so as to be impregnable against any intervention [resale] by younger heirs... were the captives of and owed their services to only their supreme masters in the capitals, their residences, and that by right they were the regular and perpetual guards of these masters, the kings and the elected lords.[9]

In other words, the captives of the crown were exempt from being sold. Indeed, it was from their ranks that the *ceddo* warriors were to be recruited. The role of such warriors would be increasingly important due to the political, social and economic crisis of the slave trade era.

At the bottom of the hierarchy of the enslaved individuals were the domestic captives. Living with the family of the master, they experienced strenuous conditions. The sixteenth- through nineteenth- century authors unanimously recognize, however, the mildness of slavery in Senegambia. While men were generally charged with fieldwork and women with housekeeping, these enslaved individuals lived until adulthood with the family of the master. Marriage permitted them to establish their own hearths. The sole obligation was to pay homage every year to the master, and to pour for him on that occasion twenty measures of millet as payment, called *yène*, "charge per head." The master also received an important part of the marriage dowry.[10]

Although slavery in Waalo was above all the punishment for theft or some other crime, prisoners of war also provided an important source. Slavery was perpetuated by heredity, for the transmission occurred through the mother— except when the father was also the master of the mother. Liberation was possible; indeed, the slave might even achieve liberty from a too-severe master through the system of *fañu*: the principle was to cause great shame to the master. After all, as Jean Suret-Canale remarked concerning African slavery, within the great agricultural domain, the servile workforces of the artisans were always unknown or were only apparent under special ownership titles.[11] The condition of the captive, having then an essentially legalistic nature, did not take into account the features of grim exploitation by the master within the economic framework of subsistence. However, its existence as a social phenomenon contributed largely to the development of the commerce in enslaved peoples.

The Traditional Religion

Regarding the traditional religion of the Wolofs, we have very little documentation that would have allowed us to identify an organized institution or precise religious theology. We have only some descriptions that shed light on the practices arising from an indigenous ritual. Chambonneau, in 1675, remarks that each family had a totem representing an animal: "…about their surnames, amongst which are the names of several beasts and birds which bear the same name as themselves. They believe that there is such great affinity and connection between them, that they would not eat them or kill them for anything in the world, or even touch them…for example the man or woman who has as his surname Guiop, will never dare eat or touch a peacock, because it is also called Guiop, he who is called Boy, a civet cat, he who is Fal, a snake and so of other names."[12]

The belief in divinities (which European observers called "the devil") is equally prevalent. According to Chambonneau, "…Not long ago the Master of the islet of Jambaar our neighbor, sacrificed an ox to the Devil every year by the seaside so as to make the tidal wave favorable. Yamsek, Master of the Forests, feeds daily a viper ten feet long. He says that it is his ancestor, and that whoever other than himself desired to see it would encounter evil. There are just such vipers on the River Bifeche that are fed. They have a tree between their village and our Settlement at which as they pass they must leave something."[13] Those several elements of their beliefs reveal a profound symbiosis with nature, one barely controlled by humans. The veneration of ancestors constituted the foundation of this traditional religion, which remains not too well understood, but which resisted Islam for a very long time.

The Marabouts and Islam in Waalo

At the margins and often in the interior of this traditional division of society, Islam appeared as a new class consisting of the marabout and his followers. It is a fact that the origin of the empire of Jolof is linked by that tradition to a definite phase of Islamization, the Almoravid movement. Before launching its conquest of Morocco and Spain, the movement left behind numerous proselytes on the banks of the river. The Portuguese reports in the fifteenth century also inform us about the expansion of Islam into Senegambia. This expansion was, however, very relative and unequal. Indeed, as Dapper says: "The religion is little observed by them; there is neither a church nor open places where they could hold some assemblies, each one follows his own sensibility and sentiment which however leans towards the Muslim doctrine."[14] Islam was still typically the monopoly of the uneducated marabouts. Thus Chambonneau describes them to us in 1675: "The Marabouts have little learning and many say they scarcely know how to write Arabic. The majority of them are wizards and fortune-tellers, who pass off on to the Negroes the stories that ever were seen for truth, abusing them by promising them a paradise of milk."[15]

Nevertheless, Islam began increasingly to supplant the traditional religion, which itself remains little known. Indeed, the role played by the marabouts in the social life ended up acquiring a considerable dimension. Some believe that this role included presiding over the majority of baptisms, weddings and funerals.

However, this Islamic influence still remained superficial. Beginning in the sixteenth century, the European voyagers were struck by the attractive force and spiritual use of amulets that made for a lucrative object of trade among the marabouts. The magical and therapeutic powers of the amulets (charms) had such significance in their eyes that the marabouts were frequently able to convince the local people of almost everything. According to one seventeenth century observer, the local people:

> They will be happy in it, will become rich and brave in war, without being able to be hurt, that they will revenge themselves on their enemies and in a word they will succeed in all their aims, in as much as these poor deluded persons would not believe their lives to be safe unless they fixed them upon their person and clothes. There are some who are more loaded than adorned with them, particularly when they go to war Also they hang some round the necks of their horses and other animals and even put them in their fields in this way, believing that this will preserve their grain from being damaged by birds and grasshoppers. The marabouts charge more or less for these amulets according to their nature and greater of lesser importance; the marabouts would not give some for less than the value of a slave, a great sum amongst them.[16]

The pilgrimage had become a common practice, for Chambonneau tells us also that he had "spoken to old marabouts who have returned from this journey. The people esteem them as nothing less than saints."[17] Thus the marabout occupied more and more a prominent place in the society, so that one finally observes the formation of a new caste—this time in the arts and sciences. Dapper suggests in the following passage: "No one among the priests has the permission to marry outside of his priestly type, neither can a priest teach someone to read or write outside of his order, so it is that no one in that land knows how to read or to write except those who are of the priestly type."[18]

It is surprising, however, that the marabouts renounced the opportunity to increase the number of converts to Islam through the caste mentality. Dapper has certainly tried to evoke the fact that the marabouts constituted often a more or less closed minority, living in the shadow of a ruler. Concerning this point, Le Maire in 1682 is very explicit when he tells us: "They have taken the Muslim religion of the Azoages or Arabs, who I have told you about. It is pretty badly practiced by the lesser people, who have only a light complexion. The nobles are more attached to it because they are usually close to one of the Moorish marabouts and thus these scoundrels take full credit for their spirit. They make their Sala, the minor people do not do anything or do it only more or less in a mosque. The king and the nobles have them, they are covered with straw like the other houses. The marabouts exploit them with charms because there are such that cost them three enslaved individuals or four or five pieces of cattle according to more or less the value which they attribute to it."[19]

In other words, we are dealing here essentially with an Islam of the royal court. However, insecurity, a consequence of the slave trade, very soon provided another image for the Islam of the royal court; it transformed into a belligerent Islam. During 1673 and 1677 this transformed Islam became the origin of the most extraordinary holy war that Waalo and the nations of northern Senegambia would experience.

THE POLITICAL STRUCTURES

Only Waalo "has the configuration of a political system so closely adapted to the structural realities, secret and at the same time made explicit by the social experience…The exercise of a political function, the possession of rights by the political and social unit, which is a lineage-family, involves necessarily the possession of a status, which justified such privileges."[20]

The Royalty

After Njaajaan Njaay ascended to the throne, the political powers of *lamane* Diaw, the former master of Waalo, were handed over to the *brak*. This inaugurated the system of elective monarchy.

The Election

In Waalo the elected *brak* must belong to the M'Bodje clan through his father. Even more crucially, he must belong to one of the three *meen* families through his mother: *Loggar*, *Dios*, and *Teejekk*. The chroniclers concur in giving a Berber origin to the *Loggar*, a Serere to the *Dios* and a Fula to the *Teejekk*. As Robin suggests, one can only see in this interpretation a concession to the agitated neighbors of the Waalo: "The brak finds himself always being a relative or ally of the ones or the others or else of all of them."[21] Chambonneau did not neglect to reveal the hereditary and elective character of the monarchy in Waalo: "There are only kingdoms (they know nothing of a republic) which are hereditary in the Royal Family, and although the king may have sons, they are no more sure of becoming king than the furthest off member of the family, for after the death of the king the great man assemble and look about for the most capable of his relatives or as at Brak, they usually take him who in the king's life time was 'Brieux,' which is the name of a principality of the country."[22]

The election of the *brak* had to be conducted by one of the two viceroys, or *bumi*. The election took place in three steps under the direction of three noble electors of the region—the *jogomaay*, the *jawdin*, and the *maalo*— who formed the *seb ak bawor*. The three *seb* or electors were the descendants of the former *lamane* or Diaw, the master of the land. The *jogomaay* was the master of the waters, president of the assembly and governor of the kingdom during the interim reigns. The *jawdin* was, at the same time, the master of the land, a type of military chief with executive power, as much during the life of the *brak* as during the interim reigns, during which he was guardian of the royal *tam-tams* (drums). The *maalo* was the treasurer-general of the kingdom. Yoro Diaw describes this election as being the result of a preliminary secret conference between the principal notables, or a plenary assembly of the three highest noble families of the land. Afterward there was a second assembly, equally secret, attended by the principal notables as well as by the *Diinye* and the *Diinyela* at Mpeytyo. The two families along with the three preceding ones constituted the five families of *meen* in the second order of nobility. A third meeting decided on the election of the *brak*. In addition to the aforementioned notables, who had voting powers, the captives of the king participated in the election with consultative powers. So did the notables of the two *lof*, but their participation was to a lesser degree.[23]

We can clearly see that this process included a definite participation of all social levels of the society, based on the hierarchy of rank and caste. Does this not show that sovereignty was at the onset a collective right, the result of a compromise between more or less autonomous groups?

The Ceremony of Enthronement

Charles Derneville, who was on a mission to Waalo on October 30, 1840, described the occasion of the coronation of the *brak*. His account largely confirms that given by oral tradition at the time of the formation of Waalo.[24] The ceremony took place on the right riverbank, at Jurbel, the first capital of Waalo. In Janje (Jandie) on Thursday evening, the evening before the day of enthronement, the *brak* could spend the night with his wife of the evening, the *ndonde,* in a specially constructed house in memory of the marriage of Njaajan Njaay with Offe, a Fula. The following day the *brak* went to Jurbel in a canoe rowed personally by the *montel,* the chief of the fishermen, accompanied by the *jawdin* and a captive. Coming in another canoe were the *jogomaay,* the *maalo* and the others in hierarchical order of the dignitaries. Derneville tells us that the prince-elect, "before embarking the canoe with which he must traverse, is obliged to jump over a bull, a ram or a billy-goat of the same color without touching [either of them], lying on the ground, and whose sacrifice is indispensible."

Once in Jurbel, the *brak* was led straight to the mound of earth, the *jal* or tumulus of his family *meen,* where he was coronated. This was the occasion for all the groups to reaffirm their rights, which the new *brak* has to recognize before his definitive consecration. Before that the *brak* had to plunge into the backwater of Kham, in memory of the long sojourn of Njaajan Njaay in the waters, and retrieve a fish (which a servant carefully slipped to him). The *brak,* according to Yoro Diaw, had also to pay a tax of ten captives, called *jëg,* as a land lease payment to the *meen* families of the second rank of nobility. He had already paid, on the path leading to the mound, two loincloths per person to the *cawdin,* i.e. "loincloths for seven people" to the *meen jar* and to the *meen jeder*. Thus, after having paid the amends for acts of violence committed by his predecessor or his agents, the new *brak* accepted *mipp* from the ranks of *maalo*: a shield of light wood, a bow, some javelins and some arrows, a cob of millet, and seeds of diverse plants cultivated in the kingdom.[25]

Then the *brak* could proceed to nominate noble dignitaries. In most cases, this meant simply re-electing the previous ones. Actually it is at that level that rivalries arose between different dignitaries possessing rights within their family for a well-determined post. Thus F.Y. B. Gaby, who visited Waalo in 1686, remarked, "All these offices are given to the highest bidders."[26] For that matter, the existence of three rival families, each having a right to the crown, fostered the formation of a coalition around each of them. This would become a factor in the instability of power.

THE ADMINISTRATION OF THE KINGDOM

The Brak

The *brak* appeared to be a sacred person whose principal role was to bring abundance to the land. This role is represented in the ceremony of enthronement by the seeds, which he receives in his left hand. Moreover, the indigenous rituals of the sacred bath and the different sacrifices also indicate the original sanctification of the *brak.* The European voyagers did not neglect to point out the prostration which one also encounters at the court of the *mansa* of Mali. Le Maire, in 1682, makes clear that "One approach[es] the king only with great difficulty and circumscription, also few of the people have the privilege to be admitted to the interior of his palace."[27] This restriction in part led the European voyagers to wrongly compare the African monarchies with those of Asia, assuming the absolutist and even tyrannical character of the kings. In 1827 Baron Roger remarked accurately that "The *Waalo-Waalo* have for the *brak* a respect out of habit and superstition all the more remarkable since the sovereign, clothed and housed nearly as simple as his subjects, is not separated as in Europe by prestiges of pomp and magnificence. The trust, which the people have in the royal family, goes as far as to suppose that he has healing powers. The *brak* and his family never proceeded to eat in public."[28]

As far as we know, the *brak* was not a cult figure. The only annual feast, the Gamu, inspired by Muslims and indigenes, was meant to reunite the different chiefs of the kingdom to assert control over them and to receive the taxes from their hands. Until the beginning of the eighteenth century, the *brak* resided at the right riverbank, in the capital of Jurbel, where he resided over a considerably large court.

The *brak*, ruler of Waalo, fulfilled numerous functions. He was primarily a warlord. He had under his command the captives of the crown, whom the *jawadin* presented to him at the time of his enthronement saying: "We submit ourselves to your authority with this guard of all of your predecessors who are as loyal to you as they were to your grandparents."[29] The *brak* was also the quintessential chief of the land, *suuf as buur*, but only on credit, because he had to pay a tax for its lease at the time of his enthronement. This proves that the land actually belonged to the community. As Abdoulaye Diop suggests, the monarchy did not fundamentally change the inalienable law of the land. But the *brak*, completely respecting the entitlements of the *lamane* (masters of the land), disposed of more and more free land to redistribute it among allies forming his clientele (warriors, dignitaries, marabouts). Eventually, he was even compelled to encroach upon the land of the *lamane*. This practice gave rise to a system of privileges: "The *lamanes* are held to give to sovereigns a part of the royalties which they obtained from their land as a form of property tax; this is one of the reasons why the taxes were raised. The masters of privilege: nobles, war chiefs, feudality living with raised taxes, seigniorial and no longer patrimonial, who took their lands as 'leases,' a portion of which had to be given to the sovereigns; they placed also their crops coming from their own fields, cultivated by a workforce which was in part servile…The introduction of Islam and the allocation of lands to the marabouts favored the elevation of the property taxes and the 'feudalization' of the conditions under which the land was occupied."[30]

This process must have difficult to comprehend at the time due to the self-sustaining character of the economy—and most of all because of the wealth of the lands, which during several centuries overcame all crises. Nevertheless, the system of privileges, superimposed on the *lamanal*-system, favored the rise of a new type of affiliation, which we will call for the sake of convenience "semi-feudal" as per how Abdoulaye Diop details it: "The type of land tenure did not change (thus) during the monarchy in its fundamental aspects, which seem to us to be that distinction between the master of the land and the master of the law of cultivation, the preeminent ownership existing then of these two 'holders,' consisted of one and the same person."[31]

La Courbe gives in 1685 an example of *Brieux* or *Brio* (*Briok*), which shows clearly that the conceded territory constituted the foundation of the bonds of "vassalage." Thus "this prince who is of the family the king of Houal, elevates also the king of Cayor, because of a sovereignty or principality, which he holds for the one that one calls Gaugël and which is not far from Biër."[32] In any case, the *brak* received taxes (*jëg*) from different families. This created a long chain of relations of a feudal type that defines the system of privileges. Indeed, the largest part of the kingdom was divided into regions of privilege; the chiefs, generally appointed by virtue of their hereditary rights, would become empowered by the reigning *brak*.[33]

In theory the power of the *brak* was absolute, but in practice it was largely mitigated by that of the members of *seb ak bawor* and by multiple rights held by different social groups, even those of servile origin. At the occasion of the enthronement, the *seb ak bawor* made the limits of the *brak*'s power clear through the voice of the *mipp*: "The preference which was given to you today by all the *jaambur* among whom all are equal to you, raises you above us and them and, for the most important reason over the *baadolo*; your present position is a testimonial which proves that if you do not stray from the normal path towards your subjects, you will give us your entire life; if you act contrary to this you will attract discord among your electors and necessarily the hate of your people."[34]

The *jawdin* did not neglect to remind the captives of the crown, who constituted a kind of regular army for the *brak*: "Keep your king, serve him well and know us, him and yourselves."[35] This demonstrates the extent of power of the *seb ak bawor*, who could dispose of the *brak* if they wanted. This possibility of control is confirmed by La Courbe, who, speaking of the *maalo*, a member of *seb ak bawor* in 1685, called him the greatest ruler of the land—one who establishes and dispossesses the king as he pleases and who is like the controller of his actions.[36] Thus when confronted with the atrocities of the *linger* Jamburgel against the *baadolo*, the *seb ak bawor* when ordered by the *brak* to kill her, replied simply: "It does not befit us to kill, to spill the blood of a noble (*tuur deret u garmi*) but it lies within our power to reduce her to being a beggar (*yelwaan*) with those of her kind."[37] This illustrates that in the oligarchic monarchy of Waalo, the *seb ak bawor* established themselves as a more or less permanent organization that controlled the sovereign, or at least shared with him the exercise of power.

The administration of the *brak* was based on the distribution of responsibilities pertaining to multiple offices, each with corresponding privileges. The *brak* was in reality only a coordinator, exercising his control over independent personnel in most cases, because of inherited duties. In the political apparatus of the nation, one distinguishes three major categories of personnel corresponding to three social groups: the noble personnel, the personnel of servile origin, and the personnel of people of castes.[38]

The Noble Personnel and the Apparatus of the Nation

The dignitaries of noble origin participated directly in the exercise of power on the basis of the hierarchical order in the entire kingdom. Among them were the holders of offices and the beneficiaries of privileges. The office holders were the chiefs of provinces, appointed by the family of the *brak* in agreement with the *kangam* or the nobles of second rank having the right of command by heredity. The *kaddj* or *kadjekk*, eventual successor to the *brak*, had states extending from Beepar Ndeeker to St. Louis. A son or a nephew of the *brak* stood at the helm and held titles analogous to the nobility. The *briok* or *bër yok* had the command from Sanent to Alsegu, namely the eastern banks of Lake Guiers. He was a son of the *brak*. Therefore he called himself M'Bodje but did not necessarily have his father's titles of nobility. The *bade*, whose domain extended from Sen Baowal to Siringe, was the last of the three *samba linger* who could claim succession to the *brak*. Then came the *maarosa*, who governed the Richard-Toll at the riverbank of Goram with residence at Rosso; he was chosen from among the paternal brothers of the *brak*.

After the *maarosa* came the *beeco* who lived first at Pum, and then at Roos Beeco where his position, near Saint-Louis—between the lands of the Moors and Kajoor—gave him a prominent place in the kingdom. Indeed, he played an important role in the solution of crises of succession and in the defense of the land against external menaces. Then came the *riket*, who commanded Khomak or Lake Cayar as far as Tene u Buur and Gura-Jey. Next came the *kangam* of lesser importance: the *bërlof,* the *biño*, the *botal Njaay,* the *bar ganjool* or *njamal ganjool,* the *jawdin ngangum,* the *bërci,* lastly the *man gass* on the right riverbank. Finally, the political chiefs, representing the noble families, ruled over independent domains—birthplaces of the families of great nobility.

The banks of the Senegal River were the birthplaces of the *Seb* and were only taken dominated by them. The states of the *jawdin* extended from Ndiugar to Ndiaw: the *maalo* commanded the Marwayal at Ndiugar on the left bank. Finally, the *jogomaay*, who had as its only state the village of Tungen in Jurbel, the capital, was personally tied to the *brak*. All the meetings, and all receptions at the court, were conducted in the home of the *jogomaay*.

This distribution of the offices, covering a well-defined territory, evolved over the course of time owing to the shrinkage of the borders of Waalo; a significant portion would be seized by the neighboring countries of Fuuta Toro, Trarza and Kajoor.[39]

Moreover, the three members of *seb ak bawor* did not have power so much due to the extent of their territory as through the political power which bestowed unto them the possibility of electing or deposing the *brak*. The evolution of the administration of the kingdom had thus been marked by the conflict between the *seb ak bawor*, who wanted to perpetuate the double-headed character of power; the great chiefs of the province who strove to preserve their autonomy and the *brak*, who attempted (often by force) to establish an autocratic monarchy.

The Beneficiaries of the Privileges

Among the noble women one distinguishes two dignitaries: the *linger* and the *awo*. The *linger* was the first lady of the kingdom and was most often the mother or the maternal sister of the *brak*, who had to choose her. The *awo* was the first wife of the *brak* and occupied second place in the female hierarchy. The *linger* and the *aawo* governed those areas that were by hereditary attached to their titles. They would appoint a *farba* or a *jaraaf*, captives of the crown, to manage the areas: "Those housekeepers, charged with the role of maintaining the food supply and the cleaning of the laundry of the surrounding family-circles of the kings and the hosts of the large cities, were expected to live at their own expenses in the royal residences called Pehi."[40]

These heavily attended princesses, through the large sumptuous feasts which they gave, and through the gifts which they made to the nobles as allowances, contributed largely to establishing the authority of the *brak*. They played thus an important role in the succession of the throne. The *linger*, in particular, played a major political role in the history of Waalo, because she was above all the keeper of the possessions of the family *meen*—the good management of which assured victory in the pursuit of power.

The Personnel of Servile Origin

As underlings subjected to the central authority, the functionaries of servile origin played a fundamental role as obedient instruments in the war between the authority of the *brak* and the hereditary authority of the nobles. Among the most important were the *bëknéég Jurbel*, the *badj*, and the *alkaati*. The *bëknéég jurbel* was the chief of the captives of the crown; the *jaam u buur i* dealt with the royal cabinet and transmitted the orders and instructions of the *brak*. Le Maire described him in 1682 as being the grand master and the first gentleman of the council. He managed in times of trouble to take a predominant position and to occupy—with the victory of the *ceddo* warriors—the position of prime minister. The *badj* was the chief of the *doom u jaambur*, in charge of the royal household.

Thanks to Atlantic slave trade, a very important office emerged: the *alkaati*. It was entrusted to a slave of the crown, who received the taxes paid by the European merchants to the *brak* in order to trade freely. Although dependent on the sovereign for whom he kept a large portion of the revenues, the *alkaati* also served as minister of foreign affairs. Indeed, it was he who in 1638 proposed peace to Captain Lambert in the name of the *brak*.[41]

The Personnel of People of the Castes

In Waalo, each caste had a chief in charge of relations with the political power. The *brak* nominated a *bitique* or *fara tëgg i jurbel* for the blacksmiths, a *ngala i jurbel* for the musicians and a *farba jun jun* for the "griots."

The Chiefs of the Muslim Minorities

These individuals were called *sëriñ* and often had concessions with which they could establish and organize their followers. They achieved integration with the system of feudal relations and thus came to pay the same fees as the other chiefs.[42]

The Judiciary Apparatus

The *brak* was the supreme chief of justice, but the judiciary apparatus was divided among different social statuses: "The chief of the lineage, the lord of the land or the waters, the chief of an ethnic minority, of an order or a caste are also judges specialized in the domains where one does not contest their competence."[43] However, at the end of the seventeenth century, the marabout took on an important role in the exercise of justice. Concerning this, Chambonneau says, "As for justice, it is administered by their Marabouts to whom alone this right belongs. Justice is called in the Negro language *Hione Hialla*, which means 'The way of God'. So they render justice freely and at the time that the parties ask for it...it is they (the Marabouts) who make the distribution of inheritances, which consist merely of furniture, cattle, millet and other things there being no immovables among the Negroes, and none of the heirs will touch anything before the deceased's debts are paid. So one does not see among them any riots, plundering, thefts or murders, or indeed if there are any, they are so rare that they are not considered to deserve punishment by death. It is only when it happens that one man has killed another, or has committed some other crime, that he either becomes a slave of the relatives of the dead man, or, if he has some property, he can ransom himself by giving a slave to the king and another to the relatives."[44]

The Military Apparatus

Formed at the outset through massive recruitment, the military apparatus transformed itself quickly into a professional army that mainly consisted of the captives of the crown—the warriors called *ceddo*. La Courbe, in 1685, noted that the *brak* could, when needed, deploy: "ten thousand men on foot including the auxiliary troops of the Moors who lived on his land."[45] The cavalry played an important role within this army. In 1681 Barbot noted that the *brak* maintained "five or six thousand horses after this manner, which enables him to make frequent excursions into the dominions of his neighbors to get cattle, slaves or provisions."[46] Le Maire described the cavalrymen as "armed with zagayes, which are a type of big and long darts, and three or four javelins, equipped with a piece of iron larger than that of the arrows and having several small hooks piercing the wound when one wants to remove them. They throw their javelins and the zagayes far enough, they rarely go without them. Besides that they have a saber and a Moorish knife, a cubit long and two thumbs wide. They ward off strikes with a shield made of strong thick leather. Although these many things could hinder them, they never leave their arms and their hand free and they are ready to attack."[47] The largest portion of the army, whose soldiers carried weapons, consisted nevertheless of foot soldiers that carried "a saber, javelins, and a quiver equipped with fifty or sixty poisoned arrows of which the injury is always fatal if one does not burn it."[48]

The goal of the campaigns often was to pillage and share the loot. They did not last a long time. However, due to the slave trade, war became the primary activity of the kings and thus lay at the center of relations between the different kingdoms of Senegambia. Hunting for individuals in the name of the Atlantic slave trade thus contributed a permanent factor of instability to Waalo until the nineteenth century.

The Fiscal Apparatus

The first European voyagers unanimously recognized the vulnerability of the revenues of the *brak*. Chambonneau noted: "All the revenues of these kings consist of cattle, slaves, and several estates where they sow millet…"[49] F. Y. B. Gaby noted: "The kings do not have the right to impose any monetary taxes on their people. All their revenues consisted of captives and cattle."[50] Indeed, in the framework of a self-sustaining economy, the only fees imposed were the *lamanale* payments, which the peasants paid to the lords of the waters and the land. The *lamanes* for their part paid at each new inauguration a tax called *jëk* to the *brak*, considered the temporary owner of the land.[51] Lastly, each year during the feasts of *Gamu*, all the *kangam* "were held to present themselves to the *brak* to bring the *moyal* (or part of pillage). The *moyal* was divided in the following way: 1/3 to the *brak*; 1/3 to members of the *seb ak bawor* and 1/3 to cover the expenses of the feast."[52]

But as the Atlantic slave trade grew, the revenues of the *brak* grew considerably and consisted primarily of the taxes, which the foreign merchants paid so as to trade their goods on the Senegal River. The payment of these taxes lay at at the center of the relationships between Waalo and the French trading post of Saint-Louis ever since the latter was founded circa 1659.

PART II
WAALO SINCE 1659 UNTIL THE END OF THE EIGHTEENTH CENTURY: THE ERA OF THE SLAVE TRADE AND THE FORTIFIED COMMERCIAL TRADING POSTS

In the fifteenth century, the Portuguese discoveries gave a new dimension to the world by putting into permanent contact Africa, Asia, and the Americas with a Europe that frantically pursued new markets. In this global race, Portugal became the first European nation to carve out a huge empire that unleashed a long and passionate rivalry with the other European powers. The Portuguese also aspired to have power among the colonists, which the Pope had bestowed on Portugal so easily without parceling the colonized lands amongst the European nations. As Eric Williams said, "The Black had himself also found his place in the sun, although he had not asked for a place under the burning sun of the sugar, tobacco and cotton plantations of the New World."[1] Indeed, with the development of the sugar industry came the formation of privileged companies conducting three-way commerce during the second half of the seventeenth century. In this system, African commerce played a significant role in the economy of a mercantile Europe that would usher in modern capitalism.

This was the era of the slave trade, and for more than two centuries it would create the framework of Waalo's historic evolution. Indeed, the French trading post of Saint-Louis, constructed around 1659 at the mouth of the Senegal River and at the edge of Waalo, responded above all to this intractable need for an African workforce for the Americas. Gum also played a predominant role at the end of the eighteenth century.

During that entire period, Waalo remained a secondary source for the slave trade. However, its geographical position subjected it to the consequences of that trade to a significant degree. This was partly through the pressure of neighboring peoples (particularly the Moors of Trarza), the atmosphere of insecurity-generating famines, and the internal dissentions and civil wars, which sparked the economic, political and social crisis that raged throughout that period.

This crisis gave rise to two antagonistic and often interdependent forces. The first was composed of the warrior party of the *ceddo*, influenced to a large degree by the Atlantic commerce—which provided arms and ammunition for their wars—and was monopolized by the traditional aristocracy, always divided into rival clans. The second consisted of the party of the marabouts who, with their followers, attempted without success to oppose the trade and to reorganize the traditionally undermined society on the foundation of Islamic principles. These are the major evolutionary traits of the kingdom of Waalo, which we trace from 1659 to the end of the eighteenth century.

CHAPTER 3

ATLANTIC COMMERCE IN THE ERA OF THE FORTIFIED TRADING POSTS

The competition between the various European powers in the aftermath of the decline of Portuguese commerce began in the second half of the seventeenth century, after the founding of Goree by the Dutch. The process of dividing the coast into zones of influence ushered in an era of fortified commercial trading posts. Thus, "After Richelieu again the maritime and colonial politics of France in hand, the first French establishment was founded at the mouth of the Senegal River."[1] This became the French trading post of Saint-Louis, which, by reserving the commerce of the Senegal River exclusively for France, played an important role in the history of Waalo.

The Trading Post of Saint-Louis: History and Role

The historic problem presented by the unknown dates and sites of the different establishments at the mouth of the Senegal River, and before the definite establishment at the actual island of Saint-Louis-du-Fort (Ndar), is to a large degree studied by Cultru, Rosseau, Abdoulaye Ly and Jean Boulègue.[2] In the lack of any new evidence, we will content ourselves with summarizing their results so as to reach an arguably essential goal: identifying the economic and political function of this trading post in relation to the nations of the Senegal River and in particular Waalo.

We have already noted that at the end of the sixteenth century and the beginning of the seventeenth century the Portuguese sounded a cry of alarm at confronting the threatening invasions of the Dutch, the English and most of all the French in the commerce of the Senegal River. In response to these threats, Lavanha proposed the construction of a fort. This project did not see the light of day because of the victory of the merchants of Rouen and Dieppe, whose efforts we are able to follow thanks to the chronicles in the town of Dieppe by David Asseline.

The naval war between France and England expanded down to the river where the inhabitants of Dieppe "wanted to repair the damages and miseries, which that city had suffered, captured from the English in 1628 with Captain Bontemps two ships, which transported a cargo of 100 Blacks and a cargo evaluated at 130,000 pounds."[3] On June 24, 1633, the Company of

Cape Verde, Senegal and the Gambia was formed with a trade monopoly of ten years.[4] But from March 11, 1634 onward, the assembly of the council drew attention to the detrimental competition of the Dutch, who had been in a position to banish the French.[5] This precipitated the construction in 1638 of the first permanent French habitation at the mouth of the Senegal River. It was the work of Captain Thomas Lambert, who had made several voyages to Senegal, and it is recounted to us by Jannequin de Rochefort.

However, it is difficult from the actual documentation to clearly define under what conditions or balance of powers the first fort was erected. However, Jannequin informs us that Thomas Lambert "received two envoys, one from the part of Damel, a close good friend of our captain who came offering all assistance and safety on his lands, the other from the part of the king brak with whom he had been at war before the voyage, which he undertook to give the dan-samba, who wanted to say hello in their language and he asked him to no longer remember their old quarrels and as at each time if he still wanted war he would then like peace in which he would be very content."[6]

This is proof that there were hostilities among the Waalo and Captain Lambert for as yet unknown reasons. But one can say that it was the cannon that convinced the *brak*. Jannequin adds: "It is necessary for you to know that these nations which fear us because of our artillery, sixty of us, well entrenched, are able to destroy six million men of that country, who have nothing but arrows and sagayes as weapons."[7] Moreover, some years later Captain Lambert did not hesitate to employ artillery against the Waalo. It is conceivable that the demand for European merchandise and especially the superiority of European firearms facilitated the establishing of this habitation, all the more so because it was located on an island.[8]

Thus we surmise there must have been a *modus vivendi,* in so far as Jannequin specifies it: "Our captain who had no other plan than to load his ship with their merchandise and not to conquer their territories, and not to exterminate them there, did not have difficulties to accept the conditions of peace with the *brak* but always with distrust."[9] Indeed, the relative power of the military monarchies on the coast prevented any European settlements on the continent; distances and conditions of the voyages of that era did not allow for maintenance of a considerable ability to resist attacks. It was not by accident that Europeans sought extensively to establish themselves primarily on the islands, given the commodities of defense against the indigenes.

In this manner, the same Captain Lambert returned to Senegal to complete the settlement, begun in 1638.[10] Finally, in 1643 Captain Lambert left for Senegal again, where "having happily arrived he unloaded his supplies of weapons and food and decided to stay and fortify his habitation in such a good way which put him into a condition not to fear the insults of the

Blacks of that country. While he did that, he made it appear that he was very resolute and brave in war and magnificent in his habitation."[11]

This passage leads us to presume that the establishing of the fort encountered a certain resistance on the part of Waalo. Therefore Captain Lambert, in the final analysis, used the war to establish himself there. Resistance broke out anew following his refusal to pay taxes at Waalo. Indeed, the chronicle continues: "This haughty and ambitious attitude which the captain affected, was (so it seemed) the reason why he refused to pay dues or customs which certain small kings demanded from the inhabitants of Dieppe when barks were stationed there at the river and passed in front of their lands and that someone was there, who would undertake to make an attempt at their life and their goods. What happened secretly took place at night in 20 locations, with 200 Blacks planning to surprise captain Lambert and to set fire to his barques, as they would have done, had he not kept alert and not pushed them back through the continual fire of his musketeers, who killed most of these savages and forced others to retreat to the land where they had come from."[12]

Chambonneau confirms this pugilistic response of Captain Lambert, and contrasts it with the conciliatory manner of Du Boulle after the massacre on the riverbank, on November 14, 1675, of six whites and Laptots (African colonial troops). He noted: "There was not even one, but particularly M. Du Boulle, who did not mourn the death of his son and that of the others, and the consequence of this action, which, if left unpunished and if one did not burn and ransack like Captain Lambert had done a very long time ago, that there would no longer be any hope to escape."[13] Similarly, La Courbe in 1685 recalls that the *brak* "remembered what had happened to the little brak at the time of captain Lambert who, before the residency was built had nothing but a little wooden hut, defended himself twice against more than two-hundred Blacks who came to attack him, of whom he killed ten of twelve."[14]

Was it not partly this fear of artillery that prevented the *brak*s for a long time from returning to the habitation in Saint-Louis? It is written that in 1685 the *brak* declined the invitation from La Courbe: "He let it be said to me that he was strictly obliged to my visit only if it would have been permitted for him to enter the dwelling of whites, he wanted to inform me, but that neither his father nor his grandfather nor his great-grandfather nor any his predecessors would never have let him do so and that for that reason he is not permitted to go there."[15] The trade of Dieppe continually grew stronger: "The inhabitants of Dieppe handled the trade of Senegal…They filled their storage facilities of merchandise and they loaded their ships off Dieppe which came from time to time and from which the residents of that town as well as those of Rouen obtained great profits and the entire kingdom many of its commodities."[16]

The trafficking continued thus until 1660—the date that to our understanding marked the first mention of the definite establishment of the fort on the Island of Saint-Louis by Sieur Caullier, placed by Cultru to 1659.[17] The fort already had the name of the island, because the ship that arrived in Senegal was named the *Saint-Louis*. Indeed, until the vessel departed for Senegal, "it left the settlement of the people of Dieppe in very good condition, under the command of Sieur Louys Caullier, commissary of the Company of merchants of Dieppe and of Rouen and its surroundings. Incidentally, I will say that this settlement is on a little island on the Senegal River, a league away from the ocean, and that the people of Dieppe have been constrained to establish themselves there and derive their merchandises from there, seeing that the ocean had broken the sandbar of the mouth of that river and that it knocked down the buildings of the settlement which Sir Caullier had constructed in about 1658 after those of Captein Lambert, who we talked about elsewhere, was swept away by the waves of that element and fell into ruins after his death."[18]

Thus, we have accounts of three successive settlements: the one of Lambert (1638), the one of Caullier (1658)—both of which were on the Island of Bocos— and a third constructed by Caullier on the present island of Saint-Louis in about 1658.[19] Chambonneau, in 1675, largely confirmed this hypothesis of Cultru and the chronicle of Dieppe: "Mr. Demuchins spent some time in the old settlement, otherwise Bakosse, which is close to the Island of the British, about a league from the settlement, which he had left several years ago, because it had been inundated and half destroyed by the sea of the sandbar, which changed, nothing remained there except one steeple. At this place he had stayed quite often and he called it therefore his 'Versailles,' he employed always a commissary to do the trading, he himself had the old lodgings restored and started a little fort there to command the entry to the river."[20]

In summary, after more than half a century of tight competition between diverse European powers and especially after the numerous hostilities with Waalo, the first French trading post on the West Coast of Africa was born. The Fort of Saint-Louis "[t]ruly like an immobile barge anchored on the river" was to a great extent a response to the exigencies of the era's Atlantic commerce. First, the island of Saint-Louis presented the advantage of protecting the entrance to the Senegal River, the commerce of which was exclusively reserved for the French. Secondly, its reduced surface area allowed for stronger defense against the threats from Waloo and the neighboring kingdoms. Lastly, the island served as a stronghold for the storage of enslaved individuals, discouraging all attempts to escape. These multiple advantages explain why other powers coveted this key site of commerce in the Senegal River, at a time when the slave trade had already begun to dominate African commerce. Saint-Louis, like an octopus, stretched its tentacles over Waalo, and thus its history can no longer be examined from this point on without taking the Atlantic commerce into account.

THE ATLANTIC COMMERCE

We have seen that since the fifteenth century, Waalo became an avenue for Atlantic commerce, which had bit by bit supplanted the Trans-Saharan commerce. But in the last stretch of the seventeenth century, the Atlantic commerce suddenly took on a new dimension with the development of the slave trade. Let us first attempt to define the origin of this commerce, which came to dominate the trading with Waalo.

Development of the Slave Trade

We know already from Godinho that Senegal was not like Gambia in terms of the *resgate* (ransom) for gold. It was most of all a source for enslaved individuals. Turning away through Arguin the majority of Trans-Saharan traffic, the Portuguese traded each year between 800 and 1000 enslaved individuals.[21] The importance of this activity of slave trading during the first years of the Portuguese occupation of the African coast had often been neglected. A recent study of one of the first attempts to establish a sugar plantation on the island of St. Thomas with slave labor revealed the existence of slave trafficking with Arguin during the entire sixteenth century.[22] In 1600, Lavanha, describing the advantages of the Portuguese trade on the Senegal River, mentions that enslaved individuals represented the main item of trafficking.[23]

The Dutch, who infiltrated the Portuguese colonies in the first part of the seventeenth century, particularly the sugar-producing area of northeast Brazil, pursued the slave trade in the Senegal River, where their powerful competitiveness became visible. It is nevertheless difficult to clearly define the importance of that commercial; one can only remark that the cargo taken in 1628 by the inhabitants of Dieppe to the English in Senegal included 100 enslaved individuals.[24]

Unfortunately, Dieppe, the only one to report the French activities in Senegal in that period, is silent about that trafficking. One cannot, however, deny that the commerce in enslaved individuals did not very soon constitute an important activity. Indeed, it did so to the extent where, as Abdoulaye Ly remarks, the African workforce played a non-negligible role in the colonization of the Americas during the first half of the seventeenth century.[25] But it was not until 1664, the date of the founding of the French West India Company (*Compagnie des Indes occidentales*), that the slave trade dominated African commerce. Indeed, this date coincides with the resumption of colonial politics by Colbert; since 1660, sugar, which supplanted tobacco, required an increasing workforce for cheap.

The commerce in enslaved individuals inaugurated thus "one of the most important transports of people which had ever taken place on the surface of the oceans," and with its economic advantages was integrated into the cogwheel of mercantile politics that would prevail during the seventeenth and the entire eighteenth century in France. Testimonies that correctly identify the weight of the slave trade in the economy of Western powers are not lacking. Indeed, this "economic commodity," which was the slave trade and Euro-American in origin, had "already in the course of the seventeenth century…developed into a necessity of international competition" because the war was then "a war of sugar, and consequently a war of enslaved individuals, but also a war for the markets."[26]

In 1684 the importance of that commerce was defined in this way: "This trade, which strictly served as the base and the foundation of all others, because it were the slaves who cultivated the land and who produced the merchandises of the land in such a way that if they went on missing, the Islands would fall into ruins."[27] That need was constant, because in 1762 another account used the same terms to describe the importance of African commerce as "one of the principle foundations of commerce and navigation of France and England. It provides them with enslaved individuals for the cultivation of the colonies, which produced sugar, indigo, cocoa, cotton. It is only through the work of the slaves that one can obtain these precious goods from the Western colonies …. Indeed, this commerce is not only precious through gold and ivory, it is infinitely more so through the Blacks, who show themselves solely capable to endure the difficult labors, which cultivation and refineries demand in the colonies where the heat alone of the climate is an overwhelming load. What commerce can indeed be compared to that the result of which is to obtain men in exchange for merchandises! One should really regard it as the foundation of the colonies and consequently as the principal resource to our maritime commerce."[28]

Citing Eric Williams, we add that the argument of climate does not hold up well; Amerindians and Europeans preceded the Africans in the plantations. In the final analysis, the profitability of the slave labor and the accompanying racial distortion has been labeled a fundamentally economic phenomenon. "Slavery is not due to racism. Racism is rather the consequence of slavery."[29]

This shows nevertheless the permanence of that need, and above all the magnitude of the slave trade to the Americas during that time. Considering its economic consequences, one can scarcely compare it to the much earlier Trans-Saharan commerce. Therefore there is no point in affirming, as per Brunschwig, that "Africa had nothing to offer except people."[30] One knows that Europe could not during all these centuries satisfy its "craving for slaves" and that it did unceasingly utilize an African workforce for its sugar colonies. This need of Europe for such trafficking ceased only with the appearance, in the nineteenth century, of new economic necessities incompatible with the slave trade.[31] Jean Suret-Canale states that "in place of the activity of production the most lucrative occupation became the war with its stream of destruction of people and materials, the war for the acquisition of slaves to trade with the risk for the slave hunter, of his luck turning to become himself captive and to follow with shackles on his legs the paths strewn with bones leading to ports where he had previously followed his brothers. This is when the permanent insecurity, the wars and the incessant raids, generating misery and famine became permanent features of black Africa and only then."[32]

There has been a tendency to minimize the importance of Senegambia in the slave trade, but a detailed examination shows us both the antiquity of that trafficking and its permanence due to the proximity of the Americas. A chronicle before 1790 recounts: "The extraction of the Blacks from Senegal is all the more beneficial for its colonies as the crossing is much shorter from the coast of New Guinea achieving lower mortality rates."[33]

This requires us to rethink the issue of the slave trade which, in the final analysis, is less important in terms of the number of enslaved individuals sold than in the atmosphere of insecurity that it engendered—which was considered secondary during the centuries when the slave trade was the permanent feature of that area.

The recent work of Philip Curtin concerning the slave trade tends to disproportionally underestimate the total number of enslaved individuals sold in the New World and thereby to minimize the impact of this trade on the development of African societies. This study of a case limited to a secondary zone of slave trading indicates that the problem does not reside in the number of enslaved individuals, but in the total economic system engendered by that trade. This trade, where a person became the equivalent of merchandise, constitutes a stand-alone phenomenon with its exigencies, which would spark in Africa over the centuries a particular revolution. It is the impact of the slave trade that explains the economic, political and social blockade at the end of the nineteenth century.[34]

Le Maire in 1682 drew a comprehensive picture of that trade in Senegal: "In exchange for these negroes we trade cotton baft, copper, tin, iron, spirits and a few glass trinkets. From such trading we make a profit of 800 percent. Hides, ivory and gum go to France. As for the slaves, they are sent to the French islands in America to work on sugar plantations. Good quality slaves can be had for ten francs apiece, to be resold for over a hundred ecus [French coins]. Often enough, you can get a pretty good slave for four or five jars of alcohol. So one spends less on purchases than on transport, since outfitting the ships costs a great deal."[35] Such is then this trade: "a particular genre where the slave serves more and more as a monetary equivalent at the same equity as a piece of cattle, a bar of salt or cowry shells."[36]

Since the beginning of the eighteenth century, the interior region of Galam constituted the major source of enslaved individuals exported from Saint-Louis. However, it is within Waalo that we attempt to better comprehend the importance of this Atlantic commerce of slave trade.

LOCALIZATION AND IMPORTANCE OF ATLANTIC COMMERCE IN WAALO

The existing body of documentation makes it difficult to define the commerce of Saint-Louis in Waalo, given the scant sources that are generally centered on trafficking as a whole on the Senegal River.

Description

Until the French conquest in the nineteenth century, almost all commerce took place on the river, where aboard their boats the merchants of Saint-Louis could profit while protecting their goods and themselves due to superior weapons. Ritchie notes that the ship of the trader in Senegal "was a home as well as a means of conveyance besides being a warehouse, shop, and fortress, heavy armed with cannon and carrying a body of loptots who acted as marines trained in the use of European weapons."[37] The navigation was seasonal and one could not travel back on the river to Galam more than once a year. But one could travel almost continuously throughout the year through Waalo, because of its proximity and primarily because of the numerous branches of the river. The transport was generally conducted on small 12-ton boats; a typical crew consisted of seven or eight Frenchmen, ten or twelve Laptots (African troops under France colonialism), and one linguist who played the important role of interpreter and broker.

Localization of Points of Trade or Ports in Waalo

The trading was generally conducted in Biërt, in Maca, which La Courbe calls: "The stopover of the little junket, is a stopover or port on the river at eight leagues from our settlement."[38] Trading also occurred at Bouscar, situated at twelve locations in Saint-Louis, forming a cluster of several villages in a great plain on the edge of the water. This commerce took place primarily at the crossroads of the desert, which was the major market of Waalo and of which the European voyagers provided numerous descriptions. In 1686 La Courbe wrote it is situated at two places in Jurbel, the capital: "This is a place which we call the desert, because it is a large sterile plain, which has as a tree only one big fan-palm planted on the riverbank…This is the place where it is the custom to trade Arabic gum with the Moors. My barque was immersed at two fathoms from the bank at a deep spot, forbidding its occupants the entire space to my surprise and dismay. No day went by in which no gum arrived. We saw long caravans of ten, twenty or thirty camels or cattle as carriers approaching."[39]

Lastly, there was the stopover at Jurbel, not far from the village of Ingrin on Lake Cayar. During that period there were few attempts to trade in the interior of the land, even at Lake Guiers. Thus, over the course of centuries, the river provided a unique and major artery for the commerce of Saint-Louis. One can say that each village on its banks was a possible stopover as a result of the Atlantic trade.

Goods and Currents of Trading (Flows of Exchange)

River commerce was dominated by the slave trade and the gum trade. This duality of two markets, coming from two often antagonistic worlds, formed the backdrop of its economic history. Indeed, as suggested in an account of the Senegal Company, "Climbing up the riverbank one has on the left hand side the land of the Moors. They were those who made the commerce of gum, which they transported on the camels around the month of June over the edge of the riverbanks …on the right hand side is the land of the Negroes with who there is not any commerce except that of captives and elephant teeth. The trade in captives has not until now been that strongly dominating in this region. But the company hopes to increase it considerably."[40] In 1693 La Courbe talks of "two-hundred captives traded, costing no more than thirty pounds a piece and which are sold on the islands at three hundred pounds making at least a sum of 60 000 pounds."[41]

It is difficult to estimate the total number of enslaved individuals sold by Waalo because of the absence of precise documents. The number varies, contingent on wars and other circumstances, but the demand was permanent. Pruneau de Pomme-Gorge, who was in Senegal from 1740 to 1752, said of Waalo: "The women are beautiful and well-shaped, of a singular intelligence. They learn with the greatest facility... This aptitude to understand readily makes them so esteemed by our inhabitants of America that the small number of them that are taken to them there sell for 20 or 30 pistoles above the price of the women from other countries…As for the men, they are more suitable for hunting and fishing than for anything else. As a rule there are very few captives in this country, not only because of its small size and because it is poorly populated, but even more because the chief would not dare to have his subjects carried off openly without risking a revolt by his country."[42]

Such circumstances did not stop British Governor O'Hara from trading; in less than six months there were 8,000 enslaved individuals after a raid of Waalo in 1775.[43] This further proves the impossibility of establishing any firm statistic, because the payment of 52 captives of *brak* Yeerim Mbañik, in 1718, to the trading post of Saint-Louis, showed the enslaved person had become the equivalent of the quintessential piece of merchandise. Moreover, the *brak*'s pledge to go to Fuuta to pay off the debt, which he had taken as the equivalent in merchandise, shows that war had become the primary means of procuring enslaved individuals.[44] He made war with his neighbor, and in retaliation the neighbor made war against him.

The manhunt is universally about insecurity. Barbot in 1681 described the different ways to obtain enslaved individuals, citing the 47 enslaved individuals sold by the *brak*: "Those sold by the blacks are for the most part prisoners of war, taken either in fight, or pursuit, or in the incursions into their enemies territories; others stolen away by their own countrymen and some there are, who will sell their own children…or neighbors.… The kings are so absolute that upon any slight pretense of offenses committed by their subjects, they order them to be sold as slaves without regard to rank, or profession.…Abundance of little Blacks of both sexes are also stolen away by their neighbors, when found abroad on the roads, or in the woods; or else in the Cougans, or cornfields at the time of the year, when their parents keep them there all day, to scare away the devouring small birds, that come to feed on the millet…"[45]

This atmosphere of insecurity explains the detrimental consequences of this slave trade to productive strength, at a time when Europe was constructing an economy that would lead to modern capitalism. The famines that punctuate the history of Waalo are innumerable, and the wars to procure enslaved individuals are constant; nothing can be explained outside this economic context, except the slave trade. The rest of the trading represents little, often merely complementing the slave trade.

Indeed, the next significant trade after the slave trade was that of leather. La Courbe wrote in 1685: "In the past one traded at this river twenty-five to thirty thousand hides and no one can hardly trade twelve thousand."[46] One traded also "Gray amber…and the elephant's teeth," the value of which is difficult to ascertain. Then there is gum, the monopoly of the Moors and an important factor in the relationship with Waalo. We have a few scattered figures that can give us an idea of the importance of the commerce of Saint-Louis in Waalo. On January 11, 1724, "Sir Jean Demion arrived to trade at Serimpate, dependent on *Bequio* Maly Coury, from where he brought back 15 captives all of sufficient beautiful appearance, 330 fur-hides and 251 pieces of cattle."[47] Nevertheless, Sir Jean Demion's list of the products traded at the desert stopover from April 3 to June 4, 1724 is more indicative of the nature of this commerce:

327 Moorish fifth of gum, a
cubic measure for 550 £, total
net weight 179 – 850 lbs   6,369 £ 10s

50 captives as they are listed in the text of the journal	2,259 £
131 pieces of cattle	884 £
120 leather hides	100 £
200 lbs. butter	152 £
400 lbs. couscous	62 £
106 sheep	256 £
4200 lbs. millet	503 £
50 lbs. millet	24 £
40 lbs. of chicken	18 £
70 lbs. soap	32 £
60 lbs. tobacco	43 £

These various purchases, in addition to the costs of the voyage, the maintenance, and the taxes paid to the *brak*, resulted in a total sum of 14,299 £ 10s, representing the capital invested at that stopover.[48] This table also reveals another aspect of the commerce between Waloo and Saint-Louis—that of restocking the island with food supplies. Remember that the island of Saint-Louis, while hosting an ever-increasing population, was also a storage facility for enslaved individuals; they had to be stored there for weeks before transported by ships to the Americas. Thus the port of Saint-Louis depended solely on the continent for supplies of all kinds, even on drinking water.

This gave Waalo a place in the commerce in Saint-Louis, namely that of millet. Chambonneau writes that from December 1675 to March 10, 1676, he occupied himself with the single aim to resupply the island after the departure of the Biërt with "millet of which we had great need for the great number of captives which we traded everyday."[49] The transport of millet was also "made on little boats. They carry a hundred *matas* of the big *moule* of millet, which is the measure of the country, which we use at the settlement to accommodate ourselves to them. This comes to seventy barrels or thereabouts."[50] Cattle and other food supplies were also crucial trafficking items. Thus Saint-Louis lived constantly in fear of famine, especially because of the delays of the ships coming from France corresponded with periods of hostilities with the hinterlands.

The table below lists the merchandise that Waalo received in exchange for its enslaved individuals: millet, cattle and other diverse items. Sir Demion provided these items for the purchase of the 50 enslaved individuals:

201 hides at 4 £ per piece	804 £

1 small silver trinket and its chain	25 £
1 trumpet	50 £
5 light shot guns at 50 £ per piece	250 £
8 strings of round red agate at 6 £ per string	48 £
1 ell and 1/2 of scarlet cloth at 32 £ each	48 £
24 pints of brandy at 3 £ per pint	72 £
12 flat iron rods at 6 £ per rod	72 £
75 lbs. gun powder at 2 £ per lbs.	150 £
104 lbs. lead bullets at 1 £ per lbs.	104 £
225 ells of blue and black cloth at 2 £ per ell	450 £
69 ells of cloth from Rouen at 2 £ per ell	138 £
12 metric tons of red pebbles at 4 £ per ton	48 £[51]

One notes the prevalence of iron, firearms, fabrics and "brandy" in the trading—all articles destined to assure continued manhunts in the context of continuous wars. This would help to establish the authority of the traditional aristocracy, the only beneficiary of the advantages of Atlantic commerce.

Such were more or less the main features of the commerce of Saint-Louis with the kingdom of Waalo. This important observation notes that the river formed the nexus of that commerce, constantly animated at its stopovers by the incessant journeys of small boats. But, despite this intensity of trading, it is not entirely different from the old Trans-Saharan commerce, which involved the same articles, albeit in smaller quantities. Firearms constituted the only great novelty of Atlantic trade, and they contributed more to establish military aristocracies than to foster a development of productive forces. Moreover, this Atlantic commerce did not totally eliminate the Trans-Saharan commerce, which continued for a long time to compete with the trafficking, primarily that of slaves, at the trading post of Saint-Louis. La Courbe, in 1686, remarked that "[t]he Moors are great horse dealers and feed many of the horses, which they barter with the blacks against captives who they then go to sell very far from these lands."[52] In 1736 the director of commerce at Saint-Louis added: "He has made few captives at the river this year, brak has made 5 to 6 efforts, which have produced nothing, the majority has past into the hands of the Moors for their horses. We want to try the commerce of horses in this season and to make a little profit we will continue dividing them, besides the black kings, with the Moors."

It did not take long for the conflict between the two economies to explode. In 1673, it happened under the guise of war with the marabouts, which we will later examine in greater detail. Moreover, the gum trade, which progressively took a prominent place in the commerce of Senegal, helped consolidate the position of the Berbers, whose pressure could be felt in Waalo. Indeed, the ascension to power of the Trarza people is one of the major consequences of the Atlantic commerce of Waalo.

The Taxes

While Waalo was strong enough to defend its territory, the trading post of Saint-Louis paid taxes to the *brak* for the protection of its commerce and free navigation on the river. The absence of documents, primarily during the first period of the Atlantic commerce, does not permit us to follow their development. But these payments were often at the center of the relations between Saint-Louis and Waalo. As mentioned, in 1643, the non-payment of taxes sparked the hostilities between Waalo and Captain Lambert. La Courbe is the first to describe the payment of certain of these taxes, which became quite diverse. For example, at the stopover in the desert, one had to pay a tax of this nature: "For each quintal (100 kilos) which was measured he has the right to take five of the largest balls of gum, and he has a man doing that and after he has a 100 kilos he demands the payments." At the same stopover, Demion writes that he paid the *brak* a tax of 69 £ and that he made him a present of 291 £. It is very difficult, however, to distinguish between these types of payments and particularly to discern the development of these multiple taxes.

One reason why records of the beginning of commerce at Saint-Louis are rare is the fact that many were burned at the time of the British occupation of Saint-Louis, so as to hide economic information relating to the trafficking on the river. There does exist a description by Father Labat of his experience in West Africa that gives us an idea of these taxes between 1697 and 1702. He wrote: "I reserve for the last chapter of departure from Senegal the indispensible taxes which one pays to kings and to nobles if one wants to have good connections with them and practice free trade. Although the blacks do not write and have no one to register so that they can recall the details of the merchandise and trinkets, which one has to give them, they have such a fortunate memory, which never betrays them. They try, on the contrary, to increase their customs when persecuted. Nevertheless I have renewed since the year 1697 until 1702 to pay only what is listed in the following table."

We have extracted from this table of total taxes those that were paid in Waalo. This table indicates that the nature of the merchandise is the same as that of those in the ongoing commercial trading. But more importantly, the total value of the taxes is actually higher than that of the total commerce of Waalo with Saint-Louis. Waalo, indeed, was far from being an interested commercial partner in comparison to the land of Galam. But, due to the strategic importance of its situation at the gate of Saint-Louis, it undeniably held the key to commerce on the river.

Taxes to pay each year to the king and the nobles at the shores of the Senegal River as to the following merchandises:	Trading for salt at Bïer	To the king Brac [brak] and his officers	To the little Brac [brak]
leg chains		2	
trumpets and their chains		1	
twisted bangles		6	
connected bangles		5	
pataques d'allemagne (German leather)		1	
escalins (coins)		15	
four pieces of coins		122	
bonnets of red wool		7	
fire swatter		10	
corral		4 ounces 4.9. 1/2	
flemish knives		15	
hats		1	1
red copper kettles of six pounds		6	6
chests of balsam pine		2	
fine crystal – no. 18		18	
scarlet jacket with fringes and label of rank			1 string (or rope)
scarlet cloth		1 and 1/8 ell	
berry-red cloth	3/4 ell	1 and 1/4 ell	
red Mazamet cloth		1/4 ell	
whiskey	12 pints	81 pints	20 pints
flat iron bars	8 bars	30 bars	2 bars
clove		1 lbs. 4 ounces 1/2	
small copper bells		5	5
copper bangles		3	3
spun wool		15 ounces 1/2	
two-bladed sabers			1
mirror with card board			2
honey			2

paper	12 mains [pack of 25 sheets of paper]	37 mains	6 mains
pewter plates		3	1
frizzed wool fabric		26 ells 3/4	9 ells
drapes of Damask silk		8	1
sabers		10	1
copper bells		2	2
linen cloth		395 ells	71 ells
glass jewelry, wool cloth, glass	4,000	43,000	11,000
precious stones		500 stones	
red cabet		39 strings	
false crystals		3 strings	

Certainly, the party that pulled the traditional aristocracy into this commerce was fairly weak inasmuch as the majority of the trading goods consisted of cheap junk, firearms and brandy, divided among a multitude of chiefs. The customs payments lay at the root of the power of the *beeco*, the chief of the province in the proximity of Saint-Louis. That led to numerous internal dissensions about sharing, heightening the rivalries of families for power. As La Courbe suggests, the *brak* attempted to monopolize the benefits of Atlantic commerce to reinforce his power and profit. Thus in 1686, the *brak* "also demanded from him the taxes of the master of the island which is close to the desert, it is he who is responsible of making the huts where one deposits the gum after it has been traded, and that of Chamchy, who guards on the island the cattle, which we buy, and for this, one pays him something every year, which one calls customs, but he has almost nothing, because the *brac* receives it and does not give him much."

Taxes did not cease to play an important role in the relations between the Waalo and Saint-Louis. Moreover, the traditional aristocracy became increasingly dependent on the connection to that commerce to maintain power. Le Maire, as early as 1682, grasped well the harmful consequences of this Atlantic commerce at the onset of the political and social crisis in Waalo. Talking about the *brak* he said in particular, "As he cannot practice his tyranny on his neighbors, he makes his subjects feel it, he travels through his own land, stays two days in one village, three days in another, where he has himself fed with his entire escort. It consists of two hundred scoundrels, most educated by the commerce they had with the whites, from which they have acquired only the bad qualities. When they ruined the villages, they often made enslaved individuals based on the slightest hint of wrongdoing."

And so those remaining in Africa had no better a plight than of their brothers sold to enslaved traders for cultivating the plantations of sugar cane and cotton in the Americas. The same individuals was shared by people forever separated by the ocean. Those who remained lived constantly in fear of famine and of war, a fear intensified by the daily anxiety of leaving one day for the unknown hell beyond the oceans from where no one ever returned. The fear was all the greater because the enslaved individuals long believed that the whites were going to eat them on the other coast; the slave traders had great difficulty convincing them otherwise.

Such were the general conditions of that transatlantic commerce. We turn now to the internal history of the kingdom of Waalo to grasp all the economic, political and social consequences of the commerce of Saint-Louis, a deciding factor in the development of the land.

CHAPTER 4

THE EVOLUTION OF THE KINGDOM OF WAALO FROM THE MIDDLE TO THE END OF THE SEVENTEENTH CENTURY

Side by side with the trading post of Saint-Louis, Waalo encountered during the second half of the seventeenth century an internal evolution, linked largely to the fluctuations of Atlantic commerce. First we see, in 1673, the reaction of the Trans-Saharan commerce against the commercial monopoly of the Senegal River at Saint-Louis. This reaction, under the cover of Islam, attempted to establish in this entire region of the Senegal River theocratic monarchies that favored the old relationships of Trans-Saharan commerce. The failure of this movement, directed by the great marabout Nàsir Al-Din, would assure the triumph of Saint-Louis as along with the birth of the military monarchy of Waalo, dominated by the *ceedo* warriors. Saint-Louis became increasingly involved in the rivalries between the three great royal families for the conquest of power. This was primarily the civil war between Bër Caaka and Yrim Mbañk who, in addition to the harmful consequences of the slave trade, markedly weakened Waalo and encouraged Moorish pressure at the end of the seventeenth century.

The Individualization of Waalo since the Breakdown of the Jolof

After the disintegration of the Jolof, Waalo became the object of Kajoor's and Fuuta's covetousness. Still, in 1638, Waalo remained a vassal state vis-à-vis Fuuta, while Kajoor possessed a part of the mouth of the Senegal River up to the level of Biërt. Chambonneau confirmed this in 1676: "The country of Biërt depending on the realm of Hamet is four leagues away from the habitation."[1] For this reason, the *damel* in 1638 sent an ambassador to Captain Lambert in order to assure him of his protected lands. Yet around 1659, as Saint-Louis was founded, Waalo apparently regained its independence vis-à-vis Fuuta and Kajoor. The Atlantic commerce and the proximity of Saint-Louis must have contributed to assure a certain power to Waalo— to the detriment of Fuuta, relegated further into the interior of the lands.[2] This appears to be the same phenomenon that caused the break-up of Jolof.

During this period Waalo's independence was more or less assured. Although Waalo continued to pay a tax as did its predecessors, the refusal of the *brak* Yérim Mbañk in 1715 suggests that this vassalage was mostly symbolic.³ Unfortunately, no documents exist for 1673 that permit us to grasp the evolution of the trade of Saint-Louis since its founding, nor that of the history of Waalo. It is only thanks to the richness of Chambonnneau's report on the marabouts' war, since 1673, that we can study the first manifestations of the consequences of the Atlantic trade— and above all try to understand the process of Waalo's evolvement from a military power.

THE WAR OF THE MARABOUTS IN THE SENEGAL RIVER, 1673 – 1677

Beginning in 1673, the entire region of the Senegal River was submerged in a maraboutic movement that tried to forcibly convert the African populations and to oppose the monopoly of Saint-Louis on trade. We will look at the genesis of this movement in Mauritania, which tended to disrupt the economical, political, and social aspects of the states of the Senegal River in the name of Islam.

The Maraboutic Movement of Nâsir Al-Din in Mauritania: Genesis and Role

The history of Mauritania is punctuated by the successive waves of Moroccan peoples toward the south in search of new pastures. Since the fourteenth century, there was a regular infiltration of Arabic or Arabo-Berber peoples, such as the Awlâd Rizg, the Awlâd Mubàrak, and finally the Hassan warriors or the Banu Maghfar around the seventeenth century. These various migrations, always caused by a certain political and social malaise in the north, were the source of the seventeenth century-era subjection of the marabouts or Zouaïa of Zenatien origin—that is to say, of the Sanhadja Berbers including the Lemtouna. They were the descendents of the Almoravids, who remained in the desert and had therefore retained their characteristic religion, and, up until that point, the Berber language.

During this time period, the Muslim world, notably Morocco, underwent a terrible crisis as a consequence of the decline of the Trans-Saharan trade. We know that in 1591 the Saadian monarchy of Morocco had conquered Gao and Timbuktu in order to obtain the gold and the enslaved individuals at their source, in an attempt to regain its dominance. But this conquest resulted in nothing more than the destruction of Songhaï (Songhay) without any benefit for Morocco, which had not been able to seize the gold mines situated further south. The remoteness of this province, which was difficult to govern at a distance, caused the economic stagnation of the Trans-Saharan traffic to reach the entire length of the caravan trails. As Ismaël Hamet said, "this poverty is aggravated by the fact that the workforce of Blacks, indispensable for the exploitation of the Saharan riches, is missing or has diminished to a great extent."⁴

In Morocco, the end of the Saadian monarchy was marked by the development of a puritanical movement under the leadership of Sidi Muhammad Al-Ayyashi. This crystallized for the first time the fight against the Christians, whose commerce was ruining the country, and the movement also opposed Saadian power until its defeat in April 1641 at Ayn Al Qasab.[5] Although unable to determine the religious and political links that might have existed between Morocco and Mauritania, we witness at the same period the birth of a similar reactionary movement in the south against the Atlantic commerce. This was the war of Shur Bubba, led by the marabout Nâsir Al-Din.

The essential elements of the Moorish tradition concerning the war of the marabouts have been compiled by Basset, Paul Marty, Ismaël Hamet and much later by Norris. We will content ourselves with summing up this movement in its Mauritanian phase, in order to address its phase of conquest in the region of the Senegal River.

Indeed, the economic crisis accentuated the domination of the marabouts by the Hassan warriors, who with their commercial, religious and herding activities constituted the most hard-working class of the nomadic world. Galvanized by the steely will of the great marabout Nâsir Al-Din and united under his *baraka* (special blessing), the marabouts or Zouaïa rose up in large numbers against the domination of the Hassan warriors. During periods of economic and social crisis, it is common in the Islamic world to see puritanical movements rise up in response. Such was the case with Nâsir Al-Din, whose principle objective was to reconstitute Berber society in the image of the greatness and simplicity of the first ages of Islam. Nàsir Al-Din, an educated and pious marabout, was tasked to lead this social and religious reform as an *imam* elected by the Islamic community. But the circumstances of the marabouts' seizure of power are still not entirely clear. It has traditionally been said that the Hassan warriors submitted for a time, until the day when they refused to pay the *zakka or zakat* (an obligatory Islamic tax)— it was then that the period of war began. This armed conflict between the marabouts and the Hassan warriors pushed the theater of military operations back to the Senegal River where the four kingdoms—Waalo, Fuuta, Kajoor and Jolof as well as the trading post of Saint-Louis—represented assets that could determine the outcome of the war.

We will attempt to study this movement in its Senegalese phase by limiting ourselves to Waalo. It would be necessary to study this war in the context of each of the kingdoms in order to clarify all aspects of the conflict.

The Success of the "Toubenan" Movement in the Senegal River, and the Reign of the Buur Jullit, 1673-1677

The texts prior to the seventeenth century have already suggested the existence in Waalo, and in the kingdoms of Senegal, of a courtly Islam in the elite circles. But, starting in the mid-seventeenth century, a shift apparently occurred in terms of a greater responsiveness of the people to Islam. This change was due in large part to the state of insecurity and the crisis, which arose from the increase of the slave trade. Indeed, the second half of the seventeenth century corresponds to the organization and development, in its *pro-slavery* form, of the sugar commerce of the islands—and thus to a frantic search for labor. During this period, the major concern of the different French companies of Senegal regarded the islands' supplies. In any case, the pretext of the fight against Atlantic commerce and the unorthodox practices of dogmatic Islam, invoked by Nâsir Al-Din, attest to the existence of a crisis which alone can explain the success of his *jihad* against the African kingdoms of Senegal.

The main objective of Nâsir Al-Din was to bring the African populations back to Islamic orthodoxy, and thus to a strict observation of Islamic principles. Chambonneau called the movement *toubenan*, using the Wolof word *tuub*, which means, as it does in Arabic, to convert oneself to Islam. Chambonneau describes the mystical character of Nâsir Al-Din, describes as the one who had "abandoned the world in order to dedicate himself to God."[6] The message that he sent to the *satigi* of Fuuta explains quite well the reformist character of the movement. He had as the mission of a great servant of God, "to show all the kings how to change their lives, by making *sala* (Islamic prayer) better and more often, contenting themselves with three or four wives, chasing away all the wandering griots and pleasure-seekers around them, and finally that God did not want them to pillage their subjects, let alone kill them or take them captive..."[7]

The pretext for the holy war was within arms' reach, because the messengers specified that "their master had God's power in case of insubordination to use the sword and any other means against them to chase them out of their kingdoms as enemies of God and of his law and to put in their place whomever he may please."[8] Thus, these messengers respected the previous forms of conversions prior to the *jihad* itself, which were possible because of the political and social conjunctures favorable to the overthrow of traditional monarchies. Indeed, Nâsir Al-Din, under the pretext of propagating an orthodox Islam, proceeded to orient his movement toward the fight against the tyranny of kings in order to increase the awareness of the masses: "God does not permit kings to pillage, kill, or enslave their people; on the contrary, to maintain them and guard them from their enemies, the people are not made for the kings, but the kings for the people."[9]

This constituted the principle theme of his religious and political propaganda. It is beyond dispute that these were the first signs of the consequences of the slave trade: increasing wars and pillaging in order to obtain European merchandise, which came in ever greater quantities to Saint-Louis. Moreover, according to Chambonneau, all the European voyagers involved in this war were taking into account the effects of the trade that assured the success of the *toubenan* party. LeMaire in 1682 described the *brak* who enslaved individuals of his country for the least offense, and demonstrates quite well that the success of the marabout is due to the promise made to the Waalo-Waalo of "avenging them for the tyranny of their kings."[10]

F.Y.B. Gaby in 1689, after La Courbe in 1685, said the same: "The kings do not have the right to impose any taxes on their people. All their revenue consists of captives and of livestock. They often go to pillage their subjects, under the pretext that they spoke badly of them or that they have stolen or killed, in such a way that nobody is safe with his possessions or in his freedom because they take them captive; and that is what caused the revolution in their kingdom."[11] And so the movement of Nâsir Al-Din benefited within all these kingdoms from the complicity of numerous indigenous or foreign marabouts, whose power was a function of the degree of Islamisation in each nation. The principle objective of Nâsir Al-Din was to overthrow the traditional kings everywhere and replace them with the partisans of the maraboutic party. We will look at the shape that this war assumed in Waalo.

Chambonneau is the only contemporary author to describe the war of the marabouts. It began on the Senegal River in 1673, before the date of his arrival at Saint-Louis, February 18, 1675. After 1673, Nâsir Al-Din, having in vain tried to convert the *satigi*, started a military conquest of the country, inciting a popular uprising. The *satigi* was chased away, and Jolof, Kajoor, and finally Waalo were subjugated one by one. Waalo was conquered last, after having put up more resistance—no doubt because of the fact the *brak* Fara Kumba had more time to prepare his defense.

Chambonneau describes the war of the marabouts in Waalo: "Later he crossed the Niger again and came to the kingdom of *brak* for the same thing, but he found more resistance there. Because the king named 'Brak-fara' is much loved and respected by his people, most of them armed themselves in order to guard him. These people are very skillful with weapons and are brave in war, more than any of the aforementioned people, they twice fought the large army of the Bourguli of four or five thousand, gathered from countries that he had already taken; but finally, no longer able to hold up against so many people, who returned endlessly with new forces to attack him even in his own village, like one morning when these *toubenans* entered his village by surprise, even the most faithful were scared of the great noise and fled, thus leaving their king alone except for two or three of his servants, who would rather have died with him than abandoned him, realizing that he had to die, bold and courageous as he was, he got on horseback and sold his life dearly, thrusting into the crowd of the enemies rather than being taken, many of which he killed with his *saguayes* until, having been pierced by many shots, he fell dead from his horse. Those two servants also lost their life there, and thus the kingdom fell to the level of the others, that is to say, it was reduced to a province under the power of this Bourguly."[12]

La Courbe goes on to confirm the death of this *brak,* noting that in 1685 at the stopover of the desert he encountered "two daughters of the dead king, father of the one they called Fara Coumba, who was killed as I said while fighting against the Moors."[13] The Moorish tradition reports the successive conquest of the Fuuta, Jolof, Kajoor in the same period; regarding the Waalo, it says in particular: "the *chama* was subjugated by El Fadhel ben Mohamed El Kaoury with the help of the Oulad El Hadj and a contingent of sixty men of Oudjfet. They killed Bourigrig (the king)."[14]

After the defeat of the four kingdoms, Nâsir Al-Din proceeded to replace the kings with marabouts that supported his cause. Chambonneau calls them the *bourguli,* a word meaning great "master of prayers."[15] This word is actually nothing more than the French deformation of the Wolof word *buur jullit* that we find in the chronicle of Amadou Wade. It simply means an *imam,* who is simultaneously an earthly leader and a spiritual leader of the Muslim community. But Vincent Monteil places the reign of Fara Koy Jon, who could be the Fara Kumba cited by La Courbe, between 1542 and 1549. This gives us a gap of more than a century in the chronology; the arrival of the *buur jullit* at Waalo can actually be dated precisely to 1673.[16]

The Moorish tradition says that the "Ottoman Cadi gave the commandment from the Waalo to Intay Sarr, the maternal uncle of Hamet Fall who was the brother of the lingeer."[17] This Intay Sarr is no other than the prince Yerim Koodé, who then succeeded Fara Kumba in taking the title of *buur jullit.* Waalo was from this time on governed by the maraboutic party. Chambonneau brings us more details about this succession: "Some time afterwards, the Bouguly said to his people that although he was master of all these four kingdoms it was nevertheless only with regret that he had had the kings obey God's order and that they would not be deprived, that if there were even any of their relatives, who wanted to do what he ordered, he would give something back to them, he presented himself to this bourguly, the prince Hierimkode, father-in-law of the dead king *brak* who had just been killed, told him that he was a good toubenan, in doing all these things, and following what he had promised to the relatives of the kings, he came to ask him for this kingdom, it was necessary for political reasons that this great marabout gave him what he wanted, but with so many conditions, that it was obvious that this king was still more enslaved and subjected to this bourguly and to the Moors than if they had remained in an individual state because thereafter when one found out that his predecessors had changed and instead of giving him some Moors and marabouts, so that he had only the title of sovereign and those Moors the command. He raced, chased the griots around him and shook without stopping the large prayer beads he had on his belt; that is, according to the toubenane fashion, like the kings did it."[18]

The Moorish tradition clearly states that Intay Sarr was the brother of the *linger* and therefore could be the uncle and the brother-in-law of the old *brak,* considering that the *linger* was always the mother or the sister of the *brak.* This relationship is confirmed by two sources. This then leads us to identify the Intay Sarr of the Moorish tradition as the Yerim Koodé of Chambonneau; it was common for princes to change their names when they quit the indigenous *ceddo* party to become marabouts. Chambonneau understood this process quite well and it generated the appointment of local followers to the position of dethroned kings.

It seems clear that Nâsir Al-Din, unable to rule the conquered nations himself, preferred to act through intermediaries in order to avoid the conflicts and resentments that direct Moorish domination would provoke. He did not control the countries less, all the more since Yerim Koodé was king in name only: "Doing nothing now than shaking his prayer beads while the people of that bourguly, who are beside him, look him closely and command for him."[19]

Unfortunately, we cannot ascertain the importance of the maraboutic party among the Waalo-Waalo to assess correctly what influenced Nâsir Al-Din to place local marabouts everywhere as the heads of the conquered lands. In any case, the Moorish tradition shows that this posed a problem, because "The tolba resolved to entrust the government of the inhabitants of Chamama (Waalo) to one of the notables, Ganar, but this one refused saying 'the people are our close relatives, it is true, but we will choose you the most fair-minded man among them and you will give him the command.'"[20] Indeed, the Waalo choice was Intay Sarr, who was no other than Yerim Koodé—the maternal uncle of the children of Hamed Fall, descendents of a Moorish family long established in Waalo and entirely assimilated. That family, after the old Moctar Ould Hamidoun, had nevertheless preserved their traditional religion, and thus served as foothold of the Moorish domination. Moreover, Chambonneau mentions a certain Serim Faly (Sëriñ Fall) who traded grey amber of the land of Bouksar, which confirms the existence of this marabout family in Waalo.[21] It always had been the maraboutic party. From then on, and because of its weapons, it became master of the entire river. As such, its attitude vis-a vis the trading post of Saint-Louis ultimately determined the outcome of the movement. Let us now look at the role the commerce of Saint-Louis played in the defeat of Nâsir Al-Din.

The Affiliations in Saint-Louis and the Maraboutic Movement

The attitude of Nâsir Al-Din toward Saint-Louis and its commerce is not without ambiguity. One knows that the conquest of the Senegal River was made in large part under the pretext of preventing the kings from selling their subjects as enslaved individuals; the marabouts thus opposed the commerce of Saint-Louis, which had been practically suspended during the entire duration of the hostilities. Chambonneau wrote in 1677, "On the contrary, the great marabouts find their glory in fleeing from us to show to their people that they have withdrawn from earthly goods, that nothing but the eager service of God and his law guides them, beyond that they despise us very much because of the difference our religion with their superstition, making the people believe that we trade the captives in order to eat them; since they are masters of the land until now the land was not entered in other way than by our boats, without the nobles it is impossible that we can establish a big trade for all goods."[22]

Here, the professed faith of Nâsir Al-Din conceals a deeper economic reality. Beyond the religious difference, there was a reaction of self-defense from the economy of Trans-Saharan commerce when faced with the increasingly more powerful commerce of Saint-Louis. The Senegal River had been for centuries the source of millet, green pastures and ultimately of enslaved individuals for the Moors. The life of the Moors was regulated by the complementary exchanges of the two economies between the nomads and the sedentary population. But, from the second half of the seventeenth century onward, this region of the Senegal River turned entirely to Saint-Louis, with its enormous demands for food supplies, livestock and enslaved individuals.

This powerful shift in the commercial current inevitably dried out the old circuit to the north, and starved the Sahelian people. The commerce of Arguin during the Portuguese period had still permitted the Moors to retain their roles as intermediaries between the interior and the Atlantic commerce. But now the trading post of Saint-Louis, where small boats could travel far up the Senegal River, eliminated them unmercifully from the commercial circuit. It is understandable that from then on, under the pretext of religion, the Moors opposed the commerce of Saint-Louis, and were tempted to seize control of the Senegal River.

Chambonneau vividly describes this attitude of self-defense within Moorish commerce, which sought above all to satisfy its own internal consumption: "If an individual kills a piece of cattle he should also eat the hide. If he has a captive, he keeps him for his work. If he is from the land or he is harvesting gum. If he has hardly anyone he will not be able to harvest the tree."[23] The oral tradition transmitted by Amadou Wade also confirms this conflict between the Moorish commerce and that of the trading post of Saint-Louis. Talking about the first contacts between Waalo and the French, the tradition reports that "then the *buur jullit*, the chief of the Muslims, sent a message to *brak* Fara Koy Jon, to warn him about the newcomers (the whites) who, said the message, under the pretext of making commerce, were in reality nothing but future conquerors, coming to explore the place. The *buur jullit* concluded in advising the *brak* to chase them out of his nation."[24]

Thus, at the religious level, the movement of Nâsir Al-Din was entirely inspired by the memory of the golden times of the Ashab (companions of the Prophet Muhammad). Moreover, at the economic level, it also took inspiration from a past revolving around Trans-Saharan commerce, which had assured equilibrium in the Moorish society. This explains his ambiguity regarding Atlantic commerce, especially the slave trade. Indeed his opposition to the slave trade, especially toward the form that it assumed at the end (namely, a massive deportation of enslaved individuals) does not at all signify a fight against enslavement per se. The Muslims, while opposing the sale of those sharing their religion, never attempted to abolish slavery itself; they permitted the enslavement of so-called "pagan" populations who refused conversion.

In declaring a holy war on the Senegal River, the Moors wanted primarily to eliminate the trading post of Saint-Louis and assure their fresh supplies of food and labor—all the more so because the Muslim front, even when increased, constantly confronted local non-Muslim populations that could still provide enslaved individuals. Sieur De Muchins witnessed in 1674 a massive transfer of goods, pillaged from Mauritania: "In a village named Hallahou Akbar, the first village of the Foules, when one leaves the kingdom of the brak, one perceived from afar around five-hundred Moors of the river Niger who were struggling to make a great number of cattle, camels and donkeys loaded with millet, cross to the other bank of the river, for transporting to their land Barbary, where because of the sand of the desert and the vicinity of the ocean no millet can be harvested."[25]

Moreover, the will to control this region so vital to the Moorish economy is clearly visible. After the military conquest of the four kingdoms, Nâsir Al-Din dispatched in early 1674 envoys to Saint-Louis. The goal was to negotiate with De Muchins the new forms of commerce on the Senegal River. According to Carson I. A. Ritchie, these envoys were sent in "August 1674 and at the end of the sojourn of the munir Eddine at Saint-Louis coincided with the death of the grand marabout Nasir Al Din."[26] But this date conflicts with the chronological sequence of events that show De Muchins went up the river at "the beginning of May 1674," trying to persuade the *brak* Yeerim Koodé to profit by the death of Nâsir Al-Din, to revolt, and "to return to the first nation of his predecessors."[27]

Starting in May 1674, the timeline is intact until a definite return of the boats in "the month of August 1674," marking the end of the campaign.[28] The sending of the envoys and the death of Nâsir Al-Din would have occurred before May 1674. The sending of the envoys show also that Nâsir Al-Din was from then on the suzerain of the Senegal River and was perceived to be the only intermediary in commerce of Saint-Louis. Munir Eddine, his brother, was responsible for this undertaking with De Muchins, to "assure that he will have with him the same friendship which the kings whose places he occupies had always had with the white commanders to who he has never lost anything and on the contrary he could come and send all his lands to trade with as much or more assurance than in the past, he asked him also to act the same towards him and his people and how he has arrived here only for trading he will render him a great service not to mettle in his affaires, in adopting the party of one or another of the Toubenans or of those who he still does not have, that God would want that he has so well achieved what he had so well advanced, that he has not wanted to chase out the kings that he regrets not having wanted to listen to the command that God has given."[29]

Before this was accomplished, De Munchins had to make quite clear that he did not have any intent to conquer the country (a departure from the colonial politics of the period) and "that finally he wanted to very well maintain this friendship from his side, because of the trade in merchandise as it was the custom."[30] Nevertheless, De Muchins did not cease to boast of the power of the king of France; he needed to intimidate that new political force that caused him grave concern. Instead of the divided small kingdoms continually at war, over which Saint-Louis could easily impose its law, De Muchins found himself suddenly confronted by a huge empire united behind the banner of Islam. This constituted a definite menace for his commerce. De Munchins was led to remark how much "this Toubenan did much harm to our business as one had already seen him do before, since he allowed the marabouts and again the Moors to stay in our land and scold us."[31]

The apprehensions of Saint-Louis may have been even more justified than we thought, given the hypothesis that the Dutch trading post of Arguin played an important role in the war of the marabouts. Through its geographic position, Arguin had since the Portuguese époque abandoned the role of intermediary to the Moors. On the other hand, Saint-Louis, with commerce conducted directly on the banks of the Senegal River, removed them from this advantageous role. A document written around 1670-1671 suggests an important trafficking capability capable of disturbing Saint-Louis:

> The office of Zeeland has under its command Arguin and the adjacent places situated near Cap Blanc at 200 N. This is a fortress situated at a reef in a small bay; it is administrated by a chief and a garrison of 25 men. The trade consists of gum and ostrich feathers; the means are all set for a big adventure and the place gives reasonable good revenues to the above-mentioned office. Currently that legislative house strives to reestablish fishing, which existed there previously. The fish is dried and sent to the Canary islands where it is put together in eight light pieces (a net of eight) which are very much on demand in Arguin and the surrounding areas in such a way that one receives as much for a light piece as for a heavy one.[32]

It is quite possible that the Dutch had favored the marabouts for more of the commerce than the Hassan warriors in order to get rid of the trading post of Saint-Louis, their common rival. In return, Saint-Louis supported the Hassan warriors. This has been confirmed by Chambonneau. The lack of existing documentation does not permit us today to evaluate the role that Arguin played in this war of the marabouts. However, the 1677 decision of Saint-Louis to eliminate the Dutch from Gorée and Arguin until the end of hostilities with the Moors suggests such a role. In any event, Ducasse explains after the taking-over of Arguin that its desertion was "in regards to attracting the commerce to the place of the riverbank of Senegal"; its mission, which consisted of eliminating the Dutch, had been fully accomplished.[33] It is ultimately for all these reasons that those at the trading post of Saint-Louis watched for the slightest rift in the movement of Nâsir Al-Din in hopes of an opportunity to shatter this new force. This occasion presented itself in the beginning of 1674 with the death of Nâsir Al-Din in combat, meaning the loss of the spiritual guide and the spearhead of the maraboutic movement.

As a matter of fact, the maraboutic movement did encounter in Mauritania a lively opposition on part of the Hassan warriors, who did not want to accept the supremacy of the marabouts. It is thus that Nâsir Al-Din died when fighting Heddy, the future chief of the emirate of Trarza. Chambonneau notes that at the moment when the envoys were to leave Saint-Louis, "the people arrived at the settlement who announced to us, and to this envoy the death of his brother, the bourguli had been killed with many of his circle by Hady, grand Moore of the nation, neighbor of the kingdom of the *brak*, who was absolutely not Toubenan."[34]

De Muchins was tempted for a moment to arrest Munir to ward off the possibility that he would take over as leader of the marabout movement in place of his brother. But he preferred to undertake a systematic political agenda of fighting to the death against the marabouts from the beginning of the month of May—the date during which he embarked on a small flotilla to go up the Senegal River.[35]

The Intervention of Saint-Louis in the War of the Marabouts and the Defection of Brak Yeerim Koodé

The primary objective of De Muchins was to detach Yeerim Koodé from the marabout party. He spent a few days on the Island of Palmiers, during which he tried his best to persuade the *brak* to profit from the death of Nâsir Al-Din and take his former prerogatives back. Waalo was vital for the survival of Saint-Louis, and this explains the utmost determination of De Muchins to make the *brak* his ally. He made it clear: "The land of the *Brak* which touches the settlement, which is *toubenan*, is not safe for us and the trade is almost lost because of the Moors, treacherous and perfidious people and more cunning than the black nation with which we get along very well, all these reasons made him still wait in this place, there to attempt to find a solution with the *brak* and that is what he did propose to him."[36]

But the maraboutic party was still too powerful and Yeerim Koodé hesitated to stoke hostilities against the Moors. Then, sometime later, three whites were massacred by the Waalo-Waalo, probably Muslims. Worse, Sir Fumechon announced to De Muchins that "the Moors who are the absolute masters in the land of the *brak* and also over the king Hierimkode, had made him defend the trade of the desert and they did not understand that no ships did trading."[37]

One does not know if this hostility of the Moorish marabouts was due to the failure of the envoy Munir Eddine, whom De Muchins had been tempted to retain for a while as prisoner, or to military assistance by Saint-Louis to the opposition led by the Hassan warriors: "Hady and Bakars, who with the Satigui, burned, pillaged and destroyed the livestock of the new Toubenans," even before his leaving for the riverbank.[38] In any case, the ban on commerce at the desert stopover was sufficiently upsetting for Saint-Louis to become openly hostile. De Muchins, seeing that it was impossible for him to conduct trading in the year of 1674, made the resolution to eliminate the marabouts through weaponry. He turned again to the *brak* Yeerim Koodé who, in his capacity as ally, was able to supply backups in the fight against the successors of Nâsir Al-Din. Concerning this, Chambonneau tells us:

> Because the entire country was against us it was necessary to find someone noble at least to help us with food supplies, he did make the attempt to ask the king-brak Hierimrode to come onboard his ship, he did come and he repeated to him the same reasons as he had forcefully expressed before, adding that moreover he had also linked up with all his boats to make war against Toubenan at his cost and to reestablish him in his state as had been his predecessors. Finally he did solicit him and pressured him so much that he did achieve his goal with a number of nobles of the land, who were around him or everyone left the people there as before and barely made

them humiliated according to their own will. Taking all the arms and converts to Toubenan they joined their king in the resolution to search for the Moors and those subjects who did not want to submit themselves to be obedient to him. They found them under the lead of one of the successors of Buurguly, who before killed the one called "Hiatmankaly," close to Guerouk, Province of Bifeche in the kingdom of the *brak*, they battled there and killed just that Hiatmankaly, the victory encouraged them in such a way, that they very soon did chase the rest of them out of their country...[39]

The intervention by Saint-Louis is clearly visible in the defection of the *brak* Yeerim Koodé, vis-a-vis the maraboutic party and the military assistance of De Muchins, who was unable to bribe the great dignitaries of Waalo. This fueled the reversal of the situation.

Unfortunately, we have no idea of the power of the local maraboutic party, which would have permitted us to judge the profound reasons for the massive uprising of the Waalo-Waalo. It is possible that the Moorish domination had already started to assume the restrictive form of a foreign conquest, which caused the people to take up arms against the marabout in order to reestablish their former order. Their hope of liberation against the tyranny of the kings, at any rate, was betrayed. Chambonneau suggests: "The people of all the four kingdoms began to become disgusted, because one took them captive, pillaged, burned and they suffered more than under the kings, contrary to what they had hoped for."[40]

But one should not forget the alternative perspective, in which the trading post of Saint-Louis for its own interests did all that could be done to weaken the thrust of the maraboutic movement. In that perspective, the hostility that Chambonneau harbored toward Islam, despite his qualifications as observer and against all those who responded to the movement, is remarkable. Regardless, the Moorish tradition confirms largely the circumstances of the defeat of Kadi Othmane, the third Imam, who Chambonneau calls "Hiatmankaly." As a matter of fact, Sid El Hassane, sent to recover the Zakka from the Ouland Khelif of the Ouland Rizg, was the object of a conspiracy directed by "Aoudaïka, Borigrig (brak) and the chiefs of the Reghiouatte and the Barnes...The Meghafra attacked them with the aid of the Blacks and the Oulad Khelif; they were commanded by Heddi... they surrounded the Tolba entirely and killed them to the last man. One gave the place of that encounter the name Ketsib el Koddhat or Hill of the Cadis because of the number among them who found here their death... When El-Kadi Othmane heard about the death of Sid El Hassane and his companions, he marched against the Blacks, who he found grouped together and ready to fight. But the Tolba, having been attacked in early morning by the Blacks were entirely defeated and El-Kadi Othmane perished with those who were surrounding him after fetes of bravery."[41]

This death confirms the prediction of Nâsir Al-Din, who when the Kadi Othmane chose Yeerim Koodé (Intay Saar) as *buur jullit,* remarked: "You gave him the command and you die by his hand."[42]

Following the multiple internal dissensions regarding the successor of Nâsir Al-Din, considering the opposition of the Hassan warriors and above all the intervention of Saint-Louis and its alliance with the *brak* Yeerim Koodé, the maraboutic movement was irrevocably weakened on all fronts. The defeat of Kadi Ohtmane was followed some time later by the death of one of his successors, Munir Al-Din, brother of Nàsir Al-Din, who had been defeated in a campaign against Fuuta.[43]

De Muchins benefited by pillaging and looting when the remainder of the Moorish army tried to pass through Mauritania.[44] All these events occurred between May and June 20 1674, the date on which De Munchins returned to Saint-Louis. He traveled the riverbank again, visiting up to sixty places. "In the first days of July 1674 with the same ships and other small boats, of the kind that the fleet was stronger than at the first voyage, it was intended to frighten all the black nobles who all had assembled."[45] He did not encounter any opposition on part of the Moors and he contented himself with pillaging certain villages of Fuuta. "There we obtained twelve captives and millet, which had been brought to that settlement, this naval army descended again after a month and a half or at their arrival in the month of August there were nothing but bonfires and entertainments, one burned there a bourguly made of straw."[46]

This autodafé signified that by August 1674, Saint-Louis had largely succeeded in weakening the maraboutic movement. Waalo, which had greatly benefited from the support of Saint-Louis and which had been the first to liberate itself, went on to play a considerable role in the annihilation of the military power of the marabouts.

The Actions of Brak Yeerim Koodé and His Successor in the Elimination of the Marabouts

The *brak* Yeerim Koodé, now restored to his former prerogatives, unleashed a veritable offensive against the marabouts, even outside his national territory. Indeed, the theater of his operations moved to the east, primarily to Fuuta, where: "The wars were more furious than ever between the toubenan party and the Moorish princes who aided Siratik to enter his country."[47] Yeerim Koodé waged war during the entire month of February 1675 and relentlessly stripped away, according to Chambonneau, "great advantages over the Toubenan, taking captives, killing and pillaging entire villages and by acquiring always something that he was trading to us."[48]

In May 1675, Du Boulle traded at Njurbel "fifteen captives from the markets of the brak."⁴⁹ During this occasion, the *brak* received him "with honor at his village where he lived for several days and he told him that he considered what Mr. De Muchins had done very good, that he was now the terror trampling the land of the Touban."⁵⁰ On November 15, 1675, Chambonneau observed on his return journey many villages that had been "burned again all anew by the brak-king with the great village of Fane (Fanaye) where he took many captives," which were purchased by Granger.⁵¹

These multiple victories and the enormous profits reaped by the *brak* Yeerim Koodé encouraged him to be increasingly distant from the war with the marabouts from November 1675 to January 1676. He waged war continually, but he ended up being killed in combat against Suranko, the vice-*buur jullit* of Jolof. Concerning this, Chambonneau writes:

> Hierim Kode king of Brak, was so well accustomed to victories in the war of the Blacks, that he did not want to make another army, assembled all his people and nobles, fortified his neighbors against the great number of Moors who came not to his aide, went in search of the Toubenans, always awaited on their territories, there he marched onward for three days burning, pillaging, killing or taking captives without encountering resistance until a little later he encountered in the kingdom of Bourguiolof the enemy army commanded by Suran, Marabout and vice-Bourguili of the land of Buiolof, he defeated him and made him flee. He then pursued those fleeing of who his people killed a great number and made a large number of captives. The king who considered himself victorious, who could not soil himself by stabbing and killing, left some of his people to run again after the fleeing and who were dispersing, but by bad luck it cost him his life since running thus with his retenue he found a young soldier avoiding the blows in the shelter of a tree who pierced him with a spear through his leather-vest so that he died a little later in the field. This felt like all was lost and the joy of victory turned into sadness. His people did however brought with them a good number of captives, cattle and other things of pillage which consequently always came to us.⁵²

Chambonneau actually did meet him in the month of January 1675, and reports that "this king Hierimkodé was killed in the war about two month afterwards."⁵³ Yeerim Koodé died in combat circa January 1675. He had been an example of good cooperation with the trading post of Saint-Louis; this is why Chambonneau described him as being an "old man who was very well built and very good-natured towards the whites. Moreover, his death created a void for the good reason that he had not been very demanding as far as commerce was concerned. He has been much regretted by us, as much for his plain dealing as for his generosity. We were able to content him for his customs by giving him what he wanted."⁵⁴

He had little other choice, especially since he owed all his power to the support that Saint-Louis had bestowed upon him to get rid of the Moorish marabouts. This allowed him to increase his power and to wage war against his neighbors. This bond with Saint-Louis thus created a form of dependence for the aristocracy, who awaited always certain number of gifts from the European traders to facilitate their commerce, yet without great profits. As Chambonneau said, "It is a bad costume of theirs not to get out of your boat before you have given them something, so that in order to depart one gives them a bandolier, or nine feet of linen cloth to make a shift for their wives, some pieces of coral and glassware, and to their people, three or four strings of glass beads to one, to another four inches of iron, or some sheets of paper. One always recovers this fully at the first transaction that is carried out with them. If one gives nothing one will never do anything at all."[55]

Those at Saint-Louis shrewdly exploited this habit, which had created new needs among the aristocracy. It is significant that the oral tradition regarding the initial connections of Waalo with the Europeans has preserved the story of the attachment of the traditional aristocracy to merchandise of the Atlantic commerce.

Amadou Wade vividly documents that the *brak* rejected the proposal made to him by the *buur jullit* to break with Saint-Louis: "Since his country did not produce sugar, nor tobacco, nor sangara, and until then he did only know honey, tamaka and the palm wine (songa), those did not compare to the products brought to the land by the whites, after having tasted them first he did not have any question to return to them later when he consequently refused to chase out the newcomers, but on the contrary he favored their trade, which on the day when the last merchants became the conquerors with his formidable army, he did not take the trouble to make them understand the reason. The whites remained."[56]

This confirms further the hypothesis that the rivalry between the Moorish commerce and the commerce of Saint-Louis was the principle factor, and that the refusal of *brak* Fara Kumba as well as the defection of *brak* Yeerim Koodé when facing the maraboutic party were less the outcomes of a certain hostility toward Islam than a certain attachment to merchandise supplied by Atlantic commerce. Moreover, the behavior of their successors remained true to this principle. We do not know the name of the *brak* who succeeded Yeerim Koodé, because Chambonneau tells us simply that "this brak succeeded Biër, who is the king from now on."[57] One might surmise that it was a certain Fara Penda, especially because Father Labat, as per La Courbe in 1686, tells us: "The same day two daughters of the dead king and sisters of Fara Penda came to visit the general. Their father, called Fara Coumbsa, had been killed in the war against the Moors."[58]

However, La Courbe states that the current *brak* was the son of Fara Coumba, without naming him. It is quite possible that this Fara Penda, who succeeded Yeerim Koodé in 1676, reigned until 1686. However, this *brak* did not have an attitude of benevolence regarding the commerce of Saint-Louis. Having certainly inherited a more important military power than his predecessors in the aftermath of the successful wars of Waalo, the *brak* had become very demanding. Indeed, when comparing him to Yeerim Koodé, Chambonneau states, "But the present king does not behave in the same way. He demanded the very last item of his customs when I paid him in the month of June and until then he had forbidden all trade even to the one (M. Du Boullé) who was then there (at le Dezert) to trade for gum. He (M. du Boullé) did not want to pay the customs himself for forms sake."[59] This proof of his power is still further illustrated by his numerous military activities." He did still more than his predecessor because in the entire year 1676 he did nothing but kill, take captives, pillage and burn the land of Toubenan, even the place of the residence of the Bourguli, gathered millet and cut it down while still green, in a way that the people of the land were forced to eat boiled herbs, carrion and pieces of hide."[60]

In 1677 the maraboutic movement was drawing to an end. In May 1677, Chambonneau was planning to depart for France when he heard of the re-establishment of Satigi in his kingdom and learned that the possibilities of Jolof and Kajoor to liberate themselves of the marabouts were high.[61] The defeat of the marabouts was irremediable; the time of war was over. This is what Barbot noticed at his arrival in Gorée in 1681. Summing up the events, he dated that war to 1677.[62]

Similarily, Le Maire in 1682 stated that "it has not been not five years" that the marabouts had invaded the entire Senegal River, under the pretext of religion.[63] One can safely name a date in 1677 or at the latest in 1678 regarding the end of the war with the marabouts in Senegal.

Let us now examine what the consequences were of this large religious movement, which failed to destroy the four kingdoms, together with the major role of the Saint-Louis commerce.

Consequences of the War with the Marabouts and the Reasons for its Defeat

This war of the marabouts, was localized in its combat phase and took place in a short period of five years. Yet its effects culminated in many years of gestation; they are enormous and on all levels. Regarding Mauritania, the original theater of the movement, the victory of the Hassan warriors over the marabouts or Zouaï assured them of political supremacy for centuries. Moreover, the formation of two emirates occurred— Trarzas with Heddi and Braknas with Bakar. The two military aristocracies dominated Moorish society, subjugating the marabout traders. They reached their heyday in the eighteenth century with the development of the commerce in gum and presented a permanent danger for the kingdoms on the Senegal River and the trading post of Saint-Louis.

In the south, the immediate consequence of that war of the marabouts for the four kingdoms was the great famine that followed the military operations. In 1676, the *brak* had destroyed the millet while it was still growing, and had reduced Fuuta to famine. Chambonneau described the calamity: "This is what I saw on my voyage to Foutes in the month of July 1676, and of the entire families which offered themselves to me as captives so one could feed them, while they were reduced to the extreme of killing one another for stealing food supplies, and I did not want to take on any of them that had not paid the others or even as a captive, who offered the merchandise of the value which was himself. One had to observe this formality for avoiding the very dangerous consequences which one would ensue in the manner that when we did not lack merchandise we were trading that year more than six hundred until the boats refused them and I did so first."[64]

Barbot in 1681 similarly describes this famine that destroyed several thousand inhabitants of the interior; many of them sold themselves as enslaved individuals just to survive.[65] This famine has passed into legend as a consequence of the "trickery of the marabouts." Le Maire, La Courbe and Barbot all derided the movement of the marabouts, noting that the Moors had promised millet to the populations "without that they were taking the trouble to cultivate it."[66] We see clearly that this famine was actually the consequence of wars, and not the result of some kind of illusion.

Chambonneau does not report the statistics of the commerce of Saint-Louis, but it seems clear that a great number of enslaved individuals were traded due to the war. Moreover, despite the threat of the marabouts averted, Chambonneau does not cease to worry that the source of enslaved individuals would not dry up with the end of the war. Yet he states that "because peace exists throughout these four kingdoms one cannot expect great captives."[67] Herein lays the paradox of that trade: it needed to survive the political breakup and the perpetual war between the different nations.

The defeat of the marabouts was above all a victory for the commerce of Saint-Louis. It rid itself of a powerful political opposition that had been capable of imposing heavy taxes for trafficking freely on the Senegal River. Moreover, the Moorish marabouts, adhering in this phase to a movement of self-defense, had turned back to the old forms of Trans-Saharan commerce that constituted a dangerous competition for Saint-Louis. Thus the elimination of the marabouts renewed the relationship between the trading post of Saint-Louis and the traditional aristocracy—one that was less demanding due to the growing Atlantic commerce. In such commerce essential revenues were acquired in the form of taxes and gifts, not counting the occasional opportunity to directly sell enslaved individuals.

Chambonneau clearly described the attraction of the European merchandise to the kings: "A king cannot keep anything at his own home, when he sees a boat full of good merchandise such as linen, brandy, coral, silver, iron, glass jewelry and all other things which one is accustomed to have them carry, besides this is what supports the whites in their country."[68]

The traditional aristocracy was therefore intimately linked to the new circuit of commerce of Saint-Louis, upon which it depended for security. As Chambonneau wrote, "When it occurs under a king, such a murder and treason as that of the above-mentioned whites, it must be that the entire country must pay more than three-hundred captives and thus it delivers many of the guilty ones as one would to do justice according to our custom."[69] The defeat of the marabouts assured the continual commercial expansion of Saint-Louis at the detriment of the Moors, who suffered from the commercial crisis until the eighteenth century. At that time, thanks to the gum trade, they were able to dynamically integrate themselves anew into the dominant Atlantic commerce.

As for the kingdom of Waalo, it did not emerge the victor in this war of the marabouts even though, when first liberated with the aid of Saint-Louis, it made war against neighboring kingdoms and thereby profited in consolidating its power. Even if Waalo did not conquer any territory, it had raised itself at least to the level of a redoubtable military power. Indeed, the major consequence of the intervention of Saint-Louis was without a doubt the utilization of a considerable amount of firearms and the formation of a military aristocracy. One could ask whether it is not this war from which springs the dominance of *ceddo* warriors in the society of Waalo and in the neighboring kingdoms. Regardless, Yeerim Koodé and his successor made the military their unique preoccupation, their unique source of revenue and their essential purpose.

Concerning the internal plan, Chambonneau unfortunately did not describe the evolution of different social groups and their participation in the maraboutic movement. But clearly it is hardly the case of a long-standing resistance of the maraboutic party of Waalo as it was the case in Fuuta, in Jolof and in Kajoor. Could one conclude that this was due to the weakness of Islamization in Waalo because of the absence of a powerful marabout party? We cannot confirm this at this time. Nevertheless, it is certain that the intervention of Saint-Louis was decisive in the elimination of the marabouts, be they indigenous or foreigners. In any case, this victory of the traditional political power of the *brak*s over the marabout party was followed by an anti-Islamic reaction of the aristocracy. Le Maire, in 1682, writes: "Those who had no longer marabouts present in their lands, all of those who they could capture they made into slaves."[70] This is confirmed by Barbot, who had pointed out the same reaction in Kajoor and who confirms having purchased in 1681 in Gorée one of these marabouts.[71]

The reaction of the traditional aristocracy was universal due to the internal power of the marabout party. From that time on it created an conflicting current of Islam in Waalo. Islam, which had been until then an Islam of the court, a monopoly of the nobles, was now increasingly rejected by this aristocracy, which was more or less hostile until the colonial conquest in 1855. On the other side, the oppressed people became more and more sensitive to Islam, preached at that time peacefully by the marabouts. It constituted the principal opposition against the *brak*'s regime.

Those were the consequences of that religious movement that failed to upset the political conditions of a large portion of Senegal and Mauritania. Its defeat was due to the opposition of the Hassan warriors, whose political and economic ambitions were barely obscured, and particularly due to the intervention at the trading post of Saint-Louis.

Finally, returning to the beautiful image of Godinho, this defeat of the marabouts is in essence a victory of Atlantic commerce over the Trans-Saharan commerce in a fierce struggle between "the camel caravan and the caravel"—a struggle waged up to the banks of the Senegal River. Waalo after that looked exclusively to the French trading post of Saint-Louis, which subjected it directly to the fluctuations of its dominant commerce.

Importance of the War of the Marabouts in the History of Senegal

The war of the marabouts, despite its brevity, represented an important turning point in the history of Senegal. The victory of Saint-Louis over Islam has since reinforced the struggle between the aristocracy—increasingly in solidarity with the Atlantic commerce —and the rest of the people. We witness there a clear detachment from Islam, primarily in the Wolof kingdoms and in the rise of the domination of the *ceddo* warriors, who became a permanent element of political instability as a result of the internal wars between the neighboring nations regarding supply of the slave trade. The defeat of the marabouts went on to provoke a severe repression of the followers of Islam; the sale of marabouts to slave traders is one of its manifestations. The existence of that severe suppression tends to reinforce the hypothesis, expressed recently by Nehemia Levtzion, regarding the possible mass departure of certain marabouts to Fuuta Jaloo, where they could help prepare for the first theocratic revolution at the beginning of the eighteenth century.[72]

We can say with certainty that the defeated marabouts, notably in Fuuta Toro, became the spiritual ancestors of those, who with Suleyman Baal, launched the Toorodo revolution of 1776. This revolution, directed principally against Moorish domination, aimed to end the detrimental effects of the slave trade. It represents very well the continuity of this maraboutic movement, which under the cover of Islam demonstrated the freedom of expression of a new political, economic and social ideology in the nations of Senegambia. It is from that angle that we must understand Islam in Senegal. It is to better grasp, outside the idealogy of a religion, the internal dynamism of these societies. We then hope that this study of an aspect of the maraboutic movement in Waalo will prompt other research concerning the neighboring kingdoms. That will permit us to better clarify the multiple phases of the maraboutic movement, which is of great importance in the history of Senegal.

CHAPTER 5

WAALO DURING THE LAST QUARTER OF THE SEVENTEENTH CENTURY: THE STRUGGLE FOR POWER BETWEEN BËR CAAKA AND YEERIM MBAÑIK

The victory of the traditional aristocracy over the marabouts reinforced the ties between Waalo and the French trading post of Saint-Louis, which provided in abundance the merchandise now indispensable to its lasting power. Internally, this economic dependency resulted in a bitter struggle between the three royal families—especially between Bër Caaka and the young Yeerim Mbañik Aram Bakar. The latter was backed by his uncle, the *beeco* Maalixuri. These two aspects of the history of Waalo during the last quarter of the seventeenth century will be the focus of this chapter. The development of commerce in Saint-Louis will be discussed first.

Development of Commerce in Saint-Louis in the Last Quarter of the Seventeenth Century

Our purpose is not to write a history of commerce in Saint-Louis, but rather to attempt to understand how it evolved in the context of the development of Waalo. During this period, the study of Abdoulaye Ly is our primary reference; it establishes the importance of the Company of Senegal (Compagnie du Sénégal) that replaced the Company of the West Indies (Compagnie des Indes occidentales) in 1673. As in the case of the trade company that preceded it, the main purpose of the Company of Senegal was to satisfy the enormous needs of the French islands for African manpower, with the possibility of selling any surplus to the Spanish colonies of America.

In order to retain exclusive rights over the trade of enslaved individuals and gum, the post of Saint-Louis took control of Gorée in 1677 and Arguin in 1678, thus eliminating the Dutch from trade in Senegambia. The Company of Senegal set for itself the goal of providing two thousand Africans a year to the islands. Abdoulaye Ly suggested that, despite vicissitudes, one must cease to minimize the slave trading activities of the company between 1673 and 1679.[1] This comment is all the more significant considering that the company's activity was restricted to the market in Senegambia; Saint-Louis thus played a primary role.[2] According to patent letters dated June 1679, however, the Company of Senegal was expected to create a monopoly of

French trade along the African coast—one that was as extensive as that of the Company of the West Indies. The Atlantic slave trade remained a priority; as Abdoulaye Ly writes, "in the conditions prevailing in August 1684, the product of slave trade is twice as important as the product of other merchandises in Africa."[3]

In September 1684, the Company of Senegal was broken up in order to reserve the southern section of the African market for a second company—the Company of Guinea (Compagnie de Guinée) in 1685. However, this did not in any way modify its objectives. Nevertheless, starting in 1693, the Company of Senegal experienced a crisis. This crisis was manifested by the easy conquest of the trading posts of Saint-Louis and Gorée in 1693 by the English governor James Island Booker. Immediately after Saint-Louis was recaptured, the Company of Senegal was completely reorganized in order to move from a tightly monopolistic system to a more liberal economic system. Only then did liberalism in the Atlantic slave trade assert itself. Less than ten years later, Europe would experience the "era of the slave trade."[4]

Such is the evolution of the Company of Senegal, which aimed to monopolize trade along the Senegal River for a quarter of a century. During this entire period, the Senegal concession—restricted as it was to Saint-Louis and the island of Gorée—carried out a policy of trading posts without territorial conquest. Nevertheless, Saint-Louis attempted to extend its commercial influence all the way to the starting point of the Senegal River. In 1687, Chambonneau explored the falls of Félou, and in 1693, La Courbe tells us that "Galam has been visited for seven years and the slave trade has already brought in fifty captives."[5]

However, the province of Galam did not lead the trade along the Senegal River until the beginning of the eighteenth century. From the beginning, Chambonneau envisioned a large project of agricultural colonization in the Senegal valley. We are told that he pushed aside the customary slave trade along the Senegal valley for this vision. "He does not talk about this traffic, but about taking over a tract of land along the river in the name of the king, sending men and women to live there, and giving them acreage as they do in America to plant and grow tobacco, indigo, cotton, white sugar canes... [to settle white men in the area] in order to raise silk worms, or mine iron and gold, or pursue anything else that can be pursued there."[6] Occupation of the land would facilitate land travel and make it easier to overcome the obstacles to river navigation, represented by the Félou falls and the river's irregular water flow. Abdoulaye Ly highlighted the modern ideas of Chambonneau who, on this level, was a precursor of Brüe—the figure for whom colonial historiography reserved the role of "pioneer of colonization." For Chambonneau, "Senegal would become a colony in the modern sense of the word, the Company of Senegal limiting itself to trading... Such is the plan we can legitimately call 'revolutionary.' It aspired to nothing less than a radical transformation of the Senegal concession under the Ancien Régime and envisioned in this region a French presence very much like the one that was envisioned in France during the Restoration."[7]

This project of agricultural colonization, which would necessarily have encompassed Waalo, was not actually implemented before the beginning of the nineteenth century, under Governor Schmaltz. Indeed, at this time, Europe was not interested in or prepared for a direct colonization of Africa. This state of affairs is due to the fact that, according to Samir Amin, Africa was admirably playing its economic role of "periphery of the periphery"—the islands of the Americas being the "periphery" of Europe, which was the nerve "center" of the global economy. Through the Atlantic slave trade and for the unique profit of Europe, Africa had integrated itself in a commercial triangle that represented, until the end of the eighteenth century, the very foundation of its mercantile economy.

Within this context, the Company of Senegal played "a pioneer role in the slave trade era in France" and, despite continual deficits, also played an important role in the context of the mercantilism of the Grand Siècle ("Big Century").[8] Let us now consider the relationships that developed between this company, based as it was in Saint-Louis, and the neighboring kingdom of Waalo.

The Conflict between the Brak and La Courbe in 1685

We have previously tried to evaluate the volume of exchanges between Waalo and the trading post of Saint-Louis. We have noticed the relative importance of this commerce and, at the same time, the role played by Waalo—although due to its geographical position, the kingdom might have interfered with the traffic of Saint-Louis along the Senegal River. From then on, the policy of the Company of Senegal directors was to give gifts and pay customary fees to Waalo chiefs in order to navigate freely on the whole length of the river. This unstable compromise was frequently violated by one or the other of the two parties and often triggered open conflicts, such as the one in 1685.

In November 1685, according to La Courbe, Monsieur La Marche reported "an incident which had happened and could have unfortunate consequences. He told me that the individual named La Jeunesse, an assistant who had gone into the Bifèche river in order to treat some oxen which were very much needed at the dwelling... had allowed one of his white men to walk into a negro village and to cause a home to be burnt down while he was trying to shoot a bird... As the hunter attempted to go back to his boat, the villagers arrested him and put him in irons along with a *laptot* (a soldier of the Senegalese light infantry) who had accompanied him, and then, at the request of Gyobo, one of the important people of

Bifèche, they forced the said La Jeunesse to pay 36 *cuirs*, that is, 36 pounds, to compensate for the loss of a home that was not worth 10. This being done, the men were freed."[9]

By way of reprisal, La Jeunesse captured a fisherman who had the misfortune of being a prisoner of the *brak*. In order to avoid a conflict similar to the one during the days of Richmot, La Courbe sent Monsieur La Marche with a well-armed boat to request a refund of the 36 *cuirs* from Gyobo on November 27, 1685; he offered to pay only 15 *cuirs* instead. In case of refusal, La Marche's instructions were to allow the *brak*'s prisoner to go free and seize a subject of Gyobo. But the *brak,* who was absent at the time, did not appreciate La Courbe's attitude and demanded the return of "the boat which had been taken to Bifèche" before considering any negotiation.[10]

Having obtained no redress, La Courbe sent the Waalo-Waalo *laptots* away from the dwelling. He was prevented from starting hostilities only by the presence, in the Fuuta valley, of a boat that was at risk of being pillaged. In the meantime, La Marche failed to follow the instructions of La Courbe and looted "about 100 *cuirs* worth of cotton and tobacco in a few homes, even before calling Gyobo to account... Having noticed how small the number of white men was, the Negroes, who numbered about 500, attacked them with fury, wounded and killed a majority and obliged the others to retreat towards the boat, but as the boat was far away, the white men were all killed on the way."[11]

Upon receiving this disturbing piece of news, La Courbe sent away the remaining two *laptots* and actively prepared to defend the island. This is perhaps partly what prevented the *brak* from attacking the island, and made negotiation possible. "It was agreed that the looting of M. La Marche, which amounted to approximately 100 *cuirs*, would remain with the Company to compensate for what had been exacted from his assistant and that the *brak* would retain what had been loaned to him and which amounted to perhaps 50 or 60 *cuirs*, that his prisoner would be returned to him, and that Gyobo would return the 'perrier' (swivel gun) and the weapons of those who had been killed; on top of it all, the harm that had been perpetrated on both sides would be forgotten."[12]

This is an example of those originally minor disputes that very often ended in generalized hostilities. Ultimately, however, the desire of Saint-Louis not to endanger its trade and the *brak*'s fear of reprisals facilitated compromise. As a matter of fact, the belligerent policies of Captain Lambert were still very much alive in the memory of the *brak,* who dared not face the canons of Saint-Louis that had always overcome his predecessors. Finally, the never-ending debt in merchandise of the *brak* toward the trading post of Saint-Louis limited his claims. Little by little, the traditional aristocracy integrated itself into the system of Atlantic trade. Let us now look at the harsh competition for power between the different royal families during the last quarter of the eighteenth century.

The Reign of Brak Bër Caaka (Loggar)

We have no archival documents pertaining to this reign that would enable us to criticize the oral tradition as reported by Yoro Diaw Azan and Amadou Wade. Although they agree overall on the historical framework, they often contradict each other when it comes to details of the events. Thus, we shall only retain the main lines of their narratives in order to understand the social and political facts.

According to Azan, Bër Caaka, from the royal branch of the *Loggar*, was the son of Uram Dialo and Caaka Mbodje. His father died at the moment when he was about to be named *brak*, and so the son took his place.[13] According to Yoro Diaw, "*brak* Tiaka M'Bodj (Bër-Tiacka), after receiving a gift from a European sailor named Sambare composed of a few guns with grenade sleeves and two trumpets during the third year of his reign, developed an avocation from these instruments..."[14]

Rousseau believes that Sambare was the nickname given to a certain Le Maître, Brüe's temporary deputy, who had agreed to pay the customary fee of 100 iron bars. However, this might be a distortion of the name Chambonneau, whom *brak* Yeerim Koodé already called "sa Dome Samboné" in 1675, though it could refer to his son, Chambonneau, who was still living in Senegal in 1688.[15] The reign of Bër Caaka, nonetheless, can be placed in the last fifteen years of the eighteenth century. Azan reports that, from the beginning of his reign, Bër Caaka had to fight Yeerim Mbañik, the son of Fara Condama and Aram Bakar. When still in his youth, Yeerim Mbañik was put forward as a false king by *beeco* Maalixuri, his cousin, who wanted to rule in his name.[16] In this competition, the triumph of Bër Caaka, from the *Loggar* family, over Yeerim Mbañik, of the *Teejek* family, was politically strengthened through the elimination of all the offices in the kingdom that had once been attributed to the vanquished party. Indeed, Bër Caaka "entrusted the highest dignities in the realm to his maternal nephews (*doomi ndeyam*), at the expense of his paternal nephews (*doomi baayam*)... Naatago Deegón and Dembanee Deegón, the sons of Deegón Fara, uterine sister of the *brak*, were therefore named *kaj* and *briyot*."[17] *This policy of elimination was largely suggested by linger* Jambur-Gel, who never stopped reiterating to Bër Caaka that "the *kaj*, the first dignitary in the country after the *brak*, whom he eventually succeeds, must be chosen among the members of his family on his mother's side (*meen*). Thus, after the death of the *brak*, power always remains in the family..."

The sons of Aram Bakar, whose interests as well as their honor (*jom*) had been damaged, sought revenge. They formed an alliance with their parent, the former *beeco* Maalixuri, who had also been dismissed at the time of Bër Caaka's accession to power. Maalixuri often repeated to the children of Aram Bakar the following statement: "If I had [had] a Mboj last name, I would have taken up arms against the *brak* a long time ago. But unfortunately, I am a Jop."[18] They eventually accepted the help of Maalixuri and planned the assassination of Bër Caaka. They failed in their attempt and only escaped the death sentence through the complicity of the *Jogamaay* Ali Caaka. They found an initial refuge in Fuuta, and from there helped Jam assume the authority of *satigi* against his brother Koli.

The sons went to settle in Wul (Ouli), a land rich in gold. According to Amadou Wade, "during their long stay in this land, they often sent gifts of gold powder (*bol-u-wurus*) in bulk (*baar-u-wurus*) or in wrought form (*wurus bu ñu ligey*) to their parent Altyaka Jogomaay of Waalo."[19] Azan confirms this: "They brought [Altyka] two ostrich necks filled with gold powder in order to propitiate him."[20] Also, during their exile, the *linger* Jambur-Gel never stopped engaging "without any shame in the pillage (*móyal*) of the *baadolo* of Waalo; no one was spared (*Kenn muccul*) and everyone was mercilessly plundered."[21] The multiple complaints of the *baadolo* to the members of the *seb ak bawor* did not change the behavior of the *linger*, especially regarding the *brak*. Dominated by his sister, he attempted to smother the whole affair through corruption by giving them, after each meeting, ten captives each.

However, as these instances of extortion persisted, and as the members of the *seb ak bawor* felt personally threatened, the latter decided to bring Aram Bakar's sons back from exile and reinstate them in power. The circumstances of the war that ensured the victory of Yeerim Mbañik over Bër Caaka are reported differently by Amadou Wade and Azan. According to Azan, Bër Caaka was "surprised while completely defenseless in Jurbel by Yeerim Mbañik who had come from the right shore with his army. He managed to escape and ran away almost alone to Dioraye. The next day, he came back alone to the fort at Diek, where someone called Ndoun Macodé Gaye helped him cross the river and, with the help of the Jolof, he returned to pursue Yeerim, but the latter succeeded in having him poisoned... The followers of Bër Caaka continued a war of revenge under the leadership of a brave warrior named Thiéka Yeerim Ndiaye; they attacked Yeerim near Ndombo, beat him up and pursued him almost all the way to M'Poumou. There, however, the *beeco* Maalixuri, his cousin, came to his rescue, the army of Yeerim Ndiaye was scattered, Yeerim was killed during the action and Yeerim Mbañik had himself proclaimed *brak*."[22]

According to Amadou Wade, the army of Yeerim Mbañik arrived during the feast of the Gamu and "all the discontent (*ñi-mer*), all the partisans (*ñi-anda ak*) of their uncle and a man who was obliged to them, the *jogomaay* Altyaka, warned by the latter, joined the army of Yeerim Mbañik.

They attacked the *brak*'s house... After several charges, their ammunitions being exhausted, the *brak* returned to Njurbel to replenish his supplies. While they were getting gunpowder, the *jawdin* Tañ Ngilee, who was a personal friend and first counselor of the *brak* (*diisoo ak Brak*) and who, on his mother's side (*ci wallu meen*), was a close parent of the *jogomaay* and of the *malo*, both supporters of Aram Balar's sons, the *jawdin* Tañ Ngilee pointed the gunpowder reserve (*njëg-u putar*) to Yeerim Mbañik and advised him to set fire to it... A huge fire was lit... The *brak* Bër Caaka, lacking ammunition, was vanquished. With a few followers, he escaped from Njurbel and took refuge at the home of his uncle Yatma Demba in Pum. Upon seeing him, the latter said to him, 'What is happening to you today is fatal (*xamoon nga ne lii dana ñów*), you gave too much licence to the *linger* Jambur-Gel and you have never wanted to take my advice into account...'[23]

However, his wife Maram Njaay, sister of the former *beeco* Maalixuri, followed the example of Tañ Ngilee: she set fire to the gunpowder reserve, thus forcing Bër Caaka and Yatma Demba to flee to the Jolof. They eventually found refuge in the Fuuta, where they asked for the help of the *satigi* Gaydi. Although backed by the Fuuta, Yatma Demba and Bër Caaka both met their deaths while attempting to re-conquer Waalo. Their ally, the *satigi* Gaydi, continued the war and repelled the Waalo-Waalo back to Ndioo twice. In the end, Yeerim Mbañik only won due to the help of the *beeco* Maalixuri who, at the head of his brave army, drove the soldiers of the *satigi* all the way back to the Tawey marshland "where they were massacred with such fury and cruelty that the bodies of their dead were used to make a bridge for the warriors of Waalo across the 'marigot' (African marshland)."[24]

Even though they differ in some details, Amadou Wade and Azan concur in showing the main sources of this power struggle. They both refer to the death of the *brak* Bër Caaka. However, an allusion in the plan of the Ormans, in November 1720, leads us to believe that things did not unfold like this. Indeed, Alichandora, king of the Trarzas, gave the Ormans a mission to "restore on the Waalo throne Kiaçafara, formerly overthrown by Yeerim Bagnic, and who lived as a refuge near the Siratic."[25] It is therefore probable that this Kiaçafara was the *brak* Bër Caaka, who, once vanquished, went to live in Fuuta where he died a natural death. A dispatch dated May 24, 1721, tells us that "the candidate of Alichandora to the throne of Waalo, the former *brak* Kiaçafara, having died two months before the return of the Trarza chief in Mauritania, it was necessary to find him a substitute."[26] During his long exile, his attempts to regain power did not cease. This account of Bër Caaka's death agrees with the narrative of Amadou Wade, who says that Bër Caaka died in a house that collapsed on his body "in the village of Añam."[27] This, however, supposedly took place during his campaign against Yeerim Mbañik. The fact remains that Yeerim Mbañik took power and the *brak*, or so Amadou Wade tells us, "brought back his troops to Njanay, which, from then on, he turned into his capital (*péey*) instead of Njurbel."[28]

Yoro Diaw reports that "Njurbel, the true capital of Waalo, had become depopulated since 1697 as a result of the numerous family feuds in many of which the Trarza Moors had taken part."[29] Azan also links the transfer of the capital of Jurbel on the right bank to the town of "Nguianguie" on the left bank as a consequence of the Trarza Moors' pressure.[30] Indeed, it is possible that the destruction of the left bank villages, which formed the setting for the civil war, increased the pressure of the Trarza Moors. Their power increased during the first quarter of the eighteenth century as a consequence of the increasing importance of the gum trade. However, the civil conflicts described above already reveal a permanent factor of dissension in the history of Waalo—that is, the power struggle between the *Loggar*, *Teejekk* and *Dios* families. The conflict arose from the fact that Bër Caaka had given the most important positions in the state to his nephews on his mother's side, in order to ensure succession within his *meen* family. Such an approach always provoked reactions from the other candidates and thus gave rise to unending civil wars that ultimately weakened Waalo.

In the context of this permanent conflict, the importance of the *meen* family is clear. It is first revealed in the attitude of the *jawdin* Tanñ Ngilee, who threw himself in the fire he had lit as a result of his loyalty to his *meen* family. The *linger* Jambur-Gel deemed his action treacherous and "all the more criminal as he was the most intimate and best adviser of the *brak*." But he told her: "I am not the son of a noble (*du ma doom u garmi*), but I am worthy of being the son of a *sek ak bawor* (*Yelloo naa di doomu Seb ak Bawor*)... When the town has burned down, search in its ashes and you will find my bones. Possessions and honors are good (*alal, teranga, baax nañu, dëgg la*), but for nothing in the world would I allow my maternal relatives to be massacred (*Waande dara ci addina du tax ma bayyi ñu jeexal sa mbooki ndey*)."[31]

Maram Njaay had a similar attitude. Upon betraying her husband, she destroyed the gunpowder reserve, saying that "she would die contented (*danaa dee ak baneex*) knowing that this powder would not be used against her brother and her cousins."[32] The conflict also demonstrates another aspect of the political tensions in Waalo: the power of the *seb ak bawor* to conduct intrigue on behalf of their chosen candidates for the throne. Despite his gift-giving, Bër Caaka did not succeed in restraining the members of the *seb ak bawor*; Yeerim Mbañik, having found a source of gold, was able to give them even more, and therefore ensured their support. Gifts given to different dignitaries clearly played an important role in the race to power. Finally, it appears that the rise of a new *brak* to power was very often followed by a change in political responsibilities within the provinces, which reflects the different alliances built during the elections. In this case, the *beeco* Maalixuri was pushed aside at the same time as his cousin Yeerim Mbañik. More to the point, the decisive intervention of Maalixuri, who ultimately determined the end of the competition between Bër Caaka and Yeerim Mbañik, shows that his province—a fiefdom of the *beeco*—played an important role in Waalo.

The proximity of Saint-Louis explains the power of the *beeco,* whose role would be even more significant in the first quarter of the eighteenth century, during the gum war. But even at this point in the story, it is possible to believe that the trading post of Saint-Louis played a role in this conflict. Indeed, the soon-to-be-determined assignment of Brüe to the *beeco* Maalixuri, a supporter of Yeerim Mbañik, suggests an alliance of Saint-Louis with his party; it has been noted that the *beeco*'s intervention was a determining factor. In any case, the participation of Saint-Louis in the victory of Yeerim Mbañik is confirmed by a dispatch in 1717. It states in particular that "a kinglet from the Waalo country, acting against the good faith of the treatises, the sincere exchange he (Brüe) was having with him, and the gratitude that he (the *brak*) owed to the company which had helped him climb on the throne, has just taken a double longboat loaded with merchandise that he (Brüe) had sent upriver for the gum trade."[33] This proves that the role of the Saint-Louis trading post was, from then on, a determining factor in any succession crisis in the kingdom of Waalo, which had become the key to trade on the river.

The end of the seventeenth century marked an important stage in the development of political institutions in Waalo. Family rivalries launched a long civil war that resulted in the destruction of the capital's military power, which had been acquired after the marabout war. The transfer of the capital from the right to the left bank of the river was a sign of the decline of Waalo, which would henceforth always be under Moorish pressure. From then on, Waalo would no longer be more than a small kingdom wedged in a vise between two imperialistic forces: the Trarza Moors in the north, and the French at the mouth of the Senegal River. Rivalry between these two imperialistic forces would be constant in the history of Waalo. From the beginning of the eighteenth century, that rivalry manifested itself with the gum war.

THE REIGN OF BRAK YERIM MBAÑIK IN THE FIRST QUARTER OF THE EIGHTEENTH CENTURY: THE ARABIC GUM WAR

The reign of *brak* Yeerim Mbañik, who succeeded Bër Caaka after a long civil war, corresponds to an important phase in the history of Waalo. The transfer of the capital from Jurbel to Ndiaw, and from the right bank to the left bank of the Senegal River, coincided with the beginning of the pressure of the Trarza Moors. This pressure would thereafter be a constant threat, very much related to the growing importance of gum. The monopoly of gum, which had become indispensable to European manufacturers, launched a serious competition between France, England and Holland throughout the eighteenth century. The Trarza emirate thus became the center of French colonial policy.

The French, unable to eliminate competitors on the coast of Mauritania, attempted to at least redirect the gum trade to the trading posts along the Senegal River. In order to fulfill this objective, the different trade directors in Saint-Louis attempted, according to circumstances, to create alliances with the *brak* Yeerim Mbañik or with the *beeco* Maalixuri. The latter was a powerful provincial chief who, through his independence from royal power, symbolized an aspect of the internal life of Waalo. Beyond the Trarza pressure, the invasion of Ormans disturbed the peace in Waalo for a few years. Such are the different aspects of the reign of Yeerim Mbañik that will be discussed in this chapter.

The Arabic Gum War

As André Delcourt pointed out, "in the first half of the eighteenth century, the seizure of the Mauritanian coast section included between Cap Blanc and the mouth of the Senegal river was a main objective in the African colonial policy of the three European powers who were then sharing the great maritime trade and textile industry: France, Holland and Great Britain."[34] During this period, arabic gum, a plant sap, was an indispensable raw material in the making of almost all dyestuffs and painted fabrics. Arabic gum was used "in the preparation of silks, ribbons, gauzes, batistes and hats; was also used in the preparation of medicines and confectionery; was used for the making of pigments as well as gildings, and in many other occasions, and to all those many uses added also the precious advantage of being a sane and very substantial food."[35]

Thus, in the eighteenth century, gum along with enslaved individuals became an increasingly popular product in the Galam region, fueling the main trading activity along the Senegal River. In order to monopolize this trade activity, France applied from 1713 to 1763 the "doctrine of exclusiveness, the most outrageous version of what has been called 'the colonial pact'" and thus constantly opposed the ambitions of other European powers.[36] This competition sparked the gum war, the first phase of which took place from 1717 to 1727. During that decade, the French sought by any means necessary to shove the British out of Portendick and Arguin—and especially to thwart the Dutch interlopers who came to trade gum. As early as July 29, 1717, Brüe signed a friendship treaty with Alichandora, the Trarza emir. This treaty was intended to confirm, for the Company of Senegal, the exclusive privilege of the European commerce along the Mauritanian coast. Brüe was nonetheless obliged to inaugurate a series of cruises along the coast of Mauritania in order to turn away the competition. This ended in failure; the capture of Arguin by Salvert in February 1721 did not drive away the Dutch from the coast. The Dutch built another fort in Portendick. Most importantly, the French had to confront the hostility of Trarza Moors.[37]

Waalo played an important role in the gum war as a result of its geographical location. Indeed, since they could not seize the whole Mauritanian coast, André Brüe and his successors attempted to restrict the entire gum trade to the shores of the Senegal River. This explains the unfolding of a political as well as a military offensive against the Waalo chiefs.

Waalo Policy of Brüe

The policy of Brüe concerning Waalo consisted of fostering the conflict between the *brak* Yeerim Mbañik and the powerful provincial chief, the *beeco* Maalixuri. The latter, due to his geographical position near Saint-Louis, was able to act as an intermediary between Brüe and the Trarza emir, Alichandora. Most importantly, he could oppose the territorial and political pretensions of the *brak* and the *damel* in Saint-Louis.

Relationship between Brüe and the Brak Yeerim Mbañik

We saw that Brüe intervened in favor of Yeerim Mbañik in the power struggle, thus becoming an opponent of the *brak* Bër Caaka. Ultimately, it was the trading post of Saint-Louis that contributed most to his ascension to power. However, the subsequent friendly relationships, established by way of gratitude and in order to facilitate the slave trade along the river, were soon interrupted. As a matter of fact, as early as the spring of 1717, Brüe announced that Yeerim Mbañik had captured a double longboat loaded with merchandise that Brüe had sent upriver for the gum trade.[38] In response, Brüe asked the maritime council for a ship with 200 soldiers in order to bring the *brak* back to reason.[39] It was not until 1720 that Brüe, accused by Nicolas Desprès de Saint-Robert of having provoked this attack because of the "gallant relationship" he had carried on with one of Yeerim Mbañik's wives, justified himself by foisting the responsibility onto Alichandora. According to Brüe, Alichandora had incited Yeerim Mbañik to "interrupt the gum trade that I was carrying out on the river and to shift it to Portendick for the benefit of the interlopers."[40]

Brüe ordered reprisals and had the *brak*'s lands pillaged as compensation for the loss of the longboat, *La Curieuse*. Later, Yeerim Mbañik disclosed to Saint-Robert that, in order to express his hostility toward Brüe, he was ready to dispense with his customary fees, "but that never would he have had any commerce with the Whites, or tolerated the gum trade in his country or any other thing."[41] This explains why Yeerim Mbañik refused to pay his debt that, according to the accounts of Brüe in January 1718, amounted to "56 captives 10/50 which make 2,810 pounds."[42] By 1719, Yeerim Mbañik had only paid an installment of 13 captives 10/50, i.e. a value of 660 pounds, while promising to discharge his debt regularly in order to benefit from his yearly custom of approximately 2,000 pounds.[43]

In April 1720, Brüe attempted to retrieve the 40 promised prisoners by capturing the 68 captives that the *brak* had intended to sell him. Bataille, who was charged with this mission aboard *The Union*, was unable to execute the plan because the *laptots*, subjects of the *brak*, refused to do it. The ship came back empty and, despite the efforts expended later on to buy the captives with merchandise, Yeerim Mbañik was so irritated that he resolved never to do any more trading with Brüe.[44] It seems that Brüe then incited Alichandora, who had gone to request help from the sultan of Morocco, to chastise his enemy.[45] Brüe had definitely alienated Yeerim Mbañik, most probably as a result of his alliance with *beeco* Maalixuri.

Relationship between Brüe and the Beeco Maalixuri

In Waalo, Brüe had chosen as the main pawn of his policy the powerful *beeco* Maalixuri, who was the *kangam* of the most important province located near Saint-Louis. The position of that province between the lands of the *brak* and those of the *damel* of Kajoor made *beeco* Maalixuri an interesting partner, capable of balancing the pretensions of the two rulers. As a matter of fact, Maalixuri had "so many good feelings, worth and courage" for Brüe that Brüe attached to the service of the company a man "rare among Negroes."[46] Indeed, since his very first visit to Saint-Louis in February 1716, the *beeco* Maalixuri never ceased to help Brüe. First of all, he delivered a certain Jean de Booth who had been captured by the Moors. In 1719, when the pirates threatened Saint-Louis, Maalixuri put 150 men at Brüe's disposal to defend the island in case of aggression.[47]

As a reward, Brüe encouraged the marriage of the *beeco* with Famiguiau, the niece of a certain Bourié Bergame. He also gave his protégé millet for the feast, a dozen barrels of lime to cover the walls of the nuptial dwelling, two swivel guns and four fireboxes for the festivities.[48] This affinity was endangered, however, when the *beeco* Maalixuri returned to the Moors some oxen that Brüe had seized as reprisal. Brüe was obliged to make restitution from his own cattle. According to Saint-Robert, in reality the handsome wife of Maalixuri had merely obtained a show of restitution to make Brüe appear viable in the eyes of the public.[49]

It is this positive relationship between the two men that, according to Saint-Robert, explains why Maalixuri and his wife conducted after Brüe's departure "a considerable amount of trading of prisoners, gold and smuggled supplies in the country of Oual, because they are well provided with the most beautiful and necessary merchandises, especially iron for which the Negroes are clamoring in order to make '*lougans*,' this being the season when they sow millet."⁵⁰

Despite the rebuttals of Brüe, one must agree with Saint-Robert that the power of the *beeco* kept increasing. As a matter of fact, Maalixuri admirably played a double game. For example, after advising Yeerim Mbañik to pillage the longboat *La Curieuse*, the *beeco* "refused to be a part of the expedition although he too shared in the pillage; he did even more since he sent one of his deputies, a man named Bona, to Mr. Brüe to tell him that he was sorry about the *brak*'s affront."⁵¹ According to Saint-Robert, the *beeco* "behaved with so much guile that he advised both men and both were his dupes; he wanted to usurp the kingdom from the *brak* with the help that Mr. Brüe gave him and enrich himself at the same time with the Company's goods that Brüe showered on him..."⁵²

This conclusion is all the more plausible when we see the event that occurred a few years later. In 1724, the *beeco* Maalixuri, strengthened by the power acquired through his alliance with Brüe, actually took up arms against his own king, *brak* Yeerim Mbañik.⁵³ In the interim, after the departure of Brüe, Saint-Robert attempted to take an opposite course and to form an alliance with *brak* Yeerim Mbañik.

WAALO POLICY OF SAINT-ROBERT

The Waalo policy of Saint-Robert was not fundamentally different from that of Brüe, since it also involved creating internal divisions among the chiefs in order to ensure the security of his trade.

Saint-Robert's Attempted Alliance with Yeerim Mbañik

Immediately after the departure of Brüe, Yeerim Mbañik let it be known that he wished to renew relationships with the new director. Contradicting previous practice, he intended to pay him a visit in Saint-Louis. Saint-Robert received this piece of news with joy; *brak* Yeerim Mbañik became his guest on the island of Saint-Louis from July 4 to July 8, 1720. The *brak* brought along gifts of 19 captives and 80 oxen. This visit provided him with an opportunity to vent about all the vexations he had incurred with Brüe; it did not take him very long to gain Saint-Robert's sympathy. Saint-Robert later conveyed his impressions: "I have found this king to be so reasonable that I promised to wait for the orders of the Company in this respect and I believed it to be my duty to pay him the entire amount of what he swore was owed to him. I also promised him his customary fees for the year 1720, the same amount Brüe had paid him the year before, without requiring him to pay that which he (Brüe) said he owed."⁵⁴

The relationship continued to improve. In 1721, Violaine, the director of Galam, paid the *brak* the yearly customary fees according to the best interests of the Company. Indeed, he convinced Yeerim Mbañik to accept "poor smuggled supplies and leftover pieces of blue cloth which had been lying about the store for three years, instead of Rouen cloth, as well as cheap metal instead of iron." He also convinced the *brak* to subtract from his receipt the value of four captives that had been loaned to him in the form of merchandise. The *brak* declared that he was satisfied, even though what he had received "was not worth half of what he had been paid during previous years."[55] However, the restoration of good relationships between Saint-Louis and *brak* Yeerim Mbañik also coincided with an external threat in the form of Orman bands, who invaded the entire region of the Senegal River.

Orman Invasion

From the beginning of the eighteenth century, bands of pillaging warriors called Ormans or Saletins swept through Senegal and Mali's Sahelian region in order to extract ransoms from the population. These groups of Moroccan origin invaded the region in successive waves. In 1716, through his son, Bubakar Siré asked for help from the sheriff of Morocco in order to overthrow Gelajo Jegi. In 1720, it was the turn of Alichandora, the Trarza emir, who had been expelled from his country by troops of Oulad Delims, to ask the sultan of Morocco for reinforcements. Incited by Brüe, Alichandora was also planning to restore Kiaça Fara (most probably Bër Caaka), a refugee in Fuuta, to the Waalo throne. On this occasion, Bubakar Siré, the *satigi* of Fuuta, sent Gaku as an ambassador to dissuade the sultan from sending any kind of help to Alichandora; such help might meet with a veritable wall of opposition from the Wolof kingdoms.

Gaku's arguments were that "the *brak* having wed a sister of the *damel*, king of Cayor, and Thin, king of Baol, and also a relative of Bourba-Yolof, those three powerful kings, whose kingdoms border that of the *brak*, would not fail to join their forces to his in order to fight the army he [the sultan] might lend to Alichandora; also the *damel* and Thin had just shared a great reserve of gunpowder and guns after the death of *damel* Latir Fal Soucabé, their father, and those four kingdoms were capable of arming more than 50,000 men; also, if the Bambaras, who are not as numerous and only have arrows and swords for weapons, have managed to defeat twice already his [the sultan's] army, there was no hope that the men he [the sultan] would send might have a better fate..."[56] However, Alichandora won his case; the sultan of Morocco sent him reinforcements of 9,000 men[57] that Saint-Robert would reduce to a mere 5,000.[58]

Alichandora drove out Oulad Delims and defeated the Braknas several times. However, the former *brak* Bër Caaka passed away before Alichandora's return, and a replacement had to be found for him. Waalo did not escape the danger; Bubakar Siré, newly re-installed on the throne, led the Ormans toward the lower part of the Senegal River as early as February 13, 1722[59] "because for the past seven years *brak* Yeerim Mbañik had been refusing to pay him the custom he had always paid to his predecessors."[60] The existence of these customary fees is confirmed by Father Labat, who noted while discussing the *satigi* that "This prince is powerful; the *brak* king and all the nobles of the kingdom of Oual are his vassals and pay him every four years a tribute of 43 captives and a set number of oxen."[61] However, Labat's 1728 writing does not mention the date of the payment of these customary fees, which must certainly have existed without reducing Waalo to a vassal state. Let us say that Bubakar Siré directed allies, who were too cumbersome in his own country, to attempt the conquest of the lower river region—without taking into account the fact that the Ormans, uniquely attracted by the lure of profit, constantly changed partners.

On February 13, 1722, Julien Dubellay learned that "the Ormans, numbering from 200 to 250, along with approximately as many Arabs from Fuuta who have joined them, were in the country of Oual; that they had already conquered the Fula land located about 30 leagues from Senegal. Some time later, the *brak* king sent us a messenger to let us know that the Ormans had surprised him at Enguiane, that he had fought a good battle and had killed Barena and about 40 of his men, but had lost at least two or three times as many of his men and was obliged to surrender his village, where they settled for a few days, and to withdraw with his valets on the island of Bissèche which belonged to Bequio Malikoury."[62]

A formidable Wolof opposition front, including the *buur-ba jolof*, the *tagne* and the *damel*, had been necessary for the Ormans to withdraw from combat toward Galam. But their brief passage had "caused horrible disorder everywhere they had gone and the country of Fuuta and Oual will remember it for a long time because they kidnapped some of the women and children and because they killed most of the cattle; everything is consternation, including the *brak*: two of his wives have been kidnapped and many of his men have been captured."[63] The Ormans did not remain intimidated for long; a few months later, they took advantage of the war between their allies, the Trarzas and the Braknas, and once again invaded the lower section of the river. Fleury reported that "100 Ormans or Moroccans with approximately 1,200 gunmen, Moors from the Fula country, had been looking for Alichandora and had forced him to flee with his Moors all the way to the 'maringoins' (mosquito-infested lands) some 10 leagues from the Senegal."[64]

Alichandora then asked for the help of *brak* Yeerim Mbañik and *beeco* Maalixuri, whose forces consequently routed the Ormans and their allies. They "took flight at full speed after having lost many of their men; Alichandora, the *brak* and *beeco* also lost many men, but they took possession of the battlefield, tents, baggage, horses and weapons, and Alichandora shared the spoils with the *brak* and *beeco*."[65] This victory allowed Yeerim Mbañik to exchange two of his wives for three Brakna chiefs who had been captured during the fighting. Once peace had been restored, Yeerim Mbañik had his *alkaati* in Saint-Louis, Dimbouguay, announce the restoration of the slave trade in all of Waalo.[66] In fact, this success would give Yeerim Mbañik a new foundation upon which he would attempt to capitalize during his second visit to Saint-Louis.

Brak Yeerim Mbañik's Second Visit to Saint-Louis

Accompanied by 300 men, Yeerim Mbañik visited the island of Saint-Louis from August 24 to September 3, 1722. Saint-Robert opposed this visit, but could not refuse to host him. His stay was a source of concern for the Company of Senegal, as its members suspected the *brak* wanted to attack the fort. Indeed, "a few White Men had overheard several of the *brak*'s men who were saying among themselves in the Negro language, without mistrusting the Whites, that Alichandora had wed a sister of the *brak* king to whom he had given a great deal of presents and that at the same time, they had pledged to take the fort of Senegal by surprise in order to turn it over to the Dutch of Portendick with whom they would then trade along the coast."[67]

Their suspicions were reinforced by the abrupt departure of Yeerim Mbañik's brother with about thirty men to join the Moors, and the suspicious behavior of a Dutch deserter, Jean de Booth. In the ensuing panic, Saint-Robert immediately implemented new measures of security. His defense preparations must have led the *brak* to hide his intentions because, in the course of two long palavers, Yeerim Mbañik assured Saint-Robert that he had no bad design against him.

Yeerim Mbañik nevertheless requested that the cost of river captives be raised to 10 bars instead of 8 and that the cost of traded spirits be brought down from 3 to 2 pounds. Saint-Robert thrust aside the request. Julien Dubellay, who was to succeed him, asked the company to reinforce the Saint-Louis garrison, because it was difficult to forbid the *brak*'s visits without interrupting trade.[68] This, by the way, explains why Saint-Louis attempted to renew relationships with *beeco* Maalixuri.

Relationship between Saint-Robert and Beeco Maalixuri

From the beginning of Saint-Robert's directorate, his hostility toward Brüe's policy manifested itself in his refusal to cooperate with Brüe's former ally in Waalo, *beeco* Maalixuri. In fact, Saint-Robert immediately informed the *beeco* that he would no longer welcome him in Saint-Louis with escorts of 50 or 60 men, as had been done in the time of Brüe. Moreover, the *beeco* was asked to bring along captives for trading, could not be accompanied by more than 5 or 6 men, and had to leave on the day after his arrival. Saint-Robert also thought of depriving him of spirits in order to enforce his conditions. But Maalixuri did not pay a single visit to Saint-Robert for two years.[69]

However, the suspicious visit of *brak* Yeerim Mbañik in September 1722 obliged Saint-Robert to renew relationships with *beeco* Maalixuri, who came to Saint-Louis a few days after the departure of the *brak* with an escort of 15 men. He come to offer the Company "his services by the side of the *damel* who had given him a large part of his realm of Cayor to command and one of his aunts, Nouissiné, for a wife, as much as his services by the side of the *brak* under whom he was a legitimate second in command."[70] The influence of Brüe on the Senegal committee of the West Indies Company, and the presence of Dubellay, the designated successor of Brüe, surely contributed to this sudden change. In fact, Julien Dubellay himself explains the return to Brüe's policy and justifies it in the following terms: "The *beeco* is the only lord of the country capable of maintaining peace between the two kings and to serve as a mediator between them in case of trouble or war and it is through his instrumentality that Mr. Brüe has honorably managed with his two kings for six and a half years during the last administration without any restriction on trade; thus, one should always retain him on the side of the Company which he never abandoned."[71]

This alliance was all the more necessary since the hostility of *brak* Yeerim Mbañik toward Saint-Louis had increased. It would indeed manifest itself during his third visit to Saint-Louis.

Brak Yeerim Mbañik's Third Visit and his Hostility toward Saint-Louis

At the beginning of 1722, war broke out between the *damel* of Kajoor and his brother, the *tagne* of Baol. After the defeat of his ally, the *damel*, Yeerim Mbañik came home on January 30, 1722. In order to keep Yeerim Mbañik indebted to him, the *damel* had given him as a present the Bétoubé (Tuubé) near Saint-Louis. Yeerim, who needed to visit his new subjects, announced on February 4, 1723 that he intended to pay a third visit to the island of Saint-Louis. Saint-Robert tried to prevent this visit by all possible means, and sent him regular rations of spirits. However, on February 9, after having received his daily present of spirits, Yeerim Mbañik demanded to be received in Saint-Louis and threatened to "have all the *laptots* move back on land and to interrupt the slave trade; this was agreed to rather than letting him come on the island."[72] Nothing could shake the decision of Yeerim Mbañik, who entered the island under the cover of night. Thanks to his entourage of a hundred or so men, Saint-Robert was forced to comply.

Yeerim Mbañik demanded a boat to conduct his dealings at Enguiane, his place of supply, but this was refused because he had earlier taken advantage of the Company "three or four times under the same pretext without ever sending any captive; however, he exacted a promise that once they were certain he had completed his plundering, they would send him a boat along with the trade goods he would request."[73] He then proceeded to seize nine of his subjects who had found refuge in Saint-Louis; he sold six of them to the Company, even though they had been previously extradited. Yeerim Mbañik returned on February 12 and 13 for three reasons: "1) to demand a loan for the value of 10 captives; 2) to be paid in advance the customary fees of Guiongo and Betoubé, two of the nobles the *damel* had given him, as has been mentioned earlier; 3) to raise the coast tariff, that is to say, to be paid 10 bars instead of 8 for river captives, as he had already proposed during his earlier visit."[74]

Yeerim Mbañik was eventually granted a loan based on the value of the captives and the payment of the customary fees, but received no more because he was still indebted to the Company. He finally left the island on February 13. His visit had cost 400 to 500 pounds.[75] The hostile act of Yeerim Mbañik would serve to bring *beeco* Maalixuri back into the sights of the Company on the occasion of Brüe's visit in May 1723.

La Rigaudière's Expedition and the return to Brüe's Policy toward Beeco Maalixuri

In 1722, the Moors of Alichandora forced the French to abandon the fort of Arguin. Booth left Arguin on January 11, 1722 and returned to Saint-Louis with 26 survivors from the French garrison. From then on, the Dutch were undisputed masters of the two Mauritanian stops for the gum trade. This unfortunate situation prompted the Marine Council to prepare a re-conquest expedition. As a result, "the colonial expedition under the leadership of La Rigaudière and Brüe was one of the best prepared of all operations of this type during the Ancien Régime."[76] One million pounds were spent and five ships left France on January 13, 1723. La Rigaudière's attempt to seize Arguin from February 17 to 22 failed, however, due to lack of water. The failure of the naval expedition gave rise to tentative negotiations to convince Alichandora to deliver the fort to the French. Brüe used his Senegal stay in May 1723 to entrust this mission to his ally, *beeco* Maalixuri.

Maalixuri had actually asked Julien Dubellay to seize Omar Ayba and Ely Ahmed, the Brakna Moor chiefs, who were at war against Alichandora. The latter had promised "to leave his children as hostages in Senegal until he had delivered the fort of Arguin in the hands of the Company."[77] Julien Dubellay was then expected to pay him the value of "300 captives in merchandises, that is to say, 200 for Alichandora and 100 for the *beeco*."[78]

In his report, Brüe is more explicit about the role of the *beeco* and his intention to take possession of Arguin at all costs. He wanted a renewal of the alliance forged with Alichandora on July 29, 1717, and was ready to pay the thousand crowns for the value of 300 captives—and even "readily double that offer if that was the only impediment to take occupancy of Arguin."[79]

However, *beeco* Maalixuri did not succeed in fulfilling his promises. On June 26, 1723, he announced that he had failed to join Alichandora. His failure was certainly due to the reluctance of *brak* Yeerim Mbañik, and especially to the refusal of his subjects to follow him in this war that pitched Braknas against Trarzas. In reality, however, Alichandora was still on the side of the Dutch. A dispatch dated December 18, 1723, states that the latter was "strongly" inciting "king Yeerim Mbañik and the Negroes of Oual to create occasions favorable to the surprise capture of the fort."[80]

To be sure, there were a few difficulties between Julien Dubellay and *brak* Yeerim Mbañik, who only accepted his customary fees reluctantly in August 1723 and threatened to form an alliance with the *damel* to interrupt trade.[81] Despite these difficulties, and especially after the regrouping on the island of 150 warriors with Yeerim Mbañik's brother, the company preferred to renew ties with the *brak*.[82] The failure of the *beeco*'s mission must also have contributed to that change. The rejection of Brüe's policy of alliance with the *beeco* Maalixuri became evident during the civil war, which erupted at the beginning of March 1724 between the *beeco* and *brak* Yeerim Mbañik.

Beeco Maalixuri's Attempt to Secede

We have already discussed the workings of the different alliances of the Company's directors with Waalo's chiefs. Their policy was a notable cause of the increasing power of *beeco* Maalixuri. As he conducted a considerable amount of trade, he played an important political role between the *damel* and the *brak* in their relationships with Saint-Louis on the one hand, and between the Trarza Moors and Saint-Louis on the other. His position conferred upon him real power, above and beyond the fact that his contribution to Yeerim Mbañik's accession to the throne had given him a choice place in the kingdom. As a result, it did not take long before he decided to profit from the situation and to seize the *brak*'s power, or at least attempt to gain autonomy for his province. The oral tradition has kept intact the record of *beeco* Maalixuri's rebellion against *brak* Yeerim Mbañik.

Amadou Wade notably tells us that Maalixuri, "made drunk by power (*nguur gi yobbu ko ba mu fatte boppam*), forgot what he owed to Yeerim Mbañik and the hardships that they had endured together (in Waalo, Fouta and Wul). He remained in Pum, his capital, for three years without paying a visit to the *brak*. He shunned the Gam of these three years and, on a more serious level, did not send to the *brak* and his council their shares of the *mooyal* (pillage) during these years."[83] The *seb ak bawor* then urged *brak* Yeerim Mbañik to relieve his cousin of the *beeco* title. Yeerim Bakar, who later became *jawdin*, was charged with the delicate mission of announcing his deposition to the powerful *beeco*.[84]

The *beeco* then officially declared his independence from the *brak*'s authority: "Upon arriving in Pum, Yeerim Bakar found the *beeco* seated under a large tree talking with the main dignitaries of his state. After the usual greetings, the *beeco* asked Yeerim if there still was a *brak* in Waalo. As Yeerim Bakar gave an affirmative response, the *beeco* turned around and said: 'If there is still one, he must be the *brak gu n'aka* (*brak* of the lower land), because I am the *brak gu ka* (*brak* of the high Waalo)."[85] Without dismounting from his fast steed, Tikri-Bomdi, Yeerim Bakar delivered the *brak*'s message and galloped away in the direction of Ndiañ. However, even before the return of the *brak*'s messenger, the fires of Rosso announced the wrath of the *beeco* and the beginning of hostilities. *Brak* Yeerim Mbañik immediately took up arms and hunted Maalixuri out of Rosso, Caggar and even Pum, his capital, which he torched in order to avenge Rosso.[86] This episode of the civil war corresponds to Maalixuri's flight toward Kajoor—a flight mentioned in archival documents.

A dispatch dated March 28, 1724, tells us that *beeco* Maalixuri, who served as an intermediary between Saint-Louis and Alichandora and had become hostile, "has been driven out of his country three weeks ago by the *brak* king Yeerim Bagnic. He is currently wandering as a vagabond in Cayor with 300 armed men who pillage everywhere."[87]

This defeat did not end the hostilities. A dispatch dated June 18, 1724, indicates that "the war between the *brak*, Alichandora and *beeco* Maalixuri is stirred up; the king has hunted out the *beeco* and the Moors of Alichandora from the island of Pum has made mincemeat of the Negroes, because the Moors abandoned them in the middle of the battle; he has hunted down the runaways very far away and had some of them drowned in the river. On the one hand, this war may provide us with a number of captives; but, on the other hand, it will harm us greatly in our ships which will be traveling to Galam, although I will ensure that they are well armed; it will also decrease the number of oxen we get and of which we are always in want."[88]

Thus, we see that from the beginning of the civil war, Maalixuri formed an alliance with Alichandora, who had become more and more hostile to Saint-Louis. In order to safeguard trade with Galam, Julien Dubellay took the side of *brak* Yeerim Mbañik. In December 1724, he justified his policy in the following terms: "The Company will dispense me, if it pleases it to respond to the item concerning the ruin of the *beeco* [and his fight] with the *brak* king or to the continuation of the war between the Thin king and the *damel*, and [it will] not ascribe to me faults into which I have never had any part. Without the *brak*, who supported me with everything available in his country, I could not have traded with Galam nor fed this garrison with millet and oxen, and if I had secretly supported the *beeco*, who was himself supported by the Moors, as the bad advice of the Company have inspired him to write to me, I would have entirely lost the Galam trade and river trade since the Siratic king belonged to the *brak*'s party."[89]

The war had deprived Saint-Louis of oxen, due to the closing of certain passages to the Moors. Moreover, the Moors "pillaged a large number of oxen belonging to the Negroes of the country of Oual during the last campaign of the *brak* with *beeco* Maalixuri who had found a refuge near Alichandora."[90] We know nothing else about the continuation of the conflict between *beeco* Maalixuri and *brak* Yeerim Mbañik. According to Amadou Wade and Azan, Maalixuri was killed in combat at Beekhar, and Fara Coro was named to replace him.[91]

Whatever the issues of the conflict—which, according to the oral tradition, ended in the defeat and death of *beeco* Maalixuri—we nevertheless observe a constant element in the political history of Waalo. It has to do with the permanent opposition of the *kangam*—powerful provincial chiefs excluded from the royal nobility—to the centralizing power of the *brak*. In this specific case, the power of the *beeco* comes from the geographical location of his province, and especially from his alliance with the French trading post of Saint-Louis—augmented by the personality of Brüe. The Company of Senegal exploited, for its own interests, the division between the Waalo chiefs—the defeat of Maalixuri was, in fact, due to his rejection by Julien Dubellay. This is evidence that the trading post of Saint-Louis directly intervened in the internal workings of Waalo and that political equilibrium greatly depended on the chiefs' alliances with the directors of the Company.

The End of Brak Yeerim Mbañik's Reign

After the conflict between Yeerim Mbañik and Maalixuri, it becomes difficult to follow the events that took place until the end of the *brak*'s reign. The oral tradition tells us that Yeerim Mbañik died of illness a few years after the defeat of Maalixuri.[92] The archives give us no information on the date of his death or the date of his heir's accession to the throne. It is, however, possible to ascribe the events that took place until 1733-1734 to the reign of Yeerim Mbañik, whose name is mentioned for the very last time on June 18, 1725. For example, a note dated July 9, 1730, mentions a certain Kiaka, the *brak*'s brother. This Kiaka could very well be Ndiak Aram Bakar, the brother who succeeded Yeerim Mbañik and whose reign ended approximately in October 1757.⁹³ Thus, if we take the 25-year reign ascribed to him by Fara Penda as a reference, we can estimate the end of Yeerim Mbañik's reign as approximately 1733.⁹⁴

According to the information provided by archival documents, the end of this reign is dominated by the relationships between the *damel* and the trading post of Saint-Louis. For example, we learn that in February, the *brak* helped the *damel* repulse the forces of the *buur-ba jolof* all the way to the borders of his kingdom. On June 30, 1730, the *brak* announced that his wife, Goné Latir, had joined her brother, the *damel* of Kajoor, who was better situated to satisfy her needs for merchandise of all sorts.⁹⁵ He then "sent a request for an extravagant gift of 'pataques' [a 'war ship' used to transport people or supplies to and from the shore or another ship], double-barrelled guns, gunpowder, and black canvas, in order to have a pretext for dispute once the trade was refused."⁹⁶

In order to achieve his goals, the *brak* obliged the *laptots* to abandon the island at the moment when the Company had the greatest need of them— for the Galam expedition. This act of hostility on the part of the *brak* was really motivated by the desire to obtain the same economic advantages as his neighbor, *the damel* of Kajoor. To this end, his *alkaati* complained "that too little consideration was shown the person of their king, and that the *damel*, besides selling his captives for 30 bars, also received a large number of presents while the *brak* barely received his customary fees."⁹⁷

Peace was restored with the help of 6 pints of spirits and a gun given to the *brak*. However, as early as July 8, 1730, exercising the same privilege as the *damel*, the *brak* pillaged a wrecked longboat.⁹⁸ The trading post of Saint-Louis retaliated on July 15 by setting fire to a village on the river shore, hoping to force the *brak* to beg for peace. Hostilities between Saint-Louis and the *brak* still prevailed as of September 11, 1730. In the meantime, the *damel* seized upon the presents the *brak* had sent to the *tagne*'s sister. The *brak* had repudiated her, because Goné Latyr was still refusing to return home.⁹⁹ The conflict that eventually erupted between the two men did not prevent the *brak* from maintaining his hostility against Saint-Louis. The fort attempted unsuccessfully to persuade Amar, chief of the Moors, to pillage Waalo.¹⁰⁰ In August 1733, the *brak* reluctantly accepted his customary fees, "after many contestations and threats to stop all the boats by forbidding his subjects to serve us [the Company]. The *brak* forced [the Company] to grant him a raise, maintaining that he had already been granted it the year before from Mr. Pellay and we were obliged to agree to everything he wanted."¹⁰¹

This hostility toward Saint-Louis most certainly found a pretext in the relative power of the *brak*—something suggested, incidentally, in a memorandum on the Senegal concession dated October 8, 1734. It notably states that the "King *brak* is the closest neighbor of the fort of Saint-Louis; his forces include between two and three hundred mounted men and three thousand infantrymen, half of whom actually carry firearms."[102]

Conclusions about the Reign of Yeerim Mbañik

The reign of Yeerim Mbañik, encompassing the first quarter of the eighteenth century, was particularly agitated. Yet it brought about no fundamental change in the relationships with Saint-Louis, whose commerce remained preponderant. However, this commerce was increasingly dominated by the gum trade, which from then on dominated politics along the Senegal River. The increasing importance of gum also contributed to the power of the Moors; during this period, they began to exert heavy and continual pressure on the people living along the Senegal River.

Waalo, merely a secondary supplier of a few enslaved individuals as well as food supplies for Saint-Louis in the form of millet and cattle, only remained important because of its geographical position. Yet despite its weakness, the *brak* remained the gatekeeper to the river, and Galam commerce still depended largely on his good will. After the failure of the Company to eliminate the other European powers from the coast of Mauritania, the Waalo chiefs played a fairly substantial role in Saint-Louis' effort to redirect all the gum trade to the Senegal River. It is within this context that the trading post of Saint-Louis attempted to associate with the Waalo chiefs.

This largely contributed to a change in the political balance of the country. The policy notably favored the rebellion of *beeco* Maalixuri against the centralizing power of the *brak*. Maalixuri's failure may have marked the beginning of the strengthening of power of the *brak,* who relied increasingly on his army of *ceddo,* which was widely provided with firearms. This would enable Waalo to intervene regularly in the wars that positioned its neighbors from Kajoor, Jolof and Bawol against each other.

But the relative authority of the Waalo chiefs still remained linked to the commercial fluctuations of Saint-Louis and the changing policy of its directors. The local aristocracy was increasingly attracted to European merchandise; possessing such merchandise constituted, from then on, a fundamental element in aristocratic power and the maintenance of that power. Thus, the reign of Yeerim Mbañik was marked by multiple visits to the fort of Saint-Louis. Each time, the *brak* attempted to obtain new advantages. However, his military forces were not powerful enough to enable him to attack the fort; his continual indebtedness to the Company thus largely limited his pretensions to power. Waalo was clearly moving toward the formation of a military state, increasingly associated with Atlantic trade. The main activity for such a state would be war.

CHAPTER 6

THE REIGN OF BRAK NDIAK ARAM BAKAR, CA. 1733–57

The reign of Ndiak Aram Bakar was primarily marked by his foreign policies. Indeed, along the border with the Trarza Moors, Waalo was constantly on the defensive. The *brak*'s military intervened several times in the internal affairs of Kajoor and Bawol, two states fighting for hegemony. As far as Saint-Louis trade was concerned, competition between the French and the British constituted the background for a period dominated by multiple wars. These wars eventually led to the weakening of the Wolof states.

The Accession of Ndiak Aram Bakar

The uneventful accession of Ndiak Aram Bakar to the throne followed the death of his brother, Yeerim Mbañik. Azan tells us that "Ndiak Aram, second son of Aram Bakou (*Tediek*) and Fara Coundama or Fara Counba Dama (*djëse*) replaced his brother Yeerim Mbañik. He was the first *brak* to settle in Nder; he turned it into the third capital of Waalo."[1]

Oral tradition and archival sources do not supply any facts relative to the internal history of the kingdom—except for a war that erupted in August 1742 between Ndiak Aram and one of his subjects, who claimed the crown.[2] However, the transfer of the capital to Ndiaw, located inland on the river shore, can only be explained by the pressure of the Moors to the north and by the need to intervene in the affairs of Kajoor in the south. Let us examine these two aspects of the reign of Ndiak Aram, whose actions are often confused by Amadou Wade with those of his brother and successor, Naatago Aram. This confusion is because of the participation of the latter in all the campaigns of his elder brother.

Relationship with the Moors

The Moorish pressure that already weighed on Fuuta began to be felt in Waalo as a result of the rivalries between its chiefs. Thus, in August 1742, Ndiak Aram had to confront the rebellion of one of his subjects, who asked the Moors for help. The latter pillaged much of the country. "It is painful to see that the [Moor] nation has become very powerful and it is to be feared that it will take over the *brak*'s country, as it has taken over and completely ruined the country of the Fula people. This can only be very detrimental to our commerce."³ Ndiak Aram must have shaken off his competitor, since we know he reigned until 1757and intervened regularly in the affairs of Kajoor.⁴

Relationships with Kajoor

During this reign, the north of Senegambia was dominated by the attempt of the Kajoor *damels* to win hegemony over Bawol. This provided a pretext for Waalo to intervene regularly, since multiple civil wars were started to gain power and went along with the *damels*' politics of annexation.

Consequently, in 1737, Bawol was under the leadership of *damel* Maïsa Teindde Ouédji, who combined two crowns until his death in 1748.⁵ His death gave rise to a bitter competition between his brother, Ma Haoua, and his nephew, Maïsa Bigé. "Ma Haoua wanted to be acknowledged as king; a section of the country acknowledged him. He entered it with his troops, [but] his nephew beat him to it and defeated him. [Ma Haoua] escaped in the land of the *brak*, who is currently at war with the *damel*. But this war had no other consequences than the pillage of a few villages on both sides."⁶

However, the struggle for power was not over. Oral tradition tells us that Maïsa Bigé went to war against Ndiak Aram in order to avenge the offense to his mother, Bigé Ngoné, wife of the *brak*. According to Amadou Wade and Azan, Ndiak Aram pursued the forces of Maïsa Bigé all the way to Ndiamsil in Bawol. "Once victorious and before leaving Kayor, *brak* Ndiak Aram decided to proclaim his brother Naatago *damel* of that country. The *seb ak bawor* opposed him, for the good reason that Waalo, too weak to defend its own borders seriously, should not take responsibility for a country as vast as Kayor. The *brak* rallied to the decision of the council and acknowledged as *damel* Dorobé Mawoo Mbat yoo Samb. Exiled from Kayor, he had been a refugee in Waalo under the protection of the *brak* (*Laky si ci Brak-bi*) for numerous years."⁷ This certainly refers to Ma Haoua who, according to a note dated June 25, 1752, had been uncomfortably seated on the throne because "his nephew, whom he has driven away from the throne three years ago quarrels with him ceaselessly."⁸ Thus, this whole period was dominated by a civil war that favored commercial activities connected with the Atlantic slave trade—as well as the rise of Waalo's power.

The result of these wars was the recrudescence of the Atlantic slave trade. The *damel* sold 400 captives in 1753, constituting an exceptionally abundant trade in contrast with that of his predecessors. However, these wars were also responsible for a generalized famine that stretched "from Bisseau all the way to Galam," and that, paradoxically, limited the trading of enslaved individuals because there was not enough grain to feed them.⁹ For example, in November 1753, "the lack of food prevented Mr. Ansseno to trade more than 100 captives who were presented to him by the kings of Kayor and Sin who are at war with each other."[10]

During these lean years, the necessity of finding grain at any cost encouraged the rising role of Waalo, which had been spared the effects of the generalized famine. Indeed, as early as June 1753, the Company commented that the "general misery of the country has rendered the neighboring king *brak* and all the people of Oual more tiresome and the fear of a potential quarrel with him has rendered us more easy-going; never has the concession experienced such a general famine; it stretches from Bisseau all the way to Galam."[11] The famine was still raging in June 1754, when Waalo became the refuge for all the hungry people from neighboring countries. This situation gave the *brak* an opportunity to take advantage of the general calamity. According to Jean-Baptiste Estoupan de la Rué, "the famine which continues to prevail in the realms of Kayor and Jolof, having forced the poor people of these lands to come and look for food in the country of the *brak*, this king has seized upon those miserable people and sold them to us. The certainty they have that they will be taken as captives has not been enough to deter them from coming to the only place where they can assuage their misery and since they have no other option than death or captivity, it can be presumed that trade will not discontinue until the millet fall harvest, that is, until the end of September; the summer harvest which is taking place right now along our river is currently attracting all neighboring peoples."[12]

This advantage allowed Ndiak Aram to intervene once more in the affairs of Kajoor—and to ruin the country completely. As early as August 1754, Ndiak Aram put Ma Haoua, harassed by his nephew Maïsa Bigé, back on the throne. In this context, Estoupan de la Rué reported that "the country of Kayor has just weathered jolts it will continue to feel for a long time. The reigning king has been overthrown by his nephew and his competitor restored himself to the throne a month later thanks to the help of the *brak*. Very little blood was shed, but there has been much pillage in the land and, what is worse, a portion of the harvest which promised to be abundant this year has been destroyed. The war apparently produces a large number of captives, but Gorée will not come out of the misery entailed by the loss of cattle and grains."[13]

Kajoor's miserable fate was thus prolonged, especially as civil war continued more ruthlessly than ever. Indeed, in the month of November 1756, Ma Haoua was assassinated by one of his prisoners; his successor, Biram Kudu, was defeated by Maïsa Bigé, who had enlisted the help of the Trarza Moors. Biram Kudu's reign lasted only a month and a few days. This civil war led to the separation of Kajoor and Bawol, and the undeniable weakening of the *damel* worked to the advantage of the *brak*.[14] However, Ndiak

Aram did not benefit from this advantage for very long, since he died a year later in 1757.[15]

Conclusions about the Reign of Ndiak Aram Bakar

The dominating factor of this reign was undeniably the civil war in Kajoor. While ruining this country, the war also made it possible for Waalo to establish its power in neighboring realms. This advantage was especially furthered by Ndiak Aram's successor, Naatago Aram Bakar, whose efforts would nonetheless be ruined by the double intervention of the British and the Moors. Indeed, the reign of Ndiak Aram ended a few months before the occupation of Saint-Louis by the British, who had never stopped threatening the French gum trade. The relationship between Ndiak Aram and the French of Saint-Louis suffered only a few storms; one may ask if "this perfect understanding" that prevailed did not contribute to the relative peace in Waalo.[16] The rise of Waalo would be a dominant factor during the period that marked the first English occupation.

CHAPTER 7

CIVIL WAR AND THE FINAL DECLINE OF WAALO DURING THE
FIRST BRITISH OCCUPATION OF SAINT-LOUIS, CA. 1758-83

At the end of the Seven Years' War, the competition between the French and British along the coast of Mauritania resulted in the occupation of Saint-Louis by the British. This period from 1758 to 1783 was marked by an irreversible process of the disintegration in Waalo, after a brief moment of recovery. Indeed, Waalo's failure to gain hegemony over Kajoor was followed by a long civil war, abetted by the British and the Moors. The Moor domination that increasingly weighed down the river region also contributed to the *Toorodo* revolution in Fuuta—and the final weakening of the Waalo kingdom.

The British Occupation of Saint-Louis

We saw that the entire first half of the eighteenth century was dominated by a struggle between three powerful European nations for the monopoly of gum on the Mauritanian coast. After the elimination of the Dutch in 1727, the French and the British would engage in direct confrontation. Indeed, from 1730 to 1740, the French unsuccessfully opposed the English "interlopers," and also confronted the hostility of the Moors. "In 1739-1740, the agreement concluded between the two Companies of France and England opened a truce which seemed to settle their differences and which lasted a decade or so. However, the crisis provoked in British manufactures by the high cost of French gum provoked a movement in England favoring the resumption of direct gum trade in the coastal trading posts: In 1753, antagonism between the French and the British regained strength."[1]

The British government threw its support behind the new Company of Merchants Trading to Africa, created in 1752, as soon as hostilities resumed in 1756. Isolated from the metropolis, Senegal was conquered by the British in 1756. The Company of the Indies thus lost the two forts at Saint-Louis and Gorée, which had constituted the double key of French possession in Senegal. The Paris treaty of 1763 would sanction the British seizure of the Senegal River with the forts and trading posts of Saint-Louis, Podor and Galam, while giving Gorée to the French as restitution. Gorée was immediately reoccupied by the first royal governor, Poncet de La Rivière. France also retained the right to trade along the Mauritanian coast. This clause of the treaty enabled the French to remain a constant threat on the British presence in Saint-Louis from their post in Gorée.

British occupation opened a new era in colonial politics because Senegambia, like the colonies of America, was under the direct control of the British crown.[2] However, it was not fundamentally different from French occupation, since the Company of Merchants was obliged to carry on the same commercial activities. The only difference was that, since the British were more preoccupied with the gum trade on the Mauritanian coast, they relinquished control over the traffic in the upper part of the river. This absence of British commercial activity allowed the Moors' forceful return to Fuuta. Paradoxically, the recrudescence of the Atlantic slave trade in the lower section of the river, which until then had been considered a zone of secondary importance, would bring about the complete ruin of Waalo.

In Senegambia, the British attempted to usher in a new colonial policy that depended on a plantation economy rather than the Atlantic slave trade. Indeed, as early as 1763, a very precise plan was presented to the Commission of Lords to ensure the development of commerce in the new colony of Senegal. This plan declared the failure of a slave-driven economy in the Americas. It argued that the laziness and cruelty attributed to the Africans was simply a consequence of their status as enslaved individuals. Since slavery was adverse to industry, the plan proposed the formation of a new Senegalese colony in which the enslaved individuals brought to Saint-Louis would be emancipated—in order to devote themselves freely to the cultivation of cotton, tobacco and sugar.[3]

In Saint-Louis in 1766, Governor O'Hara looked at this plan carefully to verify that Senegal was an auspicious location for all the crops of the Americas. He especially tried to convince the planters of the Americas that the low-cost sale of these products would increase their consumption, thus far reserved only for the rich. Thus, the British could dominate the huge markets in Germany and Russia, where sugar, cotton and rice did not sell well because of their high prices.[4]

However, as confirmed by the 1763 plan itself, it was nearly impossible during this period to suppress the Atlantic slave trade or to upset the slave-driven production mode in the Americas.[5] This explains the lack of implementation of this plan in Senegal, along with the fact that the British had occupied the land for too short a period to accomplish anything of lasting impact. This project would certainly have encountered keen resistance from European planters in the Caribbean islands, as well as from the military states along the African coast. The latter, whose power rested largely on the Atlantic slave trade, would not have allowed the implantation of the British on the continent. But the idea, which would only gain ground in Europe with much difficulty, found defenders among the promoters of the *Toorodo* revolution; these promoters opposed the Atlantic slave trade in 1776. The relationship between Waalo and the British would be dominated by a recrudescence of the Atlantic slave trade, which eventually brought the African kingdom to its ruin.

The Reign of Naatago Aram, 1757-1766

A letter dated March 31, 1758, tells us that "a month after the departure of the vessel *Succès, brak* Guia, king of the country of Oual, is dead and his brother Natogo replaces him on the throne without any opposition."[6] On the very day of *brak* Ndiak Aram Bakar's death, according to the note, *damel* Maïsa Bigé, who had been hunted out of Kajoor, was soliciting and had been soliciting for the past six months the help of Naatago Aram. Thus, the death of Ndiak Aram can be dated to October 1757.[7] Indeed, the oral tradition confirms that Naatago Aram, the third son of Aram Bakar, succeeded his brother Ndiak Aram.[8] His accession to the throne coincides with Maïsa Bigé's expulsion from Kajoor by the *buur-ba jolof*, who may well have been Biram Yam. Biram Yam's place in the *damel* chronology is placed between 1759 and 1760 by Yoro Diaw.[9]

In December 1758, the threat that this marabout posed to the trade in Gorée still depended on the help the *brak* might give Maïsa Bigé, who was a refugee in Waalo. Indeed, according to Adanson, the latter again seized power on December 28, 1758, a few months after his departure from Gorée and after a fight during which the *buur-ba jolof* was killed.[10]

Naatago Aram's intervention must have been a determining factor, as stated in Faidherbe's note on Cayor.[11] If we rely on a note dated November 30, 1762, we verify the rise of the *brak*'s power. Remember that he was the exceptional heir to his *meen* family's possessions, accumulated since the beginning of the eighteenth century by the successive passage to power of three brothers. Indeed, the note explains that the *brak* was now receiving 2,000 pounds of customary fees: "This king is one of the most powerful grandees in the land; he may have up to 4 or 5,000 men capable of bearing arms, half of whom have horses. This king is a swindler and a great amateur of presents."[12] Such power best explains the *brak*'s pretensions to power in his relationships with Saint-Louis, and especially his attempt to gain control over a Kajoor severely undermined by war.

Relationship of Naatago Aram with the British and Kajoor

The relationship of Naatago Aram with the British settlers in Saint-Louis was continually perturbed. Consequently, on May 6, 1764, Naatago Aram interrupted the gum trade at the trade stop in the desert with the help of 1,500 men.[13] This hostile act of Waalo is detailed in a letter by John Barnes, dated February 17, 1765. It reveals the different aspects of the conflict with

Saint-Louis and the attempt to gain control over Kajoor.[14] At that point, the British were in open conflict with the Waalo *brak* over the yearly customs paid to the *damel* of Kajoor. Naatago Aram was taking advantage of the weakness of Kajoor—now severely undermined by a state of permanent civil war—to claim the possession of all territory in the proximity of the Barre. This conquest gave him exclusive dominance over the British and allowed him to confiscate the *damel*'s customary fees from Saint-Louis for three years, by cutting off communications with Kajoor. In 1763, Captain Bumbury was forced to pay Naatago Aram the *damel*'s custom fees in order to re-establish peace between Saint-Louis and Waalo. Peace prevailed until the beginning of September 1764. But hostilities resumed soon afterward, when the British refused to continue paying the customs of Kajoor to the *brak*.[15]

The rise to power of *damel* Makuudi Kumba Diaring, who was determined to exact revenge, encouraged the British to persist in their refusal at the end of September 1764, when the *brak* attempted to claim his rights. The *brak* immediately blocked the trade of Saint-Louis on the river and attempted to withhold all supplies from the garrison. As early as the end of October 1764, the *damel* began conducting hostile activities against Naatago Aram. The latter met the *damel*'s forces at the beginning of January 1765 with the help of the *buur-ba jolof*, but was obliged to withdraw six weeks later after suffering considerable losses. Naatago Aram then came to Saint-Louis to beg for reconciliation; he promised to compensate the British for everything that he had taken from them. He failed to fulfill his promise, however. In February 1765, as his hostile attitude was still threatening to compromise trade along the river, the British began to consider a vigorous policy toward the *brak*. On the other hand, the relationship between the British and the new *damel* were good; the *damel* promised to visit the fort after the Ramadan holidays.[16]

The hostilities continued until the month of March 1765, when John Barnes announced the end of the quarrel. However, the *brak* had still not requested his yearly customary fees which had been due since January, because he had not been able to return the five or six canoes and the numerous enslaved individuals he had plundered from the inhabitants of Saint-Louis. He was expecting a complete re-opening of communications with Kajoor, considering that Naatago Aram had already abandoned the majority of the territory over which he had been disputing with the *damel*.[17] As a result, as early as August 1765, Waalo was already vanquished by the damel, who had benefited from British support during the duration of the hostilities. Concerning Naatago Aram, Yoro Diaw tells us that "a revolt broke out in the western part of his states. The inhabitants of Toubé, Ngangouné, M'Pal and N'Gaye rebelled in order to avenge the destruction of the four villages of Gandiole, N'Diol, Mouïte and N'Djélène. Their ally was the *damel*

Macoudou Coumba Diaring who took advantage of this rebellion to annex these territories to Cayor."[18]

On this subject, Yoro Diaw largely confirms the statements of O'Hara, the British governor. O'Hara, landing in Saint-Louis on April 19, 1766, wrote on September 21, 1766, that a short while after his arrival "the *brak* had plundered and burned three big and rich villages in Kajoor, near the Barre. The majority of the inhabitants of these villages, about 1,500 of them, sought refuge in the fort, where they have remained since."[19] It is therefore possible to assert that when O'Hara arrived, Kajoor had recaptured its territories. According to Yoro Diaw, Naatago Aram died soon afterwards, probably around 1766. His death "marked the beginning of wars which lasted twenty-nine years, ruined the hegemony of Waalo and steered the *braks* from the policy which had prevailed earlier and which aimed at humbling Cayor."[20] The British intervention was a determining factor, and we shall see that as early as 1766, O'Hara inaugurated a vigorous policy toward Waalo, which would experience its final decline in power.

O'Hara's Policy and the Definitive Decline of Waalo, 1766-1776

As soon as he arrived in Saint-Louis, Governor O'Hara sought new means of insuring trade security. In a letter dated May 28, 1766, he advocated the complete disarmament of African populations by forbidding the sale of arms and munitions.[21] He was also preoccupied with the competition of the French settlers in Gorée, who traded approximately 350 to 500 enslaved individuals every year at the expense of Saint-Louis. Thus, he suggested the construction of a blockhouse close to the Barre, in order to protect communications between Saint-Louis and Kajoor against the constant threat of the *brak,* who had interrupted trade several times before O'Hara's arrival.[22] In February 1769, the danger clearly still weighed on Saint-Louis; O'Hara was still writing letters to his government, calling attention to the need for building a blockhouse. He reported notably that the then-powerful *brak* often pillaged the people who regularly brought enslaved individuals, cotton and oxen to Saint-Louis, and thus regularly cut off communications between the island and the continent for several days at a time.[23]

In August 1772, O'Hara confronted the acute problem of bringing supplies to the island. He proposed forming a colony on the continent, along the Senegal River, and to have it protected by a small fort. The Senegalese would then be able to cultivate millet, rice, and cotton and thus ensure their own food supplies, the lack of which was detrimental even to the Atlantic slave trade.[24] Failing to carry out his construction project for a fort, O'Hara undertook a mission to break down the power of Waalo with the complicity of the Moors—and then to profit from the civil war, which had been raging since the end of Naatago Aram's reign.

Civil War in Waalo, 1766-1786

The death of Naatago Aram was followed by a period of civil war which, according to Yoro Diaw, lasted 29 years and completely ruined the hegemony of Waalo.[25] Lamiral, who arrived in Saint-Louis in 1779, tells us around 1789 that the war lasted more than twenty years.[26] Unfortunately, oral tradition only provides us with few details on this civil war, the study of which is necessary to understand the process of Waalo's decline. According to Amadou Wade, Azan, Bubu Sal and Yoro Diaw, six *brak* succeeded each other; each one remained in power less than a year and a half, and each were eventually eliminated by his competitors. Let us briefly survey the reigns of these different *brak* in the wake of Naatago Aram.

1. *Yérim Adaté Bubu (Teejekk)* ruled for a year and a half, according to Bubu Sal. According to Amadou Wade, he only ruled a year and was killed by the *Dios*, led by Mö Mboodi Kumba Khedi, during the famous battle of Talaata i Nder or Tuesday of Nder.[27] Azan states that Yérim Adaté, the son of Momboye Menguey Turm and Ndaté Mboje (*Teejekk*), was obliged, one year after his ascent to the throne, to confront the ambitions of Yérim Kodé, the son of Mbarika Mbodje and leader of seventeen *Dios* princes. Yérim Adaté was killed and the *Dios*, eager to destroy the *Teejekk* line, disembowelled the *brak*'s sister Feyor, one of the most beautiful women of Waalo.[28] This was evidently caused by the opposition of the *Dios* to the *meen* family of the *Teejekk*, who had kept power in the hands of the three sons of Aram Bakar ever since the beginning of the eighteenth century.

2. *Mö Mboodi Kumba Khedi (Dios)* succeeded Yérim Ndaté Bubu. Amadou Wade, who is the only person to record that reign, tells us that *jogomaay* Madiaw Xor, outraged by the assassination of *linger* Koo Ndama, organized a plot; Mö Mboodi Kumba Khedi was subsequently killed by a Moor, Salamoono, immediately after the crowning ceremony. He was *brak* in name only and had no time to exercise his functions.[29]

3. *Yérim Mbañik Anta Joop (Teejekk)* ruled for a year and a half, according to Bubu Sal. This confirms Azan's statement that he was the son of *Teejekk* Anta Diop and Tiébo-Dia Fama, who combined the functions of *brak* and *kadj*. He took up arms immediately to avenge the death of Yérim Ndaté. However, he was attacked by Yérim Kodé Mbunee (*Dios*), who vanquished him at Buur Diak.[30] According to Amadou Wade, Yérim Mbañik Anta Jop was attacked a year later by Yérim Koodé Fara Mbunee, who was allied with the Trarzas and with the valiant warrior *kaddi* Ndiak Xuri (*Loggar*), who craved power. Yérim Mbañik Anta Jop was killed along with a large number of *Teejekk* princes. Yérim Koodé was crowned *brak* and Ndiak Xuri, who had been shoved aside, found a refuge in Jolof.[31] Saugnier, who was a witness to the end of Ndiak Xuri's reign, writes that "the king of this country had been the minister of the old one whom he had assassinated

by the Moors of Alikoury."[32] In other words, this phase of the civil war was dominated by an alliance of the *Dios* and the *Loggar* against the powerful *meen* family of the *Teejekk*.

4. *Yérim Kodé Mbuné* (*Dios*) ruled for one year only, according to Bubu Sal. According to Azan, his reign lasted two years. In any case, Ndiak Xuri, a refugee in Jolof, did not stop threatening him. Ndiak Xuri beat him a first time in Mbuden, but could not find any official to celebrate the ceremony of his crowning; Waalo "had become a desert as a result of this endless series of wars, pillages and internal dissensions." It is under this reign that the Moors began to dominate the left shore of the Senegal River and to exact tributes from the Waalo-Waalo. Yérim Kodé was killed the following year near Mbuden, during a battle waged by Ndiak Xuri between that location and the island of Thionk. "A large number of *djëss* princes died during this battle which dealt a mortal blow to this family (1775)."[33] Amadou Wade tells us also that Ndiak Xuri, exiled to Jolof, allied himself with the toro *lam* and Trarza *burr* in order to exterminate Yérim Koodé.[34] Thanks to the British archives and the testimonies of Lamiral, de Villeneuve and Saugnier, it is possible to situate this phase of the civil war during a period that corresponds to increased pressure from the Trarza Moors and the British intervention—most notably in the war between Ndiak Xuri (*Loggar*) and Mambodje Kumba (*Dios*).

O'Hara's Intervention in the Civil War and Moorish Domination in Waalo

After eliminating Yérim Koodé, Ndiak Xuri was immediately obliged to fight back against another contender from the *Dios* family, Mambodje Kumba, who had found a refuge among the Trarza Moors. Azan explains that, during nine consecutive years, he never ceased to threaten Ndiak Xuri.[35] This version is largely confirmed by written sources. Indeed, the list of customary fees paid to Waalo between November 5, 1775 and May 5, 1776 clearly shows that the British were giving gifts of equal value "to the *brak* king as well as to the pretender to the *brak*'s crown, Jack Courre."[36] This is explained by the fact that the Waalo-Waalo did not know which false candidate they should choose; Ndiak Xuri, who was obliged to shuttle constantly between Kër Mbaye and Gédé, had not found a way to be crowned.[37] It is possible that Mmbodje Kumba succeeded in taking power for a while. Lamiral, who was in Saint-Louis in 1779, tells us in 1789 that "the first war I saw and the oldest one is that of the Waalo realm which had been taken over by a usurper. This usurper was supported by several important vassals of the realm and by the chief of his Trarza Moor neighbor, Elikawri. The war opposed the usurper Mamboué Coumba to the legitimate heir, Ndja Koury Phara Penda."[38]

As it happens, it was at the very beginning of this civil war that the British governor O'Hara intervened decisively. Yet Lamiral, who attempted to demonstrate that the purpose of the wars between the different kings was not always to feed the Atlantic slave trade, does not mention this war. "Governor O'Hara agreed to supply Elikawri with help in order to lay waste to the *brak*'s kingdom, because this governor had in the harbor several ships in which he had an interest."[39] In a letter dated August 18, 1775, O'Hara wrote that the Moors had completely invaded the nations of the Africans who lived along the shores of the Senegal River. They had killed and sold several thousand persons and forced many others to flee. By this means, the Moors were becoming the masters on both sides of the Senegal River. This state of distress spread for several leagues around Podor; the Moors, who were also constantly threatening Saint-Louis, had forced the British to abandon the fort of Podor.[40]

This official description by O'Hara to the British authorities was correct, but failed to mention his own contribution to the devastation of Waalo and Fuuta by the Moors. Indeed, as early as August 22, 1775, the inhabitants of Senegal sent a petition to denounce the personal commercial activities of the governor, who was ruining their trade. O'Hara was himself tracking men on the continent and had burned all the *brak*'s villages along the banks of the river.[41] Another petition, dated June 10, 1776, reiterates the same accusations against O'Hara. He was accused of indulging in private slave trading in order to supply labor for his plantations in the Dominican islands, or to sell enslaved individuals to America or the Caribbean.[42]

The determining role of O'Hara in the destruction of Waalo is undeniable. A memorandum, published around 1783, reveals that "until 1775, the Moors only took few captives who were kept busy with their *lougans* to cultivate their fields. Mr. O'Hara and Le Brasseur let them know several times that it was in their interest to sell those workers. As a result, the Moors several times devastated different kingdoms, especially the kingdom of the *brak* where they captured more than 8,000 enslaved individuals in less than six months; an enslaved person was sold for one *pagne* in the streets of Senegal. The things that convinced them to undertake those ravages are the advances in guns and blue linen that the British gave them."[43]

In April 1777, an echo of the Moorish invasion of Waalo is heard from Gorée, where French settlers lived. The French were eager to eliminate the undesirably great power of the *damel*, who had managed to reunite the two kingdoms of Kajoor and Bawol. The French expressed their plan in the following terms: "The Moors who recently devastated the *brak*'s kingdom and reduced it to a desert, have resolved to overthrow the *damel* and, if the ambassadors of Alikoury and Sidi Moctar are to be believed, they will take up arms this year and the French will be able to buy more than 3,000 captives in less than two years, while the British will have twice that number.

It is certain that the realms of Kayor and Baol are densely populated and have already been pillaged enough. Alikoury has already asked for weapons to this effect."[44]

It clearly appears, therefore, that there was an increase in slave trading in Saint-Louis as well as Gorée, and that the British and the French armed the Moors in order to destroy the power of the African kingdoms. In the specific case of Waalo, civil war contributed hugely to the invasion of the Moors, who were able to permanently destroy the kingdom's hegemony. The efforts of O'Hara were also key, as proven by the testimony of Maxwell, who was governor during the second occupation by the British. In 1811, he writes notably: "During the period that Senegal was in our possession after the peace of 1763, the inhabitants of [Waalo] then exceedingly powerful were [giving] trouble [to] some [of] the settlements and threatened to prevent communications with the upper part of the river. General O'Hara then Governor entered into a treaty with the Trarza Moors and King *damel* to assist him in attacking that nation, which they did most effectually and the Wa[a]lo country received a blow from which it has never since recovered. Its villages on the Senegal River's bank are yet deserted and abandoned; its people have been carried into captivity and those who remain are constantly subjected to the plunder of the Moors who treat [them] as a dependent and tributary state. O'Hara's name is still used by the Waalo mothers to frighten their crying chidren."[45] This unbiased testimony from a British governor, thirty-five years after the fact, reveals the importance of this event in the history of Waalo. From then on, Waalo's tragic fate was to be nothing but a kingdom in decline.

The End of British Domination and the Pursuit of Civil War

The invasion and destruction of Waalo did not end the civil war. It continued during the final years of British occupation, until about 1786. In July 1776, Governor Matthias MacNamara, who was nominated to replace O'Hara, writes that the struggle for power in Waalo had destroyed the country; it had surrendered to the Moors.[46]

However, just like O'Hara, MacNamara was accused of trading enslaved individuals privately and of having reaped exclusive profits from the Atlantic slave trade for a period of four months. A petition complains about his private purchase of approximately twenty captives in Mouït.[47] As a result of the continuing civil war, the British governor did not pay customary fees to Waalo in July 1777, since power was being bitterly disputed between two claimants.[48] The war still involved Ndiak Xuri and Mambodje Kumba, and it continued even after the French recaptured Saint-Louis in 1779. Indeed, a letter from Eyries, dated April 10, 1781, tells us "on January 10, Jacoury, a brother of the *brak* king and aspirant to the throne, made a surprising appearance on the coast of Barbari as he was returning from a campaign he had undertaken on the lands of Mambouy Comba, his brother."[49]

Saugnier, who landed in Senegal on June 13, 1785, witnessed the end of this long struggle that culminated in the death of both competitors. "The king of this country had been the minister of the previous king and had him assassinated by the Moors of Halicory... It was under the specious argument of protecting the public good that he seized the throne; however, he paid for his treachery with his own death since, having had some difference of opinion with Halicory, the latter had him strangled a few months after my departure."[50] In a similar vein, Lamiral tells us that after the death of "Mamboué Comba, Ndja Koury Phara Penda was unable to enjoy his success very long, since Elikawry had him assassinated by a Moor who shot one gunshot into his belly while he was in his home, surrounded by the main crown officials who allowed the assassin to escape, a fact which suggests that they were accomplices to this murder."[51]

Oral tradition confirms the circumstances of Ndiak Xuri's assassination. Azan reports that Ndiak Xuri "after having so dearly bought his sovereignty, was only able to enjoy it for a few months before he was assassinated. This crime is attributed to the Tiédieks, but there is no certain proof that they, rather than the Djëss, are responsible."[52] We can therefore state that the civil war, which had started in 1766, ended somewhere in late 1785. The travelers who came to Senegal after the French recapture are witnesses capable of giving us details on the consequences of this bitter struggle for power.

Consequences of the Civil War

British occupation of Senegal was marked by a series of civil wars between the three royal *meen* families, each vying for power. The *Dios* and *Loggar* had been excluded from power since the beginning of the eighteenth century by the powerful *meen* family of the *Teejekk*. But with the help of both the Moors and the British, they had taken turns trying to seize power. The self-interested intervention of their neighbors resulted in the definitive crushing of Waalo, and tightened the hold of the Trarza Moors on the country. In this respect, the testimony of Geoffroy de Villeneuve, who lived in Senegal from 1785 to 1787, is significant: "Pursuant to frequent wars, the small state of Waalo had fallen in a state of degradation maintained by the Moors who were constantly pillaging it."[53]

This heavy-handed Moorish domination, which would weigh on the Waalo-Waalo from then on, is described at length by Lamiral. The Moors "have no fixed habitations and their sole profession is to wage war... These Moors include a few castes of professional thieves who carry the name of their avocation: the Assoumas. Their sole activity is to ravage the lands of Africans, to burn villages, capture herds, men, women and children, and everything else that falls into their hands. It is not uncommon to see a single horse rider taking away five or six enslaved individuals at the same time, some thrown over the back of his mount, others attached to the horse's tail and on either sides of the saddle. The most formidable chief of the Assoumas was called Samba Fall... His name spread terror within a range of thirty leagues. I have dealt often with him. He made me buy more than five hundred Blacks."[54]

In order to forestall pillage, the Waalo-Waalo paid the Moors increasingly larger tributes. Still, the depredations did not end because the Moors, not subjected to the Atlantic slave trade, lost none of their hegemony. A weakened Waalo could offer no resistance. The country fell prey to a triple crisis: economical, political and social.

Indeed, on a political level, the civil war sanctioned the fragmentation of the centralizing power of the *brak,* who was constantly forced to resist the pretensions to autonomy of a majority of *kangam* or provincial chiefs. In order to explain the superiority of the Moors over the Africans, Lamiral tells us that "the Negroes' country is subjected to a kind of feudal system, that it contains an infinite number of important vassals almost always divided among themselves and often at war with their own sovereigns. They are unable to resist Moorish enterprises and the Moors are not afraid of retaliation because they change their dwellings as soon as they have completed an operation and because the Whites do not care to buy them."[55]

The Atlantic slave trade is, therefore, the profound root of Moorish hegemony in Waalo. The absence of a strong centralizing power and the independence of individual chiefs are also acknowledged by Geoffroy de Villeneuve. "Each state is divided into several governments. The people in authority do not hold their power from a prince; they are only vassals, power is hereditary in each family. Among the Ouolofs, they are called *lamanes*. This is an ancient title which goes all the way back to a period which precedes the foundation of principalities. Each *lamane* supports a certain number of soldiers in his service and provides them with weapons and horses. Several members of their retinue live near him and are then fed at the expense of the master; the others remain in their villages, but are obliged to march immediately as requested. They are not given a regular pay, but all receive presents and a share of the spoils of war. The loyalty of the soldiers often turns the *lamanes* into so many small tyrants who oppress the people."[56]

During the troubled period discussed here, the independence of the *kangam* is marked by the ascension to power of the *ceddo,* recruited from among prisoners of the crown. For them, war had become the principal occupation. From then on, the *ceddo* warriors constitute the agitating element—the force with which the *brak* must deal with in order to retain his power. In another respect, the *brak* lost a large part of his authority, as

Geoffroy de Villeneuve explains: "The poverty of this always devastated country ensures that the sovereign has no other source of revenue than the depredations he commits himself, every day, and the customary fees that the government of Senegal pays him on a yearly basis."[57]

According to Jean Baptiste Léonard Durand, the customs of the *brak* had reached 4,915 pounds, 19 shillings and 8 pence.[58] Waalo was in a period of decline at the same time that Fuuta Toro, which had undergone a theocratic revolution in the name of Islam, was threatening the country's border. Let us now analyze the importance of this Toorodo revolution. As early as 1776, it profoundly modified the political situation in the river region.

The Toorodo Revolution of 1776 and its Consequences for Waalo

The Moorish pressure on Waalo increased markedly during the course of the eighteenth century. As a result of its geographical position, Fuuta Toro did not escape this reality. As early as 1720, Saint-Robert stated that *satigi* Bubakar Siré was a slave to the Moors. The recent study of Oumar Kane on the chronology of the eighteenth century *satigi* shows that this reign marked the beginning of "a half century of civil wars, anarchy, insecurity and misery. The revolution of 1776 will be born from the steps taken by Bubakar Siré in 1716 and from the Moorish intervention."[59] Indeed, the Moorish domination, which would be permanent, compelled the British in 1775 to evacuate the fort of Podor. Its surroundings had been destroyed by the Moors, who had also captured hundreds of enslaved individuals.[60] In fact, just as in Waalo, Governor O'Hara had developed intense slave trading activity in Fuuta. The testimony of MacNamara of January 26, 1776 clearly indicates that O'Hara had sent many "pooles or fullas" to the Americas. After gaining its independence, this nation consequently opposed British trade in the regions of the Senegal River.[61] By January 1776, the Toorodo revolution, led by marabout Suleymann Baal, had already taken place.

Our purpose is not to explain the Toorodo revolution in detail, but rather to extract its historical significance in order to gauge its impact on the evolution of the Senegambian states. Almost a half-century after the Islamic revolution of the Fula in Fuuta Jaloo, the Toorodo party seized power in Fuuta Toro in the name of Islam. This very ancient marabout party, composed of men from all classes of society, overthrew the regime of the *deeñanke* in order to inaugurate a theocratic regime. However, in light of archival sources, this revolution now appears to have been less so an exclusively religious movement and more a movement of national independence. The Toorodo revolution was, primarily, an action undertaken first against Moorish domination and consequently against the *satigi*, who were no longer capable of guaranteeing the integrity of their country. It was also directed against Atlantic trade—most notably, the Atlantic slave trade that, through the combined action of the Moors and the Europeans, had reduced the whole country to misery. Thus, after refusing to pay the *mudo horma*, a yearly tribute in grains to the Moors in Mboya since the defeat of the Ulad Abdallah, the Toroobe rose up against British trade.[62]

In July 1776, remembering the plunder of 1775 by O'Hara, the new masters of Fuuta forbade all British trade in the direction of Galam.[63] The ferocious opposition of the first *almamy*, Abdel Kader, against the sale of Muslims is made clear in a letter to Governor Blanchot, dated May 1789. Speaking in the names of Moslem kings, Abdel Kader stated: "We warn you that all those who will come here to trade slaves will be killed or massacred if our children are not returned home. Would not someone who was very hungry restrain himself from eating if he knew that he was eating something combined with his own blood? We absolutely refuse to let you purchase Muslims near or far... I reiterate, if your intention is still to purchase Muslims, you had better stay in your country and never return to ours. Because all those who will return can be assured of losing their lives."[64]

It is true that the Toorodo revolution was limited; it did not suppress domestic slavery in the new society. This kind of slavery was very quickly blocked by the appearance of a new caste—that of the Toorobe. By replacing the ancient governing layers of society, this new caste superposed itself upon the former social organization. However, its opposition to the sale of Muslims to Christians arose from the firm determination to stop the hemorrhage of human labor that had ruined this entire section of Africa. In this respect, the results were conclusive; Fuuta immediately became a zone of relative peace wherein the people, henceforth protected, could reap their harvests in security.

In 1811, Maxwell spoke of the possibility of suppressing the Atlantic slave trade in Africa and of replacing it with a plantation economy. He suggested that it would be easy to negotiate with the *almamy* on this point, considering that he had always opposed Atlantic slave trade as being contrary to his religious principles.[65] Baron Roger noted in this regard, "nothing could convince the Foulhes that in forbidding the trading of slaves, the Europeans were determined by their example. They are proud to have anticipated us along the path of reason, justice and humanity."[66]

It is this feeling of independence that explains the increasing pride and hostility of the Toorobe toward the Whites, as well as their contempt for those African populations not converted to Islam. Testimonies attest to how attractive Fuuta was to neighboring peoples, who came there seeking the peace necessary to conduct fruitful activities. A large number of Waalo-Waalo emigrated to Fuuta at that time. In this respect, Schmaltz wrote in 1819 that a "very large percentage of the current population on the island at Morphil... is composed of individuals who have emigrated from the Waalo kingdom, where they were not treated well enough so that they returned home to work with us in their native land as soon as they were certain of finding more justice, protection and resources here."[67]

Thus, the Toorodo revolution, a movement at once political, social and religious, had a resounding effect in north Senegambia. For a long time, it provided a model for neighboring kingdoms in all realms. The story of Kélédor, as narrated by Baron Roger, illustrates well the influence of this Islamic revolution on Waalo. Baron Roger notably states, "When those events were taking place, I was no more than fourteen years of age. Although I had been born in Waalo, I was living in the village of Fuuta Toro. My father, a zealous marabout, but a poorly educated man, since his science was limited to reciting his five daily prayers and reading rather badly and without understanding the first four surahs of the Koran, my father, who loved me very tenderly, believed that the most important wealth he could leave me was a religious education. Indeed, esteem, respect, influence, power, and goods of all kinds are assured to the *serigne* who can read and write and who scrupulously fulfills all the practices of religious devotion. My father may have been thinking that Waalo should soon carry out a revolution similar to that of Fuuta; he probably hoped that his son might one day play a role in it and become one of the leaders of his country."[68]

In the absence of such an Islamic revolution, or in the absence of another solution to its crisis, Waalo continued to suffer from Moorish domination and the deadly consequences of the Atlantic trade. Traditional aristocrats, abundantly supplied with weapons and alcohol by domestic wars, became increasingly hostile to the Islamic religion—so much so that the new masters of Fuuta tried to rule by force in all neighboring kingdoms. This period corresponds with the return of the French to Saint-Louis.

Conclusion about the British Occupation

British occupation marked an important, if brief, phase in the history of Waalo. The British did not remain long enough to modify the nature of the Atlantic commerce. Yet they brought about a weakening of the power of Waalo through their intense pursuit of the Atlantic slave trade in the lower parts of the Senegal River. Ruined by civil strife and by Moorish invaders, Waalo finally renounced its attempt at gaining hegemony over Kajoor. Inland, the weakening of the *brak*'s power encouraged the multiple tendencies to independence of the *kangam* and ensured the domination of the *ceddo* warriors, who made a living by plundering the realm. Would Waalo, doubly devastated by Atlantic trade and by Moorish domination, be capable of resisting the forces of a religious war led by the marabout merchants of Fuuta Toro against the Wolof kingdoms?

CHAPTER 8

THE FRENCH RE-OCCUPATION OF SAINT-LOUIS (1783-1809)
AND THE TUKULOR THREAT IN WAALO

France had never abandoned its trade-related ambitions along the Senegal River. It eventually recaptured Saint-Louis from the British in 1779. The reoccupation of Saint-Louis coincided with the French Revolution, along with the search for new methods to improve the administration and rational exploitation of colonial lands. However, in its trade exchanges, the colony essentially retained the features of the preceding period. Still oppressed by the Moorish infiltration on the left bank of the river, Waalo was now to experience a threat from Fuuta Toro, which attempted to forcefully convert neighboring states to Islam. The *jihad* failed per se, but it cleared the way for progress on the part of Islam. The number of Islamic converts increased, and these converts tried to solve the political, social and economic crisis. This crisis had become endemic because of the consequences of the Atlantic slave trade and the internal wars of the aristocracy, who continued their bitter struggle for power.

The Issue of Suppressing the Atlantic Slave Trade

During the British occupation of Saint-Louis, the French had continually tried to recapture the domain that, since 1659, had been their exclusive monopoly. They operated from Gorée. On January 30, 1779, the squadron commanded by the Duke of Lauzun and Eyries finally conquered Saint-Louis. The expedition then re-directed its efforts to the south. It captured Fort James in Gambia on February 11, the trading posts of the Loos islands on March 9, British settlements along the Sierra Leone River on March 14, and finally, Fort Sekondi on the Gold Coast on May 24.[1] This was the result of a systematic policy to eliminate the British from the African coast. At the Treaty of Versailles on September 30, 1783, France abandoned the objective of the 1779 expedition. It was thus satisfied with the retrocession of Senegal and its dependencies, i.e., the forts of Saint-Louis, Galam, Arguin and Portendik, as well as the restitution of Gorée. France ensured the British kept possession of Fort James and the Gambia River. The British also retained the right to trade gum from the Saint-Jean River all the way to, and including, the bay of Portendik—but were not allowed to establish permanent settlements in that area.[2]

This entire period was characterized by trials and errors in colonial politics, especially with regard to privileged companies. It was dominated by the new economic doctrine of free trade, and particularly implied the suppression of the Atlantic slave trade—the economic value of which had already been questioned by the British. This then was the period when industrial capitalism began to supplant a mercantile economy. This pivotal phase, linked to the suppression of a slave trade economy, was especially noticeable in Britain, which was then the principal motor for the industrial revolution.

As we mentioned earlier, the seventeenth and eighteenth centuries saw the dominance of commercial mercantilism in which the triangular trade, dominated by sugar and enslaved peoples, provided the backdrop for colonial rivalries. In his book *Capitalism and Slavery*, Eric Williams shed light on "the role played by black slavery and the slave trade in the creation of the capital which [financed] the industrial revolution and the role that industrial capitalism, now in its mature phase, then [played] in the destruction of the same system of slavery."[3] Indeed, apart from a few philosophers of the Enlightenment, fascinated with the notions of the "noble Negro" and "good Savage," a majority of public opinion regarded slavery as an entirely acceptable institution. New economic conditions, coinciding with the first stages of the industrial revolution, were necessary before the ideas of the theoretician of free trade, Adam Smith, could triumph. The process was accelerated by the American Revolution, which marked "the first stage in the decline of the sugar cane colonies."[4] The decline of mercantilism precipitated that of slavery. The British humanists Clarkson, James Stephen and Wilberforce fought slavery with such passion that they managed "to arouse anti-slavery feelings to the point of turning them into a quasi-religion in Great Britain."[5]

Nevertheless, Britain, which had accepted free trade due to its significant technological and commercial progress, encountered resistance from other European powers. These powers continued to hang onto mercantilism for a good many years, since mercantilism was still the backbone of their economies. This was the case with France, which "in the decade preceding 1789 saw the Negro population of Saint-Domingue double at the same time as its production."[6] The growth of Saint-Domingue, which gave France control over the European sugar trade, still depended on the old law of slave production.[7] Facing this competition while attempting to ensure British control over the European sugar trade, William Pitt tried in vain to develop sugar production in India. Above all, he tried to obtain the suppression of the Atlantic slave trade, since doing so would cause the downfall of Saint-Domingue. He failed, due to the resistance of the Caribbean monopoly that heavily taxed all sugar production that did not come from the British Caribbean. He also failed because the French, Dutch and Spaniards were opposed to the suppression of the Atlantic slave trade.[8]

In fact, despite the flow of new ideas bandied about in France before and after the Revolution, especially through the intermediary of the Friends of the Africans, the suppression of the Atlantic slave trade was rejected. "Thus, slavery officially abolished in France on September 28, 1791, continued in the colonies because its disappearance would have endangered the interests of the influential plantation owners represented at the legislative assembly, the Lameth family."[9] Slavery found desperate supporters, especially in Senegal, where a veritable chorus of voices was raised to denounce the hazards of an anti-slavery policy. A prominent representative of this tendency was indubitably Lamiral, who lived in Senegal from 1779 to 1789. He expressed his main ideas in a book, *Africa and the African People*, published in 1789. He began his work with an extract from the "Complaints and Remonstrations of the Inhabitants of Senegal to the French Citizens Holding Seats at the States General," in which the traders of Saint Louis protested against the exclusive monopoly of the Guyanne Company over the gum and slave trade, and resolutely opposed the suppression of the Atlantic slave trade. "Maritime trade is threatened with the most alarming revolution if the unpatriotic and disastrous projects of the Society of Friends of the Blacks succeed in blinding the National Assembly and force it to sacrifice the precious interests of a multitude of citizens to their frenzied enthusiasm."[10]

Indeed, according to him, "sugar and coffee are pleasures without which we can no longer manage. Should we, and can we, do without the precious colonies which provide them for us? Are we to allow the advantages of an annual trade of approximately 300 million [francs] and the profits of a balance of 70 to 80 million [francs] fall into foreign hands? For this is what would inevitably happen if the slave trade were suppressed and our rich harvests, more precious than the mines of Potosi, were abandoned in order to give Negroes their liberty."[11]

As a result, in the face of anti-slavery ideology—and above all, in the face of a general lack of interest regarding the colonial problem within a France more preoccupied by its own internal problems—Lamiral defended the continuation of the Senegal colonial policy in a letter dated 1791: "This country has no interest for France except as it furthers trade, a part of which will necessarily be eliminated as the lights of philosophy become brighter. However, another consideration is that this land is the key which must introduce us to the center of Africa and help us discover the huge treasures which are hidden between the tropics, as many travelers have acknowledged. This key will open new resources for our industry and commerce and provide new discoveries for the sciences and the arts. Under this perspective this country is worthy of the highest consideration."[12]

In that same period, many writings emerged that condemned the Atlantic slave trade and proposed new ways to develop trade with Africa. Pruneau de Pomme-Gorge in 1789, after 22 years spent in Senegal, wrote that "the Senegal river is within easy access of Europe; it offers at least as many, maybe more, riches for France as America did for the Spaniards and the Portuguese. It [France] can also possess it all in a very few years by protecting what is indigenous instead of destroying it."[13] Speaking of the banks of the Senegal, Jean Baptiste Léonard Durand, who traveled there in 1785 and 1786, declared that nature "has refused nothing to the river soil and especially to the soil of the islands placed in its flow. The riverbanks are suitable for the richest harvests and only await cultivation. However, foreigners have looked away from this mine of fertility and focused instead on the products of commerce."[14] He added that, since the individual trader was a prisoner of particular and momentary interests, it is up to the state "to anticipate the future and encourage the Blacks to cultivate their land in order to reap pleasure and happiness." Thus, "tobacco, cotton, indigo, coffee and sugar, all the harvests of the West Indies, can cover a soil until now hostile to cultivation and provide France with inexhaustible resources."[15]

It is clear that the maintenance or suppression of the Atlantic slave trade was intimately linked to economic objectives—a more powerful factor than the passionate impulses of humanists. No one described the horrors of the Atlantic slave trade with more compassion than Lamiral. With brutal and disconcerting sincerity, he exposed the responsibility of White people for the destruction of the African people living along the Senegal River—most notably in Waalo, where the Moors represented an evil far worse than plague. "Even at this moment, do we not put weapons into their hands, do we not provide to this one or to this other means of destruction, according to the dictates of our interests? Is it not to deliver slaves to us that [the Moors] carry war and calamity among those miserable Negroes whose dwellings they burn, whose harvests they ravage? ...And we dare call barbarian a people we drag in irons."[16]

Yet no matter how steeped in the ideas of freedom, which he so ardently defended, Lamiral was still a partisan of slavery and was very much aware of the economic interests of the system. This is why, after asserting how necessary the Atlantic slave trade was, he confessed: "I have painted the horror with which the slave trade and its fatal consequences fill me in all sincerity. I have practiced that trade against my own will for a long time because we are not always the masters of the choice of profession we embrace."[17] Foisting the responsibility for the situation upon "the despotism of kings," Lamiral remarks that it would be impossible to compel Africans to work when they are free. Thus, in the interest of colonial plantations and maritime commerce, he concluded, "the issue of freedom for the Blacks is at least premature, if not imprudent and downright foolhardy."[18]

The British, who spearheaded the abolitionist movement, came to the rescue of the plantation owners of Saint-Domingue. Frightened by the French revolutionary wave, which was hostile to slavery, these owners called on Britain for help in 1791. From the beginning of the anti-French struggle, in 1793, Britain attempted unsuccessfully to seize the precious colony first from the French and then from the Africans.[19] French colonial supremacy was abolished; Saint-Domingue soon became the stage for a slave revolt. The enslaved individuals assumed power and proclaimed their island a republic in 1804. For all its proclamations of anti-slavery, Britain continued to profit from trade with the southern United States, the sugar plantations of Brazil, and Cuba—countries still using African slave labor. From then on, these entities took over trade from the French and British Caribbean.

In Senegal, much to the satisfaction of complaining traders, the January 18, 1791 decree cancelled the privileges of the Compagnie du Sénégal. However, this decree upset the colony management without providing any kind of new organization. It also marked the beginning of a chaotic period. As soon as the war with Britain began, the colony was abandoned to fend for itself. In the meantime, as a rebuttal to the betrayal of the Caribbean plantation owners, the law of Februrary 4, 1794, abolished slavery. Consequently, the function and purpose of the slave-trading settlements along the African coast was removed.

The instructions given to Blanchot during his first mission, on March 13, 1799, warn that "the director of Senegal will seize every opportunity to recall Article 14 of the Declaration of the Rights of Man: Any man has the right to engage his time and services, but cannot sell himself or be sold; his person is not an alienable property."[20] However, the Treaty of Amiens was signed on March 27, 1802, under the Consulate. After that, Napoléon, who harbored ambitions of colonial expansion, re-instituted slave trading under Articles one to three of the law dated May 20, 1802. Slave trading was re-instituted according to the laws and regulations that were in effect before 1789.[21]

As a result, Senegal again found a reason for existence. The balance of its yearly commerce between 1784 and 1799 indicates the importance of its transactions with France. "Senegal supplied 70,125 pounds of gum at a cost of 493,587 francs which proffered 1,767,812 francs at their arrival in France. Senegal also supplied 1,500 Negroes paid 273 francs each by the Compagnie that is a total of 409,500 francs; these were sold on the spot for 1,200,000 francs in free trade, at a cost of 800 francs each. When they were sold in the West Indies, they fetched a total amount of 2,184,000 francs, that is to say 1,456 francs each, which is the mean cost for a negro in our colonies. Moreover, 21,000 francs in gold and ivory yielded 68,670 francs. Thus, 924,087 francs yielded 3,036,482 francs or 277 percent for the immediate transactions from France to Senegal, without taking into account the benefits of loop trading in the West Indies, when the Compagnie transported its Negroes there. If we deduct 302,161 francs from this sum, that is, the total of government expenses and administrative fees for which the Compagnie was responsible, we find a net benefit of 196 percent."[22] This record clearly indicates the great importance of the slave trade. For the most part, enslaved individuals came from Galam; their number sometimes reached 3,000. This might be due to British competition, which diverted a large quantity of gum toward Portendik.

However, the slave rebellion in Saint-Domingue (Haiti) dealt a deathblow to the French sugar colonies. From that time on, efforts were made in Senegal to compensate for the loss. A plan for agricultural colonization of Senegal, written in 1802 by an anonymous author, was one attempt to suggest a solution to the crisis in colonial trade. The author followed the example of the British, who proposed in 1794 to create agricultural colonies near the mouth of the rivers in Gambia and Sierra Leone. The author of the plan wrote that the colonies, as they existed, could not give back to France the commercial luster she had lost. This was all the more evident as "one could no longer see in Saint-Domingue anything but an open arena between Negroes and the French until the absolute depopulation of this unhappy island."[23] He wondered "why could not this species of men be left on the land of their birth? With infinitely less cost, they would have given more useful results."[24]

The banks of the Senegal, as rich as the alluvial plains of Egypt, were indeed favorable to agricultural colonization. The test center would be the island of Morphil. However, the author determined that the new colony would rest on the labor of enslaved individuals, because "any attempt to give the indigenous people freedom would be utter extravagance; it would ruin the interests of the power brokers... The land of Senegal can only be cultivated by slaves, but in our colony one can ensure that these slaves are not the personal property of men, but rather that they are inseparably attached to the land: Serfdom would be a first step toward freedom."[25] This, broadly speaking, constituted the terms of this very detailed plan. Its goal was to utilize enslaved individuals who had been transported to the Americas. They would promptly be used in Africa for agricultural tasks.

Considering this proposal, it was really a bit of the Caribbean that would serve as an example for the rest of Africa. A network of trading posts would be created to support French trade. The weakness of the plan, however, lies precisely in the fact that the author wanted to reproduce the plantation colonies and their systems of cultivation in a different context. The only innovation consisted of the proposed creation of a privileged company, or "a capitalist association," which would have been a compromise between a monopoly and free enterprise. However, this project would not take place until 1819, because in the interim, the British again occupied Saint-Louis in 1809. After having officially abolished slave trading in 1807, the British attempted to impose this abolition upon other European powers. This ushered in a new era for the relationship between Africa and Europe.

However, before discussing the agricultural colonization—of which Waalo was to be the center—let us examine a few aspects that dominated the country's internal history during that period.

THE EVOLUTION OF WAALO AND THE TUKULOR THREAT

The period of French re-occupation of Waalo lasted from 1779 to 1809. During that time, Waalo was dominated externally by three factors: its relationship with Saint-Louis, the Moorish presence and the Tukulor threat. Internally, it was shaped by the continuation of the aristocracy's domestic struggles for power.

The Accession to Power of Fara Penda Teeg-Rel (1785-1795?) and the Holy War led by Abdul Kader, almamy of Fuuta

Fara Penda Teeg-Rel succeeded Ndiak Xuri, who had been killed by the Moors around 1785. Almost a year later, he had to confront the threat coming from Fuuta Toro. Indeed, the Toorodo revolution had barely been consolidated when the first *almamy* of Fuuta, Abdul Kader, proclaimed a holy war against neighboring kingdoms. There exist several testimonies, notably those of Lamiral and Durand, both contemporaries of the events. There is also the romanticized version by Baron Roger, whose hero, Kélédor, a Waalo-Waalo by birth, takes part in the expedition with the forces of the *almamy*.

Abdul Kader took advantage of the war against the Braknas and the Trarzas around 1785; he intervened in support of the former. The Trarza leader, Ali El Kory, who had formed an alliance with *brak* Fara Penda Teeg-Rel and the Kajoor *damel*, was defeated and killed during the fighting around October 1786.[26] A note dated September 8, 1786, specifies that "the inhabitants of Senegal, intimidated by the success of Amet Moctard and the *almamy* against Alikoury, whose death ended the war, did not this year show the same eagerness to travel to Galam."[27]

Abdul Kader used his victory to attempt to impose his "law not only on the Trarzas, but also on the Braknas, Dramanko, neighboring Negro kings and the French of Senegal."[28] In fact, the intervention of Abdul Kader was not intended, as in the case of Moorish interventions, to ravage the land and to capture as many enslaved individuals as possible. The goal was to convert neighboring populations to Islam. Abdul Kader had given himself the mission of liberating populations, and he had therefore "sent ambassadors to order king *damel* and the *brak* to shave their heads and wear a turban, to oblige them to renounce spirits and warn them that in eight days he would be coming in person to administer their solemn oath."²⁹ This is actually what he did after the defeat of Ali El Kori (Alikoury).

On this subject, Amadou Wade explains that "*Almamy* Abdul Kader, marching from the West, met no resistance in the states of Rikee, Caaka Fatim Borso, crossed the river and met the *brak* in Saftu, between Gi Dakhaar and Kór-Mbay."³⁰ In the face of an imminent defeat of the Waalo-Waalo, the *seb ak bawor* forced Fara Penda Teeg-Rel to capitulate. He was advised "to pretend for the moment a false conversion to Islam (*tuub-tuublu*) which he could recant as soon as circumstances allowed it."³¹

Fara Penda Teeg-Rel immediately took advantage of the war of Abdul Kader against *damel* Amari Ngonee Ndella in order to rebel and renounce Islam. The *brak*'s warriors, who had been placed at the disposal of Abdul Kader upon his request, switched sides. Once reunited with the forces of the *damel*, they succeeded in soundly defeating the *almamy*.³² This defeat is described in detail by Baron Roger. Indeed, the army of Abdul Kader, which Lamiral estimates included 30,000 soldiers, was armed for the most part with sticks. This army was decimated by thirst, dysentery and, above all, a policy of scorched earth as practiced by *damel* Amari Ngonee Ndella. The entire army was captured by the *damel*. The defeated soldiers were kept as hostages until all threats from Fuuta ceased.³³

This victory of the *damel* was due to the superiority of his weapons and of his war methods. Indeed, the *almamy* encountered a *damel* who "had a troop of horsemen determined and devoted to his person and whom he trained under arms constantly and at his own expense. This ran against the custom of a land in which permanent military corps do not exist."³⁴ The constitution of this army of *ceddo*—mercenaries hired by the *damel*, and a source of constant terror for the population—was a direct consequence of the Atlantic trade that had benefited the countries along the coast more than any others. In this respect, Lamiral tells us that "along the coastline, they are better armed because they have more direct contacts with Europeans and they are the ones who derive all the benefits from trade."³⁵

It is possible that slave traders did intervene in favor of the Wolof kingdoms, as Baron Roger suggests. Roger wrote, "When the slave traders of Saint-Louis, Gorée and Rufisque learned that there was a war brooding between Kajoor and Fuuta, they rejoiced because whoever the victor was going to be many prisoners would be captured on either side and the slave trade would benefit from it. The *damel* asked them to supply arms and ammunitions to help in his defense. In exchange for these advances, he promised to deliver the first prisoners who would fall in his hands. For such was the custom of the country in such cases."³⁶ We can then understand this conflict within the political and cultural contexts of this period, and because of the opposition of the *almamy* to the trade in Muslim prisoners. The conflict between Fuuta and Saint-Louis became permanent from then on. During this conflict, Islam was increasingly regarded as an ideology hostile to the Whites and to colonization.

Nevertheless, the military defeat of Abdul Kader temporarily eliminated the Tukulor threat. It was followed by a strong, irreversible wave of conversion to Islam in Waalo. According to Amadou Wade, "after this victory, the *brak*, who had returned to Dagana, had to confront new difficulties. The inhabitants of the village who had converted to Islam at the same time with the *brak* refused to separate from the *almamy*, and declared that their conversion, which had originally been feigned had become a reality and they now were sincere Muslims, faithful and fervent followers of the Tukulor marabout who alone was their master, after God and the Prophet. The *brak* was then obliged to acknowledge the sincerity of their faith and Dagana was divided into two very distinct villages (traces of which still exist): a Muslem Dagana and a *ceddo* Dagana. The former commanded by the Seeriñ Dagana answered to the authority of the Fuuta *almamy*; and the latter administered by the Jombé Nahk, Kangam of the *brak*, was loyal to the *brak*."[37] This Islamic wave directly challenged an aristocracy supported by *ceddo* warriors.

No sources are available to determine the precise length of Fara Penda Teeg-Rel's reign. It began around 1785 and probably ended in 1794-1795, if we accept the nine years proposed by Bubu Sal as a reference point. Indeed, in 1795, Tardieu quotes Raffennel and says that the *Dios* were completely destroyed near the village of Ntiank under *brak* Maderbi.[38] Yet, no oral tradition has kept a record of the reign of Maderbi. The sole mention comes from Azan, who notes that Maderbi, a *Dios* noble, was the bravest warrior in the land under the reign of Fara Penda Teeg-Rel.[39]

It should be mentioned that Maderbi requested help from the *almamy* against Fara Penda—and, after the death of the *almamy*, attempted to seize power in the name of the *Dios*. They were defeated in 1795. It is a *Teejekk*, Ndiak Kumba Khuri Yaye, who succeeded Fara Penda Teeg-Rel. In any case, the archives barely mention the reigns of Fara Penda Teeg-Rel's heirs all the way to that of Amar Faatim Borso, whose rise to power coincided with the beginning of agricultural colonization. Only oral tradition, as transmitted by Azan, Yoro Diaw and Bubu Sal, mentions the *braks* at the end of the eighteenth century. According to extant travel accounts, that period appears to be dominated by the Moorish presence in Waalo. The following is a list of the different *braks* and a brief discussion of their reigns.

Ndiak Kumba Khuri Yaye (Teejekk)

He was the son of Fara Penda and Khuri Yaye (*Teejekk*). Azan attributes to him the actions of Fara Penda Teeg-Rel against the *almamy*.[40] According to Bubu Sal, he reigned for ten years and eventually became insane.

Sayoodo Yacine Mbodj (Dios)

Sayoodo was the son of Yacine Mbodje and Diabo Douba-Ali. According to Azan, he paid regular tribute to the Moors during the five years of his reign. Indeed, "Waalo, ravaged and ruined, could not sustain a war against the Moors."[41]

Kuuly Mbaba (Teejekk)

The son of Mbaba (*Teejekk*) and of Ladior (from the Guedje branch of Cayor), Kuuly attempted to liberate himself from the customary fees paid to the Moors. However, Amar Ould Mokhtar, the father of Mohamed El Habib, pillaged a number of Moorish camps and crossed the Senegal. He began "a war of massacres and devastations along the left bank of the river." The Trarzas were masters everywhere, causing the utmost terror. During that period, Kuuly was in Saint-Louis.[42]

Beeco Sakura managed to liberate the river banks, where the people of Rosso had no longer dared to draw water. The Waalo-Waalo, encouraged by his example, pushed the Moors back on the right bank of the river under the leadership of the *jawdin* Tyaaka.[43]

Kuuly reigned for six years, according to Azan; Bubu Sal measures it at five years and six months. The succession of Kuuly Mlaba gave rise to a harsh competition between the three royal families. The *Teejekk* allied with the *Dios* in order to drive away the *Loggar*. Monsérat tells us in his 1839 account that "after the death of *brak* Kuuly, the princess from the *Teejekk* branch, Fatim Yamar, became the heir to the throne. Troubles were brewing. She lost no time and proposed to Amar Bouye from the *Dios* family to share her crown with him."[44] This *brak* is none other than Amar Faatim Borso, who in 1819 signed the treaty for agricultural colonization in Waalo.

This reign begins with the advent of a new era in the relationship between Europe and Africa. First, let us examine the relationship between Saint-Louis and Waalo during this period.

Evolution of the Relationships between Saint-Louis and Waalo

The period of the French Revolution and the Empire of Napoléon is rather murky. We possess little documentation of the activity of Saint-Louis in Waalo. We do know that the French reactivated their old commercial circuit, with the country of Galam as the main supplier of enslaved individuals. Yet again, Waalo became the breadbasket of Saint-Louis. Saugnier, who arrived in Senegal in June 1785, wrote that "the trade that we practice with these peoples is a very small thing indeed. We merely draw from these lands the millet necessary to the tobacco colony and a little ivory. In case of war between nations, we can export excellent and superb slaves."[45]

The payment of customary fees for the gum trade at the desert post represented the only subject of discord between Saint-Louis and Waalo. In effect, the trading post of Saint-Louis put constant pressure on Waalo by threatening to suspend the customary fees. It fulfilled that threat on April 28, 1798. Blanchot suspended the customs of Waalo until the 60 oxen pillaged from the inhabitants of Saint-Louis were returned. Waalo submitted to the law because, as Blanchot puts it, the *brak* "was the easiest prince to satisfy in the arrangement of customary fees" because of his weakness.[46] The list of the customs paid to the *brak* in 1817 demonstrates the precariousness of his revenues during this period. Every year, he received the following items "to maintain harmony and encourage commerce":

57 and a half long rods of iron
15 lengths of Guinean cloth
2 sheets of pellets
100 pints of rum
37 rifles for trade
3 pairs of pistols or 3 pairs of rifles for trade
12 pounds of powder
400 bullets
400 pieces of flints
1 and ¼ ells of scarlet cloth
30 buckets (?)
1 trunk mounted with iron and a lock[47]

These customary fees, established for the last time, were stable. Their value did not follow the evolution of the flow of merchandise, which was constantly declining. In any case, the most significant opposition encountered by Saint-Louis came from Fuuta Toro. There, the *almamy* was eager to maintain the right to visit boats transporting enslaved individuals, and attempted several times to interrupt the trade from Galam. In 1803, Blanchot declared war on the *almamy*. However, he was obliged to accept peace in 1806 without having obtained any advantage capable of improving commercial relationships.

Due to the famine that permeated the colony between 1793 and 1807, Blanchot acquired the islands of Babagué, Safal and Gueoba on November 21, 1799. The purchase act explained that "Mayout Guiab, alias Jean Barre, an inland Negro, chief and owner of the islands of Saure, Babagué, Safal and Gueba, hereby gives complete ownership [of the islands] to the French Republic in order for the Republic to establish any settlements that will be deemed appropriate and to dispose of them as it pleases, in exchange for customary fees equal and similar to the ones which have been ascribed for the possession of the island of Saint-Louis, which customary fees consist of 3 lengths of Guinean cloth, 1/3 ell of scarlet cloth, 7 long bars of iron and 10 pints of spirits."[48]

This treaty was also meant to reduce the excess population of Saint-Louis on the island of Babagué. It constituted a harbinger of the attempt to settle on the continent. That would eventually take place in 1819, with the agricultural colonization of Waalo. In the meantime, however, Saint-Louis was once again recaptured. On July 13, 1809, Commandant Lavasseur surrendered and ceded the island to Colombine, the British admiral.

The Second British Occupation of Saint-Louis, 1809-1817

The British reoccupation of Saint-Louis was not that impactual, considering that it did not last long. More to the point, it coincided with a transition period in African trade, since the British had abolished the Atlantic slave trade in 1807. From then on, the British attempted to find new products to trade in Africa. A royal commission, convened for this purpose, requested that all the governors along the African coast provide complete reports on the economic, political and social situation of their colonies and on their prospects for development.

In response, Maxwell wrote a long report on Senegal. His comments indicated the possibility of cultivating of colonial products, such as cotton and indigo. He asserted that there would be no difficulty in obtaining the cooperation of the *almamy* to suppress the Atlantic slave trade. That might encourage a return to peace, as well as the formation of a confederation of all the states. Like Waalo, these states had all been undermined by internal wars.[49] This objective was one that European powers would eventually impose at the end of the nineteenth century, during the colonial conquest.

However, the British barely had time to implement this renovation plan for Senegal. In fact, the final act of the Congress of Vienna on June 9, 1815, and the treaty of Paris signed on November 29, confirmed the re-conveyance of Senegal to France. This re-conveyance had already been acknowledged by the peace treaty of May 30, 1814, along with the obligation to suppress the Atlantic slave trade.[50] This marked the end of an era of slave trading. For almost two centuries, that era had represented the basis for the relationships between Saint-Louis and the African kingdoms.

The new era that began would bring about the agricultural colonization of Waalo. We will now examine the main lines of this economic revolution, which the Europeans desired and which constituted the prelude to colonial conquest in Waalo.

PART III
THE AGRICULTURAL COLONIZATION AND THE CONQUEST OF WAALO, CA. 1819-59

CHAPTER 9

AGRICULTURAL COLONIZATION OF WAALO, CA. 1819-31[1]

According to the documentation of Baron Portal, the governors worked to transform the economy of the settlements into a policy of agricultural colonization as soon as they regained control of the Senegal colony in 1817. On May 4, 1819, Governor Schmaltz and *brak* Amar Fati Mborso co-signed a treaty entailing the transfer of Waalo's land in order to establish agricultural settlements, thus eliminating the traditional gum, slave and ivory trades. This represented an attempt to safeguard trade with the near-bankrupt Senegal, and to help it adapt to the new conditions created by the abolition of Atlantic slave trade. Overall, it was intended to end the era of trading posts along the African coast. French settlements on the continent would open new relationships between Saint-Louis and the states along the Senegal River, and point the colony in the direction of territorial conquest. Agricultural colonization would also ameliorate the economic, political and social crisis of Waalo.

Realization of an Agricultural Colonization Plan

For multiple reasons, it was not until January 27, 1817, that the French regained control of the Senegal colony. The peace treaty that imposed the abolition of Atlantic slave trade resulted in the complete ruin of the French settlements of Senegal and the Caribbean, because it depleted the labor force necessary for tropical cultivation. Since workers could no longer be transported to the sites of work, the ideal solution was—as Schefer states it—to transport the work to the workers.[2] This marked a departure point for Waalo's agricultural colonization, which the Bourbon monarch Louis XVIII of France attempted to implement in order to save the colony. Instructions dated December 31, 1818, indicate approval of the project as presented by Governor Schmaltz, who became the pioneer of agricultural colonization in Senegal. To realize the project, Schmaltz was given a credit of 11,233,358 francs between 1818 and 1824. After that, Senegal was not to expect any kind of financial subsidy from the metropolis.[3] As soon as he arrived in Saint-Louis on March 13, 1819, Schmaltz was eager to sign treaties in order to fulfill his plan of agricultural colonization, for which he chose the state of Waalo.

The May 8, 1819 Treaty Signed in Ndiaw with Brak Amar Faatim Mborso (Dios), 1816-1825

Schmaltz' initial choice for the first agricultural settlements was Fuuta Toro, and in particular the island of Morphil. However, the unrest that prevailed there, and especially the constant hostility of the *almamy* toward Saint-Louis during the French Revolution and Empire, forced him to look to Waalo instead. Waalo apparently offered similar agricultural possibilities, and lent itself better to supervision and control because it was located close to Saint-Louis.

After two days of negotiations between Governor Schmaltz and *bëkk-néeg jurbel* Biram Kura, *brak* Amar Faatim Mborso signed the treaty transferring Waalo land to the French. Also present were major dignitaries: *jawdin* Madiaw Xor, *beeco* Sakura, *maalo* Giak Danko, *jogomaay* Giak Gio, etc.[4] Regarding this treaty, ratified on May 8, 1819 in Ndiaw, we only have the official version of Schmaltz. He claims that he explained extensively to the chiefs the advantages that Waalo, henceforth protected against the constant Moorish threat, could derive from agricultural colonization.[5] *Brak* Amar Faatim Mborso was "deeding to the King of France full ownership for all eternity of the islands and other land portions of Waalo which were deemed appropriate for cultivation in the present and in the future."[6] He also promised to facilitate the hiring of a labor force, which he would supervise. He agreed to the construction of forts in his country to ensure the protection of agricultural settlements.[7]

In order to motivate the different chiefs to respect the clauses of the treaty, the governor also promised to pay annual customary fees of 10, 358.64 francs, with the first installment on January 1, 1820.[8] These customary fees, which were added to the old ones, made up a total annual sum of 11, 715.70 francs and tripled the revenues of the Waalo chiefs. Distributed among 28 dignitaries according to their ranks in the political hierarchy, these customary fees are summarized in the chart above.

Waalo had enjoyed a state of relative peace for the past two years, because the Trarzas were entirely occupied with their civil war and their unshakeable enemies. It is therefore possible that the Waalo chiefs, who had been intimidated by the military might of Fleuriau in April 1818, were not only seduced by the bait of new customary fees, but also tempted by Schmaltz' promise to protect them from Trarza depredations. In any case, they all signed the treaty. Henceforth, Waalo was to be merely a kind of economic protectorate.

Before examining the political, economic and social implications of the treaty, let us consider how this experiment in agricultural colonization was actually implemented.

LIST OF CUSTOMARY FEES FOR 1819

Past Customary Fees	Treaty of May 8, 1819	Total	List of Items			Total Value	
				I.	S.	I.	S.
37 1/2	96	133 1/3	Lengths of blue Guinean cloth	42		5,607	
47	91	138	Trade guns	11		1,518	
	33	33	Single-barreled guns (fine)	39		1,287	
	4	4	Double-barreled guns (fine)	80		320	
3	1	4	Pairs of pistols	14		56	84
700	2,150	2,850	Lead bullets	2	10	61	
650	2,150	2,850	Flints	10	56	28	36
1 1/2	2	3 1/2	Ells of scarlet cloth	10	6	41	30
2		2	Pieces of meat [?]	10	33	21	25
		125					
24	101	25	Gun powder	1	47	166	75
	25	1	Sugar	1	50	36	50
	1	198 1/2	½ length of muslin	27	50	27	75
104 1/2	94	4	Iron rods	7	121	1,488	25
	4	4	Ounces of no. 4 amber		198	30	50
	4	55	Ounces of no. 4 coral			49	
30	25	1,092	Piastres [unit of currency]	5	50	275	
670	422	12	Pints of rum			546	60
	12	2	Pints of wine	30		3	
2		1	Iron-studded trunks	20		40	
	1		Hats with braided ornaments	12		12	
		1	(fake gold)				
	1	1	Trade saber	6		6	

1	1	4	Small case	12		12	
	4	2	Single-barreled gun (ordinary)	18	80	78	60
2			Rods	4		9	

Waalo customary fees amount to 11,715.70.[9]

The Different Experiments with Agricultural Colonization in Waalo from 1819 to 1831

Schmaltz clearly stated his objective of agricultural colonization in a letter to the ministry, dated September 4, 1819: "Our objective is to integrate ourselves in a vast country of several million inhabitants, to engage those people to work through advantages they could not have discovered without us, to attach them to their work by gradually increasing their immediate needs, and to steer them efficiently in the direction of our interests through examples tending to improve their agriculture and unobtrusively make them accept French domination."[10]

However, the actual implementation of this project, regarding which Schmaltz had made such extravagant promises to the ministry, would suffer numerous setbacks and would finally be abandoned completely in 1831.

Schmaltz immediately chose Dagana as the center of his agricultural experiment. He undertook the construction of a blockhouse along the river bank in order to ensure the protection of the settlements. However, as early as July 1819, the Trarza Moors threatened Waalo, and the Fuuta chiefs claimed ownership over the Dagana domain. As a result of these difficulties, which emerged abruptly from all sides, the French parliament voted only reluctantly in favor of the funds necessary to carry out the agricultural project. The report of Melay, who had noticed the flood danger, insalubrity, and opposition of neighboring peoples to the project, revealed his doubts concerning the likelihood of its success.[11] The minister consequently decided to reduce funds, and only granted 1,200,000 instead of 2,000,000 francs for 1820. Moreover, he suggested that Schmaltz conduct cautious trials, rather than the large-scale project he had planned.[12] Schmaltz, however, failed to contain the Trarza threat. The minister, frightened by the warmongering of his deputy, re-sent the Mackau mission to survey the situation firsthand.

On July 3, 1820, Schmaltz was called back to France. His replacement, Captain Le Coupe, arrived by ship in Senegal, with instructions to drastically reduce the scope of the colonization plan. The goal was to develop the production of cotton, and thus reduce France's heavy reliance on foreign sources.[13] The minister recommended a conciliatory policy with the indigenous population; he advised bribing the Trarzas, Braknas and Fula via annual customary fees.[14] Le Coupe's legacy in Senegal was that of inaction, the tidying up of archives, and the effort to win peace at any price. He thus abandoned the project of agricultural colonization that Schmaltz had launched. On March 8, 1821, the demands of neighboring peoples forced him to tell the ministry that "our cultivation projects have been postponed; cotton exportation is almost non-existent; in a word, colonization has been stopped and the colony is in desperate straits; it can only get out of those straits with peace and it must be said that peace will only come after a violent jolt."[15]

Following this admission of failure, the ministry appointed Baron Roger, who landed in Saint-Louis on February 28, 1822. From 1822 to 1827, Baron Roger served as the true igniter of agricultural colonization in Waalo. He gave it a new start and attempted to ensure effective development. As the first civilian governor of Senegal, his goal was to establish a powerful colony "with a pickaxe" to serve as an example for the rest of Senegambia. The baron attacked his work with all the energy and experience he had utilized during his former role as director of the royal palace of Koëler.

He began by organizing a special group of supervisors. He recruited and trained agents to study the agricultural possibilities of the country, and make improvements. Richard, the gardener who gave his name to the experimental garden of Richard-Toll, was the most notable member of this technical team. It included an overall coordinator of the colonization effort, government gardeners, surveyors, indigo specialists, botanists, chemists, accountants, and so on.

After creating the Richard-Toll experimental garden as part of his technical research, Roger considered large-scale agricultural experimentation as early as 1824. For that purpose, he attempted to acclimatize some European crops, such as potatoes, lettuce, cabbage, cherry, apple, pear, olive, fig trees and even vineyards. However, since these crops did not always thrive in the Senegalese climate, Roger spent most of his time adapting exotic tropical plants, especially cotton of Asian and Egyptian origins. He also worked on the adoption of Gambian plants for dyes and foodstuffs, and cultivated oleiferous plants, such as sesame and castor-oil plant; he created a large forest-tree nursery at Richard-Toll.

Roger also attempted to improve local cotton crops, and studied all the varieties of indigo—a product that was becoming increasingly important from 1825 onward. He was also interested in the improved cultivation of sweet potatoes, melons, mangoes, and rice to feed the country's population. From the very start, Roger was also interested in the cultivation of peanuts—which would eventually become the main export product of Senegal—as well as the cultivation of natural rubber and mahogany.

Roger's extensive studies went above and beyond plant experimentation to include operations pertaining to agriculture, soil improvement, tools, and tilling. He even dabbled in the beginning of an industry of conversion, by installing a cotton gin. Starting in 1825, he conducted multiple and methodical experiments to with indigo, and began building a large indigo factory in Saint-Louis. He did not forget livestock farming, but was satisfied with exporting cattle; he focused his efforts on the cultivation of silkworms and cochineals.

In the space of five years, Roger tried everything he could think of in Waalo. All his scientific research was aimed at building an effective improvement program. As such, he created government settlements to serve as experimental and orientation centers, in Richard-Toll, Dagana and Faf. The royal palace of Koëlel and the dwelling of the Commercial and Agricultural Society, known as the "Sénégalaise," were intended for agricultural propaganda as well as large-scale exploitation. However, except for Richard-Toll, these sites failed in those goals.

Subsequently, Roger based his hopes on the development of agricultural concessions. The distribution of these concessions, in territories stretching from the Four-à-Chaux marshland all the way to Dagana, was regulated by a May 15, 1822 ordinance. As early as September 1825, fifteen much-improved concessions existed in Waalo.[16] Every year, the number of concessions managed by local inhabitants increased. On May 14, 1824, Roger noted that, in spite of the lack of concession-holders from France, there were now several large plantations and more than three million cotton plants, which were beginning to produce. All the trials, conducted on diverse plants cultivated in other colonies, had prospered; Senegal now possessed one of the most beautiful naturalization gardens.[17]

As early as 1824, agricultural occupation was already a given reality. Thus, with the April 1, 1824 ordinance, Roger imposed an administrative framework of four counties upon the economic protectorate of Waalo; Dagana, Richard-Toll, Faf and Lampar served as the chief administrative centers. In 1826, Roger announced that there were now 42 plantations of approximately 1,200 hectares, and a concession project of another 10,000 hectares.[18] To further encourage the development of cultivated lands, the improvement of industrial conversion methods and general cultivation methods, he created a system of bonuses. However, in 1826, Roger admitted that agricultural colonization was going through a crisis; it was moving from extensive to intensive cultivation, despite the agricultural program he had established in order to raise the knowledge level of plantation managers. The program was conducted at the Agricultural and Commercial Society of Waalo, created in 1824.

Toward the end of 1826, Roger felt satisfied that he had given France a rich agricultural colony that now merely needed further development. He asked to be replaced for health reasons. His departure gave the ministry a chance to establish a balance sheet of his work. However, his successors—Gerbidon in 1827, Jubelin from 1828 to 1829, and Brou from 1829 to 1831—determined that the project was a failure, and liquidated the business. Production revenues did not match the promises of Roger. From 1822 to 1825, the cotton exports that had used up his energy did not reach 50,000 kg; the export total added up to less than 188,000 francs, for expenditures of 1,250,000 francs.[19]

Upon his arrival, Gerbidon ascertained that ministerial hopes for agricultural colonization had not been fulfilled and that Senegal did not appear destined to become a cultivation colony.[20] Jubelin, who replaced Gerbido, reached the same conclusions. Governor Brou was ordered to liquidate the agricultural colonization effort following the unrest provoked by the civil war, which tore apart Waalo from 1829 to 1831. "The budget projected for the year 1831 constituted an official liquidation of the business."[21]

Let us now examine why Waalo's agricultural colonization failed.

CAUSES OF THE FAILURE OF THE COLONIZATION PLAN

The implementation of the agricultural colonization plan failed, because unplanned difficulties abruptly confronted those who had hoped to turn Senegal into another Caribbean. Among the multiple causes for failure were the pressure of neighboring peoples, the difficulties involved in the transfer of plantations, the difficulties in hiring a labor force, and the resistance of former slave traders from the post of Saint-Louis.

The Pressure of Neighboring Peoples

After it became a center for agricultural colonization, Waalo became coveted by neighboring peoples, who resented the French presence at their expense. Indeed, *brak* Amar Faatim Mborso tried to utilize the situation to get rid of Moorish tutelage, and refused to pay the tributes that had been imposed on the country for many years. On this subject, Morenas explains that Schmaltz had convinced the *brak* that "the treaty which transferred the kingdom to the King of France completely liberated the *brak* from these customary fees worth 4,000 Francs."[22]

However, Schmaltz' advice immediately provoked retaliation from the Trarza Moors. On September 21, 1819—abetted by Pelligrin, a Saint-Louis individual of mixed heritage—they attacked the village of N'Tiaggar, where the *brak* and his main dignitaries were staying. "In a short while, the people of the *brak* were completely defeated. The *brak* had his leg fractured near the knee, his minister was wounded in the arm, one of the main chiefs in the country was wounded in the leg, and six others, as well as a score of villagers, were killed. The village was burned down by the Moors who then crossed the river again with a large number of prisoners."[23] On November 20, 1819, the *Tooro lam* staked his claim on Dagana, which had been chosen as the seat for agricultural settlements.[24]

On November 15, 1819, Schmaltz, who wanted to take advantage of the Trarza civil war, had rushed to sign a treaty with Mohamed El Koury. In that treaty, El Koury acknowledged Waalo sovereignty on the left bank of the Senegal. He promised to stop demanding tribute, in exchange for help in the war against would-be usurper Amar Ould Moctar.[25] Despite this treaty, a coalition of all the neighboring peoples—including Braknas, Trarzas, Tukulors and Kajoorians—formed on February 19, 1820 to protest the French presence in Waalo.[26] This coalition was led by *imam* Boubakar. Using the pretext of fighting against the infidels, he persuaded the Moors to force the departure of the French from Bakel and Dagana. His true goal was to ensure for himself the monopoly of trade along the Senegal River. Schmaltz also saw that this sudden uprising of neighboring peoples was partly due to British intrigues, led by Major Gray. For two months, Gray had distributed an abundance of goods in Wolof country.[27]

On March 5, 1820, the Moors and Tukulors seized the capital city of Nder despite the defense organized by *briok* Yeerim Mbañik, the heir to the throne of Waalo; *brak* Amar Fantim Mborso, who had been wounded in the thigh, was in Saint-Louis.[28] Yoro Diaw tells us that this war was ferocious. Many of the women attached to *linger Awo*, Fati Yamar, chose to burn themselves alive in a large house rather than be taken captive by the Moors and Tukulors.[29] According to Yoro Diaw, however, *brak* Yeerim Mbañik forged an alliance with the legitimate heir of the Trarzas, Mohamed el Koury. With the help of Schmaltz, the *brak* rallied the survivors of the armies beaten at N'Tiaggar and Nder. Supported on his right flank by the *jawdin* and on his left by *bëkk-néeg jurbel* Biram Kura, Yeerim Mbañik then marched through the village of Ronk. "Reinforced by a small contingent of El Guebba Moors, who were supporters of Mohamet Ould El Kewri, he entered Trarza country and ravaged it all the way to the central dunes."[30]

Amar Ould Moctar, defeated in Ouara Ouar, rushed to the Adrar, leaving almost 150 dead behind him on the battlefield. The *almamy* and the Trarza king raised a new army, but were nonetheless defeated in Dialoowali.[31] In truth, this series of victories by Moctar was due to the intervention of Schmaltz. He ordered cannon fire on a few Fuuta Toro villages, and thus succeeded in intimidating the coalition—already weakened by internal dissensions over the distribution of spoils.[32] Nevertheless, the agricultural colonization was badly compromised. On August 19, 1820, Schmaltz noted: "The war that the Waalo-Waalo are waging with us to defend their dependence [on France] saddens them much as it prevents them from clearing up their *lugan* and to begin cultivating their lands."[33]

Schmaltz was incapable of brokering a peace with the Trarzas, and was recalled in July 1820. He was replaced by Le Coupe, who sought peace at any cost. After the death of the legitimate heir El Koury, Le Coupe negotiated the treaty of June 7, 1821 with the usurper Amar Ould Moctar. With this treaty, he essentially acknowledged Trarza sovereignty over Waalo. France was merely purchasing the right to establish a few agricultural settlements in Waalo, in exchange for an annual customary fee.[34] The treaty was followed on August 21, 1821, by a written agreement in which France pledged to pay the tribute of 100 oxen that Waalo had traditionally been paying the Trarzas. It was a confirmation by France that the Trarzas had taken control of the country.[35]

The various treaties signed with the Tukulors, Braknas and Trarzas turned France into a peace-for-power broker along the Senegal River. However, the ultimate consequence of this policy was to subject Waalo to the double hegemony of the Trarza Moors and the trading post of Saint-Louis. It would severely compromise the success of the agricultural colonization plan.

As early as 1822, Moorish dissidents led by young Moctar, the son of El Koury, sought asylum in Waalo; Amar Ould Moctar soon began pillaging the country.[36] He incidentally limited his acts of depredation to the region around Portendik, thus threatening the gum trade along the river ports. This was done with the complicity of the British, who were trading from 100,000 to 115,000 kg of gum a year.[37] *Brak* Yeerim Mbañik, who succeeded *brak* Amar Faatim Mborso around 1825, hoped to use the civil war among the Trarza Moors to get rid of their dominance. According to Monserat, *brak* Yeerim Mbañik, whose bravery and hatred of the Moors were well known, never tired of saying: "Remember, people of Waalo, that it is better to fight against the Moors all your lives than to grant them one single day of peace; never forget that if you allow them to penetrate on your lands, you will all become not only tributaries of them, but the vilest of their slaves; then, you will want to remember what I am telling you today, but it will be too late; you will have been sacrificed and you will have no homeland left."[38]

This is why *brak* Yeerim Mbañik "had taken young Moctar under his wing and was serving as his mentor."[39] Indeed, "the Moors who had never abandoned his father, proclaimed him king of the Trarzas and Senegal acknowledged him as well because of the great services his father had rendered the French." However, this alliance mostly benefited the *brak* at the expense of the gum trade. Because of this, and because of the very real power of Amar Ould Moctar, the governor wrote to Berton. He asked that Berton request that Moctar delay accepting the title of king. Indeed, according to him, "As king, Moctar would be the vassal of the *brak* and the foe of Amar...the would-be king of the Trarzas, a ghost of a king who hurts us if he separates his interests from ours: I would be nothing to him anymore and if the good of Senegal required it I would become his enemy. The *brak*, who sees things differently, will push him blindly upon the throne; it is really quite simple, he enjoys dragging behind him a crowned vassal. His spirit of hatred and revenge wants to wage war against Amar and divide the Trarzas; he wants everything that binds Moctar and his people, everything which might prevent them from making peace with Amar."[40]

A letter to Brunet dated January 16, 1827, indicated that the inhabitants of Saint-Louis were worried that the Waalo-Waalo, now allied with Moctar's Moors, "might attack the caravans which bring gum along the river banks."[41] In spite of the governor's threat, Moctar and the Waalo-Waalo violently forced settlers to evacuate the Gaïe river port in February of 1827.[42] A few months later, the hostility of Yeerim Mbañik against the agricultural colonization project—and the rupture of dams by the Waalo-Waalo—convinced Gerbidon to adopt a policy of accommodating Amar Ould Moctar.

After the death of Yeerim Mbañik, around December 17, 1827, young Moctar found himself abandoned.[43] According to Monserat, "*brak* Fara Penda who had just replaced Yrim Bagnic no longer gave him any kind of protection, and after being several times harassed by negroes, he decided to surrender to his cousin."[44] In May 1828, the forces of Amar Ould Moctar entered Waalo between Gaïe and Bokol, removing all hope for the implementation of agricultural colonization.[45] Subsequently, Gerbidon signed the peace treaty of April 15, 1829 with Amar's son and successor, Mohamed el Habib. In order to eliminate the impending threat to the gum trade, Gerbidon once again acknowledged the sovereignty of the Trarzas over Waalo.[46] In Waalo, *bëkk-néeg jurbel* Biram Kura, holding firm to the hostile policy of Yeerim Mbañik toward the Moors, refused any kind of accommodation with the Trarzas.[47] His death, however, ended any effort to re-establish the rights of Waalo. Waalo was once again subjected to Moorish exploitation, since the clauses of the treaty included no protection provisions whatsoever for the country.

We can thus conclude that the lack of effective protection of Waalo against its neighbors led to the failure of agricultural colonization, because of the country's subsequent state of insecurity. Yeerim Mbañik's hope—that agricultural colonization would remove the Moorish threat—was also dashed. Moreover, the transfer of lands for cultivation also played a large role in the failure of the agricultural project.

The Land Problem

The 1819 treaty stipulated the permanent transfer of title-deeds to the Waalo islands, along with other land portions deemed appropriate for present and future cultivation projects. In the eyes of French authorities, this clause constituted a legally binding purchase of Waalo lands. However, its actual application was quite difficult as a result of the ambiguous wording. It was indeed difficult to reconcile the African community's ownership of the land with its proposed sale in perpetuity, considering that this was a country where rights to the land were still considered unalienable. Baron Roger's 1822 interpretation of the treaty assumed that the *brak* had transferred to France not a territory per se, but rather a right to establish settlements wherever France deemed it appropriate. This interpretation would inevitably create conflicts when land was actually being purchased.[48] Moreover, in 1857, Faidherbe asserted that while some French people may have taken the 1819 alleged purchase of Waalo seriously, it had never been taken seriously by anyone in Senegal.[49]

In 1862, Jaureguilberry also noted that "land in Kayor as in Waalo belongs to the sovereign as the representative of his nation. He can transfer tenure of it, but not ownership as we understand it in Europe, that is to say, the possibility of disposing of it at will, in other terms, to sell it."[50] Land, under the joint ownership of a family, belonged to all the descendants of the person who had first cultivated it.[51] The conflicting interpretation of the treaty created a constant source of conflict. The Waalo-Waalo interpreted the payment of customary fees as a land lease, while the French felt that they actually purchased Waalo lands.

In the end, in order to convince the French minister to accept his project of agricultural colonization, Schmaltz was obliged to present him with an advantageous treaty. There is no record of the conditions under which the treaty was signed. However, as Faidherbe remarked, it should not be forgotten that it was an African practice for a transfer of land to be achieved after chiefs were intoxicated.[52] In any case, conflict was inevitable in a country that had been settled for a long time, and in which every parcel of good land near water was already the inalienable property of a family. Indeed, the trading post of Saint-Louis counted rather on the greed for customary fees and, above all, physical force to obtain land concessions. As Fleuriau put it, "As soon as our forts are established, ownership will be guaranteed to us."[53]

In a memorandum written in 1823, Pichon expressed his doubts: "In the current state of things, we are sowing and building on someone else's land which is ceded to us temporarily in exchange for a very high yearly rent. It is the king and princes who receive the prices of fields which do not belong to them. The natives have already complained; planters have been insulted in the midst of their cotton workers... If we continue, in another four years, what will the Negroes say who are already complaining about the growth of plantations and the loss of their *lugan*?"[54]

The whole crux of agricultural colonization lay in the feasibility of easily obtaining concessions. Thus in 1821, facing the reluctance of the Waalo-Waalo, Le Coupe was obliged to sign a treaty that vowed to compensate those who owned sections of cleared land located within the concessions given to the Europeans.[55] However, in spite of his threats to break the clauses of the treaty, this did not prevent the governor from encountering similar difficulties concerning the lands he had demanded in the neighborhood of Mbilar.[56] In March 1824, the refusal to transfer concessions involved fallow lands in Khouma and Ndombo.[57] Worse yet, in August 1824, *serigne* Ndombo gave Carpentier a hard time regarding parcels of land for which Brunet and Pellegrin had "recently paid much too high a value."[58] Confronting panic-stricken planters who were frightened by so much hostility, Roger tried to reassure them: "This is a crisis; we had to expect crises of this type and even some that would be far more serious yet than this one has been so far."[59]

Those calming words were proven false a few years later, in August 1827. Perrottet informed the governor that the Waalo-Waalo had broken the dam that enclosed the Tawé marshland, thus channeling water to their *lugan*. This they did while disregarding the risk of flooding the best lands of the "Sénégalaise."[60] With the recrudescence of hostile acts, Brunet bitterly admitted the failure of the land concessions policy in a dispatch dated August 26, 1827. "The Waalo are determined to do us harm, and to insult us, and it is at the very moment in the seasonal cycle when we are helpless that they choose to commit outrages with the goal long recognized on their part of forcing us to leave their country. Experience teaches us that, in order to execute this project of agricultural colonization, the first thing to do was to press back the population inland."[61]

Regardless of his threat to withhold customary fees, Brunet drew the same conclusions after the Doukik dam was destroyed by the people of the *jawdin*, who had "received from Mr. Roger presents that he did not grant to other chiefs."[62] "On this occasion, they have expressed the intention they had already implied on more than one other occasion that they will resist the expansion of our cultivations and that they are quite ready to use force against us if we want to continue implementing the treaty we signed with them on May 8, 1819."[63]

In order to stop the relentless war that the Waalo-Waalo were waging against the dams, Gerbidon refused to pay the customary fees of *brak* Yeerim Mbañik and the main chiefs. Moreover, he sent a steamboat along the river to repress any further rebellion.[64] Thus threatened, Waalo chiefs were obliged to sign a new agreement on December 5, 1827. It aimed to prevent all conflicts between European and Waalo-Waalo planters and to reaffirm the clauses of the May 8, 1819 treaty.[65] Nonetheless, the agricultural colonization project was ultimately abandoned due to a lack of fertile soil, which raised the issue of irrigation on a large scale. Climate, especially the hot eastern wind, also hindered the development of plantations.

Thus, the issue of land concession created a serious obstacle to the implementation of the agricultural project—an attempt made in lieu of conquering the whole country or pushing back the population inland, as the British did later in Kenya. However, in addition to the troubles caused by neighboring peoples and the difficulties born of land transfer, another equally serious problem existed—the ineffective recruitment of a labor force.

The Labor Force Problem

The 1819 treaty stipulated that the *brak* and major Waalo chiefs would be responsible for providing and supervising a labor force. Workers' wages were to be determined freely by owners and hired hands. The village chiefs who provided workers would each receive a customary fee of four iron bars yearly, but would be obligated to replace deserters, or sick or dead workers, within two weeks to maintain their allocations.[66]

From the perspective of agricultural colonists, the recruitment of a labor force should have posed no difficulty; here was a large servile population with an opportunity to gain independence by earning wages. However, as early as September 1819, Valentin noted how difficult it was to make "free, independent people work like slaves," especially since the *brak* had limited ability to coerce his people.[67] Baron Roger eventually reached the same conclusion. Thrusting aside the well-established stereotype of the "laziness" of Waalo-Waalo people, he wrote in 1820: "It is precisely from this habit Negroes have of working for themselves that comes the difficulty of hiring them to take care of our plantations. These men are very independent; they state in no uncertain terms that they are as free as we are and their chiefs have very little authority over them."[68]

Thus from the very beginning, lack of a labor force was a very serious handicap to the implementation of agricultural colonization. The plan's supporters considered bringing in a foreign work force from the Canary Islands, or convicts from Martinique or France. However, as this attempt failed, a system of indentured servitude was selected. This intermediate status between slavery and freedom involved liberating enslaved individuals confiscated from a clandestine slave trade. They were then forced to work in Waalo agricultural concessions for fourteen years. Thus, as early as November 1823, enslaved individuals were systematically purchased. On the Bakel market alone, one hundred enslaved individuals were turned into indentured servants, and five times more were promised.[69]

This form of recruitment, so similar to that of enslaved individuals, naturally gave rise to human abuses. The merchants of Saint-Louis used the system to collect on old debts; they requested, as payment, indentured servants from the different trading posts along the river and the coast.[70] It appears that a total of 3,077 indentured servants were recruited between

1818 and 1844.[71] Despite opposition from the French ministry, this practice encouraged the development of a new form of clandestine slave trade.

In any case, the official elimination of the Atlantic slave trade did not put an end to the actual trading of enslaved individuals. The trade continued throughout the first half of the nineteenth century, as a result of ineffective and unenforceable laws. In 1820 and 1821, Morenas published two petitions denouncing the continuation of the African slave trade in Senegal. "On October 5, 1817, a slave trader from Saint-Louis provoked the attack of the village of Diman in Waalo country by a Moorish prince belonging to the Trarza tribe to whom a boat, weapons, ammunitions and *laptots* (Senegalese light infantry soldiers) had been provided. The village was burned down and in one night 47 Blacks were captured while 65 died while defending their homes and liberty."[72] In order to meet the requests of traders, the *damel* sold approximately 3,000 of his subjects.[73]

In 1821, in a letter to the French minister, the governor himself reveals his inability to prevent and repress the activities of slave traders in foreign colonies.[74] "The judges themselves are not exempt of passion and private interests as they are largely composed of merchants from Saint-Louis who are almost all of them interested in evading the intentions of the laws."[75] In a July 15, 1828 letter, the governor mentions that the Green Cape islands had become the operational center for the African slave trade along the coast.[76] A Parisian newspaper denounced the illegal activity of a certain Piecentin, who brought 600 Africans each year to the market of Saint-Louis. In response, the governor attempted to justify himself by remarking that "slavery is rampant in Africa; it is customary in the countries neighboring Saint-Louis...it is normal and fulfills the needs of the population. Contact encourages the introduction of a few captives, whatever the level of supervision by the authorities."[77] Testimonies related to the continuation of the clandestine slave trade are numerous. Agricultural colonization did not end the commerce of enslaved individuals.

Paradoxically, there was a recrudescence of the slave trade in the old Trans-Saharan circuit. In 1818, Mollien warned that the abolition of Atlantic slave trade would not produce happy results and would merely be "illusory until we can force the Moors to accept it. Let me explain: Negroes sell to the Moors prisoners that the Whites are forbidden to buy, and a king who used to have a revenue sufficient for the maintenance of his court with 200 prisoners sold 600 Francs a piece to the Europeans now makes more frequent incursions inside his neighbors' lands and even inside his own territory in order to double the number of slaves and thus keep the same revenue, since the Moors pay half the price Europeans used to give for one single captive."[78]

Thus, after the wars in Waalo and during the period of agricultural colonization, Moorish pillaging in Waalo extended the effects of the previously dominant slave trade. In 1823, Baron Roger remarked that pillage by the *ceddo* was a "continuance of the atrocious policy of the slave traders which was to have pillages done by one country over another."[79] History offered an avenging twist: after three centuries of Atlantic slave trading, now that the French planned to use an indigenous labor force, they found that there were not enough workers left in this vast and supposedly inexhaustible reservoir. The population of Waalo had been decimated by wars, trade practices, famine, and slavery. The lack of workers represented a serious impediment to the realization of the agricultural project. In March 1832, Jaureguiberry explained: "The excursions I have just undertaken in Waalo, Kayor and Diander have convinced me that one of the obstacles to the development of agricultural industries, which alone could ensure the prosperity of this colony, lies in the lack of working hands. Everywhere, one sees fallow lands and vast solitudes; the rare inhabitants, grouped in a number of centers, are content to grow only the products necessary to satisfy their yearly needs. Such a sad situation can only be explained by the continuous wars which, for centuries, have bloodied the African continent and which were motivated by the slave trade or barbarian customs."

As an alternative, he recommended the immigration of 20,000 Chinese families to assure the agricultural development of Senegal.[80] The unwillingness of the Waalo-Waalo to devote their time to reaping exportable crops—for the profit of the French, and at the expense of food crops—is understandable. Gerbidon, however, did not understand it. In 1827, he attributed local resistance to the inborn laziness of the Senegalese: "Our presence has not convinced the natives to cultivate one additional acre of land. They have remained so uninterested in our crops that for the past five years, they have provided no more than three or four workers who, pursued and ill-treated by their own people were soon obliged to stop their work."[81] In these circumstances, work could not be organized spontaneously, particularly when it involved difficult and not-very-profitable tasks. The fear of a labor shortage thus encouraged the institution of indentured servitude and later that of forced labor.[82]

We see here that, as in the case of the land problems, it was not possible to impose forced labor on free men and women without first conquering the territory. The lack of workers precipitated the failure of agricultural colonization, which was reinforced by the resistance of former slave traders at the trading post of Saint-Louis.

Resistance of Traditional Trade

Realizing that any success of agricultural colonization would disturb the commercial habits of Saint-Louis, small shopkeepers and individuals of mixed heritage actively resisted the project. Indeed, in spite of the glowing promises made by Schmaltz and Roger, commercial activities continued to dominate Senegal's economy. As early as September 1819, the Saint-Louis merchant, Valentin, opposed the concession system and proposed instead that commerce serve as a support for agricultural colonization. He wrote, "It was more simple, it seems to me, more economical for the government and more advantageous for trade in the colony to sacrifice 400,000 Francs in order to encourage, for a period of three years, the Saint-Louis inhabitants and inland Negroes to cultivate cotton and indigo which are native crops in this country... Let the Negroes remain independent and masters in their own country, so that they feel their liberty is not threatened and they are not frightened by all these grand preparations. Leave trade to do its thing, give it the protection it deserves and then there is no doubt we shall prosper at least in part in the projects which have been formulated."[83]

But the hostility of shopkeepers' and individuals of mixed heritage toward agricultural colonization became especially noticeable. Pellegrin, who called himself in Saint-Louis the "King of Mulattoes," actively participated in the invasion of Waalo by the Moors, because he anticipated that the new ideas would attract superior men to Senegal and deprive him of some of the benefits he enjoyed.[84] In his report, Mackau attempted to exculpate Pellegrin, but Morenas and Roger did not fail to point out his very real opposition to agricultural colonization. According to Roger, "the individuals of mixed heritagees, who have much influence on the chiefs of neighboring peoples, have blown up the war because they had reasons to be unhappy and worried about our colonization project."[85] Indeed, even the opposition of the Trarzas and Braknas was mainly provoked by their attachment to ancient privileges—in particular, the monopoly of gum.[86]

In spite of this opposition, many merchants rushed to grab agricultural concessions at high costs. They were attracted by the system of bonuses, instituted from the beginning to encourage the development of new crops. This practice did in fact give rise to many cases of abuse and speculation; people collected bonuses for plant numbers or indemnities for workers. The merchants of Saint-Louis, for whom cultivation in Senegal required both perseverance and preliminary expenses, preferred to hang on to the traditional commerce of gum and ivory in the different river ports. Certainly the trade involved many uncertainties due to its system of free competition, and especially due to the rivalry of the British settled in Portendik. Nevertheless, the merchants refused to encourage the economic revolution advocated by Schmaltz and Roger, which involved a growth of commerce based on agricultural development. In the face of this intransigent resistance, Roger responded by intertwining the two branches of activity. In 1824, he created the Commercial and Agricultural Society of Galam and Waalo, assigning it the obligation of creating agricultural settlements.

When the "Sénégalaise" failed, Roger tried to ensure the development of new crops in 1826 by urgently calling for the help of French capitalists.

Eventually, the failure of agricultural colonization ensured the triumph of commerce. Around 1830, a veritable fever for gum took hold of the Saint-Louis population. Gum became "the palladium of Senegalese industry and commerce"; it demanded "an exclusive cult" and any other conception of how Senegal could become a rich country was regarded as "heresy."

Agricultural colonization thus met insurmountable difficulties at all levels. This experiment from 1818 to 1831 failed in its goal to make Waalo an economic protectorate of France. However, it had an enormous impact on the economic, political and social evolution of the country.

CHAPTER 10

AGRICULTURAL COLONIZATION AND THE ECONOMIC, POLITICAL AND SOCIAL CRISIS IN WAALO

During the period of attempted agricultural colonization, the internal affairs of Waalo were dominated by the pressures from neighboring populations and by acrimonious internal conflicts over the distribution of customary fees. The project of agricultural colonization, which had opened new relationships between Waalo and Saint-Louis, was destined to transform political, economic and social life in Waalo. Its failure provided justification for the colonial conquest by the French.

Impact of Customary Fees on Political Life

The stated goal of new customary fees was meant to ensure the collaborative support of Waalo chiefs for the implementation of the agricultural colonization project. On a scale much larger than in the past, Saint-Louis began a systematic policy of division and pressure by means of customary fees. Indeed, the threat to suppress customary fees became, for Saint-Louis, an efficient means of guaranteeing adherence to treaty clauses. On the other hand, an increase in customary fees was calculated to stoke, on the part of Waalo chiefs, a greater hunger for the honors and offices to which they were attached. And at first, the customary fees did indeed enhance the authority of Waalo chiefs.

On September 1, 1820, after the triumphant return of *brak* Amar Fatim Mborso to his own country, Schmaltz confided to Vire, the commander of Dagana, that it was "essential to surround him with consideration and to make his authority as preponderant and respectable as possible."[1] The intermediary role Waalo chiefs filled was quite important. The governor stated this in strong terms in his November 16, 1823 letter to Monery: "We can only act on the Negroes of Waalo through the intermediary of their own native chiefs. This is our only means of influence, policing and government. If we alienate these chiefs and if, indulging in an attitude that is no less dangerous, we humiliate them, we discredit them in front of their people, then we destroy all species of hierarchy and discipline, we reduce the country to anarchy, and we deprive ourselves of the very first political element of our own power."[2]

This policy bore its fruit. On December 29, 1822, the *mangas* was discharged by the *brak* for having attempted to upset new French plantings. *Brak* Amar Faatim Mborso, wanting to take advantage of this opportunity to confiscate the customary fees of the *mangas*, received the support of the governor: "It is in our interest to support his pretensions."[3] Through such means, Saint-Louis managed to retain the good will of certain influential dignitaries. In response to a conflict between Neron and a Waalo-Waalo from Ndiange, Roger wrote to Ziegler on July 20, 1824, asking him to make "Diawdine as well as the new *jogomaay* intervene." He told the latter that "from his behavior in this affair would depend the esteem and presents he might expect from me."[4]

In the context of this policy, *jawdin* Madiaw Xor especially benefited from the gifts issued from Saint-Louis. This would explain his 1830 revolt against *brak* Fara Penda Adam Sal. Indeed, after having provided the *jawdin* with an additional food allowance, Roger explained: "I beg you to make him understand that this is not a customary fee that I am establishing, but instead assistance that I am willing to give him now and which will only last as long as he deserves it."[5]

After *brak* Amar Faatim Mborso died, around January 1826, he was succeeded by Yeerim Mbañik, who had opposed the Moorish hegemony. The new *brak* tried unsuccessfully to have his customs upgraded. As early as February 6, 1826, his accession to power was a cause of concern for Roger, who took advantage of the conflict over Carpentier's lands to uncover the *brak*'s intentions. "This will be a means to make him explain his intentions relative to the treaties. If he asks for an accession gift, you can tell him that my intention is to give him one as soon as he has shown a willingness to remain my friend by swearing to maintain the treaty concluded by his predecessor."[6]

This policy was more or less successful, until the Waalo-Waalo started a damaging campaign against dams in 1827. That compelled Gerbidon to exert force in order to make Yeerim Mbañik sign the convention of December 5, 1827, which confirmed the terms of the 1819 treaty. But it marked the end of attempts at agricultural colonization. This demise marked, at the same time, recognition that the politics of customary fees had failed as a means of realizing the project. In all, the payment of customs to an increasingly divided aristocracy was an indication of a political, economic and social crisis. Agricultural colonization had failed to re-establish peace in Waalo. As before, the country continued to suffer from the pressure of neighboring peoples and from warfare within its own territory.

Evolution of Political and Social Institutions

Not only did efforts at agricultural colonization effort fail to improve commercial production in Waalo, they paradoxically increased political and social conflicts between the aristocracy—still dependent on Saint-Louis—and the rest of the people. Let us look at some aspects of the political and social evolution of Waalo during that period.

Baron Roger, who lived in Waalo for a long time and who took part in the launch of the colonization plan, is well positioned to describe this evolution. Indeed, he wrote a great deal about the Wolof language and published numerous philosophical narratives. His "Note on the Government, Manners and Superstitions of the Negroes in the Country of Waalo," written in 1827, is an important testimony to the political and social crisis.

First of all, it describes, with barely contained emotion, the ills suffered by the Waalo-Waalo people under the combined weight of "odious slavery, a feudal system with ridiculous and absurd consequences, a tithe imposed by lazy chiefs and humbug priests, and finally to make matters even worse, the proximity of Moorish desert roamers."[7]

In Waalo, the domination of the *garmi*, or nobles, was still a reality. "The *brak*'s retinue is usually composed of a score of Negroes who regard themselves as aristocrats, but are really professional warriors. These people live at the expense of the people and regard any type of work as demeaning."[8] The creation of this military aristocracy is the most evident result of Atlantic commerce. The constant relocations of the *brak*'s abode, and the consequent travel of his retinue across the country, resulted in pillages. "Hens, sheep, goats, milk and food supplies are taken away from poor inhabitants."[9] Although the political institutions had not, for the most part, changed from those of earlier centuries, they had become increasingly devoid of meaning. Comparing the political organization of Waalo to the feudal regime in the French Middle Ages, Baron Roger stated, "the most significant dignities are not strictly speaking hereditary according to fixed rules, but they seldom leave the family which owes them. Chiefs grant a part of their territories to vassals who pay them yearly dues; these vassals exact a contribution from village chiefs who, in turn, levy taxes on villagers. A feudal and fiscal chain thus descends, ring by ring, from the *brak* to the last captive."[10]

As for the administration of the kingdom, Roger made a distinction between two types of villages: "Some, and let us note that they are the smallest, are subjected to lords whose order of succession is the same as that used for the crown. The others are less numerous, but more heavily peopled. They constitute free communities with their own civil officers responsible for surveying the land, levying taxes, performing police tasks, and taking care of judicial matters. In some of these places, a marabout with the title of *serigne* (or *sëriñ*) or priest, followed by the name of the village, is the head of municipal dignitaries. The inhabitants are usually required to give up one tenth of their crops and this tithe which is found everywhere is shared between the priest and a chief appointed by the *brak*."[11]

A disciple of the Enlightenment, Baron Roger sought to find in Waalo an evolution similar to that of Europe. This goal prevented him from noticing the particular trait of Waalo, in which there was no one peasant with a particular affinity for a certain piece of land. The limited efforts of agricultural colonization on that territory did not significantly modify the distribution of land, because the Waalo-Waalo quickly opposed any attempt at taking it over. Political chiefs took some advantage of this situation by collecting customary fees. The payment of fees gave more value to the land, thus unfortunately sharpening competition for power. However, Roger well understood the failure of the *brak*'s centralizing power, because such a system created a permanent state of insecurity that favored the increasing development of independent communities, each responsible for insuring its own protection.

More significant yet was the fact that some of these communities had increasing numbers of marabout leaders. Accompanied by many followers, the marabouts' dedication to Islam was often synonymous with a rejection of traditional society during a crisis. In fact, the progress of Islam was the fundamental factor in this first half of the nineteenth century.

We have seen that although the many holy wars led by the Moors or the Tukulors failed in Waalo, they were followed by multiple conversions to Islam. Thus, at the beginning of the nineteenth century, a distinct separation between Muslims and non-Muslims occurred. In 1818, the comment made by Mollien concerning the progress of Islam in Kajoor also applied to Waalo. He said notably, "Every day, Islam makes new converts and is destined to become the sole religion in Kayor." He stated that the holy stature of the marabouts—equally respected by local nobles and Muslim disciples—plus circumcision and public schools, were the three fundamental factors of Islam's progress among the Wolof people. Indeed, he witnessed a rebirth of Islam, which manifested itself in scrupulous observation of external Islamic practices by a great majority of people.[12] The progress of Islam was such that, in 1827, Baron Roger remarked on the existence of two distinct social classes in Waalo:

1. The class of "marabouts or literate people surrounded by their wives and children, lazy and peaceful owners of a horse and small herd of cattle. The head of the family developed a firm, independent personality, not devoid of dignity. There are villages in which there exist more Negroes capable of

reading and writing the Arabic language than there are peasants able to read and write French in the French countryside today.
2. The class of non-Muslims, who "they alone interact with the Europeans. They are violent drunkards. It is not useless to remark that the *brak* and other political chiefs do not participate in the intellectual and moral development of the other part of the population. They indulge in drunkenness, which the marabouts abhor, and they glory in the fact that they are illiterate. Thus, Waalo is in this respect at the same level of development France was in during the period when towns liberated themselves from their feudal lords, when one class of citizens distinguished itself by its good behavior, while the aristocracy was parading its ignorance and disorderly manners."[13]

Waalo was continually racked by warfare as a consequence of its neighbors' rivalries, and above all because of the Atlantic slave trade. These wars profoundly affected the role of the marabouts in a society torn by violence. A marabout took on the mantle of a social critic, as he generally found fault with traditional aristocracy and contrasted its behavior with the values of Islam. This situation led to an anti-Islamic reaction from the aristocracy, which clung to its old values in the face of the invading wave of Muslim reformism.

At the beginning of the nineteenth century, we see that Waalo society was indeed in a crisis in every domain. Wars destroyed crops and contributed to the weariness of peasants and artisans who increasingly turned to Islam—the only bulwark against the arbitrary ways of a constantly divided traditional aristocracy, whose power was undermined by the dominating influence of the *ceddo* and by the magnitude of external pressures. The political and social crisis, made worse by the efforts at agricultural colonization, was marked by the rebellion of *jawdin* Madiaw Xor against *brak* Fara Penda. It was also marked by the attempted coup of marabout Diile Faatim Cam, who channeled popular discontent and took advantage of the country's internal conflicts to attempt the establishment of a theocratic regime in Waalo.

CIVIL WAR AND FAILURE OF THE ISLAMIC REVOLUTION

The major consequence of agricultural colonization was the worsening of the political crisis in Waalo. It manifested itself in the rebellion of *jawdin* Madiaw Xor against *brak* Fara Penda, and the attempt of Diile to create a theocratic kingdom like that of Fuuta.

Civil War between Brak Fara Penda Adam Sal (Teejekk) and Jawdin Madiaw Xor

Upon the death of Yeerim Mbañik in December 1827, Fara Penda Adam Sal (*Teejekk*) ascended the throne with the support of his niece, *linger* Njómbót.[14] Monserrat tells us that Fara Penda, who had been the direct heir to the throne before his predecessors, "was known to be inept to the task; he had always been kept away from the crown and, if it had not been for the death of Yrim Bagnic, he would probably had never been king. *Brak* Fara Penda knew that circumstances alone called him to the throne, and that he owed his accession to no one but chance; as a result, he did not deal tactfully with other dignitaries. He changed all his attendants and sent away all former state ministers. Two parties then began to take shape. Madiawcord, an influential *N'Diawdine*, took up arms against Fara Penda, who had just removed him from office and had almost chased him out of the country when the Prophet appeared."[15] According to Yoro Diaw, the grandson of *jawdin* Majax Xor, the quarrel was caused by the multiple power abuses of *brak* Fara Penda.[16] However, Amadou Wade, less willing to excuse the actions of Madiaw Xor, comments that it was indeed the *jawdin* who, taking advantage of his title, attempted to remove Naatago Biti Koor Cam from power (*dag ko ca nguur ga*) in order to assure the nomination of his brothers, *jogomaay* Meegonë Boli and *briyot* Yeerim Mbañk Boli.[17]

In other words, we have here an instance of a political crisis caused by the accession of a new *brak*. The new *brak* intended to surround himself with the dignitaries who had contributed to his election. In this case, *jawdin* Madiaw Xor, the true beneficiary of the subsidies from Saint-Louis, was also eager to counterbalance the *brak*'s power. When the *brak* kept his *jogomaay*, a discontented Madiaw Xor sought refuge near the French fort at Dagana. A dispatch dated February 19, 1830, explains that "in order to avenge the loss of his position, Madiaw Xor, former *jawdin*, or minister to the *brak*, killed the *jogomaay*, who was the uncle of his successor and had been responsible for the change in position."[18]

From then on, two parties existed:

1. The first, made up mostly of the crown's captives, the *ceddo*, supported the new minister.
2. The second, much stronger than the first because it had the support of the most powerful and almost independent chiefs of the *brak*, did not approve of the actions of Madiaw Xor. However, they demanded the dismissal of his substitute, who had neither the power nor the steadfastness necessary to lead the country.[19]

As before, external alliances alone were capable of solving this public political crisis. Madiaw Xor soon appealed to the Moors for help.[20] In the face of this threat, *brak* Fara Penda sent Berton to Madiaw Xor, asking him to come back and restore peace. The *brak* promised to return to him all his possessions.[21] On February 17, 1830, Berton announced that the Moors, led by Ouldou Leighat himself and accompanied by Madiaw Xor, intended to attack the village of Khuma, which had been evacuated by the *brak*. Richard-Toll now served as a refuge for *linger* Njómbót and the wives of the main chiefs. Berton refused to send ammunitions to Fara Penda Adam Sal, whose forces diminished daily. On the other hand, Madiaw Xor had the support of *elimane* Boubacar of Dimar.

According to Yoro Diaw, this civil war was a series of victories for the *jawdin,* who defeated the *brak* first at Ndiange, and then at the bloody battle of N'Tohla on Lake Guiers. The *brak* was harried all the way to Mal and only stopped running in Mouï, near Marinaghen. The intervention of the two main foreign powers—competitors for the French trading post of Saint-Louis—eventually caused much worry for the governor; he had hoped to remain neutral in the conflict. We know, however, that Berton had refused to send help to Fara Penda Adam Sal, while Madiaw Xor had found refuge in Dagana, near the French fort. In a letter addressed to the *jawdin,* Brou denied the *brak*'s request to extradite Madiaw Xor, but reproached the *jawdin* for his alliance with the Moors: "I do not approve this action anymore than I would approve the action of a child who after tearing apart his mother's breast grabs a foreign weapon to finish her off. Think about what you have done, repent, if there is still time and if you wish to keep my esteem."[22]

Brou's sympathy for the cause of Madiaw Xor was lessened by the Moorish threat, which was more difficult to contain than a Waalo-Waalo threat. The governor's council, eager to wait until the slave trade ended before stopping the Moorish intervention, dispatched Berton to negotiate a peace between the different parties.

However, Berton's mission had barely made it to the river when an unexpected threat to the French position on the Senegal River arose. The entire Waalo territory was suddenly invaded by the prophet Diile, who almost succeeded in ending the *brak* regime.

Invasion of Waalo by the "Prophet" Diile Faatim Cam Kumba Djombos

In previous chapters, we have seen that although several instances of *jihad* had failed, Islam nevertheless gained many converts in Waalo. The political crisis, on top of external pressures, increased chaos in the country and facilitated a power takeover by an indigenous Muslim party. On March 5, 1830, marabout Diile Faatim Cam Kumba Djombos, in complicity with all the converts to Islam, tried to replace the *brak*'s regime with a theocratic regime.

A year before, in February 1829, Mohamed Amar had incited a religious revolution in the province of Podor. Berton, describing Mohamed Amar as gifted with all the qualities that make a man superior to others, noted that he had gained passionate proselytes all the way to Saint-Louis. His power was such that he threatened the religious and political power of the *almamy;* the combined forces of *imam* Boubacar and *almamy* Youssouf, as well as the Braknas, had been necessary to force him to retreat near the religious group of Oulad Ymar.[23] Moreover, the power of the *damel* of Kajoor was threatened—and had been threatened since 1827—by the great marabout of Koki. His name was Niaga Issa, and he was the political and religious chief of the Muslim province of Jambuur. Jambuur was a Muslim fief, an almost independent province of Kajoor. We do not know how this Muslim enclave was formed. However, as in the case of Waalo, the creation of more or less independent communities—led by a marabout sharing power with a royal officer—had become more and more frequent.

At a very early stage, Jambuur probably gathered together men from all social categories, bound together by their allegiance to Islam and their rejection of a traditional society, undermined by the violence and lack of security resulting from the slave trade. Boubacar Ly suggests that there is an analogy between the name of the province and the social significance of the word *Jambuur* in the hierarchy of values. From then on, *Jambuur* has come to refer to the new ethics of a class of people outside the old social structure.[24]

The Muslims of Jambuur had already rebelled against the *damel* in 1786, during Abdul Kader's invasion of Kajoor. The dissidents vanquished by *damel* Amari Ngoné Ndella were sold as enslaved individuals, except for those who were able to find refuge in the peninsula of Cape Vert. Those refugees contributed to the foundation of another Muslim fief, the Lébou republic. In 1827, consequently, Niaga Issa availed himself of his religious influence and took up arms against the *damel*. Ultimately forced to seek shelter on the Waalo frontier, in the village of Ndimbe, he continued to recruit many converts until 1829.[25]

Waalo was not immune to the religious fervor that had impacted all its neighbors. Indeed, in 1829, according to Montserrat, "civil war was stirred up more violently than ever. Yagayassa (Niaga Issa) took advantage of the chaos to conquer the kingdom of Waalo. From Cayor he called a man named Dilëy, a blacksmith by trade, whom he elected Prophet. He then called his other supporters from Cayor and when he had a big enough force, he fell on the first villages at the Waalo frontier, forced them through the voice of his Prophet to fight a religious war and to embrace Islam."[26]

Hostile as he was to Islam, Montserrat does not understand the phenomenon well. On March 7, 1830, Desgranges, who communicated the news of Diile's invasion, explained that the invasion had been anticipated for a long time, considering the complicity of all the marabouts in the country.[27] This was indeed a religious revolution; its goal was to take advantage of conflicts inside Waalo "to seize the country and establish a theocratic government."[28] Indeed, the speed of this surprise conquest indicates that a long preparation had taken place at the Waalo frontier, where marabout Niaga Issa never stopped recruiting new converts from 1827 to 1829.[29]

The minutes from the Government Council tell us that his army of over 3,000 warriors, swollen with felons outlawed from all countries, invaded the whole country of Waalo in an instant. "Called up by the vows and treasons of everything that was practiced by the marabouts, Diile fell on the very rich and populous villages of Paniefoul and ravaged them without any opposition. The terror he inspired was such, the secret of his operations was so well kept by the accomplices he had everywhere that we only learned of his arrival in Waalo when the whole country had surrendered and he was already threatening our settlements and issuing the order for everyone, White, Yellow or Black, to come and be shaved and acknowledge him as a second Moïse."[30]

On March 7, 1830, Berton announced the defeat of *brak* Fara Penda Adam Sal, who had come to Richard-Toll in vain to solicit help. On the same day, it was Desgranges's turn to announce that the agricultural settlement of Doukitt and its indigo plantation had been burned by Diile during the course of his total invasion of Waalo.[31]

During this time, the *brak* and *jawdin* Madiaw Xor were still refusing to reconcile, even in order to face their common enemy. Rather, each one of them wanted to derive some profit from a possible victory over Diile by seeking an alliance with Saint-Louis. While Fara Penda was in Saint-Louis demanding the governor's help, Madiaw Xor was confined near the fort at Dagana, and was still enjoying the moral superiority of not having been defeated by Diile. During the meeting of the Government Council, Brou was still hesitant about siding with one man or the other; he feared either that the *brak* might ask for help from Kaydoor, or that the *jawdin* might call again on the Moors for assistance. However, after Diile's attack on the agricultural settlements—especially the forts at Richard-Toll and Dagana, which were key to trade along the Senegal River—Governor Brou decided to put an end to the Prophet's invasion. He said notably, "The Waalo country has been invaded. Someone has had the audacity to lay hands on one of our settlements; the others are seriously threatened by this act of direct aggression. Our duty is clear: I must act."[32]

However, it seems that Brou was still inclined to help Madiaw Xor. The emissaries sent to negotiate had been assured that *elimane* Boubacar and Ould Leighat would make peace with Waalo, provided Fara Penda was driven out of the country.[33] Thus, the governor had a vested interest in treating the powerful allies of *jawdin* Madiaw Xor with circumspection—

especially since Fara Penda, hunted out of Waalo by Diile, had arrived in Saint-Louis on March 8, 1830 to beg for protection.[34] The victory of Brou over Diile eventually benefited Madiaw Xor. On March 10, 1830, Diile was already in Ndiange with his 3,000 warriors. He was preparing an attack on Dagana, one of the pillars of the French presence on the Senegal River. Meeting no resistance from the Waalo chiefs, he spent the night in the village of M'Bilor. On the morning of March 11, Brou moved in the direction of M'Bilor, where his gunners effectively burned the village.

As a result and as chief of all operations, Brou explained, "*elimane* Boubacar and the people of Dagana finally arrived and most awfully ravaged that which had escaped us—cruel, but all too just reprisals."[35] Indeed, very few soldiers of the Prophet managed to ford the Tawe; *serigne* Niaga Issa escaped and found refuge in the Lébou republic of Cape Vert. Diile was captured, tried, and hung at the foot of the great tamarind tree planted in front of Richard-Toll. Eager to have him recant in his presence as well, the governor forced Diile to acknowledge in a loud voice that he was nothing but an impostor.[36]

Causes and Consequences of Diile's Failure

The brief expedition of Diile still lives in the memories of the Waalo-Waalo; the consequences of his adventure, which threatened the very existence of the *brak* system, were crucial. Unfortunately, the different versions of the story are marked by the quarrel between *brak* Fara Penda Adam Sal and *jawdin* Madiaw Xor. According to some versions, Madiaw Xor alone triumphed over Diile. In order to make the most of his importance in the kingdom, he said to the *brak* after his victory that "the *brak* is nothing without the *jawdin*." However, Yoro Diaw himself acknowledges the alliance of Madiaw Xor with *elimane* Boubacar and Governor Brou.[37] According to others, and in particular according to the Cam or descendants of the Prophet, Diile is such a symbol of pride that the retelling of his actions takes on epic proportions. For them, Diile epitomized all the hopes of men trapped in a caste system, and held in contempt for it. His war was a reaction against endogamy.

In Dagana, this author was lucky enough to meet a jeweler whose story coincided exactly with the official version of Governor Brou.[38] The attitude of the traditional aristocracy, who have mostly converted to Islam today, is still filled with hostility toward Diile. This is proof that in the days of the Prophet, when the aristocracy was still in power, its members must have reacted even more sharply against this outcast who almost put an end to the *brak*'s regime. The existence of the *brak* system had not been questioned since Njaajaan Njaay. Until the coming of Diile, the powerful people had been restricted to members of the three great royal families. As a result,

Diile's attempt to install a new regime, similar to the religious theocracy that prevailed in Fuuta Toro, represented a triple revolution—religious, social and political.

In terms of a religious revolution, the movement led by Diile solidified the triumph of Islam in Waalo. The party of the marabouts had become so powerful that it had the audacity to take up arms in order to impose its religious views. From then on, Islam would never be an outside force, invading a country by way of holy war, but would emerge from within—spread by those very people who, merely tolerated at the beginning, would succeed via Islam in deeply transforming their society. As a social revolution, it was the first time that an outcast, upholding the values of Muslim egalitarianism, challenged the traditional social hierarchy. Even when practiced superficially, Islam seemed to be a liberating wind, blowing the discontent of society's lower classes into the face of the political and moral disorder of the aristocracy. And finally, it was a political revolution, because Diile ultimately saw that the only means of establishing a new society was to seize political power. That is why he attempted to install a theocratic regime.

When we examine the causes of Diile's defeat, we must not linger on his resounding failure. We should instead remember the fact that, far from being defeated by the aristocrats in power, he was defeated by Governor Brou. Indeed, the aristocrats in power, undermined by internal quarrels and external wars, offered no resistance to Diile's forces. Their political dissensions were such that they could not even manage to unite in order to confront a common danger. This is proof that the political system was decomposing. This decomposition was made even more evident by the breakdown of the equilibrium that supposedly existed between the *brak*'s power and that of the members of the *seb ak bawor*. In the face of this weakness, Brou was prompted to say that "it was necessary to extract all possible profit from the powerful impression our victory has left." As a result, Brou warned Mohamed El Habib to cease his incursions in Waalo to levy taxes on the people. From then on, Brou was the master of the Senegal River.

From many points of view, and in spite of his failure, Diile is the distant harbinger of a Wolof society without castes, a propagator of Islam, and finally a far-reaching politician whose success might have changed the destiny of Waalo. He failed, on the one hand, because he arrived too early to destroy the harsh restrictions of endogamy and to conquer the resistance of the indigenous aristocrats in power. On the other hand, he failed because he lived too late to oppose the interests of the French, who could no longer tolerate the presence of a hostile force along the Senegal River. The social, religious and political revolution embodied by Islam failed in Waalo. Everywhere else, it acted as a springboard for resistance against colonialism.

It is not by accident that Waalo was the first state in this area of Africa to fall under colonial conquest in 1855.

The failure of Diile's revolution also coincided with the failure of agricultural colonization. As a consequence, the interest Saint-Louis took in Waalo diminished. Indeed, for reasons we have already analyzed, the budget of 1831 represented a total liquidation of the agricultural enterprise. From then on, the traditional gum and ivory trade at the various stops along the Senegal River took on more importance than the agricultural projects. This return to traditional commercial activities suddenly relegated Waalo to a lower status. In this context, in May 1831, Brou conceded, "The affairs of this country which have such a strong impact on the Senegal River have lost much of their importance for us since we have acknowledged that it could not grow a single advantageous crop. Thus, if the banks of the river in Waalo are still ornamented with splendid settlements and expensive exploitation buildings, they no longer harbor plantations or people attached to the land... The 'Sénégalaise'... recently discharged its sole manager gardener and sold all the Black workers. Therefore, we have nothing left to protect in Waalo but stones which degrade on their own and I do believe this task does not give us the moral right to intervene, except as arbiters, in the affairs of this unfortunate territory, used as it is for the withdrawal of water and for more or less frequent pillage by the Moors or the Fula."[39]

Brou added that the trading activities taking place on the right bank of the river were safe from conflicts in Waalo. Thus, in the interest of the colony, Brou was leaving Senegal trade under the best possible terms with the Trarzas. But Waalo, undermined by an economic, political and social crisis, was abandoned. Thus the blows from a new war of succession proved even harsher than previous ones.

Conclusion on Agricultural Colonization

The attempt at agricultural colonization in Waalo from 1819 to 1831 ended in complete failure. The agricultural project was intended to save the colony of Senegal from bankruptcy after the slave trade had been abolished. But it failed to overcome the attachment of the Saint-Louis merchants to the old trade along the river. Most importantly, it failed in its objective to cultivate colonial plants for exportation by the Waalo-Waalo. Constantly threatened by war, Waalo could not be a territory favorable to the development of a plantation economy. The relative powers of the states located along the coast at the beginning of the nineteenth century prevented all European efforts to establish themselves firmly within the continent. Paradoxically, the weakness and anarchy that prevailed after slave trading was interrupted constituted a serious handicap to the development of a sustainable agricultural colonization. Once again, the economic, political and social situation made it impossible to proceed with any enterprise of this type, in the context of a simple economic protectorate. Once the agricultural project was abandoned, the crisis worsened in all domains in Waalo, while the authorities in Saint-Louis increasingly steered their efforts in the direction of territorial conquest.

CHAPTER 11

THE PERIOD OF CONFLICTS AFTER ABANDONING THE POLICY
OF AGRICULTURAL COLONIZATION, CA. 1830-40

The end of agricultural colonization did not end the civil war. It continued, harsher than ever. Left to its own devices, Waalo was dominated by the struggle between Fara Penda Adam Sal (*Teejekk*) and Kheerfi Xari Daaro (*Dios*) and by the marriage of *linger* Njómbót with Mohamed El Habib, king of the Trarzas—who nearly annexed the country to his own kingdom.

Power Struggle between Fara Penda Adam Sal
(Teejekk) and Kheerfi Xari Daaro (Dios)

The defeat of Diile encouraged the return of *jawdin* Madiaw Xor, who reaped all the profit from Brou's victory over the Prophet. Indeed, according to Monserat, Governor Brou attempted to re-establish harmony in Waalo and to end the civil war. However, "N'Diawdine was irreconcilable; he held fast onto the reins of the kingdom, so to speak. He did not want a stubborn king, but instead a king of his own choice who would not be hostile to him. Since he could not ascend the throne himself, he wanted at least to govern according to his liking."[1]

Madiaw Xor thus imposed the nomination of Kheerfi Xari Daaro, who belonged to the rival *Dios* family. This opened the door to yet another civil war, as two parties emerged. The first party, led by Madiaw Xor and Kheerfi Xari Daaro, was allied with the French colonists in Saint-Louis. The second included Fara Penda, who had found refuge in the village of N'Guik Cayor on the border of Waalo. He was supported by *linger* Njómbót, to whom the French had unsuccessfully attempted to attach the party of Kheerfi.[2] However, Kheerfi Xari Daaro "had no more ability than his predecessor to win over the affection of his subjects."[3]

Fara Penda attracted the discontented, who joined him in great numbers and, "at the beginning of 1831, he invaded Waalo. He conquered most of the country and would have captured the rest if he had not stubbornly insisted on running a partisan warfare, although N'Diawdine had called the Moors in order to hunt him out of Waalo.[4]

As a matter of fact, Brou explains in a memorandum dated May 31, 1831, that the Moors and Tukulors were still taking advantage of the division among Waalo leaders to intervene in the country. Mohamed El Habid had answered the call of *brak* Kheerfi Xari Daaro and *jawdin* Madiaw Xor.[5] According to Monserat, the Moorish intervention spurred Fara Penda to leave the country, in order to avoid its destruction. "The people thus persuaded him to return to Cayor by promising to follow him, which they did."[6] However, war soon broke out between Saint-Louis and Mohamed El Habib, following the assassination of Jacques Malivois on July 19, 1831 near Richard-Toll. Young Moktar was captured and accused of the murder. The purpose: to permanently get rid of the legitimate heir of the Trarzas. This restored peace between Mohamed El Habib and the French. This peace was guaranteed by the treaty of August 1831.[7]

But Governor Saint-Germain saw nothing in this treaty to assure the protection of the Waalo-Waalo, who had fought by his side. So he abandoned the country to constant Moorish pressure. Monserat tells us that "having succeeded in their undertakings and having made it impossible for the Waalo-Waalo to defend themselves from further invasions, the Moors attacked several villages, which until then had remained neutral, pillaged them and threw into slavery all the people who could not flee. The village of N'Dombo, where prince Bethio had chosen to reside at the time, deplored the loss of more than 1,200 subjects who were captured or massacred under the vain pretext that the prince had not agreed to side with the attackers."[8]

The misery that followed the Moorish intervention must have played a part in discrediting the party of Kheerfi Xari Daaro, and therefore encouraging the return of the former *brak*, Fara Penda. In this respect, Monserat tells us that Fara Penda and his supporters, "having spent the inclement season in Cayor, attempted again to take hold of the country's government. This time, they succeeded and in 1832 they were once again in possession of their kingdom."[9]

Abandoned by his ally *jawlin* Madiaw Xor, Kheerfi Xari Daaro found refuge in Gandiole, near Saint-Louis.[10] Amadou Wade provides ample support of Monserat's account, and says that the reign of Kheerfi Xari Daaro created nothing but a series of famines and miseries for the people. Notable officials in the country requested the return of Fara Penda; *jawdin* Madiaw Xor abandoned his ally and accepted the change, while explaining that he had fought against Fara Penda "with the sole intent of proving that he, Madiaw Xor, should not be compared with the people the *brak* had chosen and nominated instead of his brothers."[11] Defeated, Kheerfi Xari Daaro gave an account of his setbacks to Madiaw Xor, who replied: "I was able to put a country between your hands, but I cannot take bullets because of you."[12] Forsaken by everyone, Kheerfi Xari Daaro left Waalo.

Starting in April 1832, Mohamed El Habib, threatened by a revolt of the Amar Bouchanouns after the delivery of Moktar to the French, attempted to link himself to Waalo in order to use that kingdom as a potential refuge.[13]

He also tried to put Waalo at odds with the French by telling the chiefs that an alliance, both offensive and defensive, would be very advantageous to them; he told them that if their forces were united, they might exact larger customary fees from the French. However, Saint-Louis—which no longer had any interest in Waalo after the failure of the agricultural project—did nothing to relieve the country from Moorish pressure.

In August 1832, a number of dignitaries, including *beeco* Sakura, *jawdin* Madiaw Xor, and *brak* Mambodje Fanta, declared that they had formed no offensive alliance against Saint-Louis. Nevertheless, the Waalo-Waalo obtained no help from the governor. "As earlier, they were abandoned to their own devices and to the constant oppression of Fula and Moors."[14] It is then that a new party was formed. It promoted an alliance with the Moors in order to save the country from destruction. Monserat tells us that dignitaries "named Natago Boutiquer (Ndiawdine), Mafaly (Geyque), Alidoune (Boukenegue Nguiëbel) and Yaly Gaye, Natago Ndiaye, only intent on the present and not at all considering the future, decided between themselves to propose to [*linger*] Nuimbot that she marries the Trarza king; this inexperienced girl, who had been forgotten by the civil war and the neighboring powers allied against her country, accepted the advice that was proffered and agreed to the negotiation."[15]

The wedding was celebrated on June 18, 1833. This irreversible act forced Governor Saint-Germain to realize the danger that now threatened Saint-Louis, if Mohamed El Habid did in fact unite the two crowns of the Waalo-Waalo and the Trarzas. Frightened by this prospect, he declared a ruthless war against Waalo in order to break up the marriage.

Consequences of the Marriage of the Waalo Linger Njómbót to Mohamed El Habid, King of the Trarzas

The marriage of *linger* Njómbót gave rise to multiple interpretations. Even today, opinions are divided about the motivations for the alliance. According to some, Njómbót accepted this union to satisfy her inordinate ambition; she wanted to bear the name of *kumba linger* and to bear the title of heir to the combined kingdoms of Trarza and Waalo. According to others, especially the *géwél* or storytellers, Njómbót sacrificed herself to save her country from the misery of war that Mohamed El Habib was waging on Waalo. This national heroism, embodied in the gift of the most beautiful pearl in Waalo, is evoked at length by the *géwél* in their epic tales. In fact, the different interpretations are merely a reflection of the different positions of contemporary parties in Waalo, because this marriage had enormous consequences.

According to Monserat, there were only four dignitaries in Waalo, including the *bëkenkk jurbel*, who approved the marriage. "All the other chiefs and their people disapproved the initiative of the princess; several princes of the land expected to marry her; they suffered to see that their princess had given herself up to their deadly enemy, the Trarza king."[16] Moreover, this marriage had enormous consequences for the future of commerce in Saint-Louis. Reporting on this incident, which had destroyed peace in the lower region of the Senegal River, Renault de Saint-Germain wrote, "This marriage which was destined to put one day the crown for this country on the head of a Moorish king, and which effectively put it there immediately, undermines the very foundation of this colony, that is, the neutrality of the left bank of the river during our frequent quarrels with the Moors."[17] He added that the Moorish takeover of Waalo would be followed by their takeover of the salt mines of Gandiole; Saint-Louis, surrounded on all sides, would perish irremediably.[18] A French intervention was therefore unavoidable.

As early as July 21, 1833, Saint-Germain deposed *brak* Fara Penda and replaced him with his rival Kheerfi Xari Daaro.[19] Monserat tells us that Saint-Germain "called *brak* Kheerfi, who had already been crowned king of Waalo during the country's invasion by the false prophet, and put him back on the throne; he dispossessed Fara Penda and forced him to leave his capital without even listening to the chiefs or the people, letting them know that they had to acknowledge the new king he was giving them immediately or leave the country."[20]

All Waalo chiefs, even those who were hostile to the marriage, felt the blow to their national pride; they retired inland with Fara Penda and joined the Moors against Saint-Louis. Saint-Germain destroyed all the villages along the river; his successor, Quernel, attempted to break the marriage. When he failed, he finalized an alliance with *elimane* Boubacar in order to subjugate Waalo completely. This war between Fara Penda, allied with Mohamed El Habib, and Kheerfi Xari Daaro, supported by Saint-Louis, was to last more than three years. On September 11, 1833, Quernel destroyed Khouma; Fara Penda and the main Moorish chiefs were in a position to threaten Richard-Toll.[21] By November 8, the situation had not changed. Quernel prepared a large expedition with the hope of expeditiously ending a war that was ruining Saint-Louis.[22]

As early as December 4, 1833, the villages of Khouma, Ndombo and Ntiago had surrendered, with all their cattle and reserves of millet. Quernel left the banks of the river for the first time, thus surprising the Waalo-Waalo. He pushed his expedition all the way to Foss, which was also forced to surrender. So did three other villages located on the island of Ghiëlu (Yalen) in the center of Paniéfoul.[23] "There, destruction was total; everything was ravaged and burned, all the way down to the harvests which were still standing in the fields; in the whole region we surveyed, there did not remain a single barn or house. Fara Penda found a refuge in the village most remote from the border between Waalo and Cayor."[24]

At the beginning of 1834, a truce was declared. Quernel sent Monserat as a government agent, as well as Saint-Louis inhabitants Jean Derneville and Charles André, to negotiate a peace with the supporters of Fara Penda. During a meeting on January 20, the Waalo chiefs accused Saint-Louis of having ceded the country to the Moors and of causing their alliance with Mohamed El Habib. "Hadn't the governor been forewarned about the weakness of our forces? Did he not know our position? Wasn't it his duty as well as his interest to help us in time? Did he have to depose our king and force us to acknowledge the one he wanted to give us without even lending us an ear?"[25]

After a lengthy indictment against the policy of Saint-Louis, the chiefs nevertheless consented to send an embassy to make peace with Saint-Louis. It was composed of *beeco* Sakura, *maalo* Mbarrik Diagne and *bërc* Aly Thiam. This delegation had barely left Saint-Louis on January 28, 1834 when the Moors, having learned of the Waalo-Waalo's intention, invaded the country. The massive presence of Moorish forces obliged the Waalo chiefs, intent on safeguarding their families from pillage, to abandon the idea of unilateral peace with Saint-Louis.[26]

Unable to obtain the divorce of Mohamed El Habib and Njómbót or the departure of the Moors from Waalo, Saint-Louis again declared war. On March 7, 1834, Quernel destroyed all the villages that had been spared during his first campaign.[27] On March 22, 1834, he announced proudly that war on the left bank of the river could be considered finished; nothing further was to be feared from that region. Abandoned, *linger* Njómbót found refuge with all her supporters in Kajoor. However, Quernel's mission to subject the Moors of the right bank to the same fate was interrupted by the nomination of Pujol.

Pujol bitterly criticized the war-mongering policy of Quernel, whom he said had achieved no lasting goal since the true enemies, the Trarzas, were elusive creatures of the desert. He notably pointed out, "We have completely ruined Waalo, our former ally and close neighbor whose defection was only caused by our neglect and lack of willingness to support them in their differences with the Moors. They were forced to contract an alliance cemented by a marriage with the Moors."[28] His goal was therefore to break the marriage and to re-negotiate the conditions of the April 15, 1829 treaty.

Deprived of military resources, Pujol's only weapons were the long-term denial of customary fees and of gum trade with which to force the Moors to demand peace. However, his threats did not succeed. In 1834, the English traded 600 million francs of gum, a sale that reinforced the Trarzas' position for at least two years. Pujol immediately sounded the alarm, saying that "gum trade, the main resource of Senegal, cannot be shared and the country will be ruined if a blockade does not bring this to a stop."[29] But Pujol's Portendik blockade declaration for February 15, 1835, was disavowed by the French ministry. On August 11, 1835, Pujob sought another compromise solution. "Instead of requesting the king's divorce, I will declare myself satisfied if Princess Njómbót waives all her claims to the kingdom of Waalo in favor of her younger sister. I will merely request a formal renunciation by Mohamed El Habib on his behalf and that of all his heirs to all the claims to the Waalo crown that he might derive from the princess."[30]

All the parties were tired of this endless war; the chiefs exiled with Njómbót were eager to return home to Waalo, while the capture of 900 heads of cattle, 400 sheep, 30 donkeys and camels in a month's time also prompted the Moors to seek peace. Thus, Pujol signed two separate treaties with the Moors and the Waalo-Waalo.

Pujol signed the first on August 30, 1835 with Mohamed El Habib. The latter renounced all direct and indirect claims for himself and for his heirs and successors to the Waalo crown—and notably, for the children who might be born of his marriage with Njómbót. In the treaty, France promised to pay the old customary fees on the basis of previous treaties.[31] The second treaty was signed on September 4, 1835 in Saint-Louis, with the representatives of Fara Penda Adam Sal. This government in exile included *briok* Mambodi Fanta, *beeco* Sakura, *maalo* Barik Diak, *njawdin* Rike Mardiatel, *bëkk-néeg jurbel* Samba Gajol. Fara Penda pledged not to seek out or threaten the well-being of those Waalo persons who had taken part in the last war on behalf of Kheerfi or Senegal. After offering to mediate between Fara Penda and *elimane* Boubacar, Saint-Louis recognized Fara Penda as *brak* of Waalo and promised to pay customary fees, as in the past.[32]

This double peace treaty brokered by France did not mean peace for Waalo. Kheerfi Xari Daaro, abandoned by his allies, did not acknowledge defeat. Thus, on January 17, 1836, the Saint-Louis government announced that civil war was unavoidable in Waalo. Indeed, "Fara Penda, once again recognized as *brak* by the peace treaty, has refused to leave Kayor, where he has found refuge with his family, until the millet harvest is completed. This delay has given enough time to the partisans of Kheerfi, our former ally, to prepare their opposition to the *brak*'s return, and I am afraid a civil war is impending."[33]

The trading post of Saint-Louis, satisfied with the peace treaty with the Moors, had again lost interest in Waalo. Thus the events that followed have not been recorded. We only know that Kheerfi Xari Daaro, abandoned by his Saint-Louis allies, was not able to retain his power in Waalo. He found refuge with the whole royal branch of his *Dios* family near Saint-Louis. He probably died during the year 1839.[34]

The End of Fara Penda Adam Sal's Reign and the Weakening of the Brak Regime

Fara Penda Sal, re-crowned the *brak* in 1835, returned to a Waalo kingdom ruined by war. The last four years of his reign consisted of nothing but a long series of failures in attempting to rebuild his authority. The French presence and Moorish raids had forever undermined the power of the *brak*.

On March 20, 1837, a dispatch from the governor provided a gloomy description of the situation in Waalo: "Today, Waalo is devastated, its chiefs are divided among themselves, the king has lost all authority, and the Moors ravage the land and keep seizing fractions of it."[35] The lack of authority of the *brak* is confirmed in an undated letter of Fara Penda to the governor, in which he explains his difficulties. The *brak* had a hard time reining in the *ceddo*, who had become accustomed to pillaging and were making up an increasingly independent force. Indeed, the *ceddo* warriors had hunted Fara Penda from Khouma to Ntiago, then to Foss, in order to either kill or expel him and thus gain control of the country. Fara Penda urgently asked the governor for help in maintaining his authority over a country ruined by civil war.[36]

In this rebellion of the *ceddo*, one can see a sign of Moorish intervention. More importantly, one can see a direct consequence of the stark poverty of the *brak*, whose insufficient revenues no longer satisfied the requirements of his warriors. The penury of the *brak* is made evident in the desperation with which he henceforth asked for the customary fees from Saint-Louis. The need for money had become so urgent that in September 1837, Fara Penda signed a treaty abandoning all claim to kingship over the village of Sor. In exchange, he would receive a sum equal to the total of ten years of customary fees for this village—somewhere between 600 and 700 francs.[37] In a report to the French ministry, Governor Guillet remarked, "The current *brak*, an anxious old man, dissatisfied with what we have done for him in the last treaty, makes new demands every day. He has gone so far as to request an old customary fee which used to be paid a long time ago by the people of Guet Ndar although the dignity of our government and simple decorum do not allow us to continue paying such a customary fee."[38]

Fara Penda's attempt to collect money, by any means necessary, coincided with a new gubernatorial policy of refusing payment of all customary fees to Waalo chiefs. In an 1837 memorandum, Guillet challenged the "arbitrary customary fees associated with trade in ports of call." By then, customary fees in Waalo had reached over 20,000 francs. For Guillet, this dependency was ruinous; Waalo was no longer able to assure the condition that had motivated the creation of the customs in the first place—the protection of trade from the Moors. The governor therefore gave traders the choice to pay or not pay these customary fees, and asked Waalo chiefs to revise the methods of payment through a new treaty.[39] In 1839, Soret stated that many traders had refused to pay their customary fees. In order to avoid conflicts, he established a new declaration concerning the payment of customary fees; Fara Penda agreed to it with much reluctance. Soret was obliged to station three schooners in the ports of call to ensure trade security.[40]

This shows how dependent Waalo had become during the final years of Fara Penda's reign. Fara Penda no longer had any authority. In 1839, Soret noted that "Fara Penda, a blind old man who is the *brak* of Waalo, is a king in name only; it is now Princess Njómbót, married to the Trarza king who controls the policy of this whole country. She herself is under the influence of her husband and a few schemers. More than ever, Waalo is now coveted by Mohamed El Habib who oppresses the country with his troops and pushes the black population toward the south in order to gain absolute power."[41]

The impending death of Fara Penda was beginning to stir speculations about his successor in Waalo. In 1837, Guillet noted that the chiefs, who were supposed to participate in the election of a new *brak,* were all entirely devoted to Senegal. In order to regain the allegiance of Waalo, all that was needed was to ensure the election of a family member of the former *brak,* Kheerfi (the *Dios*).[42] In order to prevent the throne from being handed over to Njómbót after the death of Fara Penda, who had no male heirs, the governor sent Caille to negotiate for the return of the *Dios* family. They were refugees in Saint-Louis. After long talks, on August 26, 1839, the family returned to Nder. Then Yeerim Mbañik was proclaimed *kadj,* or heir to the throne.

The governor expressed his satisfaction in a letter to the French minister: "Thus, we will have on the Waalo throne, in a few years, a prince who has been welcome among us, who has witnessed the interest we take in his cause, and who cannot, without ingratitude, not be devoted to France."[43] However, this hope would be dashed. On October 30, 1840, the governor announced both the death of Fara Penda and his disappointment that he had not been able to bring about the election of Yeerim Mbañik. Sent to support the interests of France, Derneville arrived too late.[44]

As the January 20, 1841 dispatch explains, it appears that Njómbót had retained enough influence over Waalo to install a *brak* who was devoted to her.[45] Once again, it is Amadou Wade who describes the circumstances that surrounded the succession of Fara Penda Adam Sal. "At the time of Fara Penda Adam Sal's death, there was no man in the country from the *Teejekk* branch (*kheet*) who might be nominated *brak*. The crown should rightfully have been given to Njómbót, but unfortunately she was a woman. Thus, opinions were divided. On the other hand, the partisans (*ñi and ak moom*) of Yeerim Mbañik Mbodi, another candidate, were numerous."[46]

Three heated discussions took place in Ndiaw. To each of these meetings, Njómbót sent a man with a sum of 500 francs, intended for the assembly of the *seb ak bawor*. During the third and last reunion, *jawdin* Sharlu was persuaded; he told the other members of the assembly: "Since we have been meeting to deliberate on the question in front of us, none of the other claimants to the crown has thought of sending us anything while *linger* Njómbót has bestowed upon us three gifts in the amount of 1500 Francs. It would be only as a gesture of gratitude, [but] I believe we should turn our attention in her direction."[47] The other members of the assembly assented to the proposition of *jawdin* Sharlu and sent a messenger to Queen Njómbót to find out if she had a candidate (*kee laaj nguur gi*) to present in her stead. The queen gave them this response: "I am a woman, but before the end of this night, I will give you a man" (*Jigéen laa waande balaa bir di set ma jox leen góor*). Early the next morning, she presented her cousin Mó Mbodi Maalik, whom she had summoned from N'Dombo during the night. "As the last *brak* of Waalo, Mó Mbodi Maalik remained at the head of this country for fifteen years."[48]

The narrative of Amadou Wade has been quoted at length here, because it is the only narrative that details the intrigues surrounding this particular election crisis of the *brak*. The victory of Njómbót was obviously due to her wealth—and particularly to the fact that Derneville, who came to support Yeerim Mbañik, arrived too late. The governor hoped to make up for his defeat by having Yeerim Mbañik marry *linger* Ndate Yalla, a sister of Njómbót. "This marriage would increase the power of the *Dios* who would then be devoted to us, unless all feeling of gratitude is extinguished in them."[49]

This account makes it evident that respect for tradition had been replaced, in all domains, by violence and greed. Yoro Diaw's description confirms this state of institutional crisis, which existed in Waalo during the whole first half of the nineteenth century. He remarked, "As for real powers, they are a function of authority and material superiority. The importance of this last factor is even apparent in the election or maintenance of the *brak* as wealth is translated in the form of gifts. The most important thing for each party and for each noble is thus to be strong and rich."[50]

Thus, the stage was set in Waalo for a serious social and political crisis that culminated between 1828 and 1840. This social and political crisis left Waalo weaker than ever—at the mercy of its powerful Moorish and French neighbors, who increasingly attempted to annex its territories. The failure of the social and political revolution of Diile, and the inability of traditional aristocracy to reform itself in order to confront external danger, rendered Waalo easy prey. The Moors and the French fought bitterly for such prey between 1840 to 1855. This period of internal weakness was also marked by the reign of two powerful *linger*, Njómbót and Ndate Yalla, who relegated *brak* Mó Mbodi Maalik, *Loggar*, to a subordinate position. Waalo, however, was no longer capable of resisting either the Moors or the French, and thus was no longer capable of maintaining an independent policy.

CHAPTER 12

THE END OF THE WAALO KINGDOM AND THE EVOLUTION OF FRANCE'S COLONIAL POLITICS INTO THE SENEGAL RIVER REGION, CA. 1840-55

This period, dominated by the two *linger*, Njómbót and Ndate Yalla, is characterized by a belated and futile reaction on the part of the traditional aristocracy against the French desire to conquer the country. The *brak* Mobodi Maalik's removal from political life, before the influence of the two *linger*, would lead to the political and social system's decadence. That in turn facilitated the 1855 conquest. But above all, customs fueled the quarrel between Waalo and the French trading post in Saint-Louis. France, wishing once and for all to rid itself of these now-expensive customs and to achieve unconditional control over the river trade, would not hesitate to use force. The leaders of Waalo were ever more desperate to retain this source of income that constituted their only strength in a country ruined by war. As such, they sought alliance with the Moors in order to maintain their assets. Consequently, French action essentially consisted of attempting to separate Waalo from the Moors, whose presence on the left bank both interfered with French trade and hindered French projects of colonial expansion.

The Evolution of Colonization Projects in Waalo and the Death of Njómbót

In 1819, the attempt at agricultural colonization in Waalo had generated great hope. Its promoters envisioned a second Antilles that would maintain France's commercial dominance. Upon the failure of agricultural colonization in 1831, the commercial activities of Saint-Louis regrouped around the trade in gum, ivory, and gold. Waalo, left to its own devices, would become the stage for multiple civil wars that facilitated the progressive invasion of the Moors.

This *de facto* conquest of Waalo by the Moors concerned the governors. They perceived that this domination of the left bank posed an impending threat to the commercial projects of France. As early as 1834, Quernel, who had just destroyed all the villages on the left bank so as to cut off Waalo from the Moors, said, "The circumstances are very much in favor of making Waalo a French colony…The black populations everywhere hounded are entirely disposed to line up with the stronger side, requesting only tranquility at whatever condition."[1] Referring to the Waalo's great wealth,

Quernel added, "the time has come when Waalo must pass under French or Moorish domination, and if we abandon it, our trade should expect numerous humiliations."[2]

Essentially, Quernel was wondering aloud if France should re-enact in Waalo what it had practiced in Sierra Leone, and he proposed to transform Khouma into a Liberia-like center of this new colonization.[3] 1835 saw the end of this war against the Moors and the Waalo-Waalo—a war that had seriously threatened the French position in the Senegal River. Its aftermath was the birth of vigorous colonial politics. In 1839, commercial concerns regarding the Jolof prompted Soret to grant more importance to the affairs of Waalo. He said, "With the current state in which Waalo finds itself, our commerce is of little importance, but I believe that it is of our policies to try and prevent the Moorish invasion. The Paniefoul Lake teems with millet and we may through this subject communicate with the Jolof."[4]

In his 1839 account, Monserat is more explicit about the economical and political reasons for the conquest of Waalo by Saint-Louis. Monserat, having lived without interruption in Senegal from 1822 to 1839, was well equipped to understand the errors of Saint-Louis' policies against Waalo, and to define new colonial policies. On this subject, he insisted that Saint-Louis heavily depend on its immediate neighbor, Waalo. The latter represented, by its geographical position, a backcountry indispensable to the former's commercial expansion.

In assessing the war that Saint-Louis had waged from 1833 to 1835 against the Moors and the Waalo-Waalo, Monserat remarked, "It has in no aspect changed the State of Senegal; all the treaties have remained to the advantage of the Moors and the ruin of the Saint-Louis inhabitants, as in the past."[5] He then recommended that the government either annex Waalo to Saint-Louis or "make it be governed by a prince devoted to our cause, whom he would link himself to by the means of a few monetary assistances, and would make him act as he wished; we know that in this kingdom, any job must be bought: with certain small sacrifices on the part of the French government, a prince capable of controlling the governmental reins would be helped, the currently divided parties would be reunited, harmony would be restored, the emigrants who are still dispersed in the neighboring kingdoms would be drawn back, and this kingdom which is as of now a desert would be repopulated."[6]

Monserat felt that the threat of Moorish domination over the two banks should be pushed aside, "as we would lose all the fruits that we are to collect from this country and from the powers that border it, or we will commit to an unending war, if we wish in the future to put our interests in these kingdoms to profit."[7] These conditions would require maintaining several authorities in the Senegal River, building forts in Kemne and Ronck, restoring the royal domicile in Faf, and reinforcing the Richard-Toll and

Dagan garrisons in order to protect the Waalo-Waalo. Then they could devote themselves to cultivating the prosperity of Saint Louis's commerce. The Waalo could provide the Saint Louis's commerce with an opening to neighboring kingdoms, and guarantee the development of new commercial branches.

Moreover, Monserat warned the Saint Louis inhabitants against gum or rubber "fever": "Let us expect anything from time: one day it will be felt that the rubber trade cannot suffice anymore, and we return to indigenous cultures that have always constituted the true prosperity of a country."[8] Monserat's plan would increasingly influence the policies of Saint Louis in the Senegal River. In July 1842, however, Pageot complained that the French authorities constantly lacked the means to assure predominance on the ground, both immutable and profitable, to the development of metropolitan trade.[9] He recommended that France use force to impose its will. Pageot was then replaced by Bouet, who was to inaugurate the new policies of conquest. On October 23, 1842, Bouet announced the construction of a new, fortified trading post in Meringahen—in the heart of Waalo—to extend commercial relations.

The vision for this project dated back to 1789. It had become a necessity because, as Bouet remarked, "…the foundation of Meringahen must operate a revolution in our transactions."[10] The building of the Meringahen station provided an early hint of the austerity measures directed at Waalo. The speech given by the officer who came to inaugurate the Meringahen station echoed the French authorities' conception of the May 18, 1819 treaty. Addressing the *brak*, he said notably, "According to our treaties, you have conceded to the king of the French, with absolute ownership, portions of ground that would be fit for the founding of institutions. The lands located near Meringahen on the Paniefoul lake have been chosen to this effect by the governor, we come delegated by him to plant there the French pavilion and claim possession in the name of the king."[11]

From that point on, the desire for conquest at all levels was clearly expressed. In a March 16, 1843 letter to Caille, the governor wrote, "Since our taking over of Senegal, the efforts of many governors have aimed to maintain our domination over the regions of the left bank, the reading of treaties demand that we deliver them this justice. As such, I do not think this a new idea, but the means to action have thus far been insufficient to my predecessors in order to successfully establish their domination beyond the banks of the river. Luckier than them, I hope that within the end of the year the country's military organization will have been granted to me according to my vision, and that our intervention may be felt on this riverbank."[12]

After centuries, the policy of buying the collaboration of leaders through traditional payments ended. The governor continued his argument in favor of conquest by noting the possibility of pursuing peanut cultivation in

Waalo; peanuts would later become Senegal's prime source of wealth. "Our political and commercial interest thus presents the blacks of the left bank as our natural allies, and their lands as one day to be under our authority. This is what had been foreseen in their treaties with Schmaltz, Le Coupe, Jubelin, Brou, Quernel, although they were forced to make do with stipulations less developed than they would have hoped, owing to their humble military means."[13]

He thus expressed France's henceforth irreversible desire to conquer these countries by arms. Even as the agreement on this objective of conquest was formed, two trending justifications for the "necessary" colonization of Africa were being sketched. Ever since the suppression of the slave driver treaty, Europe had been casting a new look on Africa. It had abruptly discovered the nefarious effects of this Atlantic trade. Faced with its need for commercial expansion, Europe then looked for means to mitigate slavery's consequences by eliciting African participation in new commercial exchanges, through the production of raw materials. However, for certain colonization theoreticians, the pessimism regarding the success of this enterprise was so great that they felt the Africans were irremediably condemned to stagnation.

Pichon, who wrote in 1823 a lengthy account about the Senegal colony, represents this school of thought. He remarked that for two hundred years, Africa had made no progress, and added, "I am not at all of the opinion of people who think possible the civilization of these negroes of Africa; I think on the contrary that this race will never change, neither by the use of persuasive means nor by the sight of our European arts and products. They will be able to desire them, but the majority will never wish to subject itself to fulfilling the conditions necessary to obtain them, as it would require changing certain traits of their character, and that is what seems impossible. If the European cannot trigger this revolution by gentle means, it would be even less feasible by force? There is little doubt about that. As such, I maintain that neither the French nor the English will ever succeed in bequeathing them the qualities and inclinations required so that they may become liable to make themselves useful to the universal society of their own initiative, and thereafter contribute to the general good."[14]

Pichon even asserted that he saw the rebirth of the slave trade with indifference, because the "intensity of the negro's laziness and insouciance, the gauntness of his intellectual faculties and the rooting of his prejudices" constituted an obstacle so invincible to their civilization.[15] This pessimistic train of thought would simultaneously justify the exploitation of Africa and lead to the racism that many colonists harbored after the colonial conquest.

Those in the other school of thought believed that the Atlantic slave trade had been the principal obstacle to progress in Africa, and that its effects still handicapped the development of trade. Looking for causes of the Senegalese commerce's languor, De Moges remarked in 1841 that "we want to extend the commerce and there exists around us nothing but coarse populations subjected to the worst condition of misery on this earth: anarchy, devastation."[16] Trade would have been in better shape, he added, if Europe had worked for two centuries to integrate Christian civilization into the Senegalese borders: "We came there to find men, and then a few cargo loads of rubber and secondary items. The time has come to strive to do better, and to work for the future."[17]

The notion of imposing European civilization on Africa in order to ensure commercial expansion was thus sketched. The Prince of Joinville vehemently defended the Christianity, commerce and colonization trio in a November 1843 letter. He wrote that "three centuries of shameful traffic have fixedly introduced barbarism, but a day will come when trade will enable the penetration of civilization, healthiness will emerge of the latter's efforts, and then an immense market will open itself to the Old World's commerce, a market rich in gold, ivory, oil, and ignored products. Such is the future of Africa."[18]

Comparing the enterprising spirit of English commerce to the impotence of the French commerce, he urged France to follow its rival's example by increasing its bearing points in Africa. He invoked, for the first time, humanitarian arguments to shake French commerce out of its stasis: "Let us not forget that there are in Africa things other than commercial interest to pursue, there is also a work of reparation, and France, so fertile in generous inspiration, could not fail at this mission. It must bring to it the support of its commerce and its missionaries, for Africa is to be regenerated; if this regeneration makes its way into providence's sight, it is Christianity united with commercial progress that must be its instrument."[19] In this way, the Prince of Joinville largely explained the views of this trend as opposed to the first. It would to lead to colonial paternalism. In both cases, racism and paternalism justified the same goal: looking for the best means to restore the peace necessary to better exploit Africa's wealth. All agreed that colonial conquest was increasingly necessary to guarantee the security and the commercial expansion of Europe.

In pursuit of that goal, the governor, lacking any means to guarantee the protection of the Merinaghen station, was compelled to sign a treaty with the Trarzas on October 15, 1843. The treaty's stipulation was to respect the establishment.[20] Consequently, Bouet proposed in 1845 a plan of action to the minister, meant to definitively impose France's dominance on the Senegal River. The plan's components sought:

1. "To tolerate no band of Moors in an expedition of pillaging the left bank."
2. "To place sooner or later Waalo under our direct sovereignty, and to divide it into four counties of which the county towns would be Dagana,

Richard-Toll, Merinaghen, Lampsar, governed solely by our agents, and to this counties, link Gandiole and the salines including Dacarbango and the Fours-a-Chaux: To make of this kingdom the refuge of all the subjects ill-treated by their leaders and to encourage agriculture and the breeding of animals there."

3. "To work for the dismemberment of Fuuta…"
4. "To progressively reduce and suppress as soon as possible the state customs regarding the Moors and the black leaders."
5. "To proportion the quantity of commercial customs with the executed slave trade and not with the boat tonnage. To not exaggerate the objection to use of force; besides, more results will be obtained simply by the policy of division."[21]

His project approved by the minister, he then proceeded to create a board of external affairs for Senegal. Caille was named director of external affairs and his duty was to ensure the implementation of the colonial policies—all the more so considering that Waalo had not ceased to cause trouble for Saint-Louis.

After all, Waalo were quite familiar with economic, political and social instability. The permanent disorder that the land harbored would lead to periodical pillages—at the expense of the Saint-Louis merchants. That is why, on October 14, 1841, the governor announced the seizing of 21 cattle in Lampsar, which triggered the repression of all customs.[22] The insecurity was so extreme that the governor signed, on October 28, 1844, a convention with Njómbót in order to regulate the free transit of herds heading to Saint-Louis. Thomas documents that for some time, criminals led by Biram Sey, captive of the crown, would detain and rob the travelers. Biram Sey was arrested and shot, and the 700 oxen were returned to their owners. Thomas did not fail to specify that he owed this excellent result to the presence of his "little boats."[23]

In Waalo, Mo Mbodi Maalik was *brak* in name only, "having neither the will nor the energy necessary to prevent the evil subjects of his country from pillaging or ransoming the foreigners who traversed the country in order to reach Senegal, it is to the Princess Njómbót who governs *de facto* that the colonial authority must address itself to when it has reclamations to make or the reparation of certain prejudices to ask."[24] Queen Njómbót ruled over Waalo with the support of the *ceddo,* whom she still could not control. She died in September 1846 from a chronic chest disease.[25]

The Linger Ndate Yalla Rule and the Conquest of the Waalo by Faidherbe in 1855

Amadou Wade tells us, "at the death of Queen Njómbót, it was her sister Ndate Yalla, married to *maaroso* Tasse, who replaced her in the charges she was occupying close to and often instead of *brak* Mbodi Maalik, a flat man of little character."[26] Caille, the director of External Affairs, had assisted in Ndate Yalla's coronation. On October 1, 1846, Olivier announced that Waalo was willing to forget the resentment caused by the second war, saying, "I have just made several presents to the principal leaders in order to link them to us and to be able to dispose of them in our favor."[27] However, echoing the policies of the Njómbót rule, the relationship between Ndate Yalla and the Saint-Louis station depended on regular tax payments and on France's ability to contain the Moorish invasion on the left bank.

As early as 1847, Ndate Yalla disagreed with Saint-Louis on the subject of the free passage of the Sarakolles, who supplied the island with livestock. In a letter to the governor, she expressed her wish to defend her sovereignty over Waalo: "We have wronged no one because the country belongs to us and we must govern it; it is we who guarantee the passage of livestock in our country. For this reason, we will take a tenth and will never accept otherwise…Saint-Louis belongs to the governor, Cayor to the *damel* and Waalo to the *brak*; each of these leaders governs his country as he sees fit."[28]

The resulting hostility escalated to the extent that France was losing the means to carry out its projects. The advent of the 1848 French Republic marked a clear step backward from its colonial expansion policies. As a result, this weakness cast doubt on France's control over the Senegal River and the ensemble of states—especially after the slave emancipation act, which provoked an acute reaction. It was thus that Ndate Yalla's 1848 intervention on behalf of the Trarzas—in the war against the Braknas and the French—tarnished the relationship with the Saint-Louis station. "A great number of Waalo-Waalo were assembled in Ndombo on the Tawe. Despite my threats to Queen Ndate Yalle, the Waalo army went on, led by prince Maaroso."[29]

Yet Waalo, home to almost all the operations that opposed the Saint-Louis station to the Trarzas and the Tukulors at that time, suffered all of the consequences of this war. On March 16, 1850, Protet said, "We can only make little harm to the Trarzas. Our principal victim will be the Walo. In siding with us, it will be pillaged by the Moors; if it sides with the Moors, the wrong will come from our side…The fear of the Moor will be greater than their fear for us, and consequently, in spite of what they might say, the Waalo-Waalo will side with the Trarzas in all the wars we could have with the Moors."[30]

At this time, a national party was formed in Waalo. It was led by the *maaroso* Tasse, a resident of Kajoor who opposed the Moorish presence. The *maaroso,* through his wedding to *linger* Ndate Yalla, had become the most influential leader of Waalo. In a March 11, 1850 letter, de Pallieres, leader of the Merinaghem station, tells us that the *maaroso* was the only man capable of effectively leading Waalo in lieu of the *brak* Mo Mbodi

Maalik. "Of foreign origin," de Pallieres noted, "he [the *maaroso*] arrived only by his abilities and his good looks; like all the soldiers of fortune he has a party devoted to him and he knows that his political existence depends solely on the whims of a woman, and that he has against him the vexed ambitions of old families."³¹

De Pallieres added that the *maaroso* loved power, and that he sorrowfully watched it slip away from him upon the death of the Ndate Yalla, whose health had been ruined by alcohol. Consequently, the *maaroso* looked to guarantee his succession by Sidia, "son of Ndate Yalla; his youth would allow him to keep the supervision authority over his affairs for long."³² For that goal he needed to eliminate Ely, son of Njómbót and Mohamed el Habib, whose status as legitimate heir via his mother guaranteed the Trarzas's possession of Waalo.

As such, Waalo was divided into two parties. The first had Ely Njómbót as its leader. The Trarzas "had taken too much care to make him a Moor. In loathing the low classes he plunders with impunity, he is hated by the leaders and the lazy, intemperate population of Nder, because of his haughty and imperial character, because of his inflexible rigidity, worthy of a marabout."³³ This party, which could be called Moorish, had several Waalo several dignitaries as its allies. Incapable of shaking off the Trarzas's yoke, these dignitaries took up a common cause with the foreigners. On this subject, the report of the administrative counsel noted, "Kangam race and that of the Sibb el Bawor, the great families and the country's dignitaries, after having tried multiple times and in vain to free the Oualo from foreign domination, had ended up accepting it entirely, and having lost all power and energy to stop the Moors from pillaging their subjects, they had associated themselves with the looters to have a part of their plunder."³⁴

The *marooso* constituted the second, national party. It was led by Sidia, son of the *linger* Ndate Yalla. "Sidi alone, neglected by the Moors who count him as a zero, reunites on his head all of the country's sympathies and the general cry of all is *Sidi Walo Reck* (Sidi only for Waalo)."³⁵ This *maaroso* party opposed certain dignitaries, namely the *beeco*, who was wary of the growing influence of a Kajoorien in Waalo. Indeed, speaking of the *maaroso*, De Pallieres said, "All that is young and brave in this country belongs to him by his frankness and generosity, all the honest people opposed to the exactions of the leaders are acquitted to him by his righteousness and his justice."³⁶ This soldier of fortune had succeeded in channeling the people's discontent with foreign domination, because the "*baadolo* class, that is the workers and the producers, was thus the only one to suffer from the Moorish yoke."³⁷

Saint-Louis, eager to steer its trade away from Moorish danger, looked to associate itself with the *maaroso*, who "would be the only man capable of hampering the Saint-Louis policies, if his interest and I would almost say his sympathy did not command him to serve them."[38] However, the progressively growing wish of Saint-Louis to conquer Waalo did not favor this alliance with the *maaroso* against Moorish domination.

As the pillages on the Saint-Louis inhabitants increased, the governor attempted to threaten Waalo by suspending taxes. Ndate Yalle, previously indifferent to this threat, refused to compensate the governor for the plundering of Meringhen. "They told me that they owed nothing, that they would pay nothing, that I had the right to hold all of their taxes, but at the same time, they said, it is peace or war. The war, they don't want any of it, but they want for all the French to leave their territory, they want to prevent all trade with Waalo, all straw or wood cutting in their country."[39] The hostility between Saint-Louis and Waalo was inevitable from then on. In fact, on October 10, 1850, the governor announced the suppression of Waalo customs in retaliation for the pillaging that leaders were allowing in their territory.[40]

Henceforth, Ndate Yalle spared no effort in provoking the French by making reclamations of all sorts. The Meringhen station was pillaged while Ndate Yalla was asserting her rights over Mboye Island and Sor Island, which she guaranteed having sold to no one.[41] The Waalo, deprived of customs payments because of the Meringhen pillaging, was ready for war. On August 2, 1850, Protet stated, "all the peoples surrounding us are hostile."[42] The governor was in a precarious position, because along with the weakness of his military, he was dealing with a crisis in the rubber trade.

On November 5, 1850, after Kajoor, Waalo forbade any trade in the backwaters of its territory.[43] Faced with this threat, Protet pointed out that war had become inevitable—despite the January 30, 1851 convention signed with Ndate Yalla to compensate for the Meringhen pillage.[44] Protet wrote, "War has become indispensable today, we will wage it sooner or later; it is better to choose our time, because I am convinced that you will give me the means to make it complete and successful against the Trarzas and the entire [Senegal] River if necessary. For it is the only way to secure our lasting influence and our trade on the River."[45]

A few months later, he specified that Mohamed El Habib was the great man of the river, with absolute command in Waalo, in spite of the treaties.[46] Protet requested several times the means to begin a rigorous policy, and announced in April 1852 that a vast campaign would be launched in 1853. The goal was to extract from the riverside populations the Podor establishment, the unity of customs, and most importantly, the influence he desperately needed to remain in force in the Senegal River.[47] Previously, in 1851, the Senegal traders had addressed "to the governor of the colony a petition to complain of the intolerable situation they suffered because of the exactions and the robberies of the Wolofs, Moorish, and Tukulors natives. They asked that by a vigorous effort, he would have put an end to this state of affairs, were the trade to suffer for a couple of years. They asked especially for the suppression of short-stops and for their replacement with permanent and fortified trade establishments, one in Dagana, the other in Podor."[48]

Protet left Saint-Louis for Podor on March 18, 1854, firmly intent on becoming the feudal lord of the Senegal River. The Podor expedition was quite successful. The fort was reconstructed in less than a month, thanks to the ingenious captain Faidherbe, who had scattered the Tukulors in a relentless battle at Dialmath.

The second French Empire, which had succeeded the second French Republic, from then on had the clear objective of resorting to force. Protet, who eventually dropped his conquest program, was blamed for his inactivity and replaced in September 1854 by Faidherbe. Faidherbe used force to secure the territorial expansion of the Senegal colony. Even during his nomination, Faidherbe hammered away at Waalo. He understood that the fort in Podor in the high country would imply, first and foremost, the conquest of Waalo in the lower river and thus secure his civilian zone. Faidherbe, well-equipped to execute his policy, led operations against Waalo in 1855. The goal was to thwart the danger that Ely, son of Mohamed El Habib and Njómbót, would succeed Ndate Yalla as the head of the country. The Moorish hold over Waalo was such that Faidherbe said, "Asking the Trarzas to give up on Waalo is like telling France to evacuate the Lorraine and the Alsace."[49]

Facing the danger posed by the fact that the leaders of Fuuta had met with El Hadj Omar, already established in Bakel, Faidherbe decided to wage all-out war against the Senegal River kingdoms. "We want to free the trade of all constrained charges…Everyone must recognize that the [Senegal] River is ours and that we have nothing to pay to anyone in order to travel through it and stay there…We want to make the states of the left bank independent of the Moors…I will attempt the execution of this program with what I can find…We will try to take some millet and oxen from the enemies."[50] Waalo, already having long suffered from being the front door to Saint-Louis, would become the first to suffer from this policy of conquest.

Following the general uprising of Waalo, Faidherbe left Saint-Louis on January 31, 1855, with a retinue of 400 men. On February 25, 1855, the retinue entered the Diubuldu region, in confronting the united Moorish and Waalo armies. Waalo was defeated at the edge of the woods that needed to be crossed in order to reach Nder. This village was plundered and burned. In ten days, Faidherbe, in a bombardment campaign, had taken 2,000 oxen, 3 camels, 50 donkeys, and 150 prisoners after having burned 25 villages. Waalo was conquered. Ndate Yalla, last *linger* of Waalo, took refuge in Kajoor.[51]

Faidherbe thus became the military overlord of Waalo. In a March 1, 1855 letter, addressed to the Waalo leaders taking refuge in Kajoor, he said, "If you persist in staying united with the Moors and in holding Ely as your leader, it is useless for you to return to your country and construct houses or sheds, for I will go and burn them. It is also useless for you to harvest millet, for you will not reap it. I have told you this and I repeat it, Waalo will be separated from the Trarzas or it will remain deserted."[52] Amadou Wade says that "the *brak* Mo Mbodi Maalik and the main dignitary leaders of Waalo, accepting the defeat (*ndaq*), but being reluctant to stay, after what they thought was a humiliation, in a country where they had known only honor and glory (*teranga ag ndam*), exiled themselves to the Fouta."[53]

On March 25, 1855, Faidherbe again wrote to the minister to inform him of the results of the second expedition, which aimed to settle things in Waalo once and for all. The despairing leaders had attempted to secure themselves in Diagan near Meringhen. But they were completely defeated; with the exception of the villages occupied by the *Dios* royal family, Waalo was completely deserted. The Waalo-Waalo had fled to Kajoor and the Moors had escaped to the right bank.

Faidherbe now sought to install, in Waalo, a national party favorable to the French presence. Before we examine the initial attempts of this nature, let us determine the deeper causes and consequences of the French victory in Waalo.

Causes and Consequences of the Conquest of Waalo

The extreme weakness of the traditional aristocracy, eaten away by internal quarrels, facilitated the conquest of Waalo. Now, France's hunger for colonial expansion, established in Saint-Louis, was irreversible.

As we have seen, an economic, political, and social crisis dominated Waalo's history in this first half of the nineteenth century. The constant state of war heightened the insecurity and favored the *ceddo* warriors' dominance as rival aristocratic clans constantly struggled for power. The support that Saint-Louis consistently gave the *Dios meen* family caused the *Teejekk* to seek an alliance with the Moors, who had completely subjugated the country. The *maaroso* Tassé's attempt to rebuild a national party after 1850 failed due to this Moorish presence—supported by a number of dignitaries, angry at being robbed of their power.

Amadou Wade competently evokes this hostility of the traditional families toward the *maaroso*, who was considered a foreigner in Waalo. Wade wrote, "The Maaroso and his wife angered many. They bought off the kingdom's main dignitaries, which, since Njaajaan Ndiaay, were obtainable only by birthright (*deret, moo daan tax, nit jot ci*). The Kangam's competition (*xëcco*) ultimately discouraged those who were managing these accounts, legitimately. The disorder born of this discontent (*mer*) and the *brak*'s inertia (*néewal*) were at their worst when the general Faidherbe presented himself at the head of his troops."[54]

This allusion to the political crisis through the oral tradition does not do justice to the *maaroso*'s effort to liberate Waalo from the Moorish yoke. This attempt was also unaddressed in Pinet-Laprade's observation, when he was sent on a mission to Ndate Yalla in November 1850. Realizing that the queen had isolated the majority of the dignitaries from power, he now only felt hostility toward Saint-Louis. Pinet-Laprade wrote, "My opinion of the Queen of the Walo whom I have seen in Nder is that she is our enemy."[55] But the *maaroso*'s failure to free the country from the Moors' grip accentuated the division. This happened during the political crisis, which was the fundamental cause of Waalo's conquest. Faidherbe noted:

> Waalo was *de facto* conquered....The warriors of this country formerly so proud and contemptuous of the Whites had not opposed so great a resistance....The *jambuur* (free men) designated by the name of *seb ak bawor* reluctantly served a government that had pushed them away from any position. The *baadolo*, mere particulars, continually pillaged by the Moors and the leaders of the country, had long been discouraged and had lost all energy....The *jaam gallo* (captives of the crown), were the only ones along with the Moors to have a vested interest in defending the Ndate Yalla government, and were little more than great bandits deafened by a constant intoxication, in which they indulged in the queen's company. Used to armed pillaging, they were nevertheless liable to show courage in certain circumstances."[56]

Faidherbe had perceived the reasons behind Waalo's weakness, which facilitated the chronic lack of resistance to conquest.

Yet this internal weakness only accentuates the fact that Saint-Louis's wish to colonize Waalo constituted the fundamental cause for the country's conquest. Waalo, already plagued by so many civil and foreign wars, was in reality only the first victim of this process of colonial conquest; the entire African continent would be colonized a few years later. By 1855, the French desire to conquer in the name of commerce was clear. Faidherbe, the craftsman of these policies, set the tone in instructions left on June 12, 1856, to the temporary governor Morel: "You know that what we have undertaken here is an entire resolution. From nothing, we want to become everything. It is only by war that we have been able to set out towards this goal. As such, we wage war everywhere, and aggressive war in the [Senegal] River to take down an authority that was stifling us, and in the High River, a defensive war against the fanaticism that wishes to drive us out of the country."[57]

The opposition of the river states against conquest was a universal function of the power and of the internal cohesion of their societies. Waalo, internally weakened by a triple economic, political and social crisis, posed no significant resistance to Faidherbe's cannons when he appeared in front of Nder in 1855. From December 1855 onward, Waalo's status as first French colony in Africa affected the south of the Sahara desert and created a breach. Like an oil stain, this would spread to the neighboring kingdoms.

Before we conclude, let us address the initial consequences of this colonial administration. We can justifiably consider Waalo as the testing ground of French colonization. A few years later, the methods would be propagated by European powers throughout Africa, leading to its segmentation.

CHAPTER 13

THE ESTABLISHMENT OF COLONIAL ADMINISTRATION

Promptly after Ndate Yalla's defeat, and even before the end of the military operations, Faidherbe began attempts to structure the new colony. He still faced the resistance of the traditional aristocracy, which had fled into the neighboring countries. More importantly, he faced opposition from the Moors, who did not immediately relinquish sovereignty over Waalo.

After the second expedition of March 14, 1855, which had forced the last resisters to abandon Waalo, Faidherbe immediately planned to reconstruct a national party that supported the French presence. But Waalo was barren: the *ceddo* warriors and the great dignitaries were fomenting opposition to Saint-Louis. The people, who had long endured the Moorish yoke, allied themselves with the traditional aristocracy and were hesitant to accept new masters. "When I ask them to join themselves to us, the Waalo-Waalo reply that in six months we'll have abandoned them to the vengeance of the Moors as we did in 1835."[1] The death in April 1855 of Binier Diaram, considered the best warrior, provoked a strong reaction in Waalo—without necessarily attenuating the resistance.

Ely had refused to follow his father, Mohamed El Habib. He met with his aunt Ndate Yalla in Nimb, and according to Faidherbe, "it is his presence only and the fear he still inspires which prevent the whole of Oualo to come seek peace, accepting all of our conditions."[2] Faidherbe then summoned from Kajoor "Fara Penda Aram Guey of a great Oualo family which had always sided with us during the ancient wars. Fara Penda abandoned by us like her father and brother to the peace which succeeded Mr. Quernel's war found refuge in Cayor. He has answered my call and it is by his means that I strive to reconstruct Oualo."[3]

In June 1855, Faidherbe announced that his followers were growing strong. He started to take action in Waalo; only the three villages of Tieden Ngad and Ndimb, in the heart of the country, remain occupied by his enemies. "Eli only resists and stands firm. He holds Ndate Yalla prisoner so to speak, and has driven out her husband, Maroso, who has returned to his country of Cayor."[4] In response to this Moorish resistance led by Ely, Faidherbe organized a final expedition on June 25, 1855. He aimed, once and for all, to put an end to Waalo and the Trarzas. He planned later to take advantage of the flood waters and vanquish the Fuuta and the Galam. He led his 1,100 men into Waalo, once again deserted by the Moors and the Waalo-Waalo. After having burnt some forty villages, Faidherbe did not spend much time gloating over his victory. He came to deplore the result of his military action, which had only ruined Waalo: "You could have said that we were like the bear in the fable who, in order to free his master from the fly, knocks him out with a rock."[5]

Yet, he had nevertheless succeeded in imposing himself as sole master of Waalo. As soon as December 1855, he declared Waalo a French territory. The governor would be the supreme chief of this country—henceforth partitioned into four small territorial districts, each managed by an indigenous chief appointed by France.[6] Dagana, Richard-Toll, Merinaghen and Lampsar became the administrative centers, with each district under a "circle commander." In order to consolidate his position, Faidherbe declared Ndate Yalla the *linger* and her new husband the *beeco* along with five other chiefs of Waalo—all of whom were devoted to Mohamed El Habib and excluded from the country.[7]

However, all these measures did not hinder the Trarza opposition to the French takeover. On May 7, 1857, Faidherbe wrote Mohamed el Habib, reasserting his intention of keeping Waalo: "As for Oualo which we bought in 1819 and conquered in 1854, we'll retain it in spite of all."[8] The Trarza opposition received staunch support from the captives of the crown, or *ceddo*. They refused to accept the new French order, whose authority threatened their ancient privileges. Faidherbe wrote a March 13, 1858 letter to Nagato Fall, the *ceddo* leader. Faidherbe, who had adopted the title of *brak* of Waalo, attempted to convince them to join him: "You know that Waalo is mine and that there remains no other *brak* than me today. As such, you are my captives and must obey me. Here is what I want you to do. You must return to Walo with your families and restore the villages in which you lived before the war. With this condition, I will grant you liberty and you will live in Walo as Diambours. The old *braks* needed captives who worked for them because they had no other riches. I am powerful enough and rich enough to manage and grant you freedom. But for that, you must return to my country."[9]

Faidherbe was gravely mistaken in thinking that the promise of changing the servile condition of the *jaam* to *jambuur* (free man) could entice these *ceddo* warriors, who had been the chief supporters of the *brak* regime. The civil wars and insecurity had increased their power. The *ceddo* warriors had become the prime beneficiaries of the *brak* regime through pillaging, regardless of their traditionally servile status. Upon their refusal to return to Waalo, Faidherbe declared an all-out war on the crown captives in a March 20, 1858 letter: "Since you do not wish to obey me and return to Walo under my authority, I warn you that starting today I consider you my enemies. I will pursue you everywhere and wage war to all who grant you refuge. You claim that it is Ely who is your leader, well then, look to him for defense against me. Ely is a Moor who has done nothing but pillage and murder the Blacks. In siding with him you act like fools. You look like sheep that take a wolf to be their leader. You've already been the cause of the destruction of Walo, of Niomre, of Tarinde Mbirama, and I'll even go burn all the villages in which you'll have stayed."[10]

True to his vow, Faidherbe in May 1858 destroyed the village of Niomre in the Jambuur, where Sidia had taken refuge. This Muslim fiefdom refused to surrender. "Sidia is a despot, and a despot must only be handed to the one who entrusted it."[11] However, this resistance did not last long. On May 20, 1858, Mohamed El Habib, left bankrupt by this never-ending war, signed a peace treaty acknowledging the French sovereignty over Waalo. It moreover acknowledged the French protectorate in Dimar, Jolof, Jambuur, and in Kajoor. This treaty rang the death knell for the Moorish influence. However, it did not end the traditional aristocracy's resistance.

For a couple of years, Senegambia had once again become the stage for an important religious development—following the example of El Hajj Umar Tall, whose fame had spread beyond the borders of Fuuta. Since 1846, this leader of the *tijanya* sect had garnered numerous proselytes in Fuuta. During his second tour in 1858, he had deeply affected the country by making many of his compatriots emigrate to Kaarta.[12] His political and religious actions immediately sparked great concern in Saint-Louis. The fort saw, in Shaykh Umar Tal, a serious obstacle to the French expansion in the Senegal River region. His influence and propaganda had progressively reached the Wolof kingdoms—especially Waalo, where one could witness the concurrent, paradoxical mass adherence of the aristocracy to Islam. In a September 18, 1858 letter, Faidherbe notably wrote, "Our mortal enemy El Hadji, banished from Fouta, is going down to Saint-Louis and seeks to rouse Oualo and Cayor where we have already caught several of his emissaries, whom we've subjected to prompt and severe justice."[13]

Defeated by military might, the traditional aristocracy's adherence to Islam represented a way to oppose the French conquest. In 1858, the opposition now centered around the young son of Ndate Yalla, Sidia. The fight against the nomination of Fara Penda Aram Diey officially broke out. Sidia's supporters took up arms. The revolt, which started in the village of Bram, threatened to invade all of Waalo, and the goal became to liberate it from French domination. Faidherbe tells us that the *Teejekk* returned to Waalo after three years of exile, with the secret ambition to reclaim power. "Youga Faly, leader of the revolt, Madia Kohr and Biram Gaye, having been recognized by all as the instigators of the turmoil and having at multiple times shown themselves to be openly hostile toward us were condemned and shot immediately in the presence of a considerable public. The others were deported: Ali Tiam for two years in Assinye, Biram Sar for two years in Grand Bassam, and Biram Tiam for two years in Gabon."[14]

Faidherbe justified the severity of this repression by citing the great size of the insurrectionary movement. In fact, "this insurrectionary movement had reached troubling proportions and if I had not immediately acted against its leaders with the greatest vigor, it could have dragged down in one blow all the influence we hold over it."[15] The lesson was harsh, and Faidherbe thus discouraged any further sign of rebellion. Still, to avoid further dangers, he created a fifth district, Nder, to please Sidia's supporters. Moreover, Faidherbe tried to immediately place Sidia in Saint-Louis, so that he could be raised amongst the other children of Waalo leaders. He hoped that they would later on constitute an African elite that would act as an auxiliary to colonization: "It will be an entirely definitive result which will destroy any seed of revolution in the future."[16]

While Faidherbe progressively consolidated his power in Waalo by military force, France looked for new means and methods to perpetuate its new domination. Unlike Algeria, Waalo could not constitute a colony of populations. For this reason, the minister's February 22, 1859 dispatch defined the guidelines of colonial politics: "In general, the soil must be left to the natives. For the climate prevents any European presence. By their arms it must be cultivated and if our domination is to extend throughout the entire territory, which belongs to us, our occupation must be limited to the only items necessary to ensure the repression of banditry, the freedom of transaction, and the tranquility of the working populations. Their productions will be the object of a lucrative traffic for Europe."[17]

In other words, the country had to be organized to guarantee the security of the expansion of trade. This organization was to stand on autochthonous competition—the formation of which was to be assured at the hostage school in Saint-Louis. From December 27, 1859 onward, Faidherbe promulgated the new Waalo constitution in Wolof: "Oualo, conquered and managed by us, had need for a written law at the very least cursory, in the absence of its ancient institutions repealed by us, as incompatible with the new life conditions we are imposing on it.... This fundamental law has been made and we will publish it hereunder in the very language of the Oualo....It is not at all concerned with the internal life of the inhabitants, it leaves them with the complete liberty to observe their customs, it gives them only general policy dispositions and it limits itself to arming the public authorities necessary to repress crime, offences or any other abuses, under the superior supervision of an official designated by the governor, as commandant of Oualo."[18]

This preamble delineated an indirect policy of administration of Waalo. The publication of this constitution in Wolof demonstrated that France had not yet established the centralizing and assimilation-oriented politics that characterized the colonial era. This first sketch of an administration did take into account the particularity of the country and its language. Still, France encountered difficulties in the application of this policy preceding the total conquest of Senegambia. In fact, as long as there remained sources of resistance in neighboring countries, the deprived leaders of Waalo would always find a way to form alliances. They were determined to reclaim their societal status, and once again questioned the French presence. It was in this context that Sidia, who had been sent in 1861 to the Alger Lycée, would return to channel the opposition to the traditional aristocracy. He challenged their interests, which were increasingly more compromised by the political nominations of caste men or *cedda*.

In November 1869, Sidia led a general insurrection. He and his forces rejoined the Lat Dior forces to combat the French.[19] The governor, in a December 17, 1869 dispatch, acknowledged the failure of French domination in Waalo: "Waalo, fast abandoned, has let itself be imperceptibly carried away by clever leaders and waits only for a favorable time to shake off our authority and act as a link to our enemies of Kajoor and of Fuuta Toro. Insubordination is already on the general agenda, all the leaders who side with us have been abandoned by their people and one of the 'chef de cercle' ['county head' in the French colonial administration], circle leaders, Leon Diop (Sidia), haughtily declaring his intention to become once again sole master of the country, maintains a relationship with Lat Dior openly and publicly to all who are still submissive, just to act openly against us in spite of the exactions of the fanatics who wish, on the contrary, to combat us straight away and seize the moment when all our troops are absorbed by this war."[20]

Sidia, ironically educated in the French school, was the first nationalist to understand the implications of colonization. Thus he advocated the union of Kajoor, Waalo, Jolof and Fuuta—a united front to end the colonial conquest. But eventually, Sidia was captured under mysterious circumstances, and was deported to Gabon.

The opposition to the French conquest of Waalo had never ceased since the military defeat of 1854. Its different forms were analyzed in the board of directors' report of February 25, 1871. While they did not take up arms, Waalo-Waalo certainly used the force of inertia against the general abolition of their country's customs. "The most upset, and their number is considerable, have only hearkened to the advice of the marabouts' counsels and have converted to the Muslim faith not by conviction but out of spike and in some way in a mood of vengeance. Convinced of the dependence to which they have resigned themselves and unable to resolve themselves to abandon the country where they were born, they have found nothing better to do, to protest our authority, than to embrace the religion of the people who know only how to be our enemies."[21]

We have seen that the embrace of Islam constituted, on every level and especially for the nobles, defiance against colonial conquest. The country resisted the French authorities' attempt to govern it without the assistance of the traditional aristocracy, which the French wished to eliminate. The failure was resounding, considering that in spite of the traditional aristocracy's weakness, the nobles still retained a certain authority. In fact, no economic transformation had yet given way to a new class capable of transcending the society's traditional divide. "Fanatics for the prerogatives of birth, filled with a deep respect for the nobility, the people of Oualo aspire to see at their command a prince who is the legitimate heir of the power, because they know that with a prince, each will reclaim his rank, his hereditary post, and as much as they desire a chief whose birth calls to leadership, they submit themselves with revulsion, with anger even, to the authority of a man of the people, of a *baadolo*. Nobles and *baadolos* think themselves humbled, vilified in having to suffer the will of a chief who was long ago their inferior or at best their equal. These prejudices are strongly rooted and I think that they have not been well accounted for; they have been deemed unimportant, believed to be easily dominated and destroyed. Experience shows how mistaken we were."[22]

It is precisely for this reason that colonial politics consisted of using the old traditional aristocracy to govern the country, wherever it was sufficiently powerful to offset French authority. As such, Waalo's complete subordination would not occur before the military defeat of all the sources of resistance. Only then was the colony of Senegal formed. However, this subordination was widespread and marked by the mass adherence to Islam, but as an act of defiance against colonial conquest. The French authorities would consequently fight against Islamic influence, deemed hostile to colonization.

The threat Islam presented was described in 1871: "Today Amadou Sekhou establishes himself in Jolof...it won't be long before Jolof is lost without its resources. Oualo's turn cannot fail to come if we are not careful, as our interest is to support, to maintain in their dispositions the peoples naturally hostile to the Muslims who are our only true enemies."[23] However, noting that non-Muslim populations also opposed colonial conquest, we must add that the Islamic faith simply constituted one of many forms of Africa's resistance to colonization.

This experience of the French in Waalo is of historic importance. They tried out, on a smaller scale, the colonial administrative methods that they would later apply to the entirety of the conquered African continent. Most of the architects of these methods would gain experience during the war with Waalo. Above all, it is from the people of Waalo that the first African auxiliaries to French colonization would be recruited.

We must remember that the conquest of Waalo coincides with the economic decline of the Senegal River region, which for centuries had been the nerve center of Atlantic trade. Peanut cultivation, which would increasingly become Senegal's principal source of wealth, was established mostly in the south, in Kajoor, Sin, and Salum—with Dakar, founded as early as 1857, as an outlet. From then on, Saint-Louis would exist only in the memory of its past opulence. The Waalo-Waalo would perpetually await the promised profits of the unfulfilled dream of Baron Roger, who had striven to unite the two banks of the Senegal by means of a verdant garden.

LE MONITEUR DU SENEGAL
(TUESDAY, DECEMBER 27, 1859)*

Waalo, conquered and organized by us, had the need of a law written at least as sketch, in the absence of its former institutions, which were abolished by us, as they could not accommodate themselves to the new conditions of existence, which we imposed on them.

This fundamental law has been made and we publish here below in Waalo's own language.

It does not deal exclusively with the interior life of the inhabitants, it leaves them the entire freedom to follow their customs, it gives nothing but the commands of the general police and it limits itself to arm the chiefs with the necessary power to suppress crimes, any offense or abuse, under the superior surveillance of a functionary appointed by the governor as commander of Waalo.

LA ÉMIR NADAR TÔNAL TCHI OUÂLO

NGUÉELBEN OUAKH GUI

Ouâlo bel fou aldouna iem, français ko mom. Nit ou Ouâlo mhotay ou bour ou France laniou. Émir Ndar laniou ouar top, mom ki fi takhao ou bour France. Commandant ba fa Émir Ndar def, mou di deukke fa Taouey, mô di set réou rna ak di ko dioubbenti.

---

* Written in Wolof, this constitution is one of the earliest in an African language for an African society.

NIAREL DI

Ouâlo seddelé naniou ko, mou di djourom i tound; bou tia nek ak kélifa am bou Émir Ndar tanne.

Djourom i tound ioyalé, nio di:

Tound ou khouma, ki dalé fi Taouey bel Dagana, penkou ak soou, daléti fi dekh gui bel Djiolof. Kélifa ga Fara Penda.

Tound ou Ndiangué ki top ntak ou dekh ga, dalé fi Taouey bel Maka. Mom ki iem tchi bir Ouâlo fa Djeulleus ak mar ou gorom, ale mar ou djieus. Kélifa ga Fara Combodj.

Tound ou Ros ki tchi bir Oulllo, ki amé Tianaldé, iem, tia soou, fa mar on khassakh ak biti ndar; iem, tia penkou, tia tound ou nder ak tound ou fos, te tound ou Diangué fayté ko tia vet ou ganar ga; de na dem it bel Ndiambour. Kélifa ga Béquio Chakoura.

Tound ou Fos ki top guier, dalé fi sanente bel Mérinaghen, dadj fi tound ou nder ak bou Ros ak alle ou Mbounoun. Kélifa am loro Diao, rna nek tia diangou otas ia tia ndar. Malo Birahim Dir mo ko fâ saytoul.

Tound ou nder ki bolé Nder, Naéré, Temey, Sentch ou Beukkenek, Diobouldou, da Khalifa, bolé ak doun ou Djélaud. Kélifa-am Sidia; mom it manga fa diangou otas ia tia ndar. Ndiak Coumba roo ko saytoul, bel mou man ko saytoul bop-am.

NIAITEL BI

Kélifa tound ia nio iélif borom deukke ia, nio len di fal tchi bannekh ou Émir Ndar.

NIENENTEL BI

Diambour i Ouâlo iep, guennao ba kélifa tound ia ak borom deukke ia véyè, nio iem kep, ken guenou tia ken.

DJOUROMEL BI

Diambour bou deukke tchi Ouâlo dotou man nek diâm.

DJOUROMBENEL BI

Diàm bou Ouâlo mom, ken dotou ko man diay tchi léuen réou.

DJOUROMBENEL BI

Nâr bou amé gannay ouaroul doug tchi Ouâlo, té kélifa Ouâlo nio gaddou lou tia man am. Ndieg ià rek nio man diâr fou nek tchi Ouâlo; ouandé de naniou birel kélifa i souf sa lou di sen ion, ak naka niou day, ak lou niou seuf; guennao ga, kélifa ioyalé nio len gaddou.

DJOUROMNIATTEL BI

Kélifa i tound ia nio ouar toppetou la di ion, ak Ia Émir Ndar di santané; ouar naniou def la di atté ba, té di lou dioup; té niou téré, lou niou man, dog ion ak ntiatch tchi deukke ia. Niou khiir sen mbotay tchi mbey ak iar sen diour, ak diay ak diendou. Ouar naniou farlou, bou bakh à bakh, tchi lou di dolli sen mbotay ak sen alel i réou.

DJOUROMNIÉNENTEL BI

Aman ou kélifa i tound ia, mo di nittel ou lou di diogué tchi sen souf. Borom i deukke ia foukkel lanio diel tia sen nit i deukke, guennao ga niou diokh kélifa tound ia guenneoual ga. Kélifa i tound ia am naniou it djourom foukkel ou nag ak nkhar, ak bey iou di sam tchi sen tound.

FOUKKEL BI

Guennao bakh ioyalé, kélifa i tound ia oualla borom i deukke ia monatonniou ladj dara bel dara dtekh tchi sen i nit.

FOUKKEL BI AK BEN

Atté sey, ak ndono, ak mpacé, ak lou len nirou, khali iou kélifa tound oua fal tchi bannekh ou Émir Ndar, nio len di dogal. Khali ioyalé rek kélifa tound oua di fal, niom rek nio man sottal lef; serigne bou niou faloul atté am dou sottal dara.

FOUKKEL BI AK NIAR

Lou mel maka bôm, ntiatch ak nkor, mbouguel am ak iar am borom deukke ba oualla kélifa toud oua, oualla commandant Ouâlo, mba Émir Ndar sakh, sou réyé, nio ko amé.

FOUKKEL BI AK NIAT

Mbouguel ma nilé la démé:

Kou rey, mba ouor, mba satch amé gannay-am, dé naniou ko rey, lou ko moy, mou am lay.

Kou diâmel diambour tchi Ouâlo, mba mou diay ko, dé naniou ko bouguel mom it mbouguel ou rey.

Ienne togue iou, sen mbouguel nio di: dan mou fey alal, dan ou iaram, tetch caco bolé ak liguey, ak guenné réou sakh bel mos, mba bel diamano.

FOUKKEL BI AK NIENENT

Togne bou di ouaral de, kélifa tound oua ko atté tia kanam ou commandant Ouâlo.

FOUKKEL BI AK DJOUROM

Sou kélifa tound atté nit atté rey, bala niou ko rey taggou Émir Ndar.

FOUKKEL BI AK DJOUROM BEN

Émir Ndar rek mo man doggal atté bo guenné nit, iobou ko tchi ménen réou.

FOUKKEL BI AK DJOUROM NIAR

Kélifa tound sagne na itte kou togne bel tchi témer i sadde; ouandé borom deukke sagnoul vécou nitte i sadde ak djourom.

Togne bou niou di fey alel, borom deukke sagnou ko vècalé niar i deureum, te mou ouakh ko kélifa tound oua; kélifa tound it, defa dore tchi niar i deureum bei tchi fouk, té mou ouakh ko commandant Ouâlo; commandant mom it defa doré, sou dé dan, tchi fouk i deureum bel niément fouk, té iégueul ko Émir Ndar.

FOURREL BI AK DJOUROM NIAT

Aiel diou niou diel, seddelé ko djourom i tier: Benne ba borom deukke bâ ko diel, iar ia kélifa tound oua ko diel, iar ia tia dès niou diokhéko tia biro ba, niou def ko tchi liguey i bour.

FOUKKEL BI AK DJOUROM NIENENT

Sou kélifa feylo nit lou doul ion, de na ko dello, té de na fey lou day nonalé niénent i ion.

NITTEL BI

I nit iou top oul ion ou nâr, modi ion ou mohamédou, ken mannoul len forcé tchi nangoulo len atté alkhoran, sou niou bagné. Sen i kélifa sakh sakh nio len di atté sou lola amé. Nit ou Ouâlo hou mou man don, na top iou ou nâr oualla bou moo ko top, sou amlé ak kou nekke tchi ion ou toubab, deukke tchi Ouâlo, commandant Ouâlo mo len di atté, oualla mou diokhé affaire ba tia tirbinal.

NITTEL BI AK BEN

Bour France beuggue na béreb bou nek tchi Ouâlo guep am horom bou ver, bou niep kham; té kélifa ia ouar naniou ko dimmali tia lola.

NITTEL BI AK NIAR

Légui nek, souf sou niou beyoul ak sou niou deukkoul, bour ou France a ko mon. Souf sosalé lou tia hour ligueylo, dou diokhé foukkel.

NITTEL BI AK NIAT

Gour gou nek tia Ouâlo té di diamhour bou am nitte i at ak ben, de na amel bour deureum at mou nek, sou niou ko défé tia ndar, bel di ko fa ladj naka tchi réou i toubab iep.

NITTEL BI AK NIÉNENT

Gour ou Ouâlo gou nek gou am nitte i at ak ben, ouar na am fétal gou di tak. Nit ou Ouâlo gou mou man don, di diambour mba di diâm, amé gannay, ouar na diog hou bât ou Émir Ndar guibé. Ndégam ion la di dokh, de na len ouakh niata fan i dounde lanio djiélé tchi sen i keur.

NITTEL BI AK DJOUROM

Borom deukke mo di élif kharé deukke-am; kélita tound itam mo di élif kharé tound-am. Commandant Ouâlo, oualla office bou bokke tia biro, mba ben tchi kélifa i tound ia, kou Émir Ndar tanne, mo di élif kharé Ouâlo guep sou bolo.

NITTEL BI AK DJOUROM BEN

Lou nou fi défaroul légui, de nanou ko défar tia kanam, sou vokh am diké.

CONCLUSION

The history of Waalo from 1658 to 1859 constitutes a very interesting case study. It presents us with the internal evolution of an African coastal kingdom in relation to Atlantic and Saharan commerce. Indeed, Waalo and the neighboring kingdoms of Senegambia had experienced—ever since the founding of the trading post of Saint-Louis—an internal evolution linked to the fluctuations of Atlantic commerce, as it competed with the ancient circuit of Trans-Saharan commerce. Atlantic commerce favored the dislocation of Jolof; during the entire second half of the seventeenth century, the rise of military aristocracies in Waalo and Kajoor was dominated by the Atlantic slave trade. The defeat of the marabout Nasir Al-Din circa 1677, some years after the founding of the trading post of Saint-Louis, marked the triumph of Atlantic commerce over the former Trans-Saharan circuit. But the attraction of European merchandise promoted, in turn, internal dissensions and struggle for power. Thus, the war that pitted Bër Caaka against Yeerim Mbañik at the end of the seventeenth century originated through the pressure of the Moors of Trarzas. These Moors integrated themselves into the trans-Atlantic commerce through the sale of gum. They thus became, since the eighteenth century, a determining factor in the destiny of Waalo by occupying the right riverbank, which had been abandoned by the people of Waalo.

Waalo, once again a secondary zone in the Atlantic slave trade that benefitted Galam, served merely as a granary of millet, a source of fresh food supplies for the commerce of Saint-Louis. The *brak* became merely a gatekeeper of French commerce along the Senegal River. The customs, paid then to the *brak* and to certain *kangam* for facilitating the commerce, served as the root cause of the divisive politics of the different Saint-Louis administrators. The alliance of Brue with the *beeco* Maalixuri undermined, in 1724, the centralized authority of the *brak* Yeerim Mbañik. However, the successive rule of Yeerim Mbañik, Naatago Aram and Ndiak Aram—the three sons of Aram Bakar who represented the powerful family of the *Teejekk*—strengthened the power of the *brak*, who from then on was equipped with an abundance of firearms by the Atlantic commerce. These relative powers gave Waalo the possibility, in the second half of the eighteenth century, to profit from the civil war in Kajoor; it could now attempt to impose its hegemony on the neighboring states.

But the English, aided by the Moors, shattered that attempt in 1775. The power of Waalo was permanently reduced. It would experience, during that period, an upsurge of slave trading in its territory. This defeat, which was followed by a long civil war, resulted in the submission of Waalo to the constant domination of the Moors, who reaped many profits from the Atlantic commerce. This Moorish domination, which impacted all populations on the banks of the Senegal River, gave rise to the *toorodo* revolution of 1776. It attempted, in the name of Islam, to fight against the detrimental effects of the slave trade.

Fuuta eventually succeeded in freeing itself from the hegemony of the Moors, but it failed in its attempt to suppress their commerce. It also failed to forcefully convert the Wolof states to Islam, due to the existence of domestic slavery—and particularly the slave trade in the coastal kingdoms. Indeed, in supporting the war between the small military aristocracies, the commerce of Saint-Louis hindered the formation of great political entities that might have been capable of modifying the commercial connections. It is at the death, circa 1719, of Latir Fal Sukaabe—then serving as *damel* of Kajoor and *tagne* of Bawol—that Brue began defining the outlines of these politics of division. They would prevail until the nineteenth century. Brue, who had not benefitted from Latir Fal's excessive power, stated that "Above all it is necessary to prevent that both these crowns are not on the same head. The Company has felt the effects during the reign of Latir Fal Soucabe, it must not neglect to maintain the liberty which the people always had, that of having separate kings in order to conserve the equilibrium among the small princes. It will always be in the condition of providing the law to them, of preventing them from innovating anything, neither their customs, the tariff of the merchandise, nor the price of food, nor the liberty to interfere with waters or woods on their territories."[1]

Thus the commerce of Saint-Louis imposed its law on the states of Senegambia, either through the payment of customs to the aristocracy in power, or through force. In this context of perpetual wars, the slave trade—a secondary factor in that part of Africa—offered equally direct consequences and indirect disasters. The aristocracy waged internecine wars to procure European merchandise for themselves. This engendered anarchy and insecurity, and was unfavorable for productive labor. Three events—in 1674, following the war of the marabouts; in 1754 during the civil war in Kajoor; and in 1775 with the Moorish invasion—all came with famines, so widespread that people sold themselves to escape the hunger.

Aside from the introduction of certain tropical plants from the Indies and the Americas, no technical progress occurred to compensate for the losses—to the detriment of the productive forces that sustained Waalo. The economy retained its autarchic character, and the absence of commercial exchanges on a large scale contributed to the opposition to societal change. The Atlantic commerce did not contribute to any productive force. Rather, it gave rise to a military aristocracy supported by the *ceddo* warriors, which profited from pillaging. Islam, which triumphed in Waalo only after the colonial conquest in the nineteenth century, gave to those downtrodden classes an ideology that promised to liberate them from the aristocracy, which depended on Atlantic commerce. Thus, the Atlantic commerce's effects constituted a hindrance to all progress on the coast—and consequently, on the continent.

The appearance of the great kingdoms of ancient Ghana, Mali and of Songhai was, to a great extent, linked to the gold trade. Western Africa's trade radiated from its center, with Niani, Timbuktu, Gao, Oulata, Djenne and others serving as points of convergence for the caravan routes. From the fifteenth century onward, the diverting of the trade routes toward the coast provoked a crisis in Trans-Saharan commerce. It precipitated the decline of the Maghreb and the western Sudan. But on the coast, Atlantic commerce was not a factor of progress in these regions. They often remained on the edge of Trans-Saharan commerce, because the Atlantic slave trade was a factor of regression. The attraction of European merchandise to the coast provoked the collapse of great political entities everywhere. Examples include Jolof and the Deñanke Empire in Senegambia, where Atlantic commerce sanctioned a political breakdown and a return to anarchy. The political and economic consequences of Atlantic commerce were similar in the regions of Benin and the gulf of Guinea, where powerful military states like those of Dahomey and Asante replaced the smaller entities.

The gap between Europe, with its great expansion beginning in the fifteenth century, and Africa had always been significant; now it became further accentuated. At the beginning of the nineteenth century, the dominant commerce of an increasingly industrialized Europe imposed new relationships on Africa. Paradoxically, it was Europe that fought against the Atlantic slave trade; after the decline of the Americas, it hoped to make Africa the direct "periphery" of its maturing capitalist economy.

Because of its geographic position, Waalo was chosen as the site of the first attempts at agricultural colonization. The goal was to usher Atlantic commerce into an era of no slave trading. These attempts, between 1819 and 1831, failed because of the pressure of neighboring populations, the resistance of traditional commercial operators of Saint-Louis, and especially because of difficulties regarding the transfer of lands and the lack of labor.

This symbolized the defeat of the economic protectorate. Moreover, the agricultural colonization attempt accentuated the political, economic and social crisis of the preceding eras. The increase of customs provoked new internal dissensions. The civil war between the *jawdin* Madiaw Xor and the *brak* Fara Penda, who later fought from 1830 to 1835 against the *brak* Kherfi Xari Daaro, further weakened the traditional aristocracy. Responding to the political and social crisis, the former jeweler Diile Fatim Tiam tried to end the regime of the *brak*. In the name of Islam, which had made progress among the people, he attempted to establish a theocratic regime modeled on that of Fuuta. Despite his defeat of a divided aristocracy, Diile was defeated due to the intervention of Saint-Louis. However, agricultural colonization was defeated as well, and its collapse resulted in the abandonment of Waalo as well as Moorish domination. The marriage of Mohamed el Habib to *linger* Njómbót confirmed the control of the Trarzas over Waalo. The worried French searched in vain, until 1854, for a way to detach this land from Trarzas control.

The incapacity of Saint-Louis to hold on to the states of the Senegal River, and the increasing difficulties of its commerce, allowed the French to prepare, step by step, the conquest of Waalo. Such conquest was a prerequisite to the overall project of colonial expansion. Faidherbe easily conquered Waalo in 1855, because, as Henri Brunschwig says: "Africa was destroyed by the virus of the West."[2]

But one cannot believe him when he adds that "Black Africa was ready to surrender when it is taken."[3] Waalo did not surrender—it was seized through military force, because Saint-Louis demanded a safe territorial zone to assure the expansion and security of its commerce. In the final analysis, the fundamental cause of the conquest was the will of Europe to colonize, aided by the weakness of the African states. Remember that Waalo had been crippled for more than two centuries by a triple economic, political and social crisis. It epitomizes the disintegration of a coastal African nation, involved in Atlantic commerce, during many years after the military defeat and colonization by the French. One can say that France had wisely exploited the fundamental contradiction that existed between the traditional aristocracy and the rest of the population. The former relied on the *ceddo* warriors, while the rest of the people had suffered all the consequences of the interminable wars. The aristocracy rejected Islam, until the lack of national cohesion became a liability in face of the invader. That was also the case in Kajoor and in Jolof, where the resistance was much longer because of the adherence, at that crucial moment, of the nobles to the religion of the people.

Indeed, the internal revolution of Waalo during the periods of slave trading and of agricultural colonization was dominated by the weakness of its oligarchic monarchy. The centralizing power of the *brak* was constantly counterbalanced by that of the *seb ak bawor* and of the *kangam*. The resulting weakness was manifested in mass poverty and in the simplistic needs of the most privileged categories. These have been the fundamental features of aristocracies in Senegambia, resulting from economic stagnation over several centuries. As Pathé Diagne said, "The wealth is the granaries, of the herds and, of course, in the blood lines and the birthrights."[4] For this peasant-aristocracy, which had never entirely evolved from a society based on living off the land, material equality was a fact. The hierarchies of order remained in the early stages of development. Boubacar Ly suggests correctly, "the sentiment of honor defines an essential stimulant of the social dynamics."

The aristocracy in power dominated the history of Waalo; the *géwél* ("griots") sing of high deeds, but archives offer only traces of the connections Waalo maintained with the commerce of Saint-Louis. Poverty and the relative weakness of the aristocracy also came with tension and of contradiction at the core of the quintessentially in-egalitarian society of Waalo. The weak development of productive forces within the framework of an economy of auto-consumption attenuated the social conflicts.

There existed no landed gentry, in the Western sense, and the peasants were tied to the glebe. This explains the very strong tendency to cast the traditional African society as a model of social stability. But that is an illusion; the existence of a caste system did not constitute an element of stability. As Cheikh Anta Diop suggests, it is rather the sign of the stagnation of productive forces.[5] Except for the economic conditions, one cannot define the era as characterized by autarky. It is rather characterized by the absence of mercantile production on a grand scale, capable of scattering communal structures. Economic stagnation exists, but the exploitation of the peasants and the artisans equally affects the core of the system by way of the functions of the state.[6]

The slave trade sharpened the social contradictions, and formed the base of a productive and developmental regression. It was the primary factor in economic stagnation and the permanence of certain social structures. It affected the economic relationship with Europe and explains why the Europeans waged, at the end of the nineteenth century, a crusade against "barbarism" to justify their colonial conquest. We clearly see that the evolution of Europe's economic needs determined the diverse forms of occupation in Africa. For example, the French presence on the island of Saint-Louis was a response to the slave and gum trades of the seventeenth and eighteenth centuries. At the beginning of the nineteenth century, the suppression of the slave trade engendered attempts at agricultural colonization in the framework of an economic protectorate; the failure of these attempts precipitated territorial conquest. This conquest, which ushered in the colonial era, was borne of Europe's driving desire to make Africa the direct "periphery" of its capitalist economics.

As Europe traveled a direct path to industrialization, it increasingly needed raw materials for its factories that provided consumer products. Colonial imperialism at the end of the nineteenth century was a stark reality that resulted from the economic competition of the different European powers on the African coast. That competition existed ever since the Portuguese discoveries in the fifteenth century. The Berlin conference in 1884 was not, as one might claim, the starting point of the colonial conquest. It was simply one of the important chapters in the process of Europe's economic domination over Africa. The forms of domination varied according to the needs.

The annexation of Waalo gave France a strategic base right at the moment when the European powers prepared to engage in armed conquest of the African continent. The study of Waalo, this small kingdom at the mouth of the Senegal River, sheds a twofold light—on the evolution of the relationship between Africa and Europe, and on the internal dynamics of an African coastal kingdom. Waalo thus merits our close study.

POSTSCRIPT—1985

FROM THE AGRICULTURAL COLONIZATION OF WAALO TO THE POLICY OF THE DAMS: THE DESTINY OF THE PEOPLE OF THE SENEGAL RIVER

In 1819, France recovered the Senegal colony from the hands of the English. Henceforth, it attempted agricultural colonization in the kingdom of Waalo, at the mouth of the Senegal River. The new Governor of Senegal, Colonel Schmaltz, passionately defended this project of adaption to new economic conditions, created by the suppression of the slave trade. The governor described his project in a letter addressed to his minister on September 4, 1819:

> I have always carefully observed the lands that I have travelled through and I have never seen more beautiful, more suitable for great enterprises than Senegal. The riverbanks of Gange did not at all appear to me as more fertile than those of our River and I have not the least doubt that one could not achieve there all the cultivations that one would want there. Our project of agricultural colonization consists of introducing ourselves into a vast land, inhabited by several million people, to assign them to work through the advantages which they cannot find there without us, and to attach them there by gradual augmentation of their current needs, to direct them usefully for our interests through examples that attempt to perfect their agriculture to settle them imperceptibly under French domination.[1]

In November 1984, an entire century and a half after Governor Schmaltz, President Abdou Diouf presided over the conference of the chiefs of states and the government of the nation members of O.M.V.S. (Organization for the Development of the Senegal River). He opened the conference with an orientation on the development of the period "after the dams." In his opening speech, the president declared, "In a little less than four years the Senegal River will be totally and durably controlled. What a victory of man over nature! But above all, a marvelous adventure of that which will lead three nations to unite their energies in favor of a cause of which one can only emphasize the grandiosity and the generosity. Thanks to their obstinacy and their unwavering will to overcome misfortune, which was only a dream several years ago, [and] is now in the process of becoming reality for three Sahelian nations desiring to push back from their borders the specter of malnutrition and of famine."[2]

In the two remarks above, and over the course of a century and a half, one deals both with the Senegal River and the destiny of several million people who lived, for centuries, within a perimeter of 1790 kilometers—situated between the origin of the river in the mountainous massif of Fuuta Jallon, and its mouth at the Atlantic Ocean. After pondering the hopes and failure of Schmaltz's project of agricultural colonization, and the questions that provoked the speech of Abdou Diouf, we now must reflect on the destiny of this great Senegal River and on our profession as historians. We do so on the occasion of the reissue of our monograph on the *The Kingdom of Waalo* published about fifteen years ago by François Maspéro.

History does not precisely repeat itself. But in the case of the Senegal River, there is undoubtedly a certain historic continuity. It is necessary to recognize this continuity, in order to identify the dialectic connection between the failure of agricultural colonization at the beginning of the nineteenth century and the specter of drought and famine on the Soninke, Wolof, Moorish, Tukulor, Fula, Manding, Tenda, Jallonke, and Jaxanke populations. They lived for centuries along that great Senegal River, which is still the object of so many grandiose construction projects.

The destiny of the Senegal River is inseparable from the destiny of millions of people, nourished over the centuries by its waters, which facilitated agricultural activities of livestock farming and fishing throughout the entire valley. All these activities are now dangerously threatened by the drought, which has afflicted the region for about 15 years.

How did it come to this? Our monograph has attempted to answer this question. We could not find a full answer, due to the geographic limits of our study. It was limited to the kingdom of Waalo and hindered by the need for arbitrary divisions of chronology, which ceased in 1855 at the moment of colonial conquest. In this epilogue to our history of Waalo, we can say, "The conquest of Waalo coincides with the economic decline of the river region, which for the centuries had been the nerve center of Atlantic trade. Peanut cultivation, which would increasingly become Senegal's principal source of wealth, was established further south, with Dakar constituting the outlet market since 1857. From then on, Saint-Louis would exist only in the memory of its past opulence. The Waalo-Waalo would perpetually await the promised profits of the unfulfilled dream of Baron Roger, who had striven to unite the two banks of the Senegal by means of a verdant garden."[3]

This short excerpt was somewhat like running out of steam after having unwound, year-by-year, the three centuries of Waalo's history before its annexation by France. Nevertheless, we have tried to draw attention to the situation of neglect in the Senegal River valley. It necessitated ambitious construction projects to ensure that the populations, doomed until emigration, could feed themselves. The recent past, marked at the beginning of the nineteenth century by the failed attempts of agricultural colonization, merged then in our consciousness with the present. The present is dominated by the efforts of the riverbank nations—Senegal, Mali, Mauritania and Guinea—to establish an organization for the development of the Senegal River. But, alas! We did not have the time to evaluate the impact of the 150 years that separate the original agricultural colonization project from that of the great dams planned at the end of the twentieth century. This is despite the fact that we were fully aware of the dam's importance to the destiny of the people of the river.[4]

The Failure of Agricultural Colonization at the Beginning of the Nineteenth Century

As we have previously described, Governor Schmaltz was succeeded by Baron Roger, who, from 1822 to 1827, tried to realize the first grandiose project of development of the Senegal River. Baron Roger attempted to establish a powerful, groundbreaking colony to serve as an example for the rest of Senegambia. In 1824, he created the experimental garden of Richard Toll and launched a grand-scale experiment to cultivate cotton, indigo, sugar cane, etc. Despite his prodigious efforts, agricultural colonization was unsuccessful. From 1831 onward, Governor Brou carried out orders to liquidate the enterprise. This failure is due to multiple causes, which we will review once more.

First of all, the neighboring nations of Trarzas, Fuuta Toro and Kajoor swiftly formed a tripartite alliance against the French presence in Waalo. This created an atmosphere of insecurity that was unfavorable to the cultivation of plantations. Having failed to impose colonial peace on Waalo's neighbors, France signed a treaty on April 15, 1829, with the Emir of Trarza—Mohamed El Habib, the strongman of the river. In this way, France implicitly recognized the sovereignty of Trarza over Waalo.

The colonization also failed because of the difficulties that France encountered in the handover of territories. For France, the treaty of Ndiaw in 1819 constituted a legally documented purchase of Waalo's lands, realized via the payment of an annual tax to the *brak* and to other chiefs in the kingdom. But the inhabitants of Waalo expressed their opposition to French concessionaires through the war against the embankments.

Another factor in the failure was the lack of a workforce. At the outset, the French concessionaires, who had attempted to hire voluntary labor, continued to engage in the practice of the slave trade that had devastated the valley throughout the centuries.

Finally, the traditional commerce of Saint-Louis, consisting of small merchants and individuals of mixed heritage, opposed the arrival of large-scale capital meant to develop large-scale cultivations, because they wanted to preserve their monopoly over the traditional commerce of gum and enslaved individuals.

The failure of agricultural colonization is, first and foremost, the failure of the economic protectorate. This compelled France to conquer Waalo and establish a vast colonial empire in Africa. France attempted to organize an orderly system of production after militarily forcing the populations into submission. This is the beginning of the colonial era, which can only be fully explained by evoking the ancient history of the populations of the Senegal River—before and after the fifteenth century, during the apex of Atlantic commerce. Understanding this past is also vital in order to sufficiently grasp the reasons for the failure of agricultural colonization. It also plays a role in the problems that are now resurfacing regarding the development of the Senegal River and the regional integration of the four nations of Senegal, Mali, Mauritania, and Conakry-Guinea.

The Valley of the Senegal River: The Land, the People and their History

The valley of the Senegal River is, above all, a geographical framework determined by the union of the Bafing and Bakoye rivers at Bafoulabe. Encompassing an area of 1,790 kilometers, the Senegal River forms a large circular arc from the heights of Fuuta Jallon to the Atlantic Ocean, south of Saint-Louis. Its basin, which extends over 340,000 km2, is situated entirely in the northern tropical zone, characterized by the alternating of a rainy season with a season of drought. The river system is dominated by the climate, which increases in duration and severity according to the latitude. Thus the Senegal River, similar to the Nile in Egypt, constitutes the main factor in the livelihoods of the Wolof, Tukulor, Moorish, Fula, Soninke, and Manding populations. Centuries ago, these populations had delineated amongst themselves the territories of this valley. Diversity marks the populations, the landscapes, the patterns of relief, the vegetation and the methods of agricultural production.

The delta regions, particularly the Moyenne Valley, are influenced by the alluvial plain in the territory of Waalo. It extends some 21 km to Kaedi and the island at Morphil. The spread or reduction of Waalo cultivations are linked to the cultivations of the *jeeri*, which become increasingly random as they near the delta due to the weak pluviometry. In contrast, at the high river toward Bakel and upstream toward Bafoulabe, the alluvial valley gradually dries up again; it does not offer the populations any alternatives to the cultivations of the *jeeri*, which are favored by a great abundance of rain in the winter. The alluvial plain disappears almost entirely upstream of the Senegal River, in the hill country of Fuuta Jallon. There, the river originates at a height of 800 meters, northwest of the old capital of Timbo. The river imbeds itself deeply into the vast plateaus, made rugged by cascades and rapids. There, the extension of the rugged *bowe* considerably limits the extent of the cultivable lands of *hansanere,* or free soil, that accumulates at the foot of the escarpments of *dunkire,* the sunken valleys.

This diversity of landscape explains the diversity of settlements—and most of all, the diversity of types of occupation in the Senegal River valley, where the rainfall varies from 2,000 millimeters per year at the origin to 300 millimeters at the mouth of the river. The valley settlement is also the result of an ancient geologic history, testified by the industrial vestiges of Paleolithic stone, evidence of the Neolithic age, and the cluster of prehistoric shells. The Senegal River originates in the foothills of the massifs of Fuuta Jallon, which formed a refuge and an outlet at the same time. Fuuta Jallon constituted a crossroads for all migrations occurring from the interior toward the coast. The relative paucity of agriculture explains why this castle of water in West Africa quickly became a site for raising cattle, thanks to the existence of permanent watering places and grazable pastures during the dry season.

The Jallonke, of Manding origin, coexisted there for a long time with the Baga, Temne, Landuma and Nalu, who were pushed back toward the ocean by the arrival of the Susu and by the Pulli. The Pulli, Fula nomads, arrived progressively with their herds of cattle between the eleventh and fifteenth centuries from the Sahel, from the valleys of Senegal and Niger. The history of that massif is dominated, until the end of the fifteenth century, by the empire of Mali. It was then that the invasion by Koli Tengela upset the entire political equilibrium of this region. That preceded the conquest of the mid-region of the Senegal River valley, now Fuuta Toro, where he founded the Deñanke dynasty. The departure of Koli and his companions left the Kafu Jallonke under the domination of Kaabu from the sixteenth century to the beginning of the eighteenth century, at which point the Muslim revolution created the powerful theocratic nation of Fuuta Jallon. The power of the *almamy* consolidated throughout the entire massif, and extended progressively as far as the coast.

Thanks to its geographic position between Senegambia and the Sudanese hinterlands, the High River was successively populated, in superimposed levels, by the Soninke, Malinke, Bamana, and Xasonke. These ancient settlements are closely linked to the history of the western Sudan, which included the political, social and economic structures of ancient Ghana (Wagadu) from the eighth century onward, and of Mali in the twelfth century. Thus the Soninke, the Juula of the west, made the High River the commercial center of the ancient Ghana Empire. The Malinke farmers established themselves on the left riverbank in the wake of the empire of

Mali, until the sixteenth century. Finally, the Xasonke, the Manding-Fula combining livestock raising and agriculture, established themselves on the two riverbanks; they controlled the region of Gidimaxa in Kaarta until the Bamana invasion in about 1800. There, because of the limited acreage of alluvial lands, the appropriation of property did not constitute the basis of political life. It was characterized by the decentralization of power.

In the mid-valley region, political entities such as Tekrur had imposed themselves on the region until the founding, at the end of the fifteenth century, of the Deñanke dynasty by Koli Tengela. He gave Fuuta Toro a political unity and the durable foundations of its political, economic and social organization. The Deñanke regime consolidated the patterns of land appropriation, particularly in the rich alluvial plains, through the creation of land-owning and military gentry. The Toorodo revolution of 1776, which inaugurated a theocratic regime, superimposed itself on the Deñanke aristocracy in certain cases, and without notable structural changes. The *toorodo*-maraboutic aristocracy monopolized the largest portion of the lands of Waalo, thus ensuring until now the permanence of their political, religious and economic power. More than anywhere else, this is where the dividing of the lands lay at the center of all the political rivalries that shook Fuuta Toro. Despite these internal discussions, the maraboutic caste succeeded in retaining its privileges.

More than the Moyenne Valley, the delta belonged to the Senegambian substrata—where the influence generated by the Wolof Empire was of key importance since the twelfth century. Until the sixteenth century, Waalo remained a province of the Jolof Empire, which extended from the delta to the Senegal River to the banks of the Gambia River. There, as at Fuuta Toro, the appropriation of land was important factor in the history of Waalo. It was dominated, on the political level, by the place of choice granted to the maternal family's successive *meen*. This social matrilineal structure explains why women were assigned the right of inheritance to land; the *linger* possessed the greatest privileges.

The entire right riverbank, from the High River to the river's mouth, is marked by the influence of the Arab Berbers of Mauritania, who lived in the Chemama region. Indeed, the movements of the Arab Berbers toward the Senegal River valley regulated the history of Mauritania. But, until the Almoravid movement in the eleventh century, the history is also dominated by fierce struggle between warrior groups—Hassans of Arab origin—and the marabouts, or Zouaians of Berber origin. This fight ended with the victory of the Hassan warriors. From the end of the seventeenth century onward, after the war of Shurbubba, they founded the emirates of Trarza and Brakna. These two nomadic warrior powers progressively influenced the destiny of the Senegal River's two banks—first because of the importance of the gum trade in the framework of Atlantic commerce, and then through the Atlantic slave trade that dominated between the seventeenth and the nineteenth century.

The Burden of the Atlantic Slave Trade: The Exportation of the Producers

All states along the Senegal River were more or less subjected to the influence of the Atlantic commerce from the fifteenth to the nineteenth century. It completely upset their economic, political and social way of life. From the end of the sixteenth century, the slave trade became the principal activity of Atlantic commerce, which itself gradually supplanted Trans-Saharan commerce as a result of the victory of the caravel over the caravan. Until the nineteenth century, the Senegal River valley was dominated by Atlantic commerce. It decisively affected the internal evolution of the population's social formations. The slave trade undeniably constituted the fundamental element of Atlantic commerce during this period. The direct trade of human trafficking determined not only the relationships between the states of the Senegal River and the European powers, but also the political and social relationships within the states.

The commerce in enslaved individuals, and the subsequent war against the states, constituted a permanent element of this generalized violence. It established itself within each state as a struggle between the military aristocracy and the peasant populations, who were victims of the raids. The slave trade, which became a royal monopoly based on violence, hindered the peasant societies from concentrating on secure agricultural production.

In all domains, numerous famines marked the history of economic regression in the Senegal River states during this long era. The famines, due to wars as well as to natural disasters, emphasized the demographic drainage provoked by massive exportation of productive residents as enslaved individuals. Internally, the slave trade reinforced the inequality between free people and enslaved individuals. In this way, domestic slavery also became a component of Atlantic commerce. In Waalo, in Fuuta Toro before the Muslim revolution in 1776, in Gadiaga and in Xaaso, the enslaved individuals of the crown became arbitrary instruments of the powerful *ceddo*. But the entire valley was also the victim of raids conducted by the Moorish emirates of Trarza, of Bakna and finally the Sultanate of Morocco. This situation created a chronic atmosphere of turmoil, which hindered the formation of genuine slave production. Domestic enslaved individuals, free farmers, and even members of the aristocracy were victims of the raids. All were thus at risk of being sold as enslaved individuals.

This atmosphere of generalized violence progressively prompted the maraboutic party to organize itself for a fight against the arbitrary power of the *ceddo*. The fight would create the theocratic states capable of assuring the security and liberty of Muslims. Islam, already a strong presence in the valley due to the success of the Almoravid movement in the eleventh century, grew stronger within the Muslim communities. Muslim homes became centers for spreading Qur'anic teachings through the entire region. The maraboutic movement that developed transformed itself into a vast movement of holy war in 1673. The Moorish marabout Nacer Eddine led this war against the tyranny of the kings, who were engaged in the slave trade. This mass movement, which successively took control in Waalo, in Kaajor, in Jolof and in Fuuta Toro, was finally eliminated in 1677 by the alliance of the dethroned aristocracies with the trading post of Saint-Louis.

This defeat is nevertheless followed by the success of three glorious Muslim revolutions: in Bundu at the end of the seventeenth century, in Fuuta Jallon at the beginning of the eighteenth century, and in Fuuta Toro at the end of the eighteenth century. The new theocratic states succeeded at least in assuring the security of the Muslims, now protected against all danger of being sold as enslaved individuals. But at the same time, the slave trade continued to influence the economies of these new Muslim states.

For example, in the kingdom of Fuuta Jallon—safe from the external invasions since the success of the revolution of 1725—domestic slavery developed in direct relationship with the slave trade. The growth of the *rundes,* or villages of enslaved individuals segregated from free people, was meant both to satisfy the nutritional needs of the aristocracy and the demand for grain by slave traders' ships.

Similarly, in Fuuta Toro, the Toorodo revolution brought about domestic peace from the last quarter of the eighteenth century onward. Islam served then as an ideological basis for the cohesion of the maraboutic party. It promoted peace and wisdom, rather than the culture of drinking and violence of the *ceddo* nobles. The Toorodo organized themselves into landowners and masters of captives, but they banned the practice of pillage and effectively opposed the enslavement of Muslims. They divided all the lands of Waalo amongst themselves, and organized a land-lease payment system to replace the taxes, imposed by force at the time, of the Satigi. The peace facilitated normal demographic reproduction and thus attracted residents of adjacent regions, which had been destroyed by raids, famines and enslavement. Nevertheless, the domestic captives supplied the main portion of labor.[5]

Thus during that long period, slavery in whatever form constituted a fundamental economic, political and social factor in the states and the valley of the Senegal River. The system constantly adapted to the demands of the slave trade, which allowed for the exportation of a domestic workforce and resulted in the loss of labor at home. This demand largely hindered the evolution of domestic production into a form of pro-slavery production of the American or European capitalist type. The massive exportation of human laborers also eliminated the evolution toward a mode of autonomous production by enslaved individuals, despite the primary role of enslaved individuals as domestic producers in the theocratic states of Fuuta Jallon, Fuuta Toro, the emirates of Trarza and of Brakna—or in the army and the government of the *ceddo*, Wolof or Bamana states.[6]

During that period, war and raiding were the principal mode of surplus profit for a majority of these states. These activities spontaneously arose from the competition of kings and princes, eager to reap the profits of Atlantic commerce. These fights procured enslaved individuals for the slave traders, as well as the millet necessary for their sustenance. In this economic formation, slavery was the impetus for the work force, since the destruction of productive forces far exceeded the sole deficit of workers put into servitude. The devastation of fields and granaries provoked profound and lasting demo-economic instabilities, as well as frequent famines.[7]

The slave trade remained the cornerstone of Atlantic commerce between Europe, Africa and the Americas because of its key role in the accumulation of financial capital, which made Europe's industrial revolution possible. Consequently, Europe decided, during the nineteenth century, to abolish the slave trade in order to make Africa its direct periphery. The Senegal River valley now served as a dual source of human labor and the primary materials needed by a rapidly expanding European industry. This new phase was born out of the triumph of legitimate commerce, and most of all because of colonial conquest.

One now understands the importance of the failure of agricultural colonization in Waalo at the beginning of the nineteenth century. It preceded colonial conquest—the effective military, political and economic submission of the Senegal River social structures to France. France would impose its colonial-style peace on all Senegal River states during the second half of the nineteenth century.

The Colonial Conquest: Legitimate Commerce and Domestic Slavery

The colonial conquest of Senegambia began in 1854, with the acquisition of the Waalo area. It lasted until the end of the nineteenth century. During this long period of transition, France enlarged its colonial territory at the expense of the Senegal River kingdoms; Bordelese commercial establishments, occupied with the trade in groundnuts, dominated local economic life and stimulated the process of colonial conquest. Thanks to Faidherbe's efficient organization, these houses of commerce obtained the freedom of trade exchanges, the establishment of warrior aristocracies that collected the customs taxes, and the installation of trading posts along the Senegal River. The Bordelese commerce thus empowered itself to push aside the individuals of mixed heritage and African traders, who had been weakened by the gum crisis and the abolition of slavery. The conquest precipitated the destruction of the old social structure by eliminating the warring princes and their allies, replacing the old traders, and rebuilding forces of domestic production.

The colonial era of peace helped develop the simultaneous emergence of Bordelese commerce and a caste of free farmers. These farmers had been particularly weakened in the past centuries by the depredations of wars, but now benefited greatly from the full expansion of domestic captives. Crushed by force, the warring nobles only maintained their status via the new administrative functions they assumed. The traders were victimized by their sheer numbers, especially when facing the new forms of commerce and the remarkable business practices of the Moorish marabouts.[8]

Nevertheless, most of the valley experienced a long transition period before the definite emergence of new a dominant economy at the beginning of the twentieth century—the cultivation and export of groundnuts. From the delta to the Upper River, local growers now faced direct exploitation by capitalism, which at the same time upset the trading relationships between the Moors, Wolof Tukuleur and Soninke farmers. Ever since the failure of agricultural colonization, gum had again become the cornerstone of capital-backed commercial transactions. That was the basis for the original commercial relationships between the Moors and the Wolof farmers. With colonial support, Moors forcefully monopolized the gum harvest on the river's right bank. They also hoarded Wolof farmers' millet crops, in order to feed the very captives charged with that harvest.

Thus those with commercial interests intervened between these exchanges of gum and food, exerting control by deliberately refusing monetary transactions; that allowed for more effective price speculation in the Guinean currency. Since a Moor must use bartering to purchase his provisions of millet and imported products, he was tied to the trader who bought gum from him. In this way, the colonial state ensured the security and freedom of the commerce; it also elicited, through the institution of taxation, the farmers' participation in mercantile production while tolerating local enslavement practices.

Every entity paradoxically assisted in the expansion of domestic slavery in the entire valley from Bakel to Saint-Louis, whether because of the holy wars or because of the conquests that went on in western Sudan until the end of the nineteenth century. Despite the fact that slave trading had been repeatedly, formally forbidden in 1817-1848 and in 1901, the colonial powers favored and encouraged slave trafficking regarding areas generating exchange benefits. Domestic slavery developed not only to benefit the nobles, who maintain their dominant economic position because they owned land in Waalo, but also the farmers who acquired domestic servants. In 1904, the servile population was approximately equal to the free population in the Dagana region. Similarly, the recruitment of domestically enslaved individuals as a labor force enabled the colonial regime to fill its ranks for the army, for public institutions, and finally for the construction of railroads.[9]

The evolution is identical in the Fuuta Jallon region, at the source of the Senegal River. That theocratic state kept its autonomy until the end of the nineteenth century, far from the regions affected by the French conquest. But during the nineteenth century, legitimate trade progressed along the southern riverbanks that had been the main source of revenue for Fuuta Jallon products, as compared to groundnuts and coffee. That progress spurred the territorial expansion policy of this continental power toward the coast. Fuuta Jallon's dominating presence in the Rio Nunez and Rio Pongo, and its conquest of Kaabu and Upper Gambia, were the highlights of its political adaptation. It came to be the main supplier of enslaved individuals, following the economic imbalance between products of the coast and those of the interior.

The slave owners in the entire backcountry of Senegambia migrated toward the coast with their workforces, to devote themselves to the cultivation of groundnuts. That cultivation rapidly expanded between Sierra Leone and Gambia, prior to reaching future groundnut areas in the triangle of Saint-Louis, Dakar and Kaolack. But that expansion of Fuuta Jallon was blocked by the French presence. France consolidated itself on the southern riverbanks through the construction, since 1867, of the forts Boke, Boffa and Benc in the Rio Nunez, the Rio Pongo and the Mellakune, respectively. But it was not until 1896 that France undertook a veritable conquest of Fuuta Jallon, to assure the link between its territories in Sudan and those on the southern riverbanks. In the interim, Fuuta Jallon played an essential role as slave depot for the wars of Samori and El Hadj Umar, and for the French conquests in western Sudan. Fuuta Jallon traders purchased a tremendous amount of enslaved individuals in exchange for cattle, which served as currency to purchase arms for Samory and El Hadj Umar in Sierra Leone.

This massive concentration of enslaved individuals dates back to an era when their numbers sometimes surpassed that of free men. This abundant labor force enabled the local aristocracy and the free farmers to obtain more laborers for agriculture and for gum production, and increasingly replaced the groundnut industry on the southern riverbanks after the 1880s. Until the beginning of the twentieth century, domestic slave labor was the main source of revenue in Fuuta Jallon. During that new century, throughout the entire valley of the Senegal River, this practice was abandoned completely in favor of the groundnut industry.[10]

The Colonial Era: Migrations of Workers

At the beginning of the twentieth century, the conquest was almost over. Colonial peace reestablished normal conditions for reproducing the modes of domestic production, which had since been subjected to direct commercial exploitation. It nevertheless marked the beginning of a new era for all the Senegal River peoples. But it was not until the beginning of construction of large dams that they ceased to constitute an abandoned marginal region, outside the realm of colonial and post-colonial development. This long era is marked by an economic recession and the departure of the workforce, as described in remarkable books that eloquently depict these migrant populations' destinies. These books include Daniel Delaunay's *De la captivité à l'exil, la valle du fleuve Senegal* (From Captivity to Exile in the Senegal River Valley); Adrian Adam's *Le long voyage des gens du fleuve* (The Long Voyage of the River People) and also *La Terre et les gens du fleuve* (The Land and the River People); Abdoulaye Bara Diop's *Société toucouleur et migration* (Tukulor Society and Migration), Eric Pollet and Grace Winter's *Société dyahun du Mali* (Dyahun Society in Mali), J.Y. Weigel's *Migration et production domestique des soninke du Sénégal* (Soninke Migration and Domestic Production in Senegal), and Baldé Mamadou Saliou's *Migrations des Peuples du Fuuta jallon dans le milieu rural sénégalais* (Fuuta Jallon Peoples' Migrations within Rural Senegalese Areas). All of these works eloquently evoke, with extremely meticulous detail, the phenomenon of migration in the various parts of the Senegal River, from its source to its delta.

These works are collected in a summary edited by Lucie Colvin: *Les migrations etl'economie monetaire en Senegambie;* its English title is *The Uprooted of the Western Sahel, Migrants' Quest for Cash in Senegambia*. Claude Meillassoux's theoretical book *Femmes, greniers and capitaux* (Women, Granaries and Money) gives a good account of the dynamics of the domestic society and the imperialist and exploitative system. All of these books, used here as our references, show the role of migration in colonial development, and its place in the actual destiny of the Senegal River populations on the eve of the great dam constructions. The profits reaped by the Bordelese from groundnuts at the beginning of the twentieth century dealt a fatal blow to the river economy, which did not produce this crop as abundantly as did the groundnut basin. Consequently, the period from 1854 to 1910 is characterized by two crises: that before the conquest, when the domestic economy was ravaged by the pillaging *ceddo;* and that of the commercial economy, when gum was no longer purchased and river transport was replaced by the railroads.

Because of this marginalization, which lasted until recent developments, the twentieth century would not witness significant social transformations. As Daniel Delaunay writes, it was during the second half of the nineteenth century that the river valley populations acquired the major economic features that characterize them today.¹¹ These features include the departure of manpower, which takes on various forms to this day. The fall of gum prices provoked dwindling job opportunities in agricultural production. Since the beginning of the century, that lack of jobs prompted migration. The decay of the old social structure, accompanied the decline of captives for trade, extended into the backcountry. The ties of slavery lost their economic significance, now that enslaved individuals did not merely seek escape from their masters. From that point on, masters and enslaved individuals looked for new ways to survive in the mercantile economy through migrations. The migrants moved south toward the groundnut basin, which offered possibilities of higher incomes.

In 1884, unlike the *damel* of Kajoor, who planted millet in an area as large as the groundnut basin, the colonial powers favored the import of Indochinese rice in order to keep local land available for groundnuts. The valley migrants, impoverished by the deterioration of the trade between millet and imported products, inserted themselves easily into the groundnut-farming labor system known as the *navetane*. The *navetane* migration could take place without preliminary investment or without family solidarity. Moreover, as in the case of the Wolof of Waalo, these seasonal migrations led to permanent settlements, because of their shared ethnic identity with the populations of the groundnut basin. The most important migratory flux was certainly from the seasonal migrations of the *navetane*s, who had lived before in Fuuta Jallon; they, for a long time, provided the cheapest workforce in the groundnut area.

The typical migrant often aimed, after the groundnut picking, to obtain an urban job. That would offer the possibility to better support his relatives back in the village. After the war, industrial development replaced imports and increased employment opportunities. It increased the number of migrations to the cities, at the expense of agricultural labor. Eventually, agricultural migrations to the groundnut basin progressively dried up, since land was less available. Thus industrial development brought about the end of the *navetane* migrations. Additionally, the persistent drought considerably dried up both commercial cultivations and the expectations of income.¹² Because the groundnut area was saturated, Europeans consequently talked about the colonization of new lands to the east, in eastern Senegal.

Nevertheless, large numbers of migrants continued to leave Fuuta Jallon for the Senegalese rural area, due to the disastrous economic politics of the Parti Démocratique de Guinée (PDG, or Democratic Party of Guinea) in Guinea. Here, one dealt with the displacements in Upper Gambia due to the closing of the Guinean border, which excluded all possibilities of seasonal migration. However, a new form of *navetane* migration developed in the direction of the new cotton basin expanding in southeast Senegal, as a stage toward urban migration.[13]

On the other hand, the vivid memory of old servile relationships, maintained by the Moorish domination of enslaved individuals, hindered the temporary emigration of the Haratines to the groundnut basin or to the Senegalese cities for that entire century. But urban migration patterns became increasingly random, because of the saturation of the Senegalese labor market due to the independent interests that accelerated the balkanization of the old AOF (*Afrique Occidentale Française*), both politically and economically. Senegal, the first colony where developments took place, lost its vast AOF market. From then on, its people were condemned to migrate to foreign lands.

One witnessed a regional specialization regarding the destination of migratory waves. From west to east, the main destinations were Mauritania for Dagana and Podor, the Ivory Coast for the zone of Matam, and France for the Bakel region. This specialization is the result of the necessary channeling of the migration networks. In Senegal, migration to foreign lands became more important than migrating within the country's rural or urban areas. But in any case, by hiring field workers, businessmen achieved an economic and maintenance cost balance of physical production, now supported by the domestic economy. In France, migrants had it even worse: distance, regulations and clandestine guides considerably increased migration cost to the point that it could no longer be normally paid for at the departure point. The migrants took on the responsibility, paying for and organizing replacements based on a cycle of prepayments and on seniority status.[14]

Adrian Adams, in her remarkable book *Le long voyage des gens de fleuve*, describes the genesis of the Soninke migration. She describes the harsh living conditions of the migrants and their difficulties in re-integrating themselves into the villages from which they came. But even this transfer of workforce to foreign lands was now blocked by the crisis in France; immigrant workers were sent back to their native country in large numbers, to resolve the problem of French unemployment. This forced return unfortunately occurred at a time when the Senegal River valley was withering from a heavy drought.

For over a century and a half, nothing had been done to assure the survival of the populations of the Senegal River, or to help them to establish themselves definitively on their own lands. However, during the century and a half that separates the first experiments of agricultural colonization and the beginning of the nineteenth century, development projects of the valley did take place, albeit with many setbacks.

Multiple Development Projects for the Senegal River Valley

Timid trials occurred at the beginning of the twentieth century. The emergence of peanuts as a unique exploitation crop, an increasing population growth and the increasing needs for food supplies prompted the colonial authorities to create a Mission d'Aménagement du Sénégal (MAS, or Development Mission for the Senegal Valley) around 1938. MAS, tasked with studying the valley and implementing improvements, embarked on a rice project at Richard-Toll in the river delta. This was in response to the food shortage that prevailed during the war. From 1945 to 1955, MAS developed nearly 6,000 hectares of irrigated rice fields for mechanized exploitation. However, since the cost was clearly higher than that of either whole rice or the broken rice available on the Senegalese market, the government was obliged to subsidize a series of concessionary companies. They could not manage to make a profit, due to the low purchasing power of local consumers. Until 1964, MAS attempted, with very little success, to develop the production of rice in the easily flooded basins of the Senegal mid-valley region. During the years following political independence, this type of colonial exploitation came to an end. It was taken over in each independent state by national companies, created as a result of the division of the Senegal valley into the four sovereign states of Senegal, Mauritania, Mali and Guinea.

In Senegal, the Sociétéd'aménagementet d'exploitation des terres du delta (SAED, or Development and Exploitation Society of the Delta Lands) was created in 1965. Its goal was to encourage peasants to settle on the land, and form cooperatives. Very early, however, the failure of mechanized rice production led Senegal to convert the rice fields into a large sugar cane plantation, exploited by the Mimran Company of the Grands Moulins de Dakar (Dakar Big Mills). This sugar complex, intended to meet the country's needs, required an investment of 50 billion African francs (CFA). It was the biggest project combining agriculture and industry in Senegal since 1946. However, the Grands Moulins de Dakar also benefited from improvements in the delta made by the Senegalese public sector, with the assistance of national and international credit institutions. Moreover, the project was the result of extraordinary circumstances, specifically:

- The eviction of the industrial operator already on site, the Raffineries de Saint-Louis (Saint-Louis Refineries). It was the manager of CAPA. Another private operator was introduced, free from all prior ties to the profession.

- Uncertainty over the efficiency of industrial sugar cane production at Richard-Toll, which required considerably more expensive improvements.

In the context of a global market characterized by a tendency to over-produce, this risky operation was run jointly by the state of Senegal and the private contractor that it selected. The operation only survived because

Mimran, the private contractor, was able to discount the concession fees using the public force of extraordinary advantages.[15] As Abdoulaye Ly reports, the explanation for those extraordinary advantages delves deeply into the mysteries of Senegalese politics, especially regarding the period of the BDS and the support its directors gave to the Grands Moulins de Dakar, which was controlled by the same group.[16]

Similarly, urged by the government of Senegal to diversify their activities, Moulins Sentac (Sentac Mills) launched a project to build an agricultural and industrial complex in the basin of the Senegal mid-valley region. It garnered the financial and technical support of Grands Moulins de Paris (Big Mills of Paris), CFAO and SCOA—all companies that belonged to the same group of stockholders as SOCAS, who were the operation's managers. SOCAS owned lands made valuable by industrial exploitation, and a factory that produced food concentrates. Some of the supplies were provided by cooperatives of local producers, while the Fonds d'aide et de coopération (FAC or Fund of Aid and Cooperation) financed part of the agricultural development. From a private investor perspective, the operation had the dual advantage of insuring an outlet for sale on the Senegalese market and of allowing French industrialists or merchants to supplant foreign importations—especially those from Italy.

It was much more than a local industry substituting for imports—it was the conquest of a new market. As a consequence of state financial support, returns on the capital industrial investments were practically assured from the very beginning.[17] In both cases, the state of Senegal created start-up conditions, encouraged contractors, provided them with land, gave them a monopoly on sugar or tomatoes, protected their activities, made loans, gave warranties, and ensured the prosperity of the French industries established in Senegal.[18]

The failure of rice production, which was intended to help peasants settle on the land, prompted the state to cede lands in the Senegal valley to French private industries. The employment of some 3,000 persons cannot, in itself, justify the establishment of a sugar complex of this scope; profits were not assured in the short term. In 1964, Abdoulaye Bara Diop expressed a number of reservations about the projects of SAED, including the development of 30,000 hectares in the Senegal delta. He drew attention to the low population density in the mid-valley area of the river, and in particular to the case of the Tukulors, who would find it difficult to give up urban migration. He noted the high cost of secondary developments, especially the costs of irrigation rendered necessary by rice production. Such irrigation would be subjected to irregular flooding and the influx of seawater.[19]

Nonetheless, MAS and SAED attempted to extend the developments in the Senegal mid-valley area to Dagana, Nianga, Guede, and Matam, where the total diked surface was 23,255 hectares. On the Mauritanian side, the Sociéténationale de développement rural (SNDR, or National Society of Rural Development) played a role identical to that of SAED; it ensured the development of small surface areas in the mid-valley area of the Senegal River. The role of realization and management of irrigated surface areas was turned over to private French companies or to state farms assisted by China. However, heavy capital developments were much less extended here. The same situation applied to the border with Mali, with OVSTM, and especially on the border with Guinea, where there had been "until now no policy of development of the river valley at the national level."[20] Indeed, the high costs of hydraulic and agricultural improvements, necessary to ensure the early survival of the valley populations, compelled the states of Senegal, Mali, Mauritania and Guinea to cooperate. They put together an organization capable of continuing the public projects of the colonial powers.

Organization of the Senegal River Development:
Hopes and Worries in the Post-Dam Era

As early as 1963, an inter-state committee, which included Senegal, Mauritania, Mali and Guinea, was created to insure the development of the Senegal valley. The committee was replaced by OERS, the Organisation des étatsriverains du Sénégal (Organization of the States along the Senegal River) from 1968 to 1972. At that time, after Guinea had withdrawn from the group, OMVS, Organisation de la mise en valeur du fleuve Sénégal (Organization for the Development of the Senegal River), was created by Mali, Mauritania and Senegal. It was only in 1974 that OMVS adopted an integrated management plan for the drainage basin of the Senegal River. The OMVS program includes the construction of two dams in Diama and Manantali, the reclamation of 375,000 hectares of irrigated agricultural lands, infrastructure for navigation along the river all the way to Kayes, the production of electricity and the development of various industries. The OMVS project falls into two phases:

1. The first phase, from 1981 to 1990, was devoted to the construction of the two dams at Diama and Manantali.
2. The second phase, from 1981 to 2030, is devoted to agricultural developments, the supply of materials for agricultural exploitation, the equipment of the power plant and possible investments in navigation.

Drainage Basin of the Senegal River

The catastrophic drought of the past few years had accelerated the OMVS projects, the total costs of which are estimated at 850 billion African francs (CFA). The most important objective was to radically transform a traditional agriculture, based on the use of receding waters, into a mode of diversified, irrigated agriculture. Nevertheless, OMVS anticipated a transitional period during which artificial flooding would be maintained, to allow for traditional crops and a regulated traditional system. The first phase of the construction of the Diama dam, intended to stop the influx of salt water in the delta during the dry season, was completed in 1986. Similarly, the completion of the construction of the Manantali dam, intended to regulate the river flow, facilitate artificial flooding, ensure river navigation all the way to Kayes, and finally to progressively irrigate thousands of hectares, occurred in 1988.

The cost to build the two dams between 1981 and 1988 was estimated at 583.1 million francs. Financing was provided by foreign loans, which came, in order of importance, from Saudi Arabia, Kuwait, CEE, Germany, France, BAD, FAD, Italy, BID, and Canada. Such a global consortium, with multiple donors and loaners, had little precedence. No one debated the urgent need to develop the Senegal valley, for doing so would eliminate the risks of famine in the region due to insufficient rainfall and persistent aridity in the Sahel. Once the project was launched, it would be no longer appropriate to discuss the advisability or inappropriateness of these dams.

However, problems persisted and generated numerous concerns related to the development of the valley.[21]

While the debate on the advisability of the dams may be over, it behooves us to remember the objections raised against the project, in order to better understand the problems in the post-dams era. First of all, the debate concerning the advisability of dam construction was limited, first to the headquarters of the riparian states along the Senegal River, and then to the experts hired by the inter-state committees of OERS and OMVS. Conceived by an all-powerful state, this was a project that had not been discussed with concerned populations. The general public was not consulted about alternatives for valley development; all project criticisms were silenced. Thus, the confidential report provided to OMVS by a Canadian study group, quoted by Adrian Adams, reveals the breadth of the consequences of the river development project for the peasantry:

> It would have been possible to rescue and increase food production, to free the rural population from the revenue fluctuations caused by climactic hazards, to enable them to develop their environment according to their wishes and to re-organize the river's life collectively, to provide an alternative to the immigration of peasants toward the less well paid jobs in big cities; all this would have been possible if the development project had been linked to grass root concerns and the idea of a progressive change of weak technologies under communal control, that is, if a lighter infrastructure had been constructed as for instance a series of small dams capable of maintaining water reserves. This would have been possible with much more limited investments as long as local and regional development was put into the hands of communities. Such an alternative, however, would have been at odds with the needs of large centers in natural resources. It would also not have met the needs of investors for a production adjusted to foreign markets.[22]

In May 1980, Claude Meillassoux published an article in *Le Monde diplomatique* entitled "Wagers of the World's Food Supply System: 700,000 Peasants in the Senegal River Valley." Meillassoux attempted to explain how the construction of dams once again called into question the economic balance of the whole region. After sifting through the main objectives of the improvements as projected by OMVS, Claude Meillassoux demonstrated that the project's implementation methods were not understood by those who would be immediately impacted. In particular, the public was not aware that crops would disappear within a decade due to subsidence of the river, which produced approximately a third of the valley's total agricultural resources. The OMVS project, he noted, threatened to end their productive autonomy, and would eventually cause dislocation of their communities.

Meillassoux retold the story of how 50 percent of the valley's men emigrated toward the urban centers of Senegal, Mauritania, Zaire, Gabon or Zambia, or periodically exiled themselves to France. He showed clearly that the goal of replacing millet subsidence crops with rice production, on artificially irrigated lands, did not take into account the failures of SAED. He contended that the cost of the production would lead to financial implications that peasants could not withstand; as they become indebted, an even more acute social crisis would necessarily result. Rice production was more labor-intensive than millet production, the article pointed out, but SAED refused to plant other crops. Quoting the temporary socio-economic report of 1978, Meillassoux concluded that "irrigated crops are not a forward-looking solution; they are only a transitory step toward a development of the valley in large natural units of equipment." To this must be added the nefarious consequences of the project on fishing, cattle breeding and the ecology of the valley. These consequences were far from being controlled.

Instead of responding to the concerns raised by Meillassoux, President Léopold Senghor took exception to the so-called prophets of ill omen, the neo-colonialism of the left-wing intellectuals, etc. Nevertheless, M. Vu Van Thaï, the expert responsible for the temporary report put together in June 1978 by OMVS, was asked to provide a sufficient response. This expert, whose intellectual probity is well-known to the author of this book, and who has since left OMVS, merely corrected a few technical errors in Claude Meillassoux's article, such as the height of the Manantali dam; he went on to reiterate the overall objectives of OMVS.

Following Meillassoux, Aabonbakry Moussa Lam wrote a March 1983 article in *Le Monde diplomatique*, titled "To Be a Peasant Today in the River Area." He wrote that, alongside the ecological difficulties they create, the big dams would benefit the big food industry more than the peasants. More to the point, Lam explained that in order to function properly, the dams would need secondary equipment, networks of distribution and well-equipped infrastructure. The cost of equipment for the 350,000 irrigated hectares proposed in the project would be three billion dollars—three to four times the cost of the OMVS dams. And the implementation of those dams had already required excessive debt on the part of the states bordering the Senegal River.

So we see that even if the debate over the dam construction had ended, the ensuing debate concerning the post-dams era had already begun. It was referred to as "the second crusade," by the daily Senegalese newspaper, *The Sun*, on December 17, 1983. More recently, Adrian Adams, the author of the remarkable book *The Long Journey of the River People*, re-ignited the debate with a new book entitled *The Land and People of the River*.

In this work, Adams uses exceptional detail to describe the daily life of the Soninke along the banks of the Senegal, during eight consecutive seasons. Adams scrupulously describes the rituals at home, in the mosque and in the fields. She uses keen observational skills to document the river men's lives, sharing their pains and hopes. Moreover, Adams examines the history of conflict between the river peasants and official state organizations, as well as OMVS; she extensively discusses the development models of the Senegal valley. The descriptions reveal the full breadth of the collective drama experienced by the river people; they face climate hazards as well as inefficient state intervention. In simple, elegant prose, Adams describes how the men wait anxiously for rain every year:

> During the past months, the heat has been a fever which only abates in the early morning. At the end of the dry season, the wind brings the violent perfume that a very few drops of water manage to extract from the exasperated soil. It has rained, somewhere inland under the same mat sky, and the fine powder of dust on the path is padded under the steps of people and animals... Like many other people from the town, the men in this house cultivate parcels of land close to the river, but they also cultivate inland. As soon as the first heavy rains begin, before plowing their fields on the river bank, they will sow their *jeeri* land. A week ago, they cleared the brush and took the path that yesterday the women of the household also took. After a forty-five minute walk, they left to their right the sandy plot of land that the women cultivate, and they forded the bed of a dry marigot. On the other side stretches an area without trees, except for those which cling to two red termite hills, erected on either side of them. The area is surrounded by a fence made of thorny dead branches behind which rise the hazy new foliage of thorny trees and a live hedge of trunks with a reddish brown or olive green tender bark. The soil is grayish, smooth, spiked with strewn bushes and stumps, and striped with the long stems of last year's harvested millet still flat on the ground. This is the *jeeri* field from last planting season and it occupies a little more than one hectare. They have been cultivating it for three years now. This season, they will sow it with large millet. Next year, they will probably move their area of cultivation without leaving the spot which is called Garsingide.

The Soninke, Adams wrote, have been repeating the same series of gestures each year for centuries, inside each square of land. This was the case with the household of Issa Budu, master of the field and of the household—the oldest survivor among the men. As their ancestors did, they grew millet, corn, *ñebbe* (beans), and sweet potatoes in the *jeeri* and *collengal*, the subsidence river lands that all belong to someone. The history of those peasants goes far back, all the way to the time when ancestors left the Near East to settle in Jaxali, near Kayes, and then to Gunjurn under the reign of the Baacili, then masters of Gajaaga. Eventually, the Europeans came; they did away with warrior chiefs and liberated the enslaved individuals.

The Soninke enlisted in the French army or navy, or traded in Congo or Gabon, before undertaking the long journey to France. "This year, like last year, more than two hundred men from the town work in France. Most of them are in Paris, most of them are low-paid laborers. They live together in the 13 *arrondissement*, or the 14, in Saint-Denis. The money they send home mostly serves to buy millet or rice... Eleven of the twelve men in the household are gone, three in Ivory Coast, two in Dakar, six in France... Issa Budu [says]: 'Ma lenkigarini, o xanaxouro, o nataxu. Today, we are old, so we sit here. The young people leave. They go to Paris. Now the rain is not coming. If you plough the land, you get nothing. If you sow millet, it does not come out. If it comes out, it dries up, it does not ripen. Our children go to Paris, work for the *tubaab*, to earn a little money and bring us a little something back. Our only job here is to cultivate. If rain does not come, we have nothing.'"

Adams writes of one among the thousands of Soninke who made the long journey of the river people—Jabe So. He returned eight years before, having worked as a seasonal peanut worker and as a laborer in Dakar before the war. He then spent five years in the navy, and ten years in the merchant navy. After his return home, more than fifteen years ago, he went back to work in Paris for a period of three years and now returned home definitely. He became the president of the group that organized irrigated plantations in Samba Salu. However, as soon as Jabe So left, his group was caught in a vise between two forces: the Society for the Promotion of Social Development (Société pour la promotion du développement rural or SPDR), responsible for the re-insertion of immigrants from the region of Bakel; and the state organizations, like SAED or OMVS, responsible for implementing an integrated program of development for the Senegal drainage basin.

The group, made up of 224 members, had trouble extricating itself from the claws of the state organizations, Adams writes. These organizations increased the debt burden of the peasants in order to purchase fertilizers, fuel, and seeds. Worse yet, the agencies forced individuals to cultivate rice, at the expense of millet. Yet they forbade the peasants from organizing autonomous communities. The peasants never stopped repeating: "Couscous is the life line of our country; to abandon millet, sorghum and corn for rice alone would be a disaster."

Adams shows that the existence of the Fédération des Paysans Organisés (Federation of Organized Peasants) in the Soninke zone of Bakel "highlights, before it is too late to remedy them, the fundamental contradictions often hidden in official projects and auxiliary inquiries, contradictions between individual consumption and commercialization, between food crops and rent crops, between peasant self-management and bureaucratic management."

The bureaucracy progressively stifled the farmers' initiative of collective development. Its development projects, typical of agricultural and industrial capitalism, led to the proletarianism of the river men. Tired and powerless, peasants would now await the completion of the dams. OMVS did not bother to explain the breadth of changes that would soon impact the river valley. This might change, however—provided that a planned colloquium, devoted to the direction of development in the post-dams era, would indeed provide a long-waited response to public concerns.

The Post-Dams Era: OMVS Response

Considering the multiple concerns expressed ever since the beginning of large dam construction, the states adjacent to the Senegal River finally presented their different perspectives at the first colloquium organized by OMVS. The colloquium took place between November 19 and 23, 1984, with high-level participation of representatives from the ministries of planning, rural development, hydraulics and industry from Mali, Mauritania and Senegal, as well as OMVS experts.

M. Abdou Diouf, the president of OMVS, presided over the opening session, and reiterated the mission for enhancing the Senegal River. This great "dream, which is about to become a reality for three peoples of the Sahel eager to repel the spectrum of malnutrition and famine beyond their borders." The president recalled the great axes of the valley's integrated development, and congratulated himself—saying that in spite of its detractors, OMVS won the first part of its wager and "once the reservoir behind the Manatali dam is filled in August 1988, the after-the-dam era will effectively begin."

He continued that the "time has now come to launch a global discussion on the after-the-dams era in order to exhaustively identify all the constraints to new development work and to propose appropriate responses for additional valley enhancement." The challenges were unfortunately numerous. They include the development and protection of the natural environment, the training and management of rural populations, social and economic issues, concerns for public health, the integration of agriculture and stock breeding, the needs of the energy market and the elaboration of an electrical network, the enhancement of navigation and port installations along the river, and above all, the elaboration of a harmonized scheme of development for the river drainage basin.

Speaking in the name of Senegal, President Abdou Diouf recommended the creation of a committee that would plan, coordinate and follow up on agriculture development, while encouraging small peasant enterprises. The president insisted that "all the possible ways of development between the large agricultural and industrial exploitation and the small private family exploitation" were on the table. "Moreover, [he added,] the reduction of the role of public authority will be accompanied by a transfer of some if its functions to professional agricultural organizations. But the dams are only the first phase of a far-reaching global operation which requires financial means out of scale with our countries' economies." The president was confident that "the help of friendly countries and financial institutions will not disappoint the hopes of OMVS because, by accepting to remain at our sides during this extraordinary adventure that is the construction of the dams, our lenders have in a certain measure linked their destiny to ours. In these conditions, if they were to default in their help, they would at the same time eliminate the role planned for the dams and condemn our states to remain under-developed."

However, the colloquium did not venture any further than listing an inventory of the problems raised in the opening speech of President Abdou Diouf. After the work of the three great commissions was completed, the colloquium adopted the following recommendations as elaborated by national experts:

1 RURAL DEVELOPMENT AND ENVIRONMENT

1.1 Re-energize the permanent water commission and the inter-state agricultural research and development committee.

1.2 Urgently complete the dykes along the right bank of the river, before the reservoir behind the Diama dam is filled.

1.3 Remove all enclaves around the production zones of the drainage basin.

1.4 In order to eliminate artificial flooding as soon as possible, accelerate the yearly pace of enhancements and increase exploitation rates. As a result, it is urgent on the one hand, that all the states present a united front to the lenders in order to obtain the funding necessary to realize the program; on the other hand, that the possible inclusion of the private sector in the process of development be studied within a legal framework appropriate for each state.

1.5 Lower the costs of development with: a thorough study of the different components; the creation of work schedules several times a year; the negotiation for better financing conditions; the involvement, several times a year, of the lenders in the development financing.

1.6 Lower the costs of production by increasing yields: with more productive varieties; by using fertilizers and pesticides; by managing water use more effectively; by disengaging state agencies; by selecting equipment judiciously; by making hydraulic energy available more cheaply.

1.7 Implement a policy of agricultural prices as a stimulus to improve the revenues of peasants, and to encourage them to produce more.

1.8 Avoid the single cultivation of rice and promote diversification when agricultural conditions permit it.

1.9 Rethink the modes of land tenure in order to increase the farmers' sense of ownership inthe project.

1.10 Plan a credit union available for all farmers.

1.11 Consolidate the knowledge and understanding acquired during the meetings of expertson the subject of environmental protection and safeguard; put together the financing necessary for the program of reforestation in the basin of the Senegal.

1.12 As soon as possible, find financing for a socio-economic study on stock breeding in order to make the integration of agriculture and breeding an efficient process. The training and functional literacy in national languages being the only valid support to insure that peasants develop a sense of ownership in the project, the commission recommends that they be started and consolidated as soon as possible.

1.13 Agriculture being expected to support approximately 27 percent of the cost and fees involved in the construction of the dams, an objective tariff policy of regulated water needs to be studied at the level of the OMVS and its member states.

1.14 Elaborate and harmonize top-level development diagrams, starting from multiple sectors, thus allowing the implementation of possible scenarios for the improvement of the Senegal drainage basin, which is the fundamental basis for regional planning. Since diversified crops are to be inserted in the production system of the drainage basin, it is already necessary to coordinate a through study in this sector at the regional level.

2 NAVIGATION, ENERGY, INDUSTRIAL AND MINING DEVELOPMENT

2.1 *Navigation*

2.1.1 Adopt a strategy to be implemented by stages which will be steered toward the definition of priorities for the different components of the navigation project, as it is defined in the initial program. This strategy will especially take into account financial and rentability constraints and also, scheduling issues concerning filling the reservoir behind the Manatali dam, which make it urgently necessary to unblock the Ambidedi-Kayes section.

2.1.2 The navigation project being a regional project involving several states, it needs to be inserted into national transportation policies and especially in all the development projects which are expected to generate traffic in the basin of the Senegal.

2.1.3 Study in depth the opportunities for private sector and local collectivities participation in all activities involving freight transport and port management along the river.

2.2 *Energy*

2.2.1 Research additional financing so as to allow construction of the Manantali hydroelectric power station to start as soon as possible.

2.2.2 Harmonize the energy policies of the member states and, in particular, take into account the Manantali power station in national executive plans, avoid duplications and dispersions of efforts by initiating competitive projects at the national as well as the regional levels.

2.2.3 Update hydrological studies in order to define more precisely the volumes of water which can reasonably be expected from the dam at Manantali and to integrate the rain deficit of the past eight years.

2.3 *Industrial and Mining Development*

2.3.1 Develop an executive diagram for the industrial and mining development of the drainage basin of the Senegal, based on the national plans of industrial and mining development; in this respect, the elaboration of an executive plan of industrial and mining development for each member state is encouraged.

3 CONSTRUCTION, HUMAN RESOURCES AND TRAINING, FINANCING AND PLANNING MANAGEMENT

3.1 *Construction Management*

3.1.1 No effort should be spared to complete a management study of the dams as soon as possible. The reference terms of this study have already been approved by OMVS. The results of the study will need to be examined in depth by OMVS and its member states.

3.1.2 Give extreme care as of now to the training of the personnel (engineers and technicians) intended for the technical management (operation and maintenance) of the basic infrastructure.

3.1.3 Use technical competence as the main criterion for the selection of this personnel.

3.1.4 Update the policy of water distribution without which the management of water resources, and notably arbitration between the different sectors of consumption (agriculture, energy, navigation) will be difficult to insure.

3.1.5 Organize the collection and handling of hydrological and meteorological data and the implementation of a system of forecasting and notification of homogeneous and reliable water flows in order to respond correctly to the gradual needs of construction management.

3.2 *Human Resources and Training*

3.2.1 Complete as soon as possible the re-structuring study of the High Commission which has already been requested by OMVS. OMVS will need to clarify and identify the missions of this structure in the after-the-dams era.

3.2.2 Adopt common policies which encourage the participation and sense of ownership of peasants by initiating various training activities, such as functional literacy, management training, etc.

3.2.3 Adopt a structure responsible for animating, sensitizing and informing rural populations and to prepare them to assume predictable disruptions in their lives.

3.2.4 Study in depth the population movements in the drainage basin in order to palliate the eventual deficit in human potential and to prepare subjective conditions for settlement as well as the return of emigrants, in case of need.

3.2.5 Make very effort to insure that the dam construction will be an opportunity for the member states and the High Commission to hire sufficient and competent personnel.

3.2.6 Complete as early as possible the job and training studies conducted in the context of the High Commission in order to elaborate a training plan or program.

3.2.7 Make every effort to insure that the actions recommended by OMVS environmental studies be implemented, in particular those related to health issues.

3.3 *Financing*

3.3.1 Given the filling of the reservoir behind the dams, which will happen very soon, OMVS states need to define the priorities; ultimately their selection needs to respond to a need for regional solidarity.

3.3.2 Relaunch an active and dynamic campaign for OMVS and the member states to search for new financing.

3.3.3 Re-negotiate the conventions open to modifications as a result of the economic and financial difficulties of the member states and the difficulties of OMVS in honoring its debt service.

3.3.4 OMVS needs to study very carefully the financial implications of the decisions it might be led to take in the context of the implementation of basic infrastructure.

3.4 *Planning*

3.4.1 Organize in each member state a national committee of planning, coordination and follow-up for the development of the drainage basin.

3.4.2 Create a regional committee of planning, coordination and follow-up for the development of the drainage basin. This will gather the national committees under the authority of the High Commission whose structures responsible for planning and coordination will insure the secretarial functions.

Uncertainties Remain

Now we will describe the attempts to craft an appropriate policy for the post-dams era. First of all, the "second crusade," according to the expression used in *The Sun*, raised the problem of financing, estimated at three times the cost of the dams' construction. The riparian states still counted on international help and additional loans. Yet such financing came with the possibility of the retrocession of the lands and hydroelectric equipment to the financiers, as was the case with the Compagniesucrière du Sénégal (Sugar Company of Senegal). Hard-pressed farmers, left to their own devices for centuries, would be too poor to handle the expenses necessary for efficient development of the lands, subjected to mechanized irrigation. A proletarianization of the peasants was all the more inevitable; the state of Senegal had, for some time now, chosen to disengage itself from its initial policy of training rural populations. This happened after the liquidation of ONCAD, which left a debt of 100 billion CFA francs. The failure of state companies, which management benefited a bourgeois bureaucracy and foreign private companies, left the peasants completely helpless in the face of any agricultural modernization policy. Privatization of agriculture might have made sense if such a policy had been propped up by an expanding national economy, led by either an autonomous national bourgeoisie or an enterprising state totally independent from international capital.

The main problem was not a Cornelian dilemma between traditional agriculture and mechanized modern agriculture. Rather, the problem lay in identifying how the society, with its archaic social and technical processes, could transform itself in order to single-handedly control a natural environment—one that continued to dominate daily life, without any hope of change. It was not a question of hindering progress so that our peasant societies could remain in the equivalent of fenced-in fields, or live laboratories for anthropologists, or destinations for tourists exploring the African "bush." The main problem was that our society was incapable of thoroughly thinking this dam project through, or of repeating its benefits without seeking international aid. That aid was described as "generous" to mask its essentially mendicant nature. In another hundred years, the children of the Moors, Soninke, Wolof or Fula—those who built the dams of Diama and Manantanli—will likely be incapable of building another dam on the Gambia River. This constituted the main challenge—one not posed to an entire generation at the dawn of the twentieth century.

Numerous problems were still unresolved in the post-dams era—in particular, the integration of stock breeding, fishing and certain other economic activities attached to irrigated agriculture. Moreover, the choice of freight transport on the Senegal River needed to be reviewed, considering the intermodal possibilities: road transport, i.e. the *jeeri* road, railroad transport, i.e. the Dakar-Niger line, or river transport on the Gambia River. Indeed, since the days of great empires, the Gambia River had always been the main access route to Mali. The simultaneous utilization of both the Gambia and the Senegal rivers, from a regional perspective, would encourage better planning regarding their resources. It would also encourage greater specialization, according to the needs of the riparian states and the real possibilities of each river. The rivers are separated by a scant 100 kilometers at their sources, and less than 500 km at their mouths. But the lands of the two basins are shared by six states: Senegal, Mauritania, Mali, Gambia, Guinea-Conakry and Guinea-Bissau.

It was through the political construction of artificial borders that Mali and Mauritania were excluded from OMVG, the organization that supervised the development of the Gambia River. Gambia, Guinea-Bissau and Guinea-Conakry were excluded from OMVS, the organization supervising the development of the Senegal River. Indeed, alongside all the other constraints of the post-dams era, the most serious handicap to the realization of an integrated project remained the existence of national states, which only emphasized the fragmentation of the economic spaces created by the adjacent basins of the Senegal and Gambia rivers.

Only a unified effort of the six states, all of which belonged at least in part to the larger Senegambia, might allow the implementation of these agricultural development projects. No planning effort intended to enhance the region's natural resources could be possible within the context of national states, the legacy of centuries of colonization. Artificial borders ruptured the complementarity of the different ecological zones of forest, savannah and Sahel, which for centuries ensured the equilibrium of these societies. The desert did not always come from the north, as many believe, but also from the south—which for the past century had been subjected to ruthless deforestation.

After a twenty-two year absence, this author was shocked to see the masses of gallery forests destroyed along the dried-up streams of Fuuta Jallon, and the mountainsides stripped bare or burnt by bush fires. These examples of deforestation confirmed the danger that the land might be turning into a desert, originating from the south. The mountain mass of Fuuta Jallon—the water tower of western Africa, at the sources of the Senegal, Gambia and Niger rivers—was dangerously threatened at a time when the flow of these rivers had reached their lowest levels in centuries. That created a high risk that the concrete dams would be invaded by sand, if the construction policy did not include reforestation efforts at the river sources.

For this to happen, it was imperative that Guinea-Conakry reintegrate into the OMVS, and that the six states agree to share in the current suffering in order to benefit, later and together, from all their potential riches. Indeed, the success of the development policy of the Senegal drainage basin, however generous it might be, could only be assured if the development of the industry and energy sectors were also taken early into account. The industrial sector included important deposits of iron, bauxite, uranium, phosphate, gold, and so on, and the energy sector offered huge hydraulic possibilities. Yet, the two sectors of industry and energy were completely neglected in the project. These sectors would be vital to any future post-dams policy—once the issue of unity among the riparian states is resolved!

At the end of this brief summary of a 150-year history of the people of the Senegal River, we find ourselves firmly planted in the present. What does an historian do in this impossible situation?

Toward a New History

Fifteen years after the initial publication of our historical monograph on Waalo, it is interesting to ask ourselves some questions about the historian's job, and to locate the historian in relationship to the ever-demanding present. Adrian Adams's relevant comments in her most recent work help us to establish a dialectic relationship between the destiny of the river peoples and history. We let Daniel, the OMVS expert, answer Adams's assertion that the main function of the development expert "is not to recognize that the present lives of the people of the river are rooted in the past and open unto the future." The expert's function rests on the implicit idea that development is a transformation from the "traditional" or "under-developed" to the "modern" or "developed" model.

It is also up to Samir Amin, the theoretician of dependency, to answer this other line of questioning from Adams: "What is an auto-centered development? Is it centered on the populations along the river? By whom? Because in order to act, to transform the past into future, it is necessary to lean on the present; and an Africa that would summarize dependency, like an Africa that would summarize tradition, has no existence in the present. It has been, it will be: yesterday, pre-capitalistic social formations; tomorrow, auto-centered regional spaces, which would create the conditions of their own prosperity; but today, a vacuum."

In the same vein, Claude Meillassoux, the author of *Women, Granaries and Capitals*, also answers Adrian Adams. The anthropologist's call to save the river populations in the face of their imminent sacrifice to OMVS projects allows for a double entendre: "All things considered, doesn't this subsistence agriculture, whose loss is deplored, relate to the mode of domestic production depicted elsewhere as the condemned anchoring point of excessive pre-capitalistic and capitalistic exploitation of work?"

Adams responds, "Neither the political economy of dependency nor the economic anthropology inherited from historical materialism provide any kind of support to the people of the river because neither one nor the other recognizes that these people do exist today, so that they are denied the possibility of ever becoming once again the actors of their own history."

This legitimate obsession with the present, already visible in *The Long Journey of the People of the River*, is ubiquitous in Adams' second work. She completes her reflection with remarks on how historians have viewed the river peoples: "Doesn't the new history of de-colonized Africa turn the people of the river and their peers into our contemporaries? Doesn't she give them back their actors' roles? However, for historians also the people of the river do not have any present existence... Certainly they have existed. Several good historical studies about the river have been written during the 1970s. I am thinking of the works of Boubacar Barry on the Wolof of Waalo, David Robinson on the Halpulaar of Fuuta Toro, Abdoulaye Bathily on the Soninke of Gajaaga. These are worthy studies, but this is not what I am talking about here. Rather, I wish to remark that the studies on the Gajaaga, for example, deal, in order of publication, with the French conquest of the High River, the period between contacts and conquests, and mainly with the nineteenth century, with the ancient kingdom of Wagadu and the quasi-legendary origins of the Soninke people. This time period is the one in which is inserted all the historical studies on the people of the river; not one of them goes beyond the end of the nineteenth century. The conquest has put an end to their history."

Adrian Adams is absolutely right in stating that our monograph on Waalo stops in 1854, at the time of Faidherbe's conquest—just as the history of Fuuta Toro by Robinson, and of the Gajaaga by Bathily, do not go beyond the end of the nineteenth century. However, this justifiable reproach does not take into account the efforts of several generations of historians, who strove for a reconquest of a history that had been confiscated for centuries by Europe. The main problem is not that of a chronological break, but rather the innate fact that documentation of this ancient history has been attempted by historians living in the present. The solicitations of the present necessarily guide the historian's perspective on his or her own past, and it was necessary first to recover this past in the name of the memory of our contemporaries.

The retrospective look on our own past has its own history, which has been admirably described by Mohamed Mbodi and Mamadou Diouf in their article, "Senegalese Historiography: A Reckoning of Actual Practices and Perspectives." Mbodj and Diouf show that the process of colonization, from the seventeenth to the twentieth centuries, has been the most studied period by the historians of de-colonization. For some, the profound justification for this undertaking is existentialist. It leads to the concept of a traditional African democracy, while insisting on an inalienable African specificity. For others, Senegambia is nothing but a part of the "world's economy," dominated by capitalism since the sixteenth century—a period from which came much of its impetus. These two currents of thought privilege the oral tradition, and integrate the two drainage basins of the Senegal and the Gambia rivers into the framework of a vast socio-economic community on the scale of Senegambia, which goes largely beyond the contemporary states of Senegal and Gambia. Priority is given to the study of Islam, and political and social history, and at the expense of economic history. However, this historiography is fundamentally limited to academic studies still largely dominated by French, English and American researchers, whose competence and intellectual integrity are not questioned.

It cannot be otherwise, since our African academic world has not yet succeeded in disentangling itself from the French model. We have tried to prove to ourselves that we were capable of a corresponding model. We have been trapped by the academic system, because our society is incapable of defining the means to conduct autonomous research that could immediately be used to resolve our problems and answer our questions. The gaze of the Other always remains fixed on us, and we are not able to throw our gaze on our own daily realities. Our memory is not confiscated as much by the fact that research on Africa is made by non-Africans, as it is by our own inability to promptly produce—through our own autonomous scientific reflection—a significant alternative to solve the dilemma. We have completely failed to draw upon a long history during all our projects of national or regional development.

As Mbodj and Diouf said so eloquently, African historians must not allow others to dominate their future by monopolizing their conscience. However, this struggle for reconquered history cannot be separated from the struggle of the Senegambian peoples for political, economic and cultural independence. In April 1985, Abdoulaye Bathily brilliantly defended a doctorate thesis on the French model regarding the Gaajaga from the fifteenth to the nineteenth centuries. After approximately twenty years of thorough research, he did not cling to this past for its very sake. He was very much involved with the survivors of the great Soninke social adventure, at the intersection of paths between the Sahel, savannah and the forest. He represented not only the Juula from the west, who have been ruined since the nineteenth century, but also the militant students of 1968, the union workers of the memorable strike of SUDES, and the general secretary of his party, the Democratic League. Better still, he is one of the best representatives of the Dakar Historical School (École historique)—which is being smothered, because, ironically, the first to hold a Doctorate in History from the University of Dakar has been a PhD from the British university of Birmingham since 1975.

A quarter of a century ago, soon after our accession to international sovereignty, our generation believed, with an immature passion and hope, in an Africa soon to be regenerated by her sons—an Africa finally freed from the chains of colonialism. At that point, we sought everything in our past that might strengthen our faith in the future of Africa. Quoting Kwame Nkrumah, we used to say that Africa had not accepted its fate with crossed arms. We were seeking answers and reactions from Africa in defiance of the West. We refused the notion of specificity of African societies in relation to Europe, and the notion of the national state. We were trying, as Mbodj and Diouf explain, to master the internal ordering of the systems of domination and inequality. These systems were emerging, with internal and external solicitations, in the context of a spatial integration of African societies into the world's economy.

Mbodj and Diouf may be right when they claim the dependency perspective of Boubacar Barry gives too much weight to the influences of European solicitations since the fifteenth century, by giving them a decisive function; there, too, the major phenomenon needs to be analyzed in terms of a correlation of adoptions. We shall go further and proclaim that the current state of our societies, incapable as they are of leaving the vicious circle of dependency, confronts our generation with another challenge—that of creating a new history beyond that of de-colonization. We are still, as we were in the last century, the damned of the earth.

But that is no longer the fault of other people. From now on, it is our own fault. The gaze of the Other does not matter. The thoughts—present, past or future—of the Other do not matter either, even when it comes in the form of editorial comments in the right-wing newspaper *Le Monde*. Those comments evoked the 1985 visit of the Pope to Africa in these terms: "This visit, which certainly inscribes itself within the policy of openness undertaken by the Holy Seat since Vatican II has nevertheless another dimension in black Africa. For the Church, it is a question of confronting native cultures and trying to adapt its message to a primitive spirituality and religiosity... One of the assets of the Church in Africa is that it can constitute an element of cohesion which makes it possible to go, up to a certain point, beyond tribal solidarities."

As for us, we have simply wanted to restore, to the people of the Senegal River, their history. They are very much alive in our past as well as in our present.

The journeys we presented include the journey of Njaajaan Njaay, the mythical descendant of the Arab conqueror, who emerged miraculously from the waters of the Senegal River. He went on to unify riparian populations along the Senegal and the Gambia River in the Jolof confederation, between the thirteenth and sixteenth centuries.

It is the journey of Koli Tengela, who left the Sahel in Mali to settle for a while in the mountainous area of the Fuuta Jallon, before walking across Gambia and settling permanently with thousands of companions in the mid-valley region of the Senegal River. It is also the journey of Job Ben Solomon (Ayuba Suleiman Diallo) from Buudu, and of Abdourahmane from Fuuta Jallon—forcefully transported with thousands of other enslaved individuals by the slave ships for the plantations of the new world in the seventeenth, eighteenth and nineteenth centuries.

It is also the journey of Shaykh Umar, who left Fuuta Toro for a long pilgrimage to Mecca and came back to settle in Fuuta Jallon, before attempting to re-unite a major part of Senegambia and western Sudan in the context of a vast empire. Closer to us, it is also the journey of Jabe So, the *navetane* who became a sailor; he returned to his native Gaajaga to improve methods of cultivation so as to ensure the permanent attachment of his countrymen to the land in the face of climactic hazards.

It is also, unfortunately, the journey of our friend Mamadou Saliou Baldé, the author of the remarkable thesis on the migration of the Fula from Fuuta Jallon to a Senegalese rural environment. This *navetane* of the pen, who fled the tyrannical regime of the PDG in 1961, died in exile on the banks of the Seine in 1979, never to see his native Fuuta again. It is the destiny of all the people of the Senegal valley, tossed for centuries between captivity and exile. It is the residents of a country astride six aligned national states, yet devoid of a bright future as long as they remain excluded from a Great Senegambia.

It is finally, in a smaller measure, the journey of this author between the source of the Senegal, where he was born, and the mouth of the Senegal—where he embraced historical research for approximately twenty years. It is there, in Saint-Louis, that he found again the arms of Aida Sow. Aida Sow's embrace spared us the difficulties of that long journey of the river people beyond the ocean. This is why he is solidly anchored in Saint-Louis today. He is able to go all the way back to the river's source and to his native village of Dindeya, after a twenty-two year absence. This double experience, at the source and at the mouth of the river, confirms that there is no other alternative for the peoples of Senegambia than to turn their backs to the sea.

It is with this perspective that this author undertook a global history of Senegambia from the fifteenth to the twentieth century. He attempted to give an account of the destinies of the peoples of the Senegal and Gambia rivers, whose fates are intimately tied together. Equally tied together are the fates of the states of Senegal, Gambia, Guinea-Bissau, Mauritania, Mali, and Guinea-Conakry. All belong wholly or partially to this Great Senegambia, at the intersection between the Sahel, savannah and the forest. These links are to ensure that all Senegambians will eat their fill of millet from the valley of the Senegal River, the rice from the fields of Casamance and the Numezrio, and the *fonio* from the high plateaus of Fuuta Jallon.

Paris, June 21, 1985

POSTSCRIPT—2012

MY LAND, MY LIFE — SAMA SAMA SUUF BAKKAN

In 1985, on the occasion of the publication by Karthala of the second edition of *The Kingdom of Waalo*, first published in 1972 by François Maspero, I wrote an afterword entitled "From the Agricultural Colonization of Waalo to the Policy of Dams: The Future of the Men of the Senegal River." In the meantime, the work has been published in Spanish in 2008 by the Editorial de Ciencias Social la Habana in Cuba at the same time as the Amilcar Cabral Chair at the University of Havana was celebrating the intellectual contribution of Samir Amin, who had written the preface for the book on the Kingdom of Waalo in 1972.

Forty years later, we welcome the publication of this book in English by Diasporic Africa Press. A Portuguese version is also planned by Universidade Federal in Rio Branco, Brazil. The interest in Waalo indicates how relevant this book is in spite of the fact that we have retained the 1972 edition without introducing any new changes. However, we deem it necessary to add a postscript in order to confirm our fears and doubts already expressed in the 1985 afterword I devoted to the future of the Senegal RiverValley as it relates to the policy of dam construction within the framework of OMVS, or the Organization for the Development of the Senegal River (*l'Organisation de la Mise en Valeur du Fleuve Sénégal*).

At this time, we tried to show that the future of the men and women of the River depends on the ability of current national entities to unite and redefine a political, economic and cultural space—the potentials of which are currently undermined as a result of the fragmentation caused by the colonial heritage of the region. In the meantime, Guinea has rejoined OMVS, but Mauritania has left ECOWAS in order to attach itself to the Union for an Arab Maghreb. Worse yet, Senegal experienced a condition of rebellion in Casamance, which does not cease to upset the whole of southern Senegambia, and in particular Gambia and Guinea-Bissau. Unfortunately, we must also be the impotent witnesses to the division of Mali into two: the Northern section, controlled by the Tuareg rebellion, and a Southern section in the hands of last-minute *putschists* (coup leaders) on the eve of the presidential and legislative elections of 2012.

This situation acutely puts in question the viability of all the development projects of the Senegal and Gambia rivers in the context of a national crisis. The attempt to build a centralized model has failed in the face of multiple societies locked inside political entities, which deny the complementary character of our ecological zones. For centuries, these ecological zones—the Sahel, savannah and forest—have insured a natural balance in the region. The internal crises in each of our national states are the consequences of a policy of exclusion and bad governance, which translates without exception into a larger regional crisis because populations overflow their national boundaries. Internal as well as external conflicts compromise the equilibrium of the whole region and above all the survival of regional projects, as is the case with the efforts of OMVS.

This vital project for the populations of the Senegal valley almost collapsed during the conflict which opposed the two states of Senegal and Mauritania in 1989, after a banal incident between sedentary populations and pastoralists. Thousands of people were forced out of Senegal into Mauritania and vice versa, thus exacerbating a dividing line in the middle of the river. The result has been the deportation of large groups of black Africans from Mauritania toward Senegal refugee camps, and the grabbing and takeover of irrigated land by the Beïdanes. It took many years of negotiations before the refugees were allowed back into their country in 2010 and the conflict has left a bitter aftertaste of state racism.

Numerous documents resulting from long and patient *in situ* research by multi-disciplinary experts have been published since our afterword of 1985. They are intended to evaluate the successes and failures of the dam policy. Let us especially point out two works by Mahamadou Maïga, *Le Bassin du Fleuve Sénégal: De la Traite Négrière au Développement sous Régional Autocentré* (*The Senegal River Basin: From the Slave Trade to a Regional Auto-Centered Development*) by Harmattan in 1995, and *Le Fleuve Sénégal et l'Intégration de l'Afrique de l'Ouest en 2011* (*The Senegal River and Integration of Western Africa in 2011*) by CODESRIA in 1995.

Mahamadou Maïga, who participated in numerous occasions on the implementation of dam projects, outlined in the first volume of his work the economic history of the Senegal drainage basin from the fifteenth century, emphasizing the importance of the slave trade and the progressive submission of the local populations to the European demands, until the colonial period. Thus, he picked up the thesis of Samir Amin on the historical origins of the current dependence of local populations and proposed an auto-centered sub-regional development.

In the second volume, Mahamadou Maïga went further and recommended an appropriate and realistic planning effort as well as an integrated development policy of the Senegal River for the benefit of local populations. Above all, he cautions the authorities who give priority to agro-business at the expense of poor peasant populations condemned to emigrate in order to survive. At the time, Maïga hoped that by 2011 the four states, under the pressure of peoples who have lived together from time immemorial, might seal their reunification in a larger regional context through ECOWAS.

Unfortunately, the third volume written under the direction of Bertrand Crousse, Parel Matthieu and Sidy M. Seck, and entitled *La Vallée du Fleuve Sénégal: Evaluation et Perspectives d'une Décennie d'Aménagement* (*The Senegal River Valley: Evaluation and Perspectives after Ten Years of Development*) by Karthala in 1991, brings us back to the sad reality of the living conditions of local populations. This collective effort is the result of studies *in situ* which have the advantage of pointing out the problems which local populations have been obliged to face since the construction of the dams began. The debate between the supporters of large-scale development of intensive irrigated cultivation and the supporters of small-scale projects is still very active. However, the authors are unanimous in their identification of a number of difficulties that the states and populations encounter. Here are the most significant ones:

The slowing down, even the complete interruption, of the valley development for political, economic and social reasons.

The conflict between Senegal and Mauritania, which prevents the river development in several important aspects.

The problems of land ownership, which are sources of multiple acute tensions in inter-village developments as well as between cultural groups on either sides of the river. The reforms and land ownership legislation, which have recently been implemented, are still not accepted everywhere and actually co-exist with traditional land tenures.

All these problems, which would be fastidious to enumerate here, can only find a solution in a political will to build an integrated sub-regional entity, while taking into account the economic, political, social, cultural and environmental elements concerning all the peoples living along the Senegal River from its source to its mouth. This warning from *in situ* researchers in 1991 does not seem to have been heeded by the politicians who govern the four states which today all face the grave internal and regional crises alluded to above.

The Mauritanian refugees in Senegal, now back in their country of origin, continue to claim the lands confiscated during their exile, while a large number of refugees still live in no man's land between the two states. Very recently, Senegal has been overwhelmed by a wave of discontent from the Mbane people, in the district of Dagana, protesting against the arbitrary parceling out of their rural communities by the state with the avowed goal of dispossessing them of their ancestral lands. The protest reached a climax with the Fanaye affair, which fed the March 2012 presidential campaign. It involved the sale of river land to agro-business companies at the expense of local populations. After two persons were killed and numerous others were wounded, the government of former president Wade finally suspended the attribution of 20,000 hectares to the Italian company Tampieri Financial Group which was intent on producing bio-ethanol industrially, in spite of a preliminary agreement with the rural council. The peasant revolt and mobilization of local populations along the river with the cry "My land is my life" (*Sama Suuf Sama Bakkan*) are symptoms of the lack of consultation between central and local authorities on the subject of the future of the whole valley.

In many respects, the revolt recalls the destruction of the dikes which had been built in 1819. At that time, the Waalo peasants were rebelling against the takeover of their lands by French promoters of agricultural colonization. History repeats itself, approximately two centuries later, while the four united states of the region turn their backs unto each other, failed to take into account the survival issues of the local populations of the Senegal valley, and remain tied to a short-term political strategy. The publication of the 15 volumes of the series *The National States Facing the Challenge of Regional Integration in Western Africa*, published under our direction by Karthala, enables us today to measure more accurately the structural limits of our development projects in the context of colonial frontiers.

It will never be repeated enough that our future depends on our capacity to give the initiative for development projects back to local citizenries. This is the challenge the current national states must accept in order to avoid the disintegration that the great country of Mali suffers today.

The debate remains open and we are somewhat satisfied that this monograph on the Kingdom of Waalo, published 40 years ago, has enabled us to meet on the intellectual level with a number of great thinkers such as Samir Amin and Abdoulaye Ly, who have given a theoretical dimension to our work on the historical origins of the dependency of African nations.

Once again, I take advantage of this postscript to pay tribute to our master Samir Amin who wrote the now famous preface to *The Kingdom of Waalo* and broke the academic barrier between history and economy. I also pay tribute to our master Abdoulaye Ly who, in the preface and afterword of the second edition of his book, *La Compagnie du Sénégal* (*The Senegal Company*) by Karthala in 1993, and also in his book *La Théorisation de la Connexion Capitaliste des Continents* (*Theory on the Capitalist Connection between the Continents*) by I.F.A.N. in 1995, has given new value to the results of our modest research in the current monograph devoted to Waalo and to our synthesis on Senegambia.

Finally, I want to thank very sincerely Professor Kwasi Konadu who initiated the English edition of this work, Professor Mirta Fernandez for the Spanish edition and Professor Maria Antonieta Antonacci for the Portuguese edition, which will soon be published in Brazil.

Dakar, June 21, 2012

NOTES

PREFACE

1 For further details, see my *L'accumulation a l'echelle mondiale* (Paris, 1970), especially pp. 31, 165-8, and 341-72; also my article on "La Politique coloniale française a l'égard de la bourgeoisie commercante sénégalaise," in Claude Meillassoux (ed.), *The Development of Indigenous Trade and Markets in West Africa* (London, 1971), pp. 361-76.
2 This idea of the cumulative nature of technological progress, and the importance of the age of the social formation in assessing the significance of a mode of production to which it belongs, is stressed by H. S. Michelina, "The Economic Formation: notes on the problem of its definition," I.D.E.P. paper, Dakar, October 1971.
3 *L'Accumulation à l'échelle mondiale*, ch. 1.
4 Catherine Coquery-Vidrovitch, "Recherches sur un mode de production africain," in *La Pensée* (Paris), April 1969, rightly emphasizes the decisive role which long-distance trade played in the constitution of some African states. Cf. Ahmad El Kodsy, "Nationalism and Glass Struggles in the Arab World," in the *Monthly Review* (New York), July-August 1970; and also Antoine Pelletier and Jean-Jacques Goblot, *Matérialisme historique et histoire des civilsations* (Paris, 1969), who suggest this for Greece.
5 See A. El Kodsy, op. cit.
6 Except for Egypt and Mesopotamia, and hence the frequent mistake of speaking of "Arab feudalism" criticized by El Kodsy, loc. cit.
7 The role and the nature of this trade were highlighted for the first time by E. W. Bovill, *Caravans of the Old Sahara* (London, 1933), later revised as *The Golden Trade of the Moors* (London, 1958).
8 See A. El Kodsy, op. cit.
9 Fernand Braudel, *La Méditerranée et le monde méditerranéen à l'époque de Philippe II* (Paris, 1949).
10 See my *L'Accumulation à l'échelle mondiale*, ch. 2, section 3.
11 Boubacar Barry, *Le Royaume du Waalo, 1659-1859* (Paris, 1971, mimeo).
12 Ibid.
13 See Jan Vansina, *Introduction à l'éthnographie du Congo* (Brussels, 1967), and G. Ballandier, *La Vie quotidienne au royaume du Congo du XVI au XVIIIe siecle* (Paris, 1965).
14 See, inter alia, R. Hill, *Egypt in the Sudan, 1820-81* (London, 1959), P. M. Holt, *The Mahdist State in the Sudan, 1881-98* (Oxford, 1958), and J. S. Trimingham, *Islam in the Sudan* (Oxford, 1949).
15 For further details, see my *L'Accumulation à l'échelle mondiale*.
16 Boubacar Barry, op. cit.

17 Walter Rodney, "African Slavery and other Forms of Social Oppression on the Upper Guinea Coast in the context of the Atlantic Slave Trade," *The Journal of African History* 3, 1966.

18 Catherine Coquery-Vidrovitch, "De la traite des esclaves à l'exportation de l'huile de palme et des palmistes au Dahomey, XIX e siècle," in Meillassoux, op. cit. pp. 107-23.

19 K. Onwuka Dike, *Trade and Politics in the Niger Delta, 1830-85* (Oxford, 1956).

20 See Yves Person, *Samori* (Dakar, 1970), 3 vols.

21 This problem of the looting of natural resources is beginning to be studied with the present-day awareness of "environmental problems", although the term is ambiguous. See my *L'Accumulation à l'échelle mondiale*, afterword to the second edition, p. 594-95.

22 See my paper on "Le Modèle théorique de l'accumulation dans le monde contemporain, centre et périphérie," I.D.E.P., Dakar, 1971.

23 Thus the structures established in the Gold Coast in 1890, which have characterized Ghana up to the present day, made their appearance in the Ivory Coast only from 1950, after the abolition of forced labor. See R. Szereszewski, *Structural Changes in the Economy of Ghana, 1831-1911* (London, 1965), and Samir Amin, *Le Développement du capitalisme en Côte d'Ivoire* (Paris, 1967).

24 See Ralph Horwitz, *The Political Economy of South Africa* (London, 1967); Richard Gray, *The Two Nations* (Oxford, 1961); Serge Thion, *Le Pouvoir pale* (Paris, 1969); and above all, Giovanni Arrighi, *The Political Economy of Rhodesia* (The Hague, 1967).

25 Arthur Lewis, *Economic Development with Unlimited Supplies of Labour* (Manchester, 1954).

26 Arrighi, op. cit.

27 I have analyzed this colonial trade in my *L'Afrique de l'Ouest bloquée* (Paris, 1971). See also Osende Afana, *L'Economie de l'ouest africain* (Paris, 1966); and Andre Vanhaeverbeke, *Rémunération du travail et commerce exterieur* (Louvain, 1970).

28 As Suret Canale does in *L'Afrique noire, l'ère coloniale* (Paris, 1960).

29 See my *L'Accumulation à l'échelle mondiale*, pp. 347-8.

30 *L'Afrique de l'Quest bloguée*, op. cit.

31 See our contribution to the discussion of this problem in *The Development of Indigeous Trade and Markets in West Africa*, ed. C. Meillassoux (Oxford, 1971).

32 Elliot J. Berg, "The Economics of the Migrant Labor System," in Hilda Kuper (ed.), *Urbanization and Migration in West Africa* (Los Angeles, 1965), reflects better than anyone else this non-scientific ideology. The conventional assumption is that migrations "redistribute" one factor of production (labor) which originally was unequally distributed. If that were so, migrations would tend to equalize the rates of growth of the economies of the various regions. But we can see that they are everywhere accompanied by a growing disparity between rates of growth: the acceleration of growth *per capita* in the immigration zones, and its reduction in the emigration zones.

33 Catherine Coquery-Vidrovitch, *Le Congo français au temps des compagnies concessionnaires, 1890-1930* (Paris, 1971, mimeo); and R. Merlier, Le Congo, de la colonisation belge à l'indipendance (Paris, 1965).

FOREWORD

1 Boubacar Barry, "Le Royaume du Waalo, du traité de N'Gio en 1819 à la conquête en 1855," *Bulletin I. F. A. N.*, t. 31, series B, nr. 2, 1969, pp. 339-444.

2 Kwame Nkrumah, *Le Consciencisme* (Paris, Payot, 1965), p. 99.

3 Sénégal II.2, a copy of a letter written on 12 January 1820 by J. Roger.

4 R. Rousseau, "Le Sénégal d'autrefois, Étude sur le Qualo," *Cahiers de Yoro Dyao, B.C.E.H.S.*, 1929, Vol. XII. Nr. 1-2, pp. 144-46.

5   According to Alioune Sow, assistant inspector in Dagana.
6   Carson I. A. Ritchie "Deux textes sur le Sénégal, 1673-1677," *Bulletin I.F.A.N.*, Volume 30, séries B, nr.1, 1968, p. 323.
7   Amadou Wade, in "Chronique du Waalo...," places the reign of Njaajaan Njaay between 1186 and 1202. Boubou Sall proposes 1215 as the initial date of the reign; Yoro Diaw who gives the reign a duration of forty years (sixteen years according to Amadou Wade), placing it from 1212 to 1256. Finally, according to Le Brasseur he did not reign more than 2 years.
8   R. Rosseau, *Le Sénégal d'autrefois, Étude sur le Toubé*, Paris, Larose, 1932, p. 11.
9   R. Rosseau, "Le Sénégal d'autrefois. Seconde etude sur le Cayor," *Bull. I.F.A.N.*, 1941, Volume III, p. 143.
10 Vincent Monteil, "Chronique du Waalo sénégalais," "Esquisses sénégalaises," *Initiations et études africaines,* nr. XXI, Dakar, 1966, p. 17.
11 R. Geoffroy de Villeneuve, *L'Afrique ou histoire, mœurs, usages et coutumes des Africaines*, Paris 1814, Volume III, p. 13.
12 Le Brasseur, *Détails historique et politiques...*, 1778, Bibliothèque National, French holdings, 12080.
13 Henri Gaden,"Légendes et coutumes sénégalaises," "Cahiers de Yoro Diaw," *Revue d'ethnographie et de sociologie*, 1912, nr, 3-4, p. 15.
    1. The family of *lamane* Diaw was considered in Waalo as a second class of nobility, coming immediately after the royal family.
    2. His family took part in future years in the nomination of the kings by means of a required tax payment of ten captives.
    3. Diaw received the commanding position of the province of N'Touguene (right riverbank) and his son N'Tanye, that of Naleou (right riverbank). The inhabitants were exempt from all taxes to the king.
    4. The *maalo* Neou dat Diak, maternal cousin of Diaw, was recognized as chief of the province of Gammalo under the same conditions as the preceding chiefs.
    5. The *kangame* payed to Diaw, on the day of their nomination, a tax of two pairs of loincloths and he made them as well as the notables in the king's entourage a gift at the occasion of the two feasts Korité and Tabaski.
    6. He was in charge of government during the interims of the reigns.
    7. One third of royal revenues was given to N'Tany Diaw. These rights were recognized in the families Guenyo de Diaw and Neoudat Diak until the dislocation of the Empire of Jolof in 1549. They later crossed over to the same family and they were maintained there until 1855, the year when the wars began, which brought about the conquest of Waalo.
14 Jean Boulègue, *La Sénégambie du milieu du XVe au début du XVII siècle*, doctoral thesis, Paris, 1968, p. 35.
15 Victorino Magalhaes Godinho, *L'Économie de l'Empire portugais aux XVe et XVI siècles*, Paris, 1969, pp. 104-05.
16 Raymond Mauny, *Esmeraldo de situ orbis*...Bissau, Centro de Estudos da Guiné Portuguesa, memoir, no. 19, 1956, p. 47.
17 V.M. Godinho, op. cit., p. 189.
18 José Goncales,"Textes portugais sur les Wolof au XVe siècle (Baptism of Prince Bemoi, 1488)," *Bull. I.F.A.N.*, Volume 30, series B. no. 3, 1968, p. 832.
19 Jean Boulègue, *La Sénégambie*, op. cit., p. 202.
20 C. I. A. Ritchie, "Deux texts," op. cit., p. 323.
21 Jean Boulègue, *La Sénégambie*, op. cit., p. 212
22 Ibid., p. 207.
23 C. I. A. Ritchie "Deux texts," op. cit., p. 323

24 R. Rousseau, 1929, p. 201.
25 H. Gaden, 1912, p. 16.
26 Jean Boulègue, *La Sénégambie*, op. cit., p. 223.
27 R. Rousseau, *Étude sur le Toubé*, op. cit., p. 14.
28 Jean Boulègue, *La Sénégambie*, op. cit., cites "La Relation y suma breve de las cosas del reyno del Gran Fulo," written in about 1600.
29 Jean Boulègue, Ibid. p. 244.
30 Jean Boulègue: "Relation du port du fleuve Sénégal de Jaão Barbosa, faite par Jao Baptista Lavanha vers 1600," *Bull. I.F.A. N.*, Volume XXIV, series B. nr. 3-4, 1967, p. 499.
31 Ibid., p.503
32 Ibid., p. 509.
33 V. M. Godinho, *L'Économie de l'Empire portugais*, op. cit., p. 831.

PART I

CHAPTER I

1 G. Thilmans, *Le Sénégal dans l'œvre d'Offried Dapper*, nouvelle tradition encore inédite de la description de Afrique par O. Dapper, Amsterdam, 1686.
2 C. I. A. Ritchie, "Deux textes," op. cit., p. 320.
3 C. I. A. Ritchie, "Deux textes," op. cit., p. 320.
4 Abdoulaye Bara Diop, "La Tenure foncière en milieu rural wolof (Sénégal)" *Notes Africaines*, no. 118, April 1968, pp. 49-50.
5 C. I. A. Ritchie, "Deux textes," op. cit., p. 320.
6 G. Thilmans, op. cit., p. 17.
7 G. Thilmans; Dapper, p. 17, in detail: "These regions do not lack, however, vermine such as locusts which sometimes in June relocate from the Northeast of the coast of Arabia in such great quantities that they veil the clouds and hide the sun, and devour all vegetation that is why many of the people of the interior (while the people on the sea avoid this by fishing) die of hunger and others sell themselves as enslaved individuals to the Portuguese to keep alive, as this happened in sixteen hundred and eighty with a great loss of people."
8 P. Cultru, Premier voyage du Sieur de La Courbe fait à la côte d'Afrique en 1685, Paris 1913, p. 131.
9 Perrotet, "Voyage de Saint-Louis du Sénégal à Podor fait en 1825," *Nouvelles des voyages et des sciences géographiques*, April-May-June 1833, p. 31.
10 G. Thilmans, op. cit., p. 16.
11 C. I. A. Ritchie, "Deux textes," op. cit., p. 320.
12 C. I. A. Ritchie, "Deux textes," op. cit., p. 332.
13 G. Thilmans, op. cit., p. 20.
14 C. I. A. Ritchie, "Deux textes," op. cit., pp. 320-321.
15 C. I. A. Ritchie, "Deux textes," op. cit., p. 320.
16 P. Cultru, *Premier voyage*, op. cit., p. 131.
17 G. Thilmans, op. cit.
18 C. I. A. Ritchie, "Deux textes," op. cit., p. 331.
19 Ibid., p. 320.
20 Ibid.

21 John Barbot, "A Description of the Coast of North and South Guinea," *A Collection of voyages and travels*, volume 5, London, 1732, by Churchill, p. 55.
22 John Barbot, "A Supplement to the New Description of the Coast of Guinea," vol. 1, p. 71.
23 M. Lamiral, *L'Afrique et le peuple africain, considérés sous tous leurs rapports avec notre commerce et nos colonies*, Paris, 1789, p. 109.
24 C. I. A. Ritchie, "Deux textes," op. cit., p. 323.
25 P. Cultru, *Premier voyage*, op. cit., p. 80.
26 C. I. A. Ritchie, "Deux textes," op. cit., p. 312.
27 C. I. A. Ritchie, "Deux textes," op. cit., p. 321.

CHAPTER 2

1 Pathé Diagne, *Pouvoir politique traditionnel en Afrique occidentale: essai sur les institutions politiques précoloniales*, Paris, Présence Africaine, 1967, p. 19.
2 H. Gaden, op. cit., p. 4.
3 Le Maire, *Les Voyages du sieur Le Maire aux îles Canaries, Cap-Vert, Sénégal et Gambie*, Paris 1695, p. 160.
4 H. Gaden, *Légendes et Coutumes*, op. cit., p. 3.
5 R. Rousseau, "Étude sur le Oualo," op. cit., p. 164.
6 R. Rousseau, "Étude sur le Oualo," op. cit., p. 180.
7 Ibid. pp. 183-184.
8 Ibid. p.185.
9 R. Rousseau, "Études sur le Oualo," op. cit., p. 19.
10 R. Rousseau, "Études sur le Oualo," op. cit., p. 194.
11 J. Suret-Canale, *Afrique Noire. Géographie, civilisation, histoire*. Éditions sociales, Paris, 1961, p. 103.
12 C. I. A. Ritchie, "Deux textes," op. cit., p. 317.
13 Ibid. p. 318.
14 G. Thilmans, op. cit., p. 29.
15 C. I. A. Ritchie, "Deux textes," op. cit., p. 316.
16 C. I. A. Ritchie, "Deux texts," op. cit., p. 316.
17 Ibid., pp. 318-19.
18 G. Thilmans, op. cit., p. 30.
19 Le Maire, *Les Voyages du sieur Le Maire…*, op. cit., p. 135.
20 P. Diagne, "Pouvoir politique," op. cit., p. 19.
21 J. Robin, "D'un royaume amphibie et fort disparate," *African Studies*, vol. 5, nr. 4. December 1946, p. 254.
22 C. I .A. Ritchie "Deux texts," op. cit., p. 322.
23 H. Gaden, "Légendes et Coutumes," op. cit., p. 21.
24 2. B.18, C.G. at M., Saint-Louis, October 30, 1840, copy of a report of the ceremonies of the installation of the *brak*. His testimony shows that the enthronization ceremony of the *braks* has preserved the same features.
25 H. Gaden, *Légendes et Coutumes*, op. cit., p. 24.
26 F. Y. B. Gaby, *Relation de la négrite avec la découverte de la rivière du Sénégal*, Paris ,1689, p. 49.
27 Le Maire, "Les Voyages du sieur Le Mair," op. cit., p. 161.
28 Baron Roger, "Notice sur le gouvernement, les mœurs et les superstitions des nègres du pays du Wâlo," *Bull. Société de Géography*, Vol. 8, Paris, 1827, p. 351.
29 H. Gaden, "Légendes et coutumes," op. cit., p. 26.
30 Abdoulaye Bara Diop, "La Tenure foncière," op. cit., p. 50.

31 Ibid.
32 P. Cultru, *Premier voyage*, op. cit., p. 45.
33 H. Gaden, "Légendes et coutumes," op. cit., p. 24.
34 H. Gaden, "Légendes et coutumes," op. cit., p. 24.
35 Ibid., p. 26.
36 P. Cultru, *Premier voyage*, op. cit., p. 72.
37 V. Monteil, "Chronique du Waalo," op. cit., p. 45.
38 See the list given by Amadou Wade, "Chronique du Waalo," op. cit., pp. 34-35; Robin, op. cit., p.225; Azan, "Notice sur le Walo," *Revue Mar. et Col.*, vol. 9, Oct.-Dec. 1863, pp. 334-37.
39 Besides, the lists concerning the territorial distribution of each particular ennoblement given by Azan, Amadou Wade, and Robin do not always agree.
40 R. Rousseau, "Étude sur le Oualo," op. cit., pp. 173-74.
41 Claude Jannequin, *Voyage de Lybie au royaume de Sénégal le long du Niger*, Paris, 1643, p. 57.
42 H. Gaden, "Légendes et coutumes," op. cit.
43 Pathé Diagne, "Pouvoir politique," op. cit.
44 C. I. A. Ritchie, "Deux texts," op. cit., p. 323.
45 P. Cultru, *Premier voyage…*, op. cit., p. 126.
46 John Barbot, *A Description*, op. cit., p. 55.
47 Le Maire, *Les Voyages du sieur Lemaire*, op. cit., pp. 175-76.
48 Ibid., p. 176.
49 C. I. A. Ritchie, "Deux texts," op. cit., p. 322.
50 F. Y. B. Gaby, op. cit., p. 49.
51 H. Gaden, "Légendes et coutumes," op. cit., p. 24.
52 V. Monteil, "Chronique du Waalo," op. cit., p. 34.

PART II

1 Eric Williams, *Capitalisme et esclavage*, Présence africaine, Paris, 1968, p. 14.

CHAPTER 3

1 J. Boulègue, *La Sénégambie*, op. cit., p. 269.
2 P. Cultru, *Premier voyage*, op. cit., introduction; R. Rosseau, "Le Site et les origines de Saint-Louis," *La Géographie*, nr. 2 Vol. 44, July-August 1925, pp. 116-28; nr. 3, pp. 282-301; nr. 4-5, pp. 424-38; Abdoulaye Ly, "Sur le site et les origines de Saint-Louis," *Notes africaines*, nr. 58, August 1953, pp. 52-57 ; nr. 61, January 1954, p. 25; J. Boulègue, *La Sénégambie*, op. cit., pp. 266-70.
3 David (Preste) Asseline, *Les Antiquités et chroniques de la ville de Dieppe de 1080 à 1683*, Dieppe 1874, Vol. 2, p. 238.
4 B. N., n.a., 9396, June 24, 1633, Companie du cap Vert, Sénégal et Gambie.
5 B. N., n.a. 9339, of Saturday, March 11, 1634 at the assembly of the twenty-four of the council of the city of Rouen.
6 Claude Jannequin, *Voyage de Lybie*, op. cit., p. 57.
7 Ibid.
8 Jean Boulègue thinks, and this is not yet more than a hypothesis, that this first habitation was on the continent.
9 Claude Jannequin, *Voyage de Lybie*, op. cit., p. 57.

10 D. Asseline, *Les Antiquités et chroniques*, op. cit., p. 252.
11 Ibid., p. 256.
12 Ibid., p. 257.
13 C. I. A. Ritchie, "Deux texts," op. cit., p. 350.
14 P. Cultru, *Premier voyage*, op. cit., pp.113-14.
15 P. Cultru, *Premier voyage*, op. cit., p. 72.
16 D. Asseline, *Les Antiquités et chroniques*, op. cit., Vol. 2, p. 255.
17 P. Cultru, *Premier voyage*, op. cit., p. 29.
18 D. Asseline, *Les Antiquités et chroniques*, op. cit., pp. 316-17.
19 P. Cultru, *Premier voyage*, op. cit., p. 28.
20 C. I. A. Ritchie, "Deux texts," op. cit., p. 346.
21 V. M. Godinho, *L'Économie de l'Empire portugais*, op. cit., p. 184.
22 Marian Malowist, "Les Débuts du système de plantations dans la période des grandes découvertes," *Africana Bulletin*, Warsaw, 1969, nr. 10, p. 24, quoting J. de Barros, p. 125.
23 J. Boulègue, "Relation du port," op. cit., p. 509.
24 D. Asseline, *Les Antiquités et chroniques*, op. cit., Vol. 2, p. 238.
25 Abdoulaye Ly, "La Companie du Sénégal," op. cit., pp. 35-36.
26 Ibid., p. 64.
27 Colonies, C8 B1, Discours sur l'Estat passé et présent des Isles françaises de l'Amérique… en 1684, cited by A. Ly, p. 40.
28 Colonies, C6 29, Mémoire de 1752, Considérations sur le commerce d'Afrique.
29 Eric Williams, "Capitalisme et esclavage," op. cit., p. 19.
30 Henri Brunschwig, *L'Avènement de l'Afrique noire*, Paris, 1963.
31 We will address the circumstances of the suppression of the slave trade in a special chapter devoted to the end of the eighteenth century.
32 Jean Suret-Canale, Conséquences sociales et contexte de la traite africaine, Présence africaine, 2nd Trimester 1964, p. 142.
33 Colonies, C6 23, *Mémoire sur le Sénégal*, undated, before 1790.
34 Philip Curtin, *The African Slave Trade*, University of Wisconsin Press, 1969.
35 Le Maire, *Les Voyages du sieur Le Maire*, op. cit., p. 68.
36 Jean Suret-Canale, "Conséquences sociales," op. cit., p. 142.
37 C. I. A. Ritchie, "Deux texts," op. cit., p. 298.
38 P. Cultru, *Premier voyage*, op. cit., p. 45.
39 P. Cultru, *Premier voyage*, op. cit.
40 Colonies, C6 2, 1967, Compagnie du Sénégal et Côte d' Afrique, *État présent de la Companie du Sénégal*.
41 Colonies, C6 2. March 26, 1693, *Mémoire de sieur de La Courbe sur le commerce de Guinée*, Département du Sénégal.
42 Pruneau de Pomme-Gorge, *Description de la Négritie*, Amsterdam, 1789, pp. 28-29.
43 Colonies, C6 18, Remarques. État en aperçu des esclaves que peuvent retirer les nations de l'Europe à la Côte occidentale d'Afrique, presumed date: 1783.
44 Colonies, C6 6, Addition au *Mémoire instructif pour M. S. Robert*, director and chief commissioner of the Senegal Company, Senegal, August 1, 1720.
45 John Barbot, *A Description*, op. cit., pp. 47-55.
46 P. Cultru, *Premier voyage*, op. cit., p. 132.
47 Colonies, C6 8, March 28, 1724.
48 Colonies, C6 8, August 1724. "Extrait de la traite de gomme, de captifs et autres marchandises faites à escale du désert par le sieur Jean Demion, commis depuis le 3 avril jusqu'au 4 juin 1724." This text has been fully published by André Delcourt, "La

France et les établissements français au Sénégal entre 1713 et 1763," *Mémoire I. F.A.N.*, nr. 17, 1952, pp. 382-87.
49 C. I. A. Ritchie, "Deux textes," op. cit., p. 351.
50 Ibid., p. 320.
51 Colonies, C^6 8, August 10, 1724. Table by J. Demion.
52 P. Cultru, *Premier voyage*, op. cit., p. 146.
53 Colonies, C6 11, Senegal, June 15, 1736.
54 D. Asseline, *Les Antiquités et chroniques*, op. cit., p. 257.
55 P. Cultru, *Premier voyage*, op. cit.
56 Colonies, C6 8, August 10, 1724. Table by J. Demion.
57 Jean-Baptiste Labat, *Nouvelle Relation de l'Afrique occidentale*, Paris, 1728 , Volume 2, p. 360.
58 Ibid., Volume 2, pp. 361-64.
59 P. Cultru, *Premier voyage*, op. cit., p. 175.
60 Le Maire, *Les Voyages du sieur Le Maire*, op. cit., p. 73.

CHAPTER 4

1   C. I. A. Ritchie, "Deux textes," op. cit., p. 351.
2   Claude Jannequin, *Voyage de Lybie*, op. cit., p. 57.
3   Colonies. C6 7, Saint-Louis, May 3, 1722.
4   Ismaël Hamet, *Chronique de la Mauritanie sénégalaise*, Nacer Eddine, Paris, 1911, p. 62.
5   H. T. Norris, "Znaga Islam during the Seventeenth and Eighteenth Centuries," B.S.O.A., London, Volume 32, 3rd part, 1969, p. 517.
6   C. I. A. Ritchie, "Deux textes," op. cit., p. 338.
7   C. I. A. Ritchie, "Deux textes," op. cit., p. 338.
8   Ibid., pp. 338-39.
9   Ibid., p. 339.
10 Le Maire, *Les Voyages du sieur Le Maire*, op. cit., p. 91.
11 F.Y.B. Gaby, *Relation de la Négritie*, op. cit., p. 49.
12 C. I. A. Ritchie, "Deux textes," op. cit., p. 340.
13 P. Cultru, *Premier Voyage*, op. cit., p. 142.
14 Ismaël Hamet, *Chronique de la Mauritanie*, op. cit., p. 176.
15 C. I. A. Ritchie, "Deux textes," op. cit., p. 340.
16 V. Monteil, "Chronique du Waalo," op. cit., p. 41.
17 Ismaël Hamet, *Chronique de la Mauritanie*, op. cit., p. 176.
18 C. I. A. Ritchie, "Deux textes," op. cit., p. 340-44.
19 C. I. A. Ritchie, "Deux textes," op. cit., p. 343.
20 Ismaël Hamet, *Chronique de la Mauritanie*, op. cit., 176.
21 C. I. A. Ritchie, "Deux textes," op. cit., p. 350.
22 C. I. A. Ritchie, "Deux textes," op. cit., p. 352.
23 C. I. A. Ritchie, "Deux textes," op. cit., p. 352.
24 V. Monteil, "Chronique du Waalo," op. cit., p. 41.
25 C. I. A. Ritchie, "Deux textes," op. cit., p. 344.
26 Ibid., p. 341.
27 Ibid., p. 343.
28 Ibid., p. 346.
29 Ibid. Chambonneau calls Munir Eddine by the name "Mohamet Dine."
30 C. I. A. Ritchie, "Deux textes," op. cit., p. 351.
31 Ibid., p. 342.

32 S. Van Brakel, "Eene memorie over den handel der West-Indies compagnie omstreeks 1670," *Bijdr. Med. Hist. gen.*, vol. 35, 1914, pp. 87-104 (translated by G. Thilmans).
33 Roussier, "Mémoire ou relation du Sr Ducasse sur son voyage de Guynée avec la Tempeste en 1687 et 1688," p. 3, cited in Abdoulaye Ly, op. cit., p. 141.
34 C. I. A. Ritchie, "Deux textes," op. cit., p. 342.
35 Ibid.
36 Ibid., p. 343.
37 Ibid., p. 344.
38 Ibid., p. 342.
39 Ibid., p. 344.
40 Ibid., p. 345.
41 Ismaël Hamet, *Chronique de la Mauritanie*, op. cit., pp. 210-14.
42 Ibid., p. 176.
43 C. I. A. Ritchie, "Deux textes," op. cit., p. 344.
44 Ibid., pp. 344-345.
45 Ibid., p. 345.
46 Ibid., p. 347.
47 C. I. A. Ritchie, "Deux textes," op. cit., p. 347.
48 Ibid., p. 347.
49 Ibid.
50 Ibid.
51 Ibid., p. 350.
52 C. I. A. Ritchie, "Deux textes," op. cit., p. 351-52.
53 Ibid., p. 326.
54 Ibid., p. 325-326.
55 Ibid., p. 326.
56 V. Monteil, "Chronique du Waalo," op. cit., p. 41.
57 C. I. A. Ritchie, "Deux textes," op. cit., p. 352.
58 Jean-Baptiste Labat, *Nouvelle Relation*, op.cit., p. 101.
59 C. I. A. Ritchie, "Deux textes," op. cit., p. 326.
60 Ibid., p. 352.
61 Ibid., p. 352.
62 John Barbot, *A Description*, op. cit., p. 62.
63 Le Maire, *Les Voyages du sieur Le Maire*, op. cit., p. 91.
64 C. I. A. Ritchie, "Deux textes," op. cit., p. 352.
65 John Barbot, *A Description*, op. cit., p. 33.
66 Le Maire, *Les Voyages du sieur Le Maire*, op. cit., p. 91.
67 C. I. A. Ritchie, "Deux textes," op. cit.
68 Ibid., pp. 352-53.
69 Ibid., p. 353.
70 Le Maire, *Les Voyages du sieur Le Maire*, op. cit., p. 92.
71 J. Barbot, *A Description*, op. cit., p. 47.
72 Nehema Levtzion, *Note sur les origines de l'Islam militant au Fouta Djallon*, unpublished paper.

CHAPTER 5

1 Abdoulaye Ly, "On the site," op. cit., p. 125.
2 Ibid., p 127.
3 Ibid., p. 182.
4 Ibid., p. 214.

5   Ibid., p. 255-56.
6   Ibid., p. 257.
7   Ibid., p. 263.
8   Ibid., p. 295.
9   P. Cultru, *First Travel*, op. cit., p. 102.
10 Ibid., p. 103.
11 Ibid., pp. 107-08.
12 Ibid.
13 Azan, "Notice sur le Walo," op. cit., p. 304.
14 R. Rousseau, "Étude sur le Walo," op. cit., p. 202.
15 C. I. A. Ritchie, "Deux Textes," op. cit., p. 325.
16 Azan, "Notice sur le Walo," op. cit., p. 340.
17 V. Monteil, "Chronicle of Waalo," op. cit., p. 43.
18 Ibid.
19 Ibid., p. 44.
20 Azan, "Notice sur le Walo," op. cit., p. 340.
21 V. Monteil, "Chronicle of Waalo," op. cit., p. 341.
22 Azan, "Notice sur le Walo," op, cit., p. 341.
23 V. Monteil, "Chronicle of Waalo," op. cit., pp. 47-48.
24 Ibid., p. 49.
25 A. Delcourt, *France and the French Settlements*, op. cit., p. 153.
26 Ibid., p. 154.
27 V. Monteil, "Chronicle of Waalo," op. cit., p. 48.
28 Ibid., p. 49.
29 R. Rousseau, "Étude sur le Walo," op. cit., p. 146.
30 Azan, "Notice sur le Walo," op. cit., p. 341.
31 V. Monteil, "Chronicle of Waalo," op. cit., p. 47.
32 Ibid., p. 48.
33 A. Delcourt, *France and French Settlements*, op. cit., p. 140 or col. C6, June 6, 1720.
34 A. Delcourt, *France and the French Settlements*, op. cit., p. 180.
35 Sylvain Meinrad Xavier de Golbéry, *Fragments of an African Voyage during the years 1785, 1786 and 1787*, Paris, 1802, p. 196.
36 A. Delcourt, *France and the French Settlements*, op. cit., p. 179.
37 A. Delcourt, *France and the French Settlements*, op. cit., pp. 179-299.
38 Colonies C6, 6, August 1, 1720.
39 Marine, B1. 21.
40 Colonies, C6, 6, August 1, 1720.
41 Ibid.
42 Ibid., Colonies, C6, 6, June 6, 1720. Addition to the instructive memorandum to the attention of Mr. Saint-Robert, director and general commander of the Senegal concession.
43 Ibid.
44 Ibid, C6, 6, August 1, 1720.
45 Ibid, C6, 6, March 28, 1721.
46 Ibid., C6, 6, August 1, 1720.
47 Ibid.
48 Ibid.
49 Ibid.
50 Ibid.
51 Ibid.
52 Ibid.

53 Ibid., C6, 6, March 28, 1724.
54 Colonies, C6, 6, August 1, 1720.
55 Ibid.
56 Colonies, C6 6, March 28, 1721. Letter of Saint-Robert.
57 Colonies, C6 6, Senegal, March 28, 1721.
58 Colonies, C6 6, 1720. Observation of Saint-Robert.
59 There may have been some confusion between the troops sent to help Alichandora and older troops of Moroccan origin, who had been sweeping through Mali's Sahel since the end of the seventeenth century. It is not impossible that the descendants of the Arma of Tombouctou, attracted by the Atlantic trade, may have moved increasingly westward and be reinforced by successive waves of more or less independent warriors belonging to the king of Morocco. This might explain the changing alliances dependent upon changing circumstances. In any case, in his history of the Diawara, G. Boyer notes the siege of Diara by the Armas in 1598. The siege was still remembered as well as the intervention of the Armas, who had settled in Western Bakkounou, in the civil war of the kingdom of Diara at the end of the seventeenth century. More to the point, Bukakar Siré's allusion to the Moroccan defeat at the hands of the Bambaras confirms their presence in this region of Mali's Sahel and leads us to formulate an hypothesis according to which relationships existed between Ormas and Armas and this, all the more so as they moved eastward again, to Galam, after their defeat on the lower region of the Senegal River. This is also the hypothesis of Mohamed El Chennafi whom we met in Nouakchott.
60 Colonies, C6 7, May 3, 1722.
61 J. B. Labat, op. cit., volume 2, p. 195.
62 Colonies, C6, 7, Saint-Louis, May 3, 1722.
63 Ibid.
64 Ibid., July 16, 1722.
65 Ibid.
66 Ibid.
67 Ibid., C6, 7, December 28. 1722.
68 Ibid.
69 Ibid., C6, 6, August 1, 1720.
70 Ibid., C6, 7, December 28, 1722.
71 Ibid.
72 Colonies C6, 7, April 27, 1723.
73 Ibid.
74 Ibid.
75 Ibid.
76 A. Delcourt, op. cit., p. 240.
77 Colonies, C6, 7, Senegal, May 18, 1723.
78 Ibid.
79 B.N., F. Fr. 2422, April 14, 1723.
80 Colonies, C6, 7, December 18, 1723.
81 Colonies, C6, 7, August 18, 1723.
82 Colonies, C6, 7, December 18, 1723.
83 V. Monteil, op. cit., pp. 49-50.
84 Amadou Wade incorrectly ascribes this mission to Yeerim Ndiay. A popular song effectively narrates the courage of Yeerim Bakar, father of Yeerim Ndiay, who alone dared announce his destitution to the *beeco*.
85 V. Monteil, op. cit., p. 51. We can personally attest to this attitude of independence in the current descendant of the *beeco*, whom we met in Roos Beeco. He regarded himself

as a sovereign, with the same title as the *brak*, and would not hear any talk of their vassalage ties.

86 V. Monteil, op. cit., p. 52.
87 Colonies, C6, 8, Saint-Louis, March 28, 1724.
88 Ibid.
89 Colonies, C6, 8, December 18, 1724.
90 Ibid.
91 V. Monteil, op. cit., p. 53; Azan, op. cit., p. 344.
92 V. Monteil, op. cit., p. 53; Azan, op. cit., p. 344.
93 C.O., 267/12, March 31, 1758.
94 Azan, op. cit., p. 344.
95 D.F.C., Folder 1, Senegal, no. 30. *Historical Journal* concerning all that took place in the Senegal concession from September 1, 1729, to September 1, 1730, February 1730.
96 Ibid., *Historical Journal*, June 20, 1730.
97 Ibid.
98 Ibid., *Historical Journal*, July 8, 1730.
99 Colonies, C6, 10, *Sequel to the Historical Journal*, from September 1, 1730 to September 7, 1731. September 11, 1730.
100 Ibid., November 9, 1730.
101 Colonies, C6, 10, Senegal, August 30, 1733.
102 Colonies, C6, 11, October 8, 1734, *Memorandum on Senegal*.

CHAPTER 6

1 Azan, op. cit., p. 344.
2 Colonies, C6, 12, Senegal, August 1, 1742.
3 Ibid.
4 C.O., 267/12, March 31, 1758.
5 Colonies, C6, 11, May 31, 1737.
6 Colonies, C6, 29, undated document.
7 V. Monteil, op. cit.
8 Colonies, C6, 13, June 25, 1752.
9 Colonies, C6, 14, June 20, 1753.
10 Ibid., C6, 14, November 25, 1753.
11 Ibid., C6, 14, June 20, 1753.
12 Ibid., C6, 14, June 3, 1754.
13 Ibid., C6, 14, September 1754.
14 Ibid., C6, 14, November 16, 1756.
15 C.O., 267/12, March 31, 1758.
16 Colonies, C6, 12, August 1, 1742.

CHAPTER 7

1 A. Delcourt, *France and French Settlements*, op. cit., p. 345.
2 Eveline C. Martin, *The British West African Settlements, 1750-1821*, London, 1927, p. 74.
3 Anonymous, *A Plan for Improving the Trade of Senegal Addressed to the Lords' Commissioner for Trade and Plantation*, London, 1763, pp. 3-6, 16-18.
4 C.O., 267, A. Fort-Lewis, July 25, 1766.
5 Anonymous, *A Plan for Improving*, op. cit., p. 6.
6 C.O., 267.12, Senegal, March 31, 1758.

7   Ibid.
8   Azan, op. cit., p. 345.
9   R. Rousseau, "Étude sur le Walo," *Notebooks of Yoro Dyâo*, B.C.E.H.S., April-June 1933, p. 285.
10 Colonies, C6, 15, Memorandum on Gorée by M. Adanson, in May-June 1763.
11 Faidherbe, "Historical Notice on Cayor," *Bulletin of the Geographical Society*, 4th trimester of 1883, p. 548.
12 F. fr. 9557, B.N., November 30, 1762, Memorandum on the mines of Bambouk.
13 T. 70/37, Sunday, May 6, 1764.
14 C.O., 388/52, Copy of a Letter from John Barnes, Esqr. Gov. the Council of Senegal to the Committee of the Company of Merchants trading to Africa, dated February 17, 1765.
15 C.O., 388/52, Letter from John Barnes, February 17, 1765.
16 Ibid.
17 T. 70/37, Senegal, August 21, 1765.
18 R. Rousseau, "Étude sur le Walo," op. cit., p. 147.
19 C.O., 267/13, Senegal, September 1, 1766.
20 R. Rousseau, "Étude sur le Walo," op. cit., p. 147.
21 C.O., 267/1, Fort-Louis, Senegal, May 28, 1766.
22 C.O., 267/13, Senegal, September 1, 1766.
23 C.O., 267/14, Fort-Louis, February 25, 1769.
24 C.O., 267/15, Fort-Louis, August 1, 1772.
25 R. Rousseau, "Étude sur le Walo," op. cit., p. 147.
26 M. Lamiral, *Africa and the African people in all their Relationhips with Our Trade and Colonies*, Paris, Dessenne, 1789, p. 171.
27 V. Monteil, op. cit., p. 56.
28 Azan, "Notice sur le Walo," op. cit., p. 346.
29 V. Monteil, op. cit., p. 57.
30 Azan, op. cit., p. 346.
31 V. Monteil, op. cit., p. 58.
32 Saugnier, *Narratives of Several Voyages to the African Coast, Morocco, Senegal, Gorée, Galam, etc.*, Paris, 1791, p. 189.
33 Azan, op. cit., p. 347.
34 V. Monteil, op, cit., p. 61.
35 Azan, op. cit., p. 348.
36 C.O., 267/2, The following presents between November 5, 1775 and May 5, 1776.
37 Azan, op. cit., p. 348.
38 Lamiral, op. cit., p. 171.
39 Ibid., p. 177.
40 C.O., 268/4, Fort-Lewis, Senegal, August 18, 1775.
41 C.O., 267/1, A petition presented by the inhabitants of Senegal requesting redress for the injustice done to them by His Excellency Governor O'Hara at different times, Senegal, August 22, 1775.
42 C.O., 267/17, June 10, 1776.
43 Colonies, C6 18, presumed date of 1783. Comments. Account of slaves that European nations can retain from the western coast of Africa.
44 Colonies, C6, 17. Gorée, April 1777.
45 C.O., 267/19, *Answer to the Questions Proposed to Lieutenant Colonel Maxwell, Lieutenant Governor of Senegal and Gorée by His Majesty Commissioner for Investigating the Forts and Settlements in Africa*, Saint-Louis, January 1, 1811. "During the period that Senegal was in our possession after the peace of 1763, the inhabitants of Walo then

exceedingly powerful were trouble some the settlement and threatened to prevent communication with the upper part of the river. General Ohara then Governor entered into a treaty with the Trarza Moors and King Damel to assist him in attacking that nation, which they did most effectually and the Walo country received a blow from which it has never since recovered. Its villages on the River's Bank are yet deserted and abandoned, its people have been carried into captivity and those who remainare constantly subjected to the plunder of the Moors, who treat as a dependant and tributary state. Ohara's name is still used by the Walo mother's to frighten their crying children."

46 C.O., 268/4, Fort-Lewis, Senegal, July 1, 1776.
47 C.O., 267/4, London, November 29, 1776.
48 C.O., 267/3, Duplicate, Fort-Lewis, July 26, 1777.
49 Colonies, C6, 17, April 10, 1781.
50 M. Saugnier, op. cit., p. 189.
51 Lamiral, op. cit., p. 171.
52 Azan, op. cit., p. 348.
53 R. Geoffroy de Villeneuve, op. cit., vol. 3, p. 26.
54 Lamiral, op. cit., pp. 238-240; Ibid., p. 242.
55 Ibid., p. 242.
56 R. G. de Villeneuve, op. cit., vol. 4, pp. 28-30.
57 Ibid., vol. 3, p. 27.
58 Jean-Baptiste-Léonard Durand, *Voyage to Senegal, 1785 and 1786*, Paris, 1802, vol. 2, p. 62.
59 Oumar Kane, "Essay on the Chronology of eighteenth Century Satigi," *Bulletin I.F.A.N.*, series B, July 1970, p. 758.
60 C.O., 268/4, Senegal, August 18, 1775.
61 C.O., 268/4, Fort-Lewis, January 26, 1776.
62 Oumar Kane, *Relationships between Fuuta and the Moors*, unpublished research.
63 C.O., 268/4, Fort-Lewis, July 1, 1776.
64 Colonies, F3/62, fol. 255, copy of the translated letter from King Almamy to M. Blanchot, dated March 1789.
65 C.O., 267/29, Answer to the questions..., Fort-Lewis, January 1, 1811.
66 Baron Roger, *Kélédor*, Paris, 1829, p. 209.
67 3 B 4, Saint-Louis, September 1819, Answers of Schmaltz to Melay.
68 Baron Roger, *Kélédor*, op. cit., pp. 57-58.

CHAPTER 8

1 Christian Schefer, *General Instructions Given from 1763 to 1870 to the Governors and Directors of French Settlements in Western Africa*, Paris, 1921, p. 103.
2 Ibid., pp. 103-110.
3 Eric Williams, *Capitalism and Slavery*, op. cit., p. 6.
4 Ibid., p. 159.
5 Ibid., p. 252.
6 Ibid., p. 161.
7 Ibid., p. 190.
8 Ibid.
9 Albert Soboul, *History of the French Revolution*, Gallimard, Collection Idées, p. 209.
10 Lamiral, op. cit., p. 326.
11 Ibid., p. 375.
12 Colonies, C6, 20, Senegal, 1791, Letter of Lamiral, Senegal representative.
13 Pruneau de Pomme-Gorge, op. cit., pp. 81-82.

14 Jean Baptiste Léonard Durand, op. cit., vol. 2, p. 10.
15 Ibid., p. 327, 336.
16 Lamiral, op. cit., p. 145.
17 Ibid., p. 177.
18 Ibid., p. 222.
19 Eric Williams, op. cit., p. 192.
20 C. Schefer, op. cit., p. 171.
21 Ibid., p. 180.
22 Anonymous, "A Colonization Plan of Senegal in 1802," Yearly Report of the Committee of Historical and Scientific Studies in French Western Africa, 1916, p. 183.
23 Anonymous, "A Plan," op. cit., p. 134.
24 Ibid.
25 Ibid., p. 189.
26 Xavier de Golbéry, op. cit., vol. 1, p. 263.
27 Marine, Colonies, F3. 60, Senegal, September 8, 1786.
28 Xavier de Golbéry, op. cit., vol. 1, p. 263.
29 Lamiral, op. cit., p. 173.
30 V. Monteil, op. cit., p. 63.
31 Ibid.
32 Ibid.
33 Baron Roger, *Kélédor*, op. cit., pp. 100-24.
34 Ibid., p. 49.
35 Lamiral, op. cit., p. 165.
36 Baron Roger, *Kélédor*, op. cit., p. 129.
37 V. Monteil, op. cit., pp. 63-64.
38 Amédée Tardieu, *History and Description of all the Peoples: Senegambia, Guinea, Nubia*, 1867, p. 45.
39 Azan, op. cit., pp. 349-50.
40 Ibid., p. 350.
41 Ibid., p. 351.
42 Ibid., p. 352.
43 Ibid.
44 Boubacar Barry, "Unpublished Memoirs of Monsérat on the History of Northern Senegal from 1819 to 1839," *Bulletin I. F.A.N.*, vol. 32, Series B, n° 1, 1970, p. 11.
45 M. Saugnier, op. cit., p. 189.
46 J. Monteilhet, "Finances and Commerce in Senegal during the Wars of the Revolution and the Empire," *Yearly Memoirs of the C.E.H.S.*, 1917, p. 388.
47 13 G., 16, Balance of the Customs, 1817
48 Colonies, C6, 20, Purchase act for the islands of Babugué, Safal and Guiebair by Blanchot, November 21, 1799.
49 C.O., 267/29, Answer to the questions proposed to Lieutenant Colonel Maxwell... by His Majesty Commissioner for investigating the forts and settlements in Africa, Saint-Louis, January 1, 1811.
50 C. Schefer, op. cit., vol. 1, pp. 208-228.

PART III

CHAPTER 9

1. This subject has been abundantly treated by Georges Hardy in *The Development of Senegal between 1817 and 1854*, Paris, 1921. We shall merely repeat some aspects of the agricultural colonization which make it possible to clarify its economic, political and social consequences for Waalo.
2. C. Schefer, op. cit., vol. 1, p. 288.
3. Ibid., pp. 282-83.
4. 13 G. 2, Treaty dated May 8, 1819 signed in Ngio with Waalo Brak, article 2.
5. J. Monteilhet, "Documents relative to the History of Senegal," "A diplomatic visit of Governor Schmaltz in Senegal," May 1819, *C.E.H.S. Yearly Memoir*, 1916, pp. 72-73.
6. 13 G. 2, Treaty Dated May 9, 1819 signed in Ngio with Waalo Brak, article 2.
7. 13 G. 2, ibid., article 9.
8. 13 G. 2, ibid., articles 11 and 12.
9. 13 G. 16 files, 3 and 3, *List of Customary Fees in 1819*.
10. 2 B 4, C.G., to M., Saint-Louis, September 4, 1819, Criticisms and Observations of M. de Melay (literally extracted from the dispatch dated June 18).
11. Ibid.
12. G. Hardy, The Development of Senegal from 1817 to 1854, Paris, Larose, 1921, p. 86.
13. Schefer, op. cit., vol. 1, p. 345.
14. G. Hardy, op. cit,, p. 97.
15. Ibid., pp. 107-08.
16. G. Hardy, op. cit., p. 192.
17. 2 B 9. C.G., to M., Saint-Louis, May 15, 1824.
18. 2 B 10, C.G., to M., Saint-Louis, September 28, 1826.
19. G. Hardy, op. cit., p. 236.
20. 2 B 11, C.G., to the minister, August 25, 1827.
21. J. Morenas, Second Petition Against the Slave Trade in Senegal, Paris, 1821.
22. J. Morenas, Second Petition Against the Slave Trade in Senegal, Paris, 1821.
23. Senegal IV, 16 C, Saint-Louis, September 24, 1819.
24. 2 B 4, C.G., to M., Saint-Louis, November 1819.
25. 13 G, 2., November 15, 1819, Peace Treaty between Waalo chiefs and Hamdoul Koury, legitimate heir of the Trarzas.
26. 2 B 4, C.G., to M., Dagana, February 24, 1820.
27. 2 B 5, C.G., to Mr. Saint-Louis, March 27, 1820, Presumed Ctoses of the Events that Have Taken Place since 1819.
28. Ibid.
29. R. Rousseau, "Étude sur le *Walo*," op. cit., p. 149.
30. Ibid., p. 150.
31. Ibid., p. 150-51.
32. 2 B 5, C.G., to M., Saint-Louis, March 27, 1820.
33. 2 B 5, C.G., to M., Saint-Louis, August 19, 1820.
34. 13 G 2, Peace Treaty with Amar Ould Moctar concerning Waalo, June 7, 1821.
35. 13 G 16, File 5, August 25, 1821.
36. 2 B 13, C.G., to M., Saint-Louis, August 16, 1828.
37. 2 B 13, C.G., to M., Saint-Louis, April 11, 1823.
38. B. Barry, "Unpublished Memorandum," op. cit., p. 18.
39. Ibid., p. 16.

40 3 B 42, Letter to Mr. Berton, January 7, 1927.
41 3 B 42, Letter to Brunet, January 16, 1827.
42 3 B 42, Ibid., March 1, 1827.
43 3 B 42, Ibid., December 29, 1827.
44 B. Barry, "Unpublished Memorandum," op. cit.
45 2 B 12, C.G., to M., Saint-Louis, May 12, 1828.
46 1362, Treaty with Mohamed El Habid, April 15, 1829.
47 2 B 13, C.G., to M., Saint-Louis, April 25, 1829.
48 J. Monteilhet, op. cit., p. 66.
49 2 B 32, C.G., to M., Saint-Louis, April 9, 1857.
50 2 B 33, C.G., to M., Saint-Louis, March 8, 1862.
51 Jacqueline Soisons, *The People of Waalo*, Development Mission for the Senegal River, Bulletin no. 122, p. 11.
52 E B 32, C.G., to M., Saint-Louis, April 9, 1857, on the subject of the territory of Diawdine.
53 3 B 4, Saint-Louis, September 4, 1819, Response of Schmaltz to Melay.
54 Senegal, II, 2, Statistical Glimpses on the Senegal, a French Colony on the Western Coast of Africa by Pichon, 1823.
55 13 G.I., Treaty of February 1821.
56 3 B 23, Saint-Louis, June 17, 1822.
57 3 B 23, Letter to Mr. Sibert, March 24, 1824.
58 3 B 41, August 6, 1824.
59 3 B 41, Saint-Louis, August 14, 1824, Letter to Mr. Richard.
60 3 B 42, August 1, 1827, Letter to Mr. Brunet.
61 3 B 42, August 26, 1827, Letter to Mr. Brunet.
62 Senegal IV, 16. C., Doukik, September 16, 1827.
63 Senegal IV, 16. C., Doukik, September 16, 1827.
64 2 B 12, C.G., to M., Saint-Louis, December 14, 1827, Cover Letter for the Agreement which ended the Dispute with Waalo.
65 13 G.2, Agreement with Waalo Chiefs, December 5, 1827.
66 13 G 2, May 8 Treaty Signed at Ngio, articles 5, 6 and 7.
67 Senegal II, 2, Memorandum on the State of the Colony of Senegal until September 1819 by Valentin, inhabitant of Saint-Louis.
68 Senegal II, 2, Copy of a Letter Written from the Senegal River on January 12, 1820 by Roger.
69 2 B 7, C.G., to M., Saint-Louis, November 11, 1823.
70 2 B 10, C.G., to M., Saint-Louis, January 21, 1826.
71 F. Zuccarelli, "The System of Indentured Servants in Senegal from 1817 to 1848," *African Study Notebooks*, 1962, p. 434.
72 J. Morenas, Petition against the Slave Trade which is Taking Place in Senegal, Paris, 1820, p. 4.
73 Ibid., p. 5.
74 2 B 6, Saint-Louis, July 16, 1821, on the subject of African slave trade.
75 2 B 6, Saint-Louis, November 15, 1821.
76 2 B 13, C.G., to M., Saint-Louis, April 1, 1829.
77 2 B 13, C.G. to M., Saint-Louis, April 1, 1829.
78 Gaspard Théodore Mollien, *L'Afrique occidentale en 1818 vue par un explorateur français*, ed., Hubert Deschamps, Paris, pp. 75-76.
79 J. Monteilhet, "Documents related to the History of Senegal," "Exploration of Governor Roger in Senegambia at the end of March 1823," *Colonial Bulletin and Historical Science*, 1916, p. 85.

80 2 B 33, C.G., to M., Saint-Louis, March 1832. In this respect, it is noticeable that the cultivation of peanuts in Senegal will eventually be done by migrant workers—workers coming from Mali and Guinea.
81 2 B 11, C. G., to M., Saint-Louis, August 25, 1827.
82 F. Zuccarelli, op. cit., p. 459.
83 Senegal II, 2, Memorandum on the State of the Colony of Senegal until September 10, 1819 by Valentin, Inhabitant of Saint-Louis.
84 Senegal IV, 16 C, Paris, June 19, 1820, Mackto report.
85 Senegal II, 2, Notes requested by the Senegal by Roger in 1821.
86 Senegal II, 2, Notes requested by the Senegal by Roger in 1821.
87 2 B 11, C.G., to M., Saint-Louis, September 28, 1826.
88 G. Hardy, op. cit., p. 255.

CHAPTER 10

1 3 B 6, Saint-Louis, September 21, 1820, to M. Vire, Commander of Dagana.
2 3 B 23, Saint-Louis, November 16, 1823, Relationships with Local Chiefs.
3 3 B 40, Saint-Louis, December 29, 1822.
4 3 B 41, Saint-Louis, July 20, 1824.
5 3 B 41, Saint-Louis, August 14, 1824.
6 3 B 41, Saint-Louis, February 6, 1826.
7 Baron Roger, *Philosophical Research on the Wolof Language*, Paris, Dondé Dupré, 1829, p. 7.
8 Ibid., "Note on the Government, Manners and Superstitions of Negroes in the Country of Waalo," *Bulletin of the Geography Society*, p. 351.
9 Ibid., p. 351.
10 Ibid., p. 352.
11 Ibid.
12 Mollien, op. cit,, p. 82.
13 Baron Roger, "Note on the Government," op. cit., pp. 354-55.
14 3 B 42, Saint-Louis, December 29, 1827, Letter to M. Brunet.
15 B. Barry, "Unpublished Memoir," op. cit.
16 R. Rousseau, "Étude sur le Walo," op. cit., p. 152.
17 V. Monteil, op. cit., p. 65.
18 3 E 8, Minutes from the February 19, 1830 session of the Government Council.
19 Ibid.
20 Ibid.
21 3 E 8, Letter of M. Girardot, February 16, 1830.
22 3 E 8, Meeting of February 19, 1820 [sic], Letter of the Governor to Madiaw Xor.
23 2 B 13, C.G., to M., Saint-Louis, February 25, 1829, Report from M. Berton, December 30, 1828.
24 Boubacar Ly, Honor in the Wolof and Toucouleur Societies, PhD thesis.
25 B. Barry, "Unpublished Memoir," op. cit., p. 7.
26 Ibid., p. 8.
27 3 E 8, March 8, 1830 session of the Government Council.
28 Ibid.
29 B. Barry, "Unpublished Memoir," op. cit., p. 7.
30 2 B 14, C.G., to M., Saint-Louis, March 15, 1830.
31 3 E 8, March 8, 1830 session of the Government Council.
32 3 E 8, March 9, 1830 session of the Government Council.
33 3 E 8, ibid. Letter of Desgranges, March 7, 1830.

34 3 E 8, March 9, 1830 session of the Government Council.
35 2 B 14, C.G., to M., Saint-Louis, March 15, 1830.
36 Ibid.
37 R. Rousseau, "Étude sur le Walo," op. cit., p. 155.
38 The hostility of the traditional aristocracy against Diile is still so great today that this man refused to give us his name.
39 13 G. 22, "General Situation in Senegal 1785-1845," Saint-Louis, May 31, 1831, Memoirs of M. Brou, Saint-Germain.

CHAPTER II

1   B. Barry, "Unpublished Memoirs," op. cit., p. 12.
2   Ibid., p. 13.
3   Ibid.
4   Ibid., p. 13.
5   13 G. 22, Memorandum from Brou, May 31, 1831.
6   B. Barry, "Unpublished Memoirs," op. cit., p. 13.
7   Ibid., p. 15.
8   Ibid., p. 14.
9   Ibid., p. 13
10 Ibid.
11 V. Monteil, op. cit., p. 66.
12 Ibid.
13 B. Barry, "Unpublished Memoirs," op. cit., p. 18.
14 B. Barry, "Unpublished Memoirs," op. cit., p. 21
15 Ibid., p. 20.
16 B. Barry, "Unpublished Memoirs," op. cit., p. 21.
17 2B 15, C.G., to M..., Saint-Louis, August 7, 1833.
18 Ibid.
19 Ibid.
20 B. Barry, "Unpublished Memoirs," op. cit., p. 21.
21 2 B 15, G.G., to M.., Saint-Louis, October 3, 1833.
22 Ibid., November 8, 1833.
23 Ibid., December 25, 1833.
24 B. Barry, "Unpublished Memoirs," op. cit., p. 24.
25 Ibid, p. 27.
26 Ibid.
27 2 B 16, C.G., to M.., Saint-Louis, March 7, 1834.
28 Ibid., August 11, 1835.
29 Ibid., March 7, 1834.
30 2 B 16, C.G., to M.., Saint-Louis, May 26, 1834.
31 13 G. 2, Treaty with Mohamed El Habib, King of the Trarzas, August 30, 1835.
32 13 G. 2, Treaty with the Waalo Chief, September 4, 1835 in Saint-Louis.
33 2 B 16, C.G., to M.., Saint-Louis, January 17, 1836.
34 2 B 17, C.G., to M.., Saint-Louis, August 12, 1839.
35 2 B 16, C.G., to M.., Saint-Louis, March 20, 1837.
36 13 G. 91, Correspondence of the Waalo Chiefs, letter no. 16 by Fara Penda, Njómbót and Waalo chiefs, to the governor.
37 2 B. 17, C.G., to M..., Saint-Louis, September 13, 1837.
38 13 G. 22, Report of Governor Guillet to the Ministry Concerning the Situation in the Colony, January 15, 1837.

39 13 G. 22, Memorandum to Governor Soret upon Mr Guillet's Resignation from the Office of Temporary Acting Governor, Saint-Louis, September 24, 1837.
40 13 G. 22, Memorandum to Charmasson upon the Resignation of Soret, April 14, 1839.
41 12 G. 22, Memorandum of Governor Soret, April 14, 1839.
42 13 G. 22, Guillet's Report to the Ministry, Saint-Louis, January 15, 1837.
43 2 B 17, C.G., to M..., Saint-Louis, August 26, 1839.
44 2 B 18, C.G., to M..., Saint-Louis, October 30, 1840.
45 B 19, C.G., to M..., Saint-Louis, January 20, 1841.
46 V. Monteil, op. cit., p. 67.
47 Ibid.
48 V. Monteil, op. cit., p. 67.
49 2 B 18, C.G., to M..., Saint-Louis, October 30, 1840.
50 R. Rousseau, op. cit., p. 166.

CHAPTER 12

1 2 B 16, C. G., to M., Saint-Louis, March 7, 1834.
2 Ibid.
3 Ibid.
4 13 G. 22, Mémoire de remise de service à Monsieur le Gouverneur Charmasson par Soret, April 14 1839.
5 B. Barry, "Unpublished Memoirs," op. cit., p. 31.
6 Ibid., p. 32.
7 Ibid., p. 33.
8 Ibid., pp. 34-36.
9 2 B 20, C. G., to M., Saint-Louis, July 4, 1842.
10 2 B 20, C. G., to M., Saint-Louis, October 23, 1842.
11 13 G. 86, Merinaghen, October 22, 1842.
12 3 B 52, March 16, 1843, Letter to M. Caille.
13 Ibid.
14 Sénégal II, 2., Aperçus statistiques sur le Sénégal, colonie française sur la côte d'Afrique par Pichon officier du Génie militaire, Saint-Louis, November 1823.
15 Sénégal II, 2.
16 Sénégal II, 3., Gorée, December 16, 1841.
17 Ibid.
18 Sénégal III, 15., November 1843.
19 Sénégal III, 15., November 1843.
20 2 B 20, C.G., to M. Saint-Louis, October 23, 1842.
21 G. Hardy, op. cit., p. 325; Communication du rapport Bouet, Willtomez, November 21, 1845.
22 2 B 19, C.G., to M., Saint-Louis, October 24, 1841.
23 2 B 24, C.G., to M., Saint-Louis, November 15, 1844.
24 13 G. 22, Mémoire laissé par Thomas lorsqu'il a cessé les fonctions de gouverneur par intérim du Sénégal, Saint-Louis, December 11, 1845.
25 2 B 27, C.G., to M., Saint-Louis, October 1, 1846.
26 V. Monteil, op. cit., p. 68.
27 2 B 27, C.G., to M., Saint-Louis, October 1, 1846.
28 3 B 64, Letters of the Chiefs of Waalo to the Governor, 1847.
29 2 B 27, C.G., to M., Saint-Louis, May 25, 1848.
30 2 B 30, C.G., to M., Saint-Louis, March 16, 1850.

31 Senegal IV 19, poste de Mérinaghen, March 11, 1850.
32 Ibid.
33 Senegal IV 19, Mérinaghen Post, March 11, 1850.
34 Senegal IV 45, Board of Directors, session of October 11, 1850.
35 Senegal IV 19, Mérinaghen Post, March 11, 1850.
36 Senegal IV 19, Mérinaghen Post, March 11, 1850.
37 Senegal IV 45, Board of Directors, session of October 11, 1850.
38 Senegal IV 19, Mérinaghen Post, March 11, 1850.
39 Senegal IV 19, Board of Directors, session of June 5, 1850.
40 13 G. 23, Saint-Louis, October 10, 1850.
41 13 G. 91 Correspondence of Waalo Chiefs, letter no. 85, May 23, 1851; Correspondence of Waalo Chiefs, letter no. 95.
42 2 B 30, C.G., to M., Saint-Louis, August 2, 1850.
43 2 B 30, C.G., to M., Saint-Louis, November 5, 1850.
44 Convention of January 30, 1851 to end the payment for the pillage of Merigaghen.
45 2 B 30, C.G., to M., Saint-Louis, May 15, 1851.
46 2 B 30, C.G., to M., Saint-Louis, August 1, 1851.
47 2 B 30, C.G., to M., Saint-Louis, April 14, 1852.
48 *Annales sénégalaises de 1854 à 1885*, "Conquête du Waalo," Paris, 1885, p.1.
49 2 B 31, C.G., to M., Saint-Louis, January 19, 1855.
50 Ibid.
51 *Annales sénégalaises de 1854 à 1885*, Paris 1885, pp. 15-17; Sénégal I, 41 B, Saint-Louis, March 11, 1855.
52 13 G. 91, *Correspondance des chefs du Waalo*, "letter de Faidherbe aux gens du Waalo," Saint-Louis, March 1, 1855.
53 V. Monteil, op.cit. pp. 68-69.
54 Sénégal I, 41 B, Saint-Louis, March 24, 1855, second expedition against Waalo.
55 V. Monteil, op.cit. p. 68.
56 13 G. 33, Mission of Pinet-Laprade to the Queen of Waalo, Lampsa, Nov. 10, 1850; *Annales sénégalaises de 1854 à 1885*, p. 20.
57 13 G. 23, Saint-Louis, June 12, 1856, Instructions left by Faidherbe to Mr. M. Morel, interim governor.

CHAPTER 13

1 Sénégal I, 41 B, Saint-Louis, April 3, 1855.
2 Ibid. May 24, 1855.
3 Ibid.
4 Ibid., June 15, 1855.
5 Ibid., July 6, 1855.
6 Ibid., December 30, 1855.
7 Ibid.
8 Ibid., May 7, 1857.
9 Ibid., March 13, 1858.
10 3 B 91, Saint-Louis, March 20, 1858.
11 Sénégal I, 43, Saint-Louis, May 13, 1858, Correspondence de Faidherbe.
12 Yaha Wane, "De Halwaar àm Degembere ou l'itinéraire islamique de Shaykh Umar Tal," *Bull. I.F.A.N.*, série B., no. 2, 1969, pp. 447-48.
13 Sénégal I, 44, September 18, 1858.
14 Sénégal IV, 45, conseil d'administration, séance du 11 octobre 1858.
15 2 B 32, C.G., to M., no. 503, Insurrection au Waalo.

16 2 B 32, C.G., to M., Saint-Louis, 15 novembre 1858.
17 C. Schefer, op. cit. p. 321.
18 *Moniteur du Sénégal et dépendance*, mardi 27 decembre 1859, "Constitution de Qualo en wolof."
19 13 G. 92, Lettre de Yoro Diaw to gouverneur to sujet de la révolte de Sidia, 2 novembre 1869.
20 2 B 34, C.G., to M., Saint-Louis, December 17, 1869.
21 Sénégal IV, 45, conseil d'administration, séance du 25 février 1871.
22 Sénégal IV, 45, conseil d'administration, séance du 25 février 1871.
23 Sénégal IV, 45, conseil d'administration, séance du 25 février 1871.

CONCLUSION

1 Labat, op. cit., p. 251.
2 Henri Brunschwig, *Avènement de l'Afrique noire du XIX e siècle à nos jours*, Armand Colin, 1963, p. 176
3 Ibid.
4 P. Diagne, op. cit.
5 Cheikh Anta Diop, *L'Afrique noire précolonial*, Présence africaine, 1960, p. 12.
6 Jean Suret-Canale, "Mode de production asiatique," *C.E.R.M.*, 1959, p. 123.

POSTSCRIPT—1985

1 A.N.S, 2B 4, *correspondance du gouverneur au ministre*, Saint-Louis, September 4, 1819.
2 *Organisation de la mise en valeur du fleuve Sénégal*, Colloquesur les orientations du développement de après –barrage, Dakar, November 19-23, 1984.
3 Boubacar Barry, *Le royaume du Waalo. Le Sénégal avant la conquête*, Maspero, 1972, p. 315.
4 This gap is fortunately filled, thanks to the remarkable work of Daniel Delauney, *De la captivité à l'exil. La Vallée du fleuveSénégal*, Orstrom, Paris, 1984, p. 217. This excellent study follows the chronological plan of our monograph concerning Waalo. We are indebted to him for our analysis of the recent history of the river.
5 Daniel Delaunay, 1984, pp. 26, 180.
6 Concerning this point, we affirm our disagreement with Paul E. Lovejoy in his work *Transformations in Slavery: A History of Slavery in Africa*, who emphasizes the existence of a mode of slave production and a system of plantations. The violence created by the slave trade itself prevented a proslavery system to function in an autonomic manner outside of the satisfaction of the external need of the enslaved individuals for exportation.
7 Daniel Delaunay, 1984, p. 24
8 Daniel Delaunay, 1894, p. 34.
9 Daniel Delaunay, pp. 44-47.
10 Boubacar Barry, *Commerce légitime expansion du Fuuta Jallon vers la côte au XIXe siècle*, Séminaire Woodrow Wilson Center, 1983, unpublished.
11 Daniel Delaunay, p. 54.
12 Daniel Delaunay, pp. 69, 84.
13 Baldé Mamdou Saliou, *Les migrations des Peuls du Fuuta Jallon vers le milieu rural sénégalais*, thèse de 3e cycle, Paris, Sorbonne, 1975.
14 Daniel Delaunay, p. 86.
15 Guy Rocheteau, *Financial Power and Economic Independence in Africa: The Case of Senegal*, Karthala, p. 325.

16 Abdoulaye Ly, *Concerning Neocolonial Presidentialism in Senegal, in Favor of a Positive Approach*, And-Jëf, MRDN, p. 9.
17 Guy Rocheteau, p. 326.
18 Abdoulaye Ly, op. cit., p. 9.
19 Abdoulaye Bara Diop, *The Toucouleur Community and Migration*, IFAN, Dakar, 1965, pp. 209-11.
20 *The Senegal River*, AUDECAM, pp. 26-27.
21 *The Development of the Valley of the Senegal River*, Europe Information, Developments, DE 39, September 1984. See also *The Senegal River*, AUDECAM.
22 Adrian Adams, *The Land and People of the River*, Éditions L'Harmattan, 1985, p. 177.
23 Claude Meillassoux, "Wagers of the World's Food Supply System: 700,000 Peasants in the Senegal River Valley," *Le Monde diplomatique*, May 1980.
24 "The Development of the Senegal River Valley. Correspondence," *Le Monde diplomatique*, August 1980.
25 Abonbakry Moussa Lam, "Twenty-Two Years Later, Is Black Africa in Worse Shape? Does History Give Reason to René Dumont?" *Africa Development*, CODERS, Dakar, 1984, p. 8.
26 Adrian Adams, op. cit., pp. 9, 32.
27 Ibid., pp. 67, 83.
28 Adrian Adams, p. 150.
29 Ibid., p. 159.
30 Opening speech of his Excellency Mr. Abdou Diouf, President of the Republic of Senegal at the Colloquium on the Directions to be adopted for the Development of the After-the-Dams Era, Dakar, November 19-23, 1984, OMVS. This document is being quoted at length because of the wide range of still unresolved problems, but also because this document was not available in the official documentation structures of Senegal.
31 The breadth of the problems still to be resolved justifies, in our opinion, the concerns for the future of the Senegal River valley project, in the context of an effort led by national states.
32 Adrian Adams, op. cit., pp. 199, 218.
33 Ibid., pp. 218-19.
34 Mohamed Mbodj and Mamadou Diouf, "Senegalese Historiography: Reckoning of Actual Practices and Perspectives," April 1983, unpublished, p. 15.
35 Mohamed Mbodj, op. cit.
36 *Le Monde*, August 21, 1985, editorial entitled "Encounter."

INDEX

Adams, Adrian, 234, 239-42, 251-2
African commerce, 49, 54, 56
African history, 3, 8
agricultural colonization, 2, 4-5, 7, 90,
    136-7, 139-40, 143, 145-52, 154-5,
    158-61, 163-4, 166-7, 174, 177, 187,
    217-19, 223, 229, 234, 260
        failure of, 154, 159, 161, 174,
            187, 222, 224, 230
        project of, 91, 145-6, 149, 152,
            154-6, 163, 171, 221-3
agricultural settlements, 145-6, 152, 160,
    171
agriculture, 23, 26, 148, 150, 192, 221,
    225-6, 231, 235, 247, 249
Alichandora, 95, 98-9, 102-4, 106-9
Alikoury, 124-5, 137-8
alkaati, 42-3, 104, 110
alliance(s), 37, 39, 78, 80, 93, 95-8, 100-1,
    103, 105-9, 120, 123, 137, 152-3,
    169, 171-2, 178-82, 187, 194-5, 197,
    215
almamy (ruler of Juta Jallon), 129, 137-9,
    141-2, 146, 152, 170, 225
Almoravid movement, 15-16, 34, 226, 228
Americas, the, 2, 19, 49, 55-7, 59, 61, 66,
    90, 118, 124, 128, 134, 136, 216-17,
    222, 229, 251, 253-4
amulets, 26, 35
ancestors, 34, 241
Arguin, 17, 28, 55, 74, 76-7, 89, 98-9,
    106-7, 131
aristocracy, 82, 85-6, 131, 137, 139, 165,
    167, 172-3, 203, 216-19, 227-8
aristocrats, 165, 173
army, 27, 44, 81, 94, 102, 138, 171, 229,
    231
artillery, 52-3
Atlantic slave trade, 4, 15, 19, 43-5,
    90-1, 114, 118-19, 121, 124-5, 127-8,
    130-4, 142, 145, 158, 167, 190, 215,
    217, 227.
Atlantic commerce, 2, 59, 62, 68, 92,
    111, 128, 130, 138, 190. *See also* Atlantic
slave trade
Azan (captain), 6-8, 93-4, 96, 109, 113-14,
    122-3, 126, 139-40

baadolo, 32, 40, 94, 198, 206
Babagué, 141-2
Bakar, Aram, 93-4, 119
Barbot, Jean, 4, 27, 44, 60, 83-5
basin
    drainage, 237-8, 244-6, 248-9, 253
    groundnut, 232-4
Bawol, 14, 16, 111, 113-15, 124, 216
beeco, 41, 65, 97, 100-1, 104-9, 194, 202
beeco Maalixuri, 89, 93-5, 97-101,
    103-9, 111, 215
beeco Sakura, 140, 146, 179, 181-2
Bër Caaka, 89, 93-6, 102
boats, 58, 74, 76, 78, 82, 84-5, 91-2, 106,
    110, 158
Booker, James Island (English governor),
    90
Brak Amar Faatim Mborso, 146, 151,
    164
Brak Bër Caaka, 93, 95, 99
Brak Fara Kumba, 71, 82
Brak Fara Penda, 154, 164, 167-9, 171-2,
    177, 182, 184, 218
Brak Yeerim Koodé, 75, 78-83, 85, 93
Brak Yeerim Mbañik, 59, 93-111, 113,
    152-4, 156, 164, 184-5, 215
    army of, 94
    reign of, 98, 109, 111
Braknas, 83, 102-3, 137, 149, 152-3,
    160, 170, 193, 226, 229

brak's power, 40, 107, 119, 130, 168-9, 173, 183, 202
British, 19, 54, 98, 116-20, 123-6, 128, 130-2, 135-6, 142, 153, 157
British occupation (of Saint-Louis), 118, 125, 130
Brüe, André, 104-7
Bubakar Siré, 102-3, 128
Bubu Sal, 122-3, 139
buur jullit, 69, 72, 75, 80, 82

camels, 16, 25, 27-8, 59, 75, 182, 196
canoes, 26, 38, 120
capital of Waalo, 96, 113
Captain Lambert, 43, 52-3, 67, 92
captives, 2, 8, 27, 31-3, 37-40, 42, 44, 57, 59-62, 70-1, 74, 79-81, 83-4, 94, 100-3, 105-8, 110, 114-15, 124-5, 202
  domestic, 33, 228, 230
cattle, 27, 36, 43-4, 57, 59-61, 65, 74-5, 81, 100, 103, 111, 115, 166, 180, 182, 192, 231
Cayor, 105, 108, 119, 121, 170, 178, 181, 193, 201, 203
ceddo (warriors), 33, 43, 85-6, 127, 130, 139, 183, 197, 201-2, 217-18
Chambonneau, 4, 14, 18, 23-8, 34-5, 37, 43-4, 53-4, 61, 67, 70-4, 77-85, 90, 93
chiefs, political, 41, 166-7
civil war, 49, 67, 96-7, 107-8, 114-17, 121-8, 146, 151-3, 167-70, 177, 179, 182-3, 202, 216, 218
coast of Mauritania, 98-9, 111, 117
coastal kingdoms, 2-3, 216
colonial conquest, 2, 6, 28, 86, 142, 163, 174, 190-1, 198, 205-6, 217, 219-20, 222, 229
commercial interests, 190-1, 230
Company of Senegal, 59, 89-91, 98, 104, 109, 260
conquest,, 1, 6, 9, 34, 67-9, 72, 74, 90, 103, 120, 187, 189-90, 192, 196, 198-9, 218-19, 225, 229-32, 236, 252
conquest of Waalo, 188, 196-7, 207, 218, 222
cotton, 26, 28, 56, 66, 90, 92, 118, 121, 134, 142, 148-9, 160, 223
crown captives, 33, 202. *See also ceddo*
cubalots, 25-6
customary fees, 91, 93, 99, 101, 103, 106-7, 110, 119-20, 123, 125, 128, 140-2, 146-7, 151, 155-7, 163-4, 166, 179, 181-4
customs, 6-7, 53, 63, 65, 81, 83, 120, 128, 141, 164, 183, 187, 192, 195, 204, 209, 215-17

Dagana, 8-9, 139, 148, 150, 152, 163, 168-9, 171-2, 191, 196, 202, 234, 259
Dakar, 3, 207, 222, 231, 235-6, 242, 261
dam construction, 239-40, 248, 257
damel, 18, 52, 67, 99, 102-3, 105-7, 109-10, 114-15, 120, 124, 138, 158, 170, 193
damel Amari Ngonee Ndella, 138
damel of Kajoor, 100, 105, 110, 114, 120, 137, 170, 216, 233
dams, 154, 156, 164, 221, 237-40, 243-50, 257, 259
Dapper, Olfert, 4, 23, 25-6, 34-6
desert, 13, 17, 58, 63, 65, 68, 72, 75, 78, 119, 123-4, 173, 181, 188, 215, 251
development
  agricultural, 159-60, 236-7
  industrial, 233
  mining, 245-7
development projects, 234, 239, 243, 246, 258, 260
Dieppe, 19, 51, 53-5
  inhabitants of, 51, 53, 55
dignitaries, 38-9, 41-2, 96, 146, 164, 168, 179, 194, 197-8
Diile, 167, 171-3, 177, 185, 218
Dios, 36, 122-3, 126, 139-40, 146, 177, 184-5
domestic production, 228, 230, 232, 252
domestic slavery, 129, 216, 227-30
drought, 222, 224
Dubellay, Julien, 103-9
Dutch, 19, 51-2, 55, 77, 89, 99, 106-7, 117, 133

elimane Boubacar, 169, 171-2, 180, 182
Émir Ndar, 209-13
enslaved individuals, 4, 17, 19, 27, 32-3, 36, 43-4, 54-7, 59-62, 65-6, 74-5, 84, 118, 121, 124-5, 127-9, 135-7, 157-8, 227-9, 231, 233-4
  main supplier of, 140, 231
  source of, 58, 84
enthronement, 37-40
envoys, 16, 52, 75-7

era, post-dams, 239-40, 243, 249-50
European powers, 1, 19, 28, 49, 51, 54, 98, 111, 132, 137, 142, 199, 220, 227
European sugar trade, 132
European voyagers, 32, 35, 38-9, 58, 70
exile, 94, 182, 203, 232, 255, 259
expansion, commercial, 85, 188, 190-1

Faidherbe, Louis, 6, 119, 155, 192, 196-8, 201-4, 218, 229
famine, 14, 57, 60, 84, 115, 141, 159, 178, 216, 222, 227-8, 238, 243
Fara Penda, 154, 164, 167-9, 171-2, 177, 182, 184, 218. *See also* Brak Fara Penda
death of, 184
Fara Penda Teeg-Rel, 137-9
firearms, 62, 65, 85, 111, 215
Fleuve Sénégal (Senegal River) 237, 257-9
fort, 5, 17, 19, 51, 53-4, 94, 99, 104, 106-7, 110-11, 117, 120-1, 131, 146, 155, 171, 196, 203
freedom, 31, 71, 86, 134, 136, 157, 202, 204, 229-30
French authorities, 154, 189, 206
French commerce, 19, 191, 215
French concessionaires, 223
French conquest, 58, 203, 205, 231, 252
French ministry, 158, 182-3
Fuuta Jallon, 222, 224-5, 228-9, 231-3, 251, 255-6
Fuuta Toro, 42, 86, 128, 130-1, 137, 141, 146, 173, 205, 225-9, 252

Galam, 58, 64, 90, 102-3, 108-9, 114-15, 117, 129, 131, 136-7, 140-1, 202
Gambia River, 17, 52, 55, 131, 226, 250, 253, 255-7
Gerbidon, 151, 154, 156, 159
gold, 17, 26, 28, 55-6, 68, 90, 94, 96, 100, 135, 187, 191, 251
Gorée (Island), 77, 83, 85, 89-90, 115, 117-19, 124-5, 131, 138
Government Council, 5, 171
Governor Schmaltz, 91, 145-6, 221, 223
grains, 24, 27, 35, 114-15, 129, 228
Grands Moulins, 235-6
Greater Senegambia, 255-6
groundnuts, 229-33
gum, 17, 19, 28, 49, 57, 59-60, 63, 65, 77, 83, 89, 98, 111, 133, 135-6, 153-4, 161, 181, 187, 230

gum trade, 1, 59, 63, 85, 96-9, 106, 111, 118-19, 141, 153-4, 181-2, 219, 226
gum war, 97-9
gunpowder reserve, 95-6

Habib, Mohamed El, 140, 154, 173, 177-82, 184, 194-6, 201-3, 218, 178-9, 223
Hassan warriors, 68-9, 77-8, 80, 83, 86, 226
hierarchies, 31-3, 37, 163, 170, 219
history of Senegal, 6, 15, 86-7
horses, 16-17, 26-8, 35, 44, 62, 71, 104, 119, 127, 166

iron, 26, 44, 57, 62, 82, 85, 90-1, 101-2, 134, 141-2, 251
Islam, 2, 31, 34-6, 39, 67-70, 76, 79, 82, 86-7, 128-9, 131, 137-9, 166-7, 169-70, 172-3, 203, 206, 216-18, 227-8, 253
progress of, 166
Island of Morphil, 136, 146
ivory, 19, 25, 28, 56-7, 135, 160, 187, 191

jaam, 31-2, 42, 202
Jambuur, 170, 203
Jannequin, 18-19, 52
javelins, 38, 44
jawdin, 37-8, 40-1, 108, 152, 156, 164, 168-9, 171-2
jawdin Madiaw Xor, 146, 164, 167-8, 171-2, 177-9, 218
jeeri, 14, 23, 224, 241
jogomaay, 37-8, 41-2, 95, 168
Jolof
    buur-ba, 16-17, 103, 110, 119-20
    empire of, 7, 15-17, 34, 226
Jurbel, 37-9, 42, 58-9, 94, 96-7

Kader, Abdul, 137-9, 170
Kajoor, 7, 13-14, 16-18, 26, 41-2, 67, 69, 71-2, 83, 85, 100, 105, 108, 110-11, 113-17, 119-21, 170, 195-7, 205, 215-16
    affairs of, 113-15
Kayor, 17-18, 114-15, 155, 159, 166, 182
Kheerfi, 177, 182, 184
Kheerfi Xari Daaro, 177-8, 180, 182

La Courbe, Michel Jajolet de, 4, 24, 28, 40, 44, 53, 58-60, 62-3, 65, 71-2, 82, 90-2
lamane(s), 24, 39, 44, 127
Lamiral, Dominique Harcourt, 4, 28, 122-4, 126-7, 133-4, 137-8
land
   brak's, 99
   irrigated, 240, 258
   ownership, 24, 40, 245, 259
   parcels of, 156, 241
   subsidence river, 241
   transfer of, 154-5, 157, 217
   treaty transferring Waalo, 146
land appropriation, 226
land concessions, 155-6
law, 40, 70, 76, 135, 137, 141, 158, 204, 209, 216
lineages, 23, 31, 43
linger, 42, 73, 94, 173, 179, 187, 202, 226
linger Jambur-Gel, 93-6
linger Njómbót, 168-9, 177, 179, 181, 185, 218
livestock farming, 15, 24-7, 71, 74, 78, 150, 193, 222
Loggar, 7, 36, 93, 96, 122-3, 126, 140, 186
Ly, Abdoulaye, 6, 51, 55, 89-90, 236

Maalixuri, 94, 97, 100-1, 105-9
maalo, 37-8, 40-1
maaroso, 6, 193-5, 197
Madiaw Xor, 168-9, 171-2, 177-8
Mahamadou Maïga, 258
Maïsa Bigé, 114-5, 119
Mali, 38, 217, 223-6, 232, 235, 237, 243, 250, 255-7, 260
maraboutic movement, 68, 74, 77, 79-80, 83, 85-7, 228
maraboutic party, 34, 71-4, 78-9, 85-6, 170, 227-8
marabouts, 34-6, 39, 43, 49, 63, 68-9, 71-4, 76-81, 83-6, 89, 119, 166-7, 170-1, 173, 194, 205, 216, 226
marriage, 29, 32-3, 38, 100, 179-82, 185, 218
Mauritania, 3, 24, 68-9, 75, 77, 80, 83, 86, 98-9, 111, 117, 223-4, 226, 234-5, 237, 240, 243, 250, 256-9
Mauritanian coast, 98-9, 117-18
meen (royal) families, 36-8, 96, 122, 123, 126
mercantilism, 91, 132
Meringhen station, 189, 191-2, 195, 197, 202
migrants, 15, 233-4
migrations, 68, 225, 232-4, 255
   seasonal, 24, 233
military aristocracies, 62, 83, 85, 165, 215, 217, 227
millet, 23-4, 26, 28-9, 33, 38, 43, 60-1, 74-5, 80, 84, 109, 111, 115, 121, 141, 180, 188, 196, 229-30, 241-2
Moctar, Amar Ould 152-4
Monserat (Governor of Senegal) 5, 140, 153-4, 177-80, 188-9
Moorish
   commerce, 74, 82
   domination, 73, 79, 86, 123, 128, 130, 188, 195, 216, 218
   opposition to Waalo 202
   tradition, 69, 72-3, 79
   Saint-Louis, 107
Morocco, 16, 27, 34, 68-9, 102
Muslims, 39, 75, 78, 166, 206, 227-8

Naatago Aram, 113, 119-22
Nâsir Al-Din, 68-78, 80
   death of, 75-8
Ndate Yalla, 193-6, 198, 201-3
Ndiak Aram, 113-16, 119
Ndiak Aram Bakar, 109, 113, 116
Ndiak Xuri, 122-3, 126
neighboring kingdoms, 1, 3, 9, 15, 54, 85, 87, 91, 130, 137, 188-9, 199, 215
Njómbót, 179, 181-2, 184-5, 187, 192, 194, 196. See also *linger* Njómbót
Njurbel, 81, 95-6
nobility, 15, 31, 36-42, 63-4, 74, 78, 81, 86, 96, 103, 106, 165, 185, 206, 218, 230

O'Hara, Charles 59, 118, 121, 123-9
OMVS (Organization for the Development of the Senegal River), 237-45, 247-51, 257-8
oral tradition, 3, 6-8, 15, 37, 74, 82, 93, 107, 109, 113-14, 119, 122, 126, 139, 198, 253
Ormans, 95, 98, 102-3
oxen, 91, 100-1, 103, 108-9, 121, 141, 153, 192, 196

Paris, 3-5, 142, 236, 242, 256
peace, 43, 52, 84, 98, 104, 110, 120, 125, 129, 141-2, 149, 153-4, 164, 169, 171, 178, 181-2, 191, 195, 201
peace treaty, 142, 145, 154, 182, 203
peasants, 23, 31-2, 44, 166-7, 219, 235, 239-43, 245, 247, 249
pillaging, 44-5, 70-1, 81, 83, 94, 101, 108, 114-15, 123, 159, 165, 181, 195, 203, 228
plantations, 56, 66, 124, 150-1, 155-7, 223, 255
Podor, 117, 124, 128, 170, 195, 234
political crisis, 8, 167-9, 185, 198
populations, local, 258-6
ports, 57-8, 61, 183-4
Portuguese, 16-17, 34, 49, 51, 55, 134, 257
Portuguese commerce, 16-17, 19, 51
power struggle, 8, 95-6, 99, 177
priest(s), 35, 166
privileges, system of, 24, 36, 39-42, 110, 135, 226, 253
provincial chiefs, powerful, 98-9, 109

Quernel, Germain 180-1, 187-8, 190

racism, 56, 190-1
raids, 59, 227-8
ranks, 23, 31-3, 37-8, 41, 60, 64, 146, 206, 231
refuge, 95, 106, 109, 115, 121-3, 168-70, 172, 177-8, 181-2, 192, 196, 201, 203, 225
religion, traditional, 34-5, 73
resistance, 6, 53, 71, 127, 132, 138, 172-3, 198-9, 201, 203, 217-18
    of former slave traders, 151, 159
revolution, 57, 71, 86, 128, 130, 133, 189-90, 204, 228
    industrial, 132, 229
rice (production), 23, 118, 121, 149, 235-6, 240-2, 245, 256
Richard-Toll, 41, 149-50, 169, 171-2, 178, 180, 188, 192, 202, 235
river
    basin, 15-16, 27
    trade, 109, 187
riverbanks, southern, 231
Roger, Baron, 4-5, 39, 129-30, 137-8, 149, 155, 157, 159, 165-6, 207, 222-3

SAED (Development and Exploitation Society of the Delta Lands), 235-7, 240, 242
Sahel, 15, 225, 238, 243, 250, 254-6, 258
Saint-Domingue (Haiti), 132, 135-6
Saint-Louis
    British occupation of, 63, 131
    commerce of, 5, 58-60, 62, 66, 73-4, 76, 82-5, 215-16, 219
    countries neighboring, 158
    French colonists in, 177
    French recapture of, 125, 131
    French trading post of, 1, 3-4, 19, 45, 49, 51, 59, 62-3, 67, 69, 73-5, 77, 79, 81, 84, 86, 91-2, 97, 109-11, 215
    inhabitants of 120, 141, 154, 160, 188, 195
    intervention of, 80, 85, 218
    merchants of, 58, 157, 160, 174, 192
    occupation of, 116-17
    proximity of, 65, 67, 97
    threatened, 100, 179
    trade of, 68, 113, 120
    trading posts of, 47, 51, 89-90, 117, 151
Saint-Robert, Nicolas, 99-102, 104-5, 128
salt, 26-8, 57, 64
seb ak bawor, 2, 37, 40, 42, 45, 94, 96, 108, 114, 138, 173, 185, 198, 218
Senegal
    government of, 128, 236
    inhabitants of, 124, 137
    state(s) of, 235-7, 249, 256
Senegal colony, 145, 174, 190, 196, 206, 221
Senegal concession, 90-1, 110
Senegal drainage basin, 242, 245, 251, 258
Senegal mid-valley region, 235-6
Senegal River valley, 90, 187, 232, 235-9, 241, 255-8, 259-60
Senegalese market, 235-6
Senegambia, 4, 6-7, 16, 18, 33-4, 57, 87, 89, 114, 118, 149, 203, 205, 215, 219, 223, 225, 231-2, 253, 255-6
    kingdoms of, 18, 44
settlements, 34, 52, 54, 58, 61, 77-8, 80, 125, 141, 145, 148, 155, 171, 174, 225, 248
Sidia, 194, 203-5, 210

slave trade
- abolition of Atlantic, 86, 132-4, 145, 158, 190, 195-6, 219, 221
- clandestine, 157-8

slave traders, 66, 86, 138, 158-9, 228-9
- former, 151, 159

slave trading, 55, 57, 125, 135, 142, 174, 216-18, 230

slavery, 33, 56, 75, 118, 129, 132-5, 157-9, 178, 228-9, 233

social crisis (in Waalo), 1, 49, 65, 69, 145, 164-5, 167, 174, 197, 199, 217-18

soldiers, 44, 91, 95, 99, 127, 138, 194

Soninke, 222, 224-5, 240-2, 250, 252

stagnation, economic, 29, 68, 219

subsistence economy, 23-6, 28

sugar, 19, 49, 55-6, 82, 118, 132-4, 147, 235-6

taxes, 16, 25, 38-40, 43, 45, 53, 61, 63-5, 67, 71, 84, 96, 195, 228

Teejekk, 36, 122-3, 126, 139-40, 168, 177, 197, 203, 215

theocratic states, 227, 229, 231

Toorodo revolution, 4, 86, 119, 128-30, 137, 216, 226, 228

Toubenan, 76-80, 83

traditional aristocracy, 8, 49, 62, 65, 82, 84-6, 89, 92, 167, 172, 185, 187, 197, 201, 205-6, 218

Trans-Saharan commerce, 16-17, 27-8, 55-6, 62, 67, 74-5, 84, 86, 215, 217

Trarza king, 98-9, 102, 152, 179-80, 184, 223

Trarza Moors, 49, 96-7, 99, 113, 115, 123, 126, 148, 151, 153, 215. *See also* Moors

Trarzas, 13, 42, 63, 77, 83, 95, 103, 107, 122, 137, 140, 146, 149, 152-4, 160, 174, 177-9, 181, 193-7, 223. *See also* Trarza Moors.

treaties, 1, 98, 118, 125, 140, 142, 145-7, 151-7, 164, 178, 181-2, 188-91, 195, 223

tribute, 18, 103, 127, 151-3, 260

Tukulor threat, 137, 139

Villeneuve, Geoffrey de, 4, 7, 16, 123, 126-8

Waalo
- Atlantic commerce of, 63
- armies of 193, 196
- border of, 13, 177
- destruction of, 124-5
- French re-occupation of, 137
- French victory in, 197
- hegemony of, 121-2
- history of, 1-7, 15, 28, 42, 51, 60, 68, 89, 96-7, 125, 130, 215, 219, 222, 226
- inhabitants of, 2, 7, 15, 223
- intermediary role of chiefs in, 163
- Islamic revolution on, 130
- kingdom of, 2, 8, 10, 13, 15, 19, 31, 49, 62, 66-7, 85, 97, 117, 129, 170, 182-3, 187, 221-2, 257, 260
- policy of Governor Brüe on, 99
- population of, 14, 159. *See also* inhabitants of Waalo
- weakening of, 67, 96, 127, 181, 202
- Wolof of, 233, 252

Waalo chiefs, 91, 99, 109, 111, 146, 156-7, 163, 172, 180-1, 183, 202

Waalo customs, 141, 195

Waalo frontier, 170-1

Waalo lands, 97, 145, 154-5, 158, 165, 171, 223, 226, 228

Waalo leaders, 178, 187, 197, 204

Waalo society, 31, 85, 167

Waalo-Waalo (people), 2, 15, 25, 29, 39, 71, 73, 78-9, 95, 123, 126-7, 129, 137-8, 140, 152, 154-7, 164-6, 178-80, 188-9, 193

Wade, Amadou, 7-8, 15, 72, 74, 82, 93-5, 107, 109, 113-14, 122-3, 138-9, 168, 178, 184-5, 192, 197

West Indies, 89-90, 134-6

whites, 53, 65-6, 75, 78, 81-2, 85, 99, 104, 127, 129, 139, 158, 198

wives, 70, 82, 103-4, 166, 169

Yoro Diaw, 7-9, 16, 18, 31-2, 37-8, 96, 119-22, 139, 152, 172